The Philippine

Moluccas, Siam, Cambodia,

Japan, and China

At the close of the sixteenth century

Antonio de Morga and
Henry E. J. Stanley

Alpha Editions

This edition published in 2019

ISBN : 9789353804800

Design and Setting By
Alpha Editions
email - alphaedis@gmail.com

This book is a reproduction of an important historical work. Alpha Editions uses the best technology to reproduce historical work in the same manner it was first published to preserve its original nature. Any marks or number seen are left intentionally to preserve its true form.

THE
PHILIPPINE ISLANDS,

MOLUCCAS, SIAM, CAMBODIA, JAPAN, AND CHINA,

AT THE CLOSE OF

THE SIXTEENTH CENTURY.

BY

ANTONIO DE MORGA.

TRANSLATED FROM THE SPANISH,

With Notes and a Preface;

AND A LETTER FROM LUIS VAEZ DE TORRES, DESCRIBING HIS VOYAGE THROUGH THE TORRES STRAITS.

BY THE

HON. HENRY E. J. STANLEY.

LONDON:
PRINTED FOR THE HAKLUYT SOCIETY.

M.DCCC.LXVIII.

DEDICATED

TO

THE WORTHY SUCCESSOR OF DE MORGA

IN HIS JUDICIAL FUNCTIONS,

DON JOSÉ ENTRALA Y PERALES,

REGENTE OF THE ROYAL AUDIENCIA OF THE PHILIPPINE ISLANDS

DURING THE YEARS 1845-1854,

AND NOW REGENTE OF THE ROYAL AUDIENCIA

OF MADRID.

COUNCIL

OF

THE HAKLUYT SOCIETY.

SIR RODERICK IMPEY MURCHISON, BART., K.C.B., G.C.St.S., F.R.S., D.C.L., Corr. Mem. Inst. F., Hon. Mem. Imp. Acad. Sc. Petersburg, etc., etc., PRESIDENT.

REAR-ADMIRAL C. R. DRINKWATER BETHUNE, C.B. } VICE-PRESIDENTS.
THE RT. HON. SIR DAVID DUNDAS.
THE RIGHT HON. H. U. ADDINGTON.
Rev. G. P. BADGER, F.R.G.S.
J. BARROW, ESQ., F.R.S.
E. H. BUNBURY, ESQ.
REAR-ADMIRAL R. COLLINSON, C.B.
SIR WALTER ELLIOT, K.S.I.
SIR HENRY ELLIS, K.H., F.R.S.
GENERAL C. FOX.
W. E. FRERE, ESQ.
R. W. GREY, ESQ.
JOHN WINTER JONES, ESQ., F.S.A.
R. H. MAJOR, ESQ., F.S.A.
SIR CHARLES NICHOLSON, BART., D.C.L., LL.D.
CAPTAIN SHERARD OSBORN, R.N., C.B.
MAJOR-GENERAL SIR HENRY C. RAWLINSON, K.C.B., M.P.
REAR-ADMIRAL ALFRED RYDER, R.N.
VISCOUNT STRANGFORD.

CLEMENTS R. MARKHAM, ESQ., F.S.A., HONORARY SECRETARY.

TRANSLATOR'S PREFACE.

THE original work of De Morga was printed in Mexico in 1609, and has become extremely rare; there is no copy of it in the Bibliothèque Impériale of Paris. This translation is from a transcription made for the Hakluyt Society from the copy in the Grenville Library of the British Museum; the catalogue of which states that "this book, printed at Mexico, is for that reason probably unknown to bibliographers, though a book of great rarity." However, it is mentioned in the *Bibliotheca Scriptorum Hispaniæ*, Matriti, 1783, which says, "Antonius de Morga, juris doctor, in Philipinas, extremæ Asiæ insulas non dudum inventas & armis occupatas, perductus ut gubernatoris vices gereret anno 1598, institutæ ibidem Regiæ curiæ senator sive triumvir fuit cooptatus, quo munere functus dicitur non sine laude alacris cujusdam prudentiæ, virtutisque etiam bellicis expeditionibus compertæ. Jam vero ad prætorium urbis Mexicanæ inter quatuor viros rerum criminalium vindices fuerat translatus quando edidit: Sucesos de las Islas Filipinas. Mexici 1609 in 4 ex officina Hieronymi Balli." It is also quoted in some histories of the Philippines, and in the *Dialogo Cortesano Philipino* of P. Fr. Joseph Torrubia, of which there were two editions, Madrid, 1736, 4to., and Madrid, 1753, 8vo. In this book the inhabitant of the court of Madrid says that he has not heard of such a book nor of the author: the Philippine Spaniard answers him that the book was printed in Mexico in 1609 and is now scarcely to be found, but that he possessed a copy; and he describes de Morga as a man in whom arms and science were united in a most friendly manner, and says that he composed his book from original documents since he was the first auditor of the Audiencia of Manila. From a printed document in the British Museum, $\frac{1324\ K\ 5}{64}$, it appears that Dr. Antonio de Morga was President of the Royal Audiencia of Quito in April of 1616, seven years after he published this work in Mexico. This document, dated April 14, 1616, a legalised copy of which was made by the notary public Juan de Zamudio on the 21st March, 1617, refers to the opening of a road between Quito and Caracas; and by it the offer of P. fray Diego de Velasco and his companions to open the road is accepted, and conditions are laid down, amongst which it said that the unsettled Indians and Mulatos are to be paid for their labour and treated with gentleness.

This work of De Morga's was announced in the reports of the Hakluyt Society as in progress as long ago as 1851, but the translation of it has been deferred till the present year. Dr. De Morga is less remarkable for his literary merits than for his qualities as a jurist, and administrator, and a commander. His book is rather an historical than a geographical work; but the account of Alvaro de Mendaña's second voyage, by his pilot Fernandez de Quiros, given by De Morga, brings it entirely within the scope of the Hakluyt Society's publications. The account contained in De Morga's work has not hitherto been published in French or English, though M. E. Charton refers to it in his fourth volume of *Voyages* (Paris 1855), where he gives another account of this voyage to the islands of Sta. Cruz, compiled from two French translations of a narrative of Alvaro de Mendaña's second voyage. These French translations were—I, that of President De Brosses, in his *Histoire des Navigations aux terres Australes,* Paris, 1756; II, that of Pingré, in his *Mémoire sur le choix et l'état des lieux où le passage de Venus du 3 Juin 1769 pourra être observé*, etc., Paris, 1767. It appears from M. Charton's notes, that the text translated by De Brosses was not so complete as that which Pingré had in his hands, and he has completed De Brosses' translation by that of Pingré.

Pingré says, in a note at page 30 of his *Mémoire,* "The author of the *Histoire des Navigations aux Terres Australes,* copied by the Dutch editors of the large French collection of Voyages, in giving the account of this expedition, had under his eyes a printed copy of the sixth book of Figueroa; but that copy was terribly mutilated; two sheets (cahiers) were wanting, —the first of all, and another: so that there could not be any title-page. Nevertheless, the author says that the copy was entitled, *Descubrimiento de las islas de Salomon,* Discovery of the Solomon Isles. Was this title only in manuscript? in that case it is not a proof. Will it be said that some Spaniard has had printed separately the sixth book of Figueroa under this title? That might be; but then this title will not be that of Figueroa. What I can affirm is, that the copy which the author of the *Navigations Australes* possessed, to judge only by that author's own translation, differs in nothing from the sixth book of Figueroa, except some errors, into which the mutilation of the copy has necessarily induced the French author. Now, Figueroa nowhere says that the islands discovered by Mendaña in the second voyage were wholly or in part the same as those of Solomon, discovered in 1568. On the contrary, Figueroa insinuates more than once that the discoveries of 1595 were entirely new."

There is a fragment of a folio print of this *Descubrimiento de las islas de Salomon*, bound up in vol. ii of M. Thevenot's *Relations des Voyages*, folio, Paris, 1696, British Museum, 566, K 5. It consists of pages 5-8, 13-16, and is incomplete at the beginning, middle, and end. Now this fragment in the British Museum agrees exactly with the description given by Pingré of the copy used by De Brosses, the gap in the middle coincides with that indicated by him in De Brosses' translation, and it appears to be identical with the sixth book of Cristoval Suarez Figueroa, Madrid, 1613. The British Museum copy has the title *Descubrimiento de las islas de Salomon*, not in manuscript, but in print on the top of the pages, and this title is justifiable, since although the Sta. Cruz Islands are not the same as the

Solomon Islands, yet the object of Mendaña's voyage was to reach the Solomon Islands. The account of this voyage ends in the first column of page 16 of the fragment, and goes on to speak of two memorials of Fernandez de Quiros to Don Luys de Velasco, Governor of Peru, and successor of the Marquis of Cañete, requesting ships and men to prosecute his discoveries.

Since Figueroa's sixth book referred to by M. Pingré has no such title at the top of the pages, as is placed on this fragment, it may be inferred that it was, as M. Pingré suggests, a separate impression of the second voyage of Mendaña. This is the more probable, since, as M. Hartzenbusch, the Director of the Madrid Library, informs me, many memorials and narratives which Quiros gave to the press were, in virtue of a decision of the Council of the Indies, suppressed in 1610 by a royal order.

M. Charton says of Pedro Fernandez de Quiros: "This remarkable man still waits for his historian. If experience has shewn that his hopes surpassed the reality, the greatness of his designs is no less worthy of admiration, and the positive services which he has rendered are too undeniable for his celebrity not to increase, whenever science shall at length have presented all his claims. His name, moreover, is inseparable from that of Mendaña, who partook of his ideas and his researches, and had the honour to precede him"

M. J. Mallat published a work on the Philippines in 2 vols., Paris, 1846: it contains much that is valuable, especially of modern commercial statistics; but a very large part of his work is simply a reproduction of De Morga, or of some other author who has followed him, without any sufficient acknowledgment of the source from which this author has drawn his information. His book is accompanied by an atlas containing a large map of the Philippines, plans of Manila, etc.

In the beginning of the present year the Spanish Government gave a commission to MM. Gayangos and Vera to examine the archives of the Indies at Seville, and other archives in the kingdom, and to publish all that concerned the legislation of the Spanish settlements beyond the seas. This publication should be a very useful one, at any rate as far as it will concern the Philippines; for that colony, judging it from the result, must be considered as more successful than any belonging to any other European country, and may be claimed as a triumph for Philip the Prudent and the measures he initiated.[1] For whilst the Portuguese have lost all their settlements in those seas, the Philippines continue to increase the resources of the mother country,[2] and only require from Spain some officers and a few companies of artillerymen for their defence or retention, whilst those islands furnished a large contingent as auxiliaries

[1] Mr. Consul Farren wrote from Manila in April 1848:—"There are some things in the Spanish colonial system which are not unworthy the attention of Downing Street."

[2] Official documents state in 1844 that half a million sterling was remitted annually to the treasury of Spain.

to the French during their conquest of Cochin China. The great point in which Manila has been a success, is the fact that the original inhabitants have not disappeared before the Europeans, and that they have been civilised, and brought into a closer union with the dominant race than is to be found elsewhere in similar circumstances. The inhabitants of the Philippines previous to the Spanish settlement were not like the inhabitants of the great Indian peninsula, people with a civilisation as old as that of their conquerors. Excepting that they possessed the art of writing, and an alphabet of their own, they do not appear to have differed in any way from the Dayaks of Borneo as described by Mr. Boyle in his recent book of adventures amongst that people. Indeed there is almost a coincidence of verbal expressions in the descriptions he and De Morga give of the social customs, habits, and superstitions of the two peoples they are describing: though many of these coincidences are such as are incidental to life in similar circumstances, there are enough to lead one to suppose a community of origin of the inhabitants of Borneo and Luzon.

It would be difficult and perhaps presumptuous to attempt, amongst different causes, to say what chiefly contributed to the success of the Philippine administration: the distance from Spain, the absence of gold in any large quantities,[1] the devotion of the

[1] "Nothing is more fatal to the character than the perspective of the possibility of enriching oneself without labour: the discovery of gold in Australia, as in California, has multiplied

monks, the Spanish character and manners moulded by the Arabs of Spain, the care taken not unnecessarily to run counter to the habits of the people, the early establishment of a court of law equal in rank and dignity to some of the first tribunals of Spain—all these causes no doubt combined to secure the result of a well-ordered and contented population.

Judging, however, from the experience of modern times in our own possessions and colonies, I would humbly suggest that the cause of the well-being of the inhabitants of the Philippines is to be looked for principally in the establishment of the royal Audiencia, or High Court of Law, and that the foundation of the prosperity of the Manila Islands was that which is pointed out in the inscription over the principal gateway of the Imperial Palace of Vienna: "Justitia regnorum fundamentum." The atrocities of Pizarro were such that they have engrossed all attention, and the colonial legislation enacted to prevent the repetition of similar offences seems, from the following complaint of a modern Spanish writer, to have escaped the observation of European authors. Sr. Arias says, in a prize essay on the *Influence on*

crimes and inflamed all the bad passions; it is to it that the incredible fact must be attributed that eighteen persons on an average out of a hundred are annually taken up in the colony, and that it is almost impossible to open a newspaper from the first of January to the thirty-first of December without learning that some one has died from drunkenness that day in the town in which that newspaper is published."—*Seize mille lieues à travers l'Asie et l'Océanie*, by Comte Henry Russell-Killough.

Spain of her Dominion in America, written in 1854, —"How certain it is that if the writers of other nations, on taking up their pens to write of America, had only known the code by which that part of the world was governed, they would not have shewn so little circumspection, nor would they have allowed themselves to be led away so blindly by their imagination. We have said the code, but indeed, by reading only some of its headings, they would have formed another opinion of the colonial rule of Spain. What, nevertheless, could their information be on this matter, when, in the year 1812, Dr. Mier could not find in the public libraries of London a copy of the *Recopilacion* of the Indies, which he required to consult upon certain points upon which he was writing? In America itself there was the greatest neglect in the study of these laws, as an author of that country shews. Perhaps there is not one of them which may not be presented as an example of equity and discretion; but among them some stand forth which ought to be learnt by heart by those who take pleasure in meeting with proofs of benevolence towards peoples on the part of those that govern them, or by those who seek for models for establishing the public administration upon a basis of equity. Of this class is the Royal Order of Philip IV directed to the Viceroy and High Court of Mexico, reproduced a thousand times in different works on account of the singularly humane terms in which it is drawn up: so is also another law providing that offences committed against Indians should be punished with greater rigour than those committed against Spaniards; and the law which directed that the prelates and clergy should from the pulpit and in confession persuade Spaniards who had made their fortunes in the Indies, and who wished to assign by their wills, legacies, pious works, alms or restitutions, that they should apply these to the country to which they owed their fortunes; by this law, at the same time that America was preserved from being drained of large sums, the country of the testators deprived itself of a similar amount, and their families and relatives of considerable succours."

Though the author, De Morga, was high in the legal profession, and carried his legal habits and manner of acting with him, when on an emergency he stepped into the naval profession, he does not seem to seek to praise the High Court of Law, nor to show how useful its establishment was to the Philippines; but this appears indirectly from the narrative. One testimony to the efforts of the administration during De Morga's residence, to check oppression by the Spaniards, is not supplied by the author, but through the medium of a Dutch corsair, who intercepted letters from the Spanish governor ordering a priest to interfere in behalf of the natives against a Spaniard who was oppressing them. The intervention of the author and the legists in opposition to the views of the adventurers Diego Belloso and Blas Ruyz was most beneficial. A moral may be drawn from this for the government of our own Asiatic possessions, where the increase of European emigrants through the greater facility of access by steam, and the lesser powers now possessed by the government to control them, render it much more essential than it was in the time of our author, that the courts of law should be independent, and that they should be composed of men of such character, weight, and eminence as to make them respected. That our courts of law and judicial legislation in the colonies are not always what they ought to be, compared with what they are at home, will hardly be denied; but the assertion may be supported by the testimony of Mr. Eyre, who complains, and quotes Captain Grey, also the superintendent of Port Phillip, and several others, to the effect that the testimony of the natives was not admitted in any degree in any court of law in Australia, and that when the lives of the aborigines had been taken in the district of Port Phillip, "in no single instance has the settler been brought before the proper tribunal" (vol. ii, p. 193). The late request of the negroes of Jamaica for independent magistrates, and the governor, Sir John Peter Grant's public declaration that there was no justice in Jamaica for the poor man, are so recent as to be in everybody's recollection. Since Earl Grey's speech in July of 1864 on the deplorable lawlessness fostered in China and Japan by the impunity resulting from the abrogation of the law of the land in favour of the law of various European powers supposed to be administered by their consuls, Her Majesty's Government issued an order in Council dated March 9, 1865, for the appointment of a court of law and a judge in China, with jurisdiction over British subjects in China and Japan.[1]

This is an improvement, so long as the foreign jurisdiction treaties are not abolished; and it would appear to have had a good effect, for since then such cases as that of Dr. Rice shooting a Chinaman in June 1864, and that of another Englishman shooting a Chinese boatwoman in the public canal, reported in the London papers of February or March of 1865, in both cases with comparative impunity, have not again appeared in the public prints.

From the account of the insurrection of the Chinese, of the massacre of them, and of the disturbance of social life in Manila caused by their disappearance, De Morga was evidently of opinion that it was the result of a misunderstanding, and was forced on the Chinese by the unjust suspicions of the Spaniards which they expressed too openly. Similar suspicions and panics might arise in Singapore (where there is a large Chinese population), at any time, from as idle a story as that which caused the calamity related by De Morga. The Kong-Sis of the Straits, which are clubs and beneficent societies, and which might advantageously be regulated and encouraged, are apt to be looked upon as merely secret societies. An article which lately appeared in the *Pall Mall Gazette* (written, I believe, by a distinguished member of the Hakluyt Society), may well be added here as a commentary on such panics, and also in reference to the preceding paragraph.

[1] See Parliamentary Papers.

"THE LATE STIR AT DAMASCUS.—Some days ago it was reported in Paris that the apprehension of a massacre of Christians was prevailing in Syria. The Christians of Damascus most unquestionably were massacred seven years ago, and it is therefore anything but unnatural for them to entertain apprehensions of massacres and every other horror, or to shiver at the faintest rustle of excitement among the Mahometans. There has never been any time since the massacre, in fact, in which they have been quite free from some such apprehension in a greater or less degree; and at the present moment more especially, when rumours of Christian risings and of European material or moral support of risings all over Turkey are at their rifest in all men's minds, it would be very strange if these apprehensions were not prevalent among the Christians of Damascus, or if some justification or tangible occasion for them were not presented by the attitude of the native Syrian Mahometans, their former persecutors. Now something did really happen at Damascus to give rise to the Paris rumour, and it befell in this wise. Towards the end of last month the town of Damascus was placarded one fine day with printed papers, calling upon all the believers to come forward and contribute to the relief of the suffering Mussulman families of Crete, who had been driven out of house and home by a wicked rebellion, and were huddled together in the fortified towns in a state of complete wretchedness and starvation. The terms of this appeal would seem to have been perfectly temperate, and free from any tinge of fanaticism, even when read by the most bloodshot and panic-stricken eyes; but its tenor was undeniably such as to rouse a sense of injury in the breasts of the faithful which a native Christian, with the memory of the horrors of 1860 still fresh within him, might well be excused for deeming certain to be vented on himself as its first victim. Accordingly, to use the words of an informant, the Christians openly shewed their fear. The rest of the matter is so plain, and so inevitable of perception to even the most careless or ignorant student of modern Turkey, that it seems hardly necessary to finish the story. Of course the consuls took up the extreme view to which the natives in their panic terror had rushed, and of course they interfered at once. Of course the governor disavowed all knowledge of the placards, imprisoned the director of the printing press—a Government establishment, it should be said—and in the excess of bewildered fussiness conspicuous among consul-ridden pashas when nervously anxious to please their oppressors, put under arrest his own secretary, who had been denounced to him as the author or authoriser of the paper. Perhaps the secretary was so; or perhaps the governor himself may have been so, for the matter of that, for there is nothing in the way of trick whereof a Turkish official is not capable, at the same time that there is nothing whereof a native Christian will not accuse a Turkish official, or which a consul with a keen nose for a 'question' will not think it his profit or his duty to believe against the official on the charge of the native Christian. All these three antecedent probabilities neutralise one another, and accordingly the authorship of the placard must stand over to be decided upon direct evidence by those whom it may concern. The various morals with which the story is pointed are the only things which concern us, however, and of these the chief one is the impossibility of carrying on any government of any kind much longer in Turkey under a system of consular interference, which practically serves to put all government in abeyance without undertaking the responsibility of governing on its own account, as it were, by commission. The Mahometan population, invited under compulsion to forego all its former privileges, in the name of justice and humanity, suddenly finds itself in the present case hindered and even punished for raising a call to charity and humanity which is actually a direct imitation of similar calls recently made in Western Europe. An evil motive and an evil design are ascribed to their temperate appeal on behalf of suffering; perhaps with rightness of apprehension as regards its ultimate possible result, but, at any rate, with the utmost want of charity as regards its immediate conscious motive, and without the slightest rational ground for such conclusion beyond a sheer panic terror. They think it a monstrous and vexatious grievance that they should not be allowed to subscribe funds like anybody else for the relief of their brethren, and they see in the prohibition the dawning of a bitter day of retributary oppression. In that perhaps they are not far wrong, if words and acts may be taken as indications of future European policy in the East. We seem going the right way to have a sick continent on our hands ten times as big as ourselves. In that case, no injury and no danger to the straight march of human progress will be so great as the danger of giving the Mahometan world reason to believe that Europe has the will as well as the power to mete out a different measure of justice and morality to the Christian and to the Mahometan, the European and the Asiatic."

To revert to the comparison with Australia, Mr. Eyre, and Captain Grey whom he quotes, complain much of the inconsistency with which the Australians were put on the footing of British subjects and made amenable to British law in cases of offences against the settlers, yet were left unprotected by that law when oppressed by the settlers or by members of their own community, the law courts taking no cognisance of the testimony of the aborigines : they also complain of the barbarous usages of the Australians having been allowed to subsist which prevent them rising to a state of civilisation. This is the more inconsistent, since in other countries of Asia under our rule and amongst civilised communities we have not been so scrupulous or chary of overturning customs which we have met with, and which were not consonant with our ideas. The Spaniards in the Philippines seem to have been more happy in the choice of their measures. Whilst they did away with all customs that were contrary to natural right they allowed the others to subsist; they abolished the arbitrary power of the chiefs, but they maintained their social position, and made use of those of the higher class for their own administration. They found in the Philippines slaves, and peasants owing more than feudal service, somewhat analogous to the position of the peasantry of the Danubian principalities under the Réglement Organique;[1] though they named these two distinct classes, indifferently slaves, they left them to subsist nearly as they found them, though they prohibited Spaniards from holding any of the natives of the Philippines under either form of slavery, or from employing them otherwise than with wages and by mutual agreement; they also appear to have diminished the number of days of corvée owed by the serfs to the chiefs, and to have required a somewhat similar service from some of the natives for the civil authorities, paying wages however in return. They also prohibited all Spaniards except the officers of justice from entering the towns of the natives. Their magistrates were bound to visit the whole of their districts, and to change their residence three times in the course of the year, so as to be nearer at hand to assist with their office all the subjects within their district. The natives were allowed to change their residence when they moved to a district where religious instruction was already esta-

[1] In obedience to democratic ideas from France, the whole position of the peasants has been changed in 1864, and they have been made proprietors, paying a rent to the state which is supposed to reimburse the proprietors; but less corn is grown, and the peasants are now worse off than before.

blished, but this was not allowed when the native wished to go from a district provided with religious instruction to one where there was none. Lastly, the High Court of Justice, which had very full powers and extensive attributions, held an inquiry upon all officials on the termination of their office, and till the court had issued its sentence the official could not be reappointed. Crime also on the part of the Spanish settlers was punished, and Castilian convicts rowed on the benches of the galleys side by side with Chinese and native convicts. Several of Mr. Eyre's suggestions for the improvement of the condition of the natives of Australia are similar to the measures put in force in the Philippines. Doubtless the inhabitants of the Philippines were much superior to the Australians; but in New Zealand, where the aborigines have very great natural abilities, the result is not much more in their favour.[1] The Philip-

---

[1] The contrast between the principles that directed the government of the Philippines, and the weakness of religion which has presided over the destinies of Australia and New Zealand, may be well exemplified by the following extracts from an article in *Macmillan's Magazine* of November 1865 (p. 56) by Mr. Henry Kingsley, on Eyre's Australian journey. Comment is unnecessary, and moreover is supplied by the writer himself.

"Wylie was a very good, a somewhat exceptional, specimen of his people, as Eyre, a lover and protector of the blacks, allows. Now you know these people must *go*. God never made the Portland Bay district for *them*. All one asks is, that the thing should be done with decency, and with every sort of indulgence; whereas it is not, but in a scandalous and disgraceful manner. Of course these Australians must be improved, but let the improvement be done with some show of decency. But we may preach and preach, and the same old story will go on, now there

pines had another great advantage over our colonies in the active co-operation of the monks, who, unburdened by families, were more able to devote themselves to their labours; also (especially at that date) the monks had more influence over their own countrymen than our missionaries have ever enjoyed. From De Morga's account they do not appear to have been very numerous, but rather to have been insufficient in number for the work they had to do; but even had there been legions of them, as Monsieur Rienzi, a French writer on the Philippines, says there were, they never cost as much to the state as the protectorate of the aborigines in New South Wales and Port Phillip, which Mr. Eyre states to have been about ten thousand pounds annually.[1] It is also

is no Governor Gipps; and so we will leave preaching, and mind our business; for public opinion, unbacked by a Governor Gipps, is but a poor thing for the blacks."

"The above paragraph was written yesterday, and under ordinary circumstances I should have altered it and polished it down. But this morning I got my *Times*, and read about the massacre of the Indians on the Colorado; and that seemed to illustrate what I have said above in such a singular manner that I determined to let the paragraph stand, just as I had jotted it down as a matter of curiosity. The leading article in the *Times* this morning was remarkably sensible. When the colonists are left to administer justice in their own way, they do invariably say, 'We must fight as they fight;' and they not only say so, but do so. For very decency's sake, this improving business should be done by paid third parties, if it were only to avoid scandal. So we are going to withdraw the imperial troops from New Zealand, and do the business in a shorter and cheaper manner."

[1] Since the above was written I have found the following confirmation of what I have said of the salutary influence of the monks:—

worthy of remark, now that warlike expenditure so much exceeds what is allotted to instruction, that, of the capitation tax paid by the natives, two reals of

"The most efficient agents of public order throughout the islands are the local clergy, many of whom are also of the country. There are considerable parts of these possessions in which the original races, as at Ceylon, retain their independence, and are neither taxed nor interfered with: and throughout the islands the power of the government is founded much more on moral than on physical influence. The laws are mild, and peculiarly favourable to the natives. The people are indolent, temperate, and superstitious. The government is conciliatory and respectable in its character and appearance, and prudent but decisive in the exercise of its powers over the people; and united with the clergy, who are shrewd, and tolerant, and sincere, and respectable in general conduct, studiously observant of their ecclesiastical duties, and managing with great tact the native character." (Mr. Consul Farren, Manila, March 13, 1845.)

"Without any governing power whatever, the greatest moral influence in these possessions is that which the priests possess, and divide among the monastic orders of Augustines, Recoletos, Dominicans, and Franciscans (who are all Spaniards), and the assistant native clergy. A population exceeding 3,800,000 souls is ranged into 677 *pueblos* or parishes, without reckoning the unsubdued tribes. In 577 of those *pueblos* there are churches with convents or clerical residences attached, and about 500 of them are in the personal incumbency of those Spanish monks. The whole ecclesiastical subdivisions being embraced in the archbishopric of Manila and three bishoprics."

"The Philippines were converted to Christianity and maintained in it by these monastic orders, energetically protected by them (and at no very past period) against the oppressions of the provincial authorities, and are still a check on them in the interests of the people. The clergy are receivers in their districts of the capitation tax paid by the natives, and impose it: they are the most economical agency of the government." (Mr. Consul Farren, March 29, 1851.)

"What religion has accomplished, it alone can maintain; and

each person's tax went to religious instruction, whilst only one and a half was assigned to the expenses of the permanent military forces.

De Morga, as well as other writers of his period, refer with satisfaction to the demarcation drawn by Pope Alexander VI between the regions to be explored by Spain and Portugal. By this measure many wars were avoided; not only between the forces of those two powers, but also between the various nations of the Old and New Worlds, who would have been involved in the struggles of those rival competitors for the dominion over the newly discovered regions. Some idea may be formed of the evils which were averted, from De Morga's account of the feuds and jealousies between the Spaniards and Portuguese in China and Cambodia, even when those two nations were temporarily fellow-subjects of Philip the Second. It must however be observed that this Bull contains a grant to the

---

it is but too certain that the Philippines would be lost to Spain and to the Catholic religion if ever they were deprived of the monks who so wonderfully guard them without the assistance of a single European soldier. May so fatal a moment never arrive!"—*Mallat*, i, p. 40.

"How happy would France be if she knew how to make a suitable use of this moral force in her new colonies! What an economy of means! What security for the colonists! What happiness for the natives! Thus it is that more than once disturbances which had the most threatening appearances have been skilfully appeased only by the word of a priest. An old viceroy of Mexico used to say that—'in each friar in the Philippines the king had got a captain-general and a whole army'."—*Mallat*, i, p. 389.

Spaniards and Portuguese of all lands and islands to be discovered, which should not be already occupied by any other Christian prince before Christmas day of 1493, without regard to their having other owners and governments, or to the equal rights of all nations. This error, however, was committed before Suarez and Vattel had written, and it has not yet been entirely removed in certain quarters. Another example of the salutary action of the Papacy occurs in the history of the same period. The Zamorin was informed by the Brahmans and Mussulmans of the designs of the Portuguese on Ormuz and other towns of the Indian Ocean, and sent to ask the assistance of the Sultan of Egypt. The Sultan was already greatly irritated at the piracies of the Portuguese in the Red Sea and its neighbourhood, and at the interception of the pilgrims to Mekka; he accordingly sent for the abbot of the monks of St. Catharine on Mount Sinai, a Spanish monk named Mauro, and complained of the conduct of the Portuguese, and threatened to turn all the foreign merchants out of his dominions and to destroy the sanctuaries at Jerusalem and other places. Before resorting to reprisals, he would, he said, stay his anger if the abbot would go as his ambassador to Rome and arrange the matter pacifically. The abbot consented and went to Rome charged with letters to Pope Alexander VI complaining of the King of Portugal yearly ravaging the coasts of Africa, and of the King of Spain for having driven the Moors out of Granada without any fault of theirs or cause; and that since these two kings proceeded so tyranically against the Mussulmans, and in a manner so contrary to the laws of nations, he would blot out the name of Christian in his dominions. But if His Holiness wished to avoid this, let him call upon those kings to desist, and interpose his authority. The pontiff at once held a consistory with the College of Cardinals upon this matter, and resolved to send the ambassador with letters from himself to the King of Portugal, begging him not to run counter to the King of Egypt, if it were only not to put in danger so many merchants and so many holy places. The King of Portugal replied to the Pope that he should not let himself be alarmed at the bravado and empty threats of the Sultan, who would not injure either the merchants or the holy places on account of the losses which he would himself suffer thereby; and that as for the Moors of Granada, that matter had been quite forgotten at the end of twelve years, and the Sultan only complained of that, having nothing else to fix upon. The Abbot Mauro returned with this answer to Rome, and the King of Portugal increased his preparations against India and Egypt.

The Sultan of Egypt did not carry out his threats (if he really made them with regard to the sanctuaries), not because of the losses they would have entailed upon him, but because his laws did not permit him to do so. The remonstrances of the Pope might have had more effect if they had been based more upon right than upon expediency, as seems to have been the case, judging from the above account; nevertheless, these two acts of Pope Alexander VI, and other similar action on the part of the Holy See, shew how frequently it acted as peacemaker, arbitrator and court of appeal, and how easily it might again do so if the promised deliberations of the coming Œcumenical Council, upon the establishment of a Diplomatic College at Rome, have that happy result, which would do much to recall the rule of law in Europe, and to secure peace amongst men.

The reader is referred to Appendix II for further information about the Philippine Islands in modern times, with respect to matters treated of by De Morga.

I desire to express my obligations to Mr. Major of the British Museum for his assistance on this as on other occasions, especially since it was at his recommendation, when formerly he was Secretary of the Hakluyt Society, that I undertook this work.

Geneva, October, 1867.

SUCÉSOS DE LAS
ISLAS PHILIPINAS
DIRIGIDOS
A DON CHRISTOVAL GOMEZ
DE SANDOVAL Y ROJAS, DUQUE
DE CEA.

POR EL DOCTOR ANTONIO DE MORGA,
ALCALDE DEL CRIMEN DE LA REAL
AUDIENCIA DE LA NUEVA ESPAÑA;
CONSULTOR DEL SANTO OFFICIO DE LA
INQUISICION.

MEXICI AD INDOS.
Anno 1609.

IMPRIMATUR.

By order of the most excellent Lord, Don Luis de Velasco, Vice Roy of this New Spain, and of the most illustrious and most reverend Lord Don fray Garcia Guerra, Archbishop of Mexico, of His Majesty's Council: I have seen this book of the *Events in the Philippine Islands*, written by Dr. Antonio de Morga, Alcalde of the Court and Royal Audiencia of Mexico; and it appears to me to be agreeable and profitable, and worthy to be printed; inasmuch as the author has observed with exactitude the laws of history, and for the careful arrangement of the work; in which he shews brilliant genius, and a laconic style which few attain to, and a truthfulness in the matter, such as one might have who possessed such complete information respecting it, from the years during which he governed those islands. And I have signed this with my name in this Professed House of the Company of Jesus of Mexico, on the 1st day of April of 1609.

JUAN SANCHEZ.

Don Luys de Velasco, knight of the order of Santiago, Vice Roy lieutenant of the King our Lord, Governor and Captain General of New Spain and president of the Royal Audiencia and Chancery which resides in it, etc. Whereas Dr. Antonio de Morga, Alcalde of crime in this said Royal Audiencia, has informed me that he had written a book and treatise of the *Events in the Philippine Islands*, from their first discovery and conquest until the end of the past year of six hundred and seven; and has requested me to grant him leave and privilege that he may print it, and no other person for some time, and on my behalf I committed to padre

Juan Sanchez, of the Company of Jesus, the inspection of the said book: therefore, by this present I give it to the said Dr. Antonio de Morga, so that he, or the person who may hold his permission, may freely, during the period of ten years, the first in succession, print the said book, by means of such printer as may seem fit to him: and I prohibit that any person should do so within the said time without the said permission, under pain of losing, and that he shall lose the type and accessories with which the said impression should be made; which I apply to the Royal Chamber of His Majesty, and the said Dr. Antonio de Morga, by halves. Done in Mexico, at seven days of the month of April of one thousand and six hundred and nine years. Don Luys de Velasco,

By order of the Viceroy, Martin Lopez Ganna.

Don Fray Garcia Guerra, by the Divine Grace, and that of the Holy Apostolic See, Archbishop of Mexico, of the Council of His Majesty, etc. Having seen the opinion of padre Juan Sanchez of the Company of Jesus, which he has given, of having seen the book which Dr. Antonio de Morga, Alcalde in this Court and Chancery, presented before us, intitled—*Events in the Philippine Islands, their Conquest and Conversion*, for which we gave our commission; and as by the said opinion it is established that it contains nothing against our Holy Catholic Faith, or good morals: on the contrary, that it is useful and profitable to all persons who may read it: by this present we give license to the said Dr. Antonio de Morga that he may cause the said book of the said conquest and conversion of the said Philippine Islands to be printed in any of the printing presses of this city. Given in Mexico, the seventh of April of one thousand six hundred and nine years.

Fr. Garcia, Archbishop of Mexico,
by order of his most illustrious Lordship
the Archb. of Mexico.
D. Juan de Portilla, *Secretary*.

DEDICATION TO

DON CRISTOVAL GOMEZ DE SANDOVAL Y ROJAS,

DUKE OF CEA.[1]

I OFFER to your Excellency this small work, deserving of a good reception as much for the faithful narrative which it contains, as for its being free from artifice and ornament. Knowing my poor resources, I began it without fear, and took courage to go on with it: it is clear that if that which is given had to bear an equal proportion to him that receives, there would be no one who might deserve to place his works in the hands of your Excellency; and those deeds would remain forgotten, which in these times our Spaniards have done in the discovery, conquest, and conversion of the Philippine Islands; as well as various events which from time to time have happened in the great kingdom of the Pagans which surround them: for as these parts are so remote, no narrative has appeared in public which purports to treat of them from their beginnings up to the state in which they now are. I pray your Excellency to receive my good will, laid prostrate at your feet; and even should this short writing not give that pleasure which self love (that infirmity of human wit) leads me to expect, may your Excellency deal with me, as you are used to do with all; reading it and cloaking its imperfections with your courtesy and gentleness, as being so rich in these and other virtues, which, with Divine power, cause lofty things not to be strangers to more humble matters; and have placed your Excel-

[1] See Appendix I for the text of this dedication.

lency in your own natural greatness, in the place which you hold for the good of these realms, rewarding and favouring what is good, correcting and repressing that which is opposite: in which consists the well being of the Republic, which gave occasion to Democritus, the ancient philosopher, to say that reward and punishment were indeed gods. In order to enjoy this felicity there is no need to wish for any time gone by, but contenting ourselves with the present only to pray God to preserve your Excellency for us many years.

D. ANTONIO DE MORGA.

TO THE READER.

THE monarchy of the Kings of Spain has been aggrandised by the zeal and care with which they have defended within their own hereditary kingdoms, the Holy Catholic Faith, which the Roman Church teaches, against whatsoever adversaries oppose it, or seek to obscure the truth by various errors, which faith they have disseminated throughout the world. Thus by the mercy of God they preserve their realms and subjects in the purity of the Christian religion, deserving thereby the glorious title and renown which they possess of Defenders of the Faith. Moreover, by the valour of their indomitable hearts, and at the expense of their revenues and property, with Spanish fleets and men, they have furrowed the seas, and discovered and conquered vast kingdoms in the most remote and unknown parts of the world, leading their inhabitants to a knowledge of the true God, and to the fold of the Christian church, in which they now live, governed in civil and political matters with peace and justice, under the shelter and protection of the royal arm and power which was wanting to them:[1] weighed

[1] This boast is true of Manila, and of Manila alone amongst all the colonies of Spain or the other European states. If the natives of Manila have been more fortunate than those of Cuba, Peru, Jamaica, and Mexico, it has been owing to the absence of gold, which in other places attracted adventurers so lawless that neither the Church nor Courts of justice could restrain them.

down as they were by blind tyrannies and barbarous cruelties, with which the enemy of the human race had for so long afflicted them and brought them up for himself.

From this cause the crown and sceptre of Spain has come to extend itself over all that the sun looks on, from its rising to its setting, with the glory and splendour of its power and majesty; but surpassing any of the other princes of the earth by having gained innumerable souls for heaven, which has been Spain's principal intention and wealth. And besides much riches and the treasures which she enjoys, together with memorable deeds and victories which she has won, so that throughout the universe her great name is praised and celebrated, and the perseverance and valour of her vassals, who have accomplished these deeds and poured out their blood.

Having won America, a fourth part of the earth which the ancients never knew, they sailed following the sun, and discovered in the Western Ocean an archipelago of many islands, adjacent to further Asia, inhabited by various nations, abounding in rich metals, precious stones, and pearls, and all manner of fruit. Where, raising the standard of the Faith, they snatched them from the yoke and power of the devil, and placed them under her command and government: so that justly may they raise in those isles the pillars and trophies of *Non plus ultra*, which the famous Hercules left on the shore of Cadiz, and later the strong arm of Charles V, our sovereign, cast down upon the ground, surpassing him in great deeds of arms and enterprises.

The isles having been subjected by the sovereign light of the holy Gospel which entered there, the heathen were baptised, and the darkness of their paganism banished, and they changed their names for that of Christians. The islands also, leaving the names which they held, took (with the change of faith and baptism of their inhabitants) the name of Philippine Islands; in recognition of the great favours which they received from His Majesty Philip the Second, our sovereign: in whose fortunate age and rule they were conquered, favoured and encouraged, like a work and labour of his royal hands.

Their discovery, conquest and conversion was not accomplished without much expenditure, labour and Spanish blood, with varied events and critical moments, which make the work more illustrious, and furnish a spacious field, over which historians may extend themselves, for such is their office, and the matter is not scanty: and it possesses serious and pleasant subjects, sufficient to deserve their care, without its being prejudicial to them to treat of Indian occurrences and wars, which they who have no experience of them esteem as less than what they are. For the people of these parts are valiant and warlike nations of Asia, brought up in continual warfare by sea and land, making use of artillery and other warlike instruments, taught in this exercise by the necessity of their own defence against the great and powerful kingdoms in their neighbourhood; and (if with a few imperfections) they have become skilled and their teaching completed in the school of Spain, which lastly brought war to their doors, as has happened to other provinces of Europe in the like manner which had fallen into ignorance and neglect of the use of arms.

Some curious persons have planned to write this history, to whom (as time and resources failed me) I have given and distributed many papers and narratives which I possessed; and I hope they will publish them with more purpose than that which up to the present time we have received piecemeal from some historians of our time.

I spent eight years in the Philippine Islands, the best years of my life, serving unremittingly in the office of lieutenant of the governor and captain general, and from the moment the Royal Audiencia was founded in Manila in the office of auditor, the first who was received in it. And desirous that the affairs of these islands should be known, particularly those which happened in the time in which I dealt with them, taking them from their origin, as much as might be sufficient, I have related them in a book of eight chapters; and the first seven contain the discoveries, conquests, and other events in the islands and kingdoms and provinces in the neighbourhood, which happened in the time of the proprietary governors that there were until the death of Don Pedro de Acuña. And the eighth and last chapter is a brief summary and narrative of their qualities, inhabitants, and method of governing and converting them, and other special matters, and of the knowledge, dealings and communication which they had with the other islands and gentile communities conterminous to them. As fearful am I of the defects which will be found in this, as persuaded of being deserving of pardon, for having designed, this being my intention, to give to each one that which is due, and to restore the truth without enmity or flattery, which has been injured in some narratives which are going about the world, a fault very much to be reproved in those who relate the deeds of others, and prohibited by a penal law which Cato and Marcius, tribunes of the Roman people, established for those who in recounting their own deeds exceeded the truth, which would seem less worthy of punishment, as self love intervenes in their case.

There will not be wanting some one who will call me to account for my oversights, and I shall have already given him an answer by confessing them; and should this not be enough to put him to silence, stopping up my ears like another Ulysses, I will pass by this inconvenience (with the hurry with which I have written), and will serve whoever may read it, which will be sufficient to remove me from greater dangers.

IT IS TO BE NOTED

In reading this history, that some words may be observed, names of provinces, towns, magistrates, arms and vessels, which for more fitness have been written as they are commonly named and are current in those parts; and in the last chapter, which contains the account of the islands and their peculiarities, these words will be explained and declared.

CHAPTER I.

Of the First Discoveries of the Eastern Isles, and of the Voyage which the Adelantado Miguel Lopez de Legazpi made thither; of the Conquest and Pacification of the Philippines during his Governorship; and of Guido de Labazarris, who afterwards undertook the charge.

ACCORDING to ancient and modern cosmographers, that part of the world called Asia has adjacent to it an immense number of islands, large and small, inhabited by divers nations and peoples, as rich in precious stones, gold, silver, and other minerals, as abounding in fruit and grain, flocks and animals; in some of these all sorts of spices are produced, which are carried thence and distributed throughout the universe. They name them commonly in their books and descriptions, and charts of navigation, the great Archipelago of Saint Lazarus, which is in the Eastern Ocean; of these islands, amongst others more famous, are the isles of Maluco, Celebes, Tendaya, Luzon, Mindanao and Borneo, which are now called the Philippines.

The Pope Alexander the Sixth having divided the conquests of the New World between the Kings of Castille and Portugal, they agreed to make the division by means of a line which the cosmographers drew across the world, in order that, the one towards the west and the other towards the east, they might follow out their discoveries and conquests, and settle peacefully whatever each might win within his demarcation.[1]

[1] This demarcation was a line drawn from the North to the South Pole, at a distance of one hundred leagues west of the Azores and Cape Verde islands. Solorzano gives a translation of the Bull in his *Politica Indiana*.

After that the city of Malacca had been won for the crown of Portugal, on the mainland of Asia, in the kingdom of Jor (Johore), named by the ancients the Aurea Chersonesus, in the year one thousand five hundred and eleven, on receiving news of the islands which lie near there, especially those of Maluco and Banda, where they gather cloves and nutmeg, a Portuguese fleet set out to discover them,[1] and having touched at Banda, they went thence to the isle of Terrenate, one of the Maluco isles, drawn thither by its own king, in his defence against the King of Tidore, his neighbour with whom he was at war: this was the beginning of the settlement which the Portuguese made in Maluco.

Francisco Serrano, who returned to Malacca with this discovery, and passed on to India in order to go to Portugal and give an account of it, died before making this voyage, having communicated by letters what he had seen to his friend Fernando de Magallanes[2] (for they had been together at the taking of Malacca, and he was in Portugal); from

[1] This fleet, according to John de Barros, Decade III, lib. v, cap. 6, and San Roman, p. 217, consisted of three ships under Antonio de Abreo, who returned from Banda to Malacca, where he gave information of the Moluccas to Captain Fernan Perez de Andrada, and, returning to Portugal, he was shipwrecked and lost. Francisco Serrano, his companion, followed up the discovery in a war junk, which was wrecked on the island of Tortoises, in the islands of Luco Pino, thirty-seven leagues beyond Banda, only the men and arms being saved: here they defeated some pirates, who conveyed them to Amboyna. Thence their fame reached Ternate and Tidor. Cachil Boleyfe, King of Ternate, secured the assistance of Serrano against Cachil Almansor, King of Tidor: both of these kings and their people were Mussulmans, and had been so for some time back. Francisco Serrano died in Ternate a few days before the King Cachil Boleyfe, and about the same time that Magellan was killed.

[2] Part of the substance of these letters is contained in the relation of Francisco and Juan Serrano's voyage, an appendix to Magellan's account of the shores of the Indian Ocean, *Coasts of East Africa and Malabar*, Hakluyt Society, 1866. Perhaps the war junk of San Roman is the same as the caravel which Francisco Serrano stole at Malacca, as mentioned in the above-named narrative.

which narrative he understood what was most fitting with respect to the discovery and navigation of those islands.

Magallanes at this time passed over to the service of the King of Castille, from causes which moved him thereto;[1] and he set forth to the Emperor Charles V our sovereign that the islands of Maluco fell within the demarcation of his crown of Castille, and that the conquest of them pertained to him conformably to the concession of Pope Alexander;[2] he also offered to make an expedition and a voyage to them in the emperor's name, laying his course through that part of the delimitation which belonged to Castille, and availing himself of a famous astrologer and cosmographer named Ruyfarelo, whom he kept in his service.[3]

The emperor (from the importance of the business) confided this voyage and discovery to Magallanes, with the ships

[1] De Barros says the devil moved him; but he admits that his treatment by the King of Portugal was very aggravating. However, in seeking a south-west passage, and availing himself of the encouragement of Spain, he only followed the example of Columbus.

[2] According to De Barros, Decade III, lib. v. Francisco Serrano, in his letters to Magellan, doubled the distance from Malacca to Maluco in order to increase his reputation as a discoverer, and to obtain a reward from the King of Portugal; Magellan used Serrano's letters and distances to prove to Charles V that the Moluccas fell within his limit; but he seems to have done so in good faith, for, from Barros' account, he expected to have reached the Moluccas sooner, and thought he had run by them. Decade III, lib. v, cap. 10.

[3] According to De Barros, Magellan found Ruy Faleiro, a Portuguese astrologer in Spain, also aggrieved by King Manuel: he took him to Seville, where Magellan stayed with his relation, Diogo Barbosa, father of Duarte Barbosa, and married a daughter of Diogo. Ruy Farelo did not sail with Magellan, either as Barros says, because he repented of the expedition, or because his astrology shewed him the end which the fleet was to meet with. The astrologer of the fleet was Andres de San Martin: he and Christoval Rabelo, a Portuguese, and six or seven Castilians, were killed with Magellan. San Roman says he saw a narrative in the handwriting of the pilot himself, whom Magellan took with him in this fleet, who came to Castile by order of Don Juan de Borja; and this narrative is in the keeping of the Licentiate Cespedes, cosmographer of the king.

and provisions which were requisite for it, with which he set sail and discovered the straits to which he gave his name. Through these he passed to the South Sea, and navigated to the islands of Tendaya and Sebu, where he was killed by the natives of Matan, which is one of them.[1] His ships went on to Maluco, where their crews had disputes and differences with the Portuguese who were in the island of Terrenate: and at last, not being able to maintain themselves there, they left Maluco in a ship named the *Victory*, which had remained to the Castilians out of their fleet; and they took as chief and captain Juan Sebastian del Caño,[2] who performed the voyage to Castile, by the way of India, where he arrived with very few of his men, and he gave an account to his majesty of the discovery of the islands of the great archipelago, and of his voyage.

The same enterprise was attempted on other occasions, and was carried out by Juan Sebastian del Caño, and by the Comendador Loaisa, and the Saoneses, and the Bishop of Plasencia, without bearing the fruits that were expected, on account of the travail and risks of so distant a voyage, and the strife which those who arrived there encountered on the part of the Portuguese in Maluco.

After all these events, as it seemed that this voyage would be shorter and better by way of New Spain, a fleet was sent by that part in the year 1545 under the charge of Ruy Lopez de Villalobos, which passed by way of Sebu and reached Maluco, where it met with disputes with the Portuguese, misfortunes and troubles, by reason of which it did not succeed in the object which had been sought for; neither

[1] After the death of Magellan, Duarte Barbosa took the command: he and twenty officers were treacherously killed by the Christian king, with whom they had allied themselves, and Juan Serrano was left behind alive amongst the natives.

[2] He was a native of Guetaria in Biscay. This *Victory* was the first ship which circumnavigated the globe: it is represented on the cover of the volumes of the Hakluyt Society.

OF THE EASTERN ISLES. 15

was the fleet able to return to New Spain, from whence it had sailed, but was broken up, and some of the Castilians who remained went away from Maluco through Portuguese India, and returned to Castile. There they gave an account of what had happened in their voyage, and of the qualities and nature of the islands of Maluco, and of the others which they had seen.

As it afterwards appeared to the King Don Philip II our sovereign that it was not fitting for him to desist from this enterprise, and being informed by Don Luis de Velasco, Viceroy of New Spain, and by fray Andres de Urdaneta of the order of St. Augustine (who, being a secular, had been in Maluco with the fleet of the Commander Loaysa), that this voyage might be made shorter and more easily from New Spain, he committed it to the viceroy. Fray Andres de Urdaneta left the court of Madrid for New Spain, for, as he was so experienced and so good a geographer, he offered to go with the fleet and discover a way of returning. The viceroy equipped a fleet and men with what was most needful, in the port of Navidad in the South Sea, and gave it in charge to Miguel Lopez de Legazpi, inhabitant of Mexico, and a native of the province of Guipuzcoa, a person of quality and trust. On account of the death of the viceroy, the High Court (Audiencia), which governed in his stead, completed the despatching of Legazpi, giving him instructions as to the parts to which he was to go, with orders not to open them until he had got three hundred leagues out to sea; this, on account of differences which existed amongst the officers of the fleet, some saying that it would be better to go to New Guinea, others to the Luzon Islands, and others to Maluco. Miguel Lopez de Legazpi sailed from the port of Navidad in the year 1564, with five ships and five hundred men; he took also fray Andres de Urdaneta, and four other monks of the order of St. Augustine, and having navigated for some days to the west, he opened his instructions, and found that he was ordered to go to the Luzon Islands, where he was to endeavour to pacify them and reduce them to submission to his majesty, and to receive the holy Catholic faith. He pursued his voyage until he arrived at the island of Sebu, where he anchored, on account of the convenience of a good port which he met with, and the nature of the land. He was at first well and peacefully received by the natives and by their chief Tupas. Later they sought to kill him and his companions, because they had taken their provisions from them, upon which the natives took up arms against them; but it turned out contrariwise to what they had expected, for the Spaniards conquered and subjected them. Seeing what had taken place in Sebu, the natives of other neighbouring islands came peacefully before the chief of the expedition, making submission to him, and providing his camp with victuals. The first of our Spanish settlements was made in that port, which they named the city of the most holy name of Jesus, because they found there, in one of the houses of the natives when they conquered them, a carved image of Jesus; and it was believed that it had remained there from the fleet of Magellan, and the natives held it in great reverence, and it worked for them in their needs miraculous effects. This image they put in the monastery of St. Augustine, which was built in that city.

That same year the chief of the expedition despatched his flag-ship to New Spain, with advices and a narrative of what had occurred in the voyage, and of the settlement in Sebu, and requesting men and succour in order to continue the pacification of the islands; and fray Andres de Urdaneta and fray Andres de Aguirre, his companion, embarked in it.

One of the ships which sailed from the port of Navidad in company with the fleet, under the command of Don Alonso de Arellano, carried as pilot one Lope Martin, a mulatto and a good sailor, although a restless man; when this ship came near the islands it left the fleet and went forward amongst the islands, and having procured some provisions, without waiting for the chief of the expedition, turned back to New Spain by a northerly course : either from the little inclination which he had for making the voyage to the isles, or to gain the reward for having discovered the course for returning. He arrived speedily and gave news of having seen the islands, and discovered the return voyage, and said a few things with respect to his coming, without any message from the chief, nor any advices as to what had happened to him. Don Alonzo de Arellano was well received by the High Court of Justice which governed at that time, and was taking into consideration the granting of a reward to him and to his pilot: and this would have been done, had not the flag-ship of the commander-in-chief arrived during this time, after performing the same voyage, and bringing a true narrative of events, and of the actual condition of affairs, and of the settlement of Sebu; also giving an account of how Don Alonso de Arellano with his ship, without receiving orders and without any necessity for it, had gone on before the fleet on entering among the isles, and had never appeared since. It was also stated that, besides those islands which had peacefully submitted to his majesty, there were many others, large and rich, well provided with inhabitants, victuals and gold, which they hoped to reduce to subjection and peace with the assistance which was requested : and that the commander-in-chief had given to all these isles the name of Philippines, in memory of his majesty. The succour was sent to him immediately, and has continually been sent every year conformably to the necessities which have presented themselves; so that the land was won and maintained.

The commander-in-chief having heard of other islands around Sebu with abundance of provisions, he sent thither a few Spaniards to bring some of the natives over in a friendly manner, and rice for the camp, with which he maintained himself as well as he could, until, having passed over to the island of Panay, he sent thence Martin de Goiti, his master of the camp, and other captains, with the men that seemed to him sufficient, to the isle of Luzon, to endeavour to pacify it and bring it under submission to his majesty: a native of that island, of importance, named Maomat, was to guide them.

Having arrived at the bay of Manila, they found its town on the sea-beach close to a large river, in the possession of, and fortified by a chief whom they called Rajamora: and in front, across the river, there was another large town named Tondo; this also was held by another chief, named Rajamatanda. These places were fortified with palms, and thick *ariques*[1] filled in with earth, and a great quantity of bronze cannon, and other larger pieces with chambers. Martin de Goiti having began to treat with the chiefs and their people of the peace and submission which he claimed from them, it became necessary for him to break with them; and the Spaniards entered the town by force of arms, and took it, with the forts and artillery, on the day of Sta. Potenciana, the 19th of May,[2] the year 1571; upon which the natives and their chiefs gave in, and made submission, and many others of the same island of Luzon did the same.[3]

---

[1] I have been unable to discover the meaning of this word: the context would require *stakes*. It may be intended for areca palms, or be connected with the French *ariquier* for alizier, a thorn tree; or it might be from the Arabic '*ark*, a root.

[2] From the Spaniards having travelled westwards to the Philippines, there was an error of a day in their dates and almanacks. This was corrected in 1844, when, by order of the captain-general and the archbishop, the 31st of December, 1844, was suppressed, and the dates of Manila made to agree with those of the rest of the world. A similar correction was made at the same time at Macao, where the Portuguese who had travelled eastwards had an error of a day in an opposite direction.

[3] The Dutch *Memorable Embassies* states that the Spaniards sub-

When the commander-in-chief, Legazpi, received news in Panay of the taking of Manila, and the establishment of the Spaniards there, he left the affairs of Sebu, and of the other islands which had been subdued, set in order; and he entrusted the natives to the most trustworthy soldiers, and gave such orders as seemed fitting for the government of those provinces, which are commonly called the Bisayas de los Pintados, because the natives there have their whole bodies marked with fire. He then came to Manila with the remainder of his people, and was very well received there; and established afresh with the natives and their chiefs the peace, friendship, and submission to His Majesty which they had already offered. The commander-in-chief founded and established a town on the very site of Manila (of which Rajamora made a donation to the Spaniards for that purpose), on account of its being strong and in a well provisioned district, and in the midst of all the isles (leaving it its name of Manila, which it held from the natives). He took what land was sufficient for the city, in which the governor established his seat and residence; he fortified it with care, holding this object more especially in view, in order to make it the seat of government of this new settlement, rather than considering the temperature or width of the site, which is hot and narrow, from having the river on one side of the city, and the bay on the other, and at the back large swamps and marshes, which make it very strong.

From this post he pursued the work of pacification of the other provinces of this great island of Luzon and of the sur-

jected these islands almost without striking a blow, the inhabitants having forgotten the art of war and almost renounced civil life since they shook off the Chinese yoke. Since the Chinese had lost their dominion over these isles they had not ceased to trade with them as before and sent yearly more than twenty ships laden with cotton, silk, porcelain, sulphur, iron, copper, flour, quicksilver, cloth, and gunpowder, which they exchanged for skins of deer, buffaloes, and martens, with which these isles abounded (Part i, p. 140).

rounding districts; some submitting themselves willingly, others being conquered by force of arms, or by the industry of the monks who sowed the holy Gospel, in which each and all laboured valiantly, both in the time and governorship of the adelantado Miguel Lopez de Legazpi, and in that of other governors who succeeded him. The land was entrusted to those who had pacified it and settled in it, and heads named, on behalf of the crown, of the provinces, ports, towns, and cities, which were founded, together with other special commissions for necessities which might arise, and for the expenses of the royal exchequer. The affairs of the government, and conversion of the natives, were treated as was fit and necessary. Ships were provided each year to make the voyage to New Spain, and to return with the usual supplies; so that the condition of the Philippine Islands, in spiritual and temporal matters, flourishes at the present day, as all know.

The commander-in-chief, Miguel Lopez de Legazpi, as has been said, discovered the islands, and made a settlement in them, and gave a good beginning to their subjection and pacification. He founded the city of the Most Holy Name of Jesus in the provinces of the Pintados, and after that the city of Manila in the island of Luzon. He conquered there the province of Ylocos; and in its town and port, called Vigan, he founded a Spanish town, to which he gave the name of Villa Fernandina. So also he pacified the province of Pangasinan and the island of Mindoro. He fixed the rate of tribute which the natives had to pay in all the islands, and ordered many other matters relating to their government and conversion, until he died, in the year 1574, at Manila, where his body lies buried in the monastery of St. Augustine.[1]

[1] Ferdinand de los Rios, in a report on the Philippines, given by Thevenot, vol. ii, states that his body was removed later to another church, and that he was so good and holy that his body was found to be still entire.

The commander-in-chief having died, a sealed despatch was found amongst his papers, from the high court of Mexico, which carried on the government when the fleet left New Spain, naming (in case the commander-in-chief died) a successor to the governorship. In virtue of this, Guido de Labazarris, a royal officer, entered upon those duties, and was obeyed. He, with much prudence, valour, and tact, continued the conversion and pacification of the islands, and governed them.

In his time there came the corsair Limahon from China, with seventy large ships and many men-at-arms, against Manila. He entered the city, and having killed the master of the camp Martin de Goiti, in his house, along with other Spaniards who were in it, he went against the fortress in which the Spaniards, who were few in number, had taken refuge, with the object of taking the country and making himself master of it. The Spaniards, with the succour which Captain Joan de Salzedo brought them from Vigan, of the men whom he had with him (for he had seen this corsair pass by the coast, and had followed him to Manila), defended themselves so valiantly, that after killing many of his people they forced him to re-embark, and to leave the bay in flight, and take shelter in the river of Pangasinam, whither the Spaniards followed him. There they burned his fleet, and for many days surrounded this corsair on land, who in secret made some small boats with which he fled and put to sea, and abandoned the islands.[1]

During the government of this Guido de Labazarris, trade

[1] The *Dutch Memorable Embassies* relates that whilst Salzedo was blockading Limahon, a Chinese vessel came near, and the Spaniards were on the point of attacking it, but a Chinese merchant persuaded them first to ascertain what the ship was; and it turned out to be the Chinese Admiral Omoncon, who was cruising in pursuit of Limahon. This work states that Limahon died of fever on a desert island, to which he escaped from the island of Tacaotican when threatened by the Chinese admiral and Spaniards combined.

and commerce were established between great China and Manila, ships coming each year with merchandize, and the governor giving them a good reception; so that every year the trade has gone on increasing.

This same governor distributed all the subjected land in Luzon and the adjacent islands between the conquerors and settlers that were there, and he granted to himself the villages of Betis and Lubao in the province of Pampanga, and others of some importance. The governor who succeeded him dispossessed him of all these; and later, his Majesty, on account of his good services, did him the favour of granting them all to him; and he enjoyed them, along with the office of master of the camp of the islands, during the time that he lived.

CHAPTER II.

Of the Government of Dr. Francisco de Sande, and of the Events in his time in the Philippine Islands.

News having been received in Spain of the conquest and taking possession of the Philippine Islands by Miguel Lopez de Legazpi, and of his death, his Majesty appointed as governor and captain-general of these islands, Dr. Francisco de Sande, a native of Caceres, alcalde of the Audiencia of Mexico; and he sailed thither, and entered upon his government, in the year 1575.

During this government the pacification of the islands continued, and especially that of the province of Camarines, by means of Captain Pedro de Chaves, who several times came to blows with the natives until he subjected them, and they submitted. A Spanish town was founded in that province, and the name of city of Caceres was given to it. Amongst other enterprises, the governor in person made an expedition to the island of Borneo with a fleet of galleys and frigates. With these he attacked and took the enemy's fleet, which had come out to meet him. He then took the principal town, in which the king of the island had his house and residence. Having remained there a few days, he abandoned it on account of the sickness of his crews, and from not being able to maintain or preserve the lives of the Spaniards in the island, and returned to Manila. On the way, by his orders, Captain Estevan Rodriguez de Figueroa went into the island of Jolo (Sulu or Holo), and fought with the inhabitants and their chief, and conquered them, and they made submission to him in the name of his Majesty. From there he passed on to the island of Mindanao, and saw it, and reconnoitred the river and its chief towns; and he brought back, to peace and friendship with the Spaniards, other towns and inhabitants of the same island lying in his course of those that had before submitted. The governor despatched the ship San Juanillo to New Spain, under the command of Captain Juan de Ribera, and it was lost at sea, and never again heard of.

Dr. Sande continued in the government until Don Gonzalo Ronquillo de Peñalosa arrived from Spain as governor and captain-general. The doctor's residence having ended, he returned to New Spain to fill the office of auditor of Mexico.

CHAPTER III.

Of the Government of Don Gonzalo Ronquillo de Peñalosa; and of Diego Ronquillo, who, on account of his death, filled the office.

From the copious information which reached the court of his Majesty concerning the affairs of the Philippines, and of the great need which they experienced of being supplied with settlers and people to occupy them, for the better ordering of this, and at the least cost to the royal exchequer, an arrangement was made with Don Gonzalo Ronquillo de Peñalosa, a native of Arevalo, and alguazil-mayor of the high court of Mexico, who was at that time at the court, that he should have the government of the Philippines for life, and should take with him six hundred men from the kingdoms of Castile, married and single, to the Philippine Islands; his Majesty, at the same time, would grant him some assistance and facilities for this, and other favours, as a reward for this service.

Don Gonzalo prepared for the voyage, and having collected his people, and got them embarked in the port of San Lucar de Barrameda, when the fleet went out to the bar, one of the ships in his company was lost. He returned in order to repair his losses, and although he did not get as much as what he first started with, made his voyage to the mainland. At Panama he embarked his people on the South Sea, and set sail for the Philippines, where he arrived, and entered upon his government in the year 1580.

Don Gonzalo Ronquillo founded a Spanish town in the island of Panay, in Oton, and he gave it the name of Arevalo. In his time the trade with the Chinese was increased, and he built a silk market for them, and *parian*, within the city, to which they might bring their merchandize and sell it. He endeavoured to discover a return voyage from the islands to New Spain by a southerly course, for which purpose he sent his cousin, Don Juan Ronquillo del Castillo; but he did not succeed, for after navigating for some time, until he found himself in the neighbourhood of New Guinea, and meeting with many adverse storms, he returned to the Philippines. In like manner he sent another ship, commanded by Don Gonzalo Ronquillo de Vallesteros, to Peru with some merchandize, to obtain some goods which were required for the Philippines from those provinces. This ship returned from Peru, and found the governor already dead. He imposed two per cent. duty on merchandize embarked for New Spain, and three per cent. on the goods imported by the Chinese to the Philippines; and although this was disapproved of, and blamed for having been done without orders from his Majesty, these duties continued to be imposed and established thenceforward.

In the same governorship (his Majesty having succeeded to the kingdom of Portugal, and having ordered the governor of Manila to keep up good relations with the captain-major of the fortress of the island of Tidore, in the Moluccas, and to give it such assistance as it might require), a fleet with men-at-arms was sent from Manila to the fortress, under the command of Don Juan Ronquillo del Castillo, at the request of Diego de Azambuja, captain-major of Tidore, for an expedition for the conquest of the island of Terrenate. This fleet, after reaching Maluco, did not succeed in its object. From this time forward succour of men and provisions continued to be sent from the Philippines to the fortress of Tidore.

During this same government, the province of Cagayan in the island of Luzon, opposite to China, was reduced for the first time by Captain Joan Pablos de Carrion; and he founded in it a Spanish town, and gave it the name of Nueva Segovia; and he turned out of that province a Japanese corsair, who with some ships had taken possession of, and fortified himself in, his port.

A few days after Don Gonzalo Ronquillo had entered upon his government, he sent Captain Gabriel de Ribera with a small fleet of one galley and some frigates, to discover the coast and towns of the island of Borneo, and to go on from there to the kingdom of Patan on the mainland, from whence pepper is brought. After running down the coast of Borneo, and reconnoitring it, on account of the season being much advanced, and the provisions run short, the captain returned with the fleet to Manila. The governor sent him thence to Spain with authority from himself and from the islands, to speak to his Majesty respecting some matters which he was desirous about, and others which were advantageous to the islands. He found his Majesty in Portugal, and gave him a few pieces of gold and other curiosities which he had brought for that purpose, and treated of the business upon which he had come. The result of which was that his Majesty gratified him with the title of Mariscal de Bonbon, and other favours, for his trouble in the voyage, and took the decision which was most fitting in the business which he had come about.

Whilst Don Gonzalo Ronquillo was governor, the first bishop of the Philippines was elected, named Don Fray Domingo de Salazar, of the order of St. Dominic, a person of much literature and sanctity. When he arrived in the islands he took upon himself the ecclesiastical government and jurisdiction, which at first had been exercised by the Augustine friars who arrived at the conquest; and later, by the barefooted monks of St. Francis, who arrived at the conversion. The bishop erected his church into a cathedral, in the city of Manila, by apostolic bulls, with prebends paid by the royal exchequer until there should be tithes and ecclesiastical revenues by which to sustain them. He also established what else was necessary for the service and ornament of the church and divine service, which is celebrated there with much solemnity and display. The bishop took with him in his journey Antonio Sedeño and Alonso Sanchez, priests, and grave persons of the company of Jesus, who were the first who established that order in the Philippines; and since that time it has gone on extending itself with much profit and fruit to the teaching and conversion of the natives, and comfort of the Spaniards, and education and teaching of their children in the studies which they follow.

Don Gonzalo Ronquillo enjoyed so little health from the day in which he entered upon his government, that he died in the year 1583, and his body was buried in the monastery of St. Augustine of Manila.

Diego Ronquillo, his kinsman, succeeded him in the government, having been named thereto by Don Gonzalo in virtue of an order which he held from his Majesty. He continued all that Don Gonzalo left undertaken, especially in the matter of assistance to the Moluccas and the pacification of other islands.

In the time of Diego Ronquillo there was a fire in the city of Manila, which first began in the church of the monastery of St. Augustine, at midday, when the church doors were shut; and the fire increased so much that in a few hours the whole city was burnt, as it was built of wood, with much loss of furniture and property, and several people were in great danger. The town was rebuilt with much difficulty and labour, and after this the Spaniards remained very poor and distressed.

Of the business treated of by the Mariscal Gabriel de Ribera at court, that which was chiefly carried into effect was (though at that time the death of the governor, Don Gonzalo Ronquillo, was not known at court) was to order the establishment of a high court of justice in the city of Manila, whose president should be governor and captain-general in all the Philippines. For this purpose the necessary instructions were issued. The presidency was given to Dr. Santiago de Vera, alcalde of the high court of Mexico, a native of the town of Alcala de Henares, who went to the islands with the usual succours from New Spain, taking with him the royal seal of the court, and the auditors whom his Majesty sent, and the judge and other officials and servants for the said high court. The auditors and fiscal were the licentiates, Melchior de Avalos, Pedro de Rojas, and Gaspar de Ayala as fiscal; and at the end of two years later, Don Antonio de Ribera came as third auditor.

CHAPTER IV.

Of the Government of Dr. Santiago de Vera; and of the Establishment of the Audiencia (High Court) of Manila, until it was removed; and of that which happened in his time.

The President and Auditors having arrived at the Philippines in the month of May 1584, whilst Diego Ronquillo was governing, Dr. Santiago de Vera entered upon the government, and immediately founded the High Court, and the seal was received and placed with all solemnity and festivities that were possible. They then began to attend to business, both of justice and in matters of war and administration, with great profit to the country. During this time fresh succours continued to be sent to the Moluccas, and for the conquest of the island of Terrenate, which the captain-major of Tidore desired to make: Captain Pedro Sarmiento went from Manila for this purpose, and on another occasion the captain and sergeant-major Juan de Moron, but neither of these expeditions met with the desired result.

The President Santiago de Vera also continued to carry out the pacification of some provinces of the islands, and effected several matters that in all respects were most fitting. He discovered a rebellion and insurrection which the principal natives of Manila and Panpanga were proposing to carry into effect against the Spaniards, and justice was done upon the guilty. He built with stone the fortress of Our Lady of Guidance within the city of Manila on the land side, and he caused some artillery to be founded for arming it, by means of an old Indian named Pandapira, a native of Panpanga: he and his sons rendered this service for many years afterwards, until they died.

During the government of the President Santiago de

Vera, Thomas Escander,[1] an Englishman, passed through the straits of Magellan to the South Sea; he had captured on the coast of New Spain (close to California) the ship Sta. Ana, which was coming from the Philippines with much gold and merchandise of great value: after that he came to the Philippines, and entered by the provinces of Pintados, in sight of the town of Arevalo and of the stocks, on which a galloon was being built to perform the voyage to New Spain. Desiring to set fire to this ship he made an attempt to do so, which was resisted by Manuel Lorenzo de Lemos, who assisted in building it. The Englishman then passed on, returning towards India, by which route he made his voyage to England, having followed the same tracks which some years before Francis Drake the Englishman took when he passed through the same straits of Magellan to the coast of Peru, where he made many prizes.[2]

[1] Thomas Candish: in a letter dated September 9, 1588, published by R. Hakluyt, vol. iii, p. 837, he says he burned and sunk nineteen sail of ships. "The matter of most profit unto me was a great ship of the king's which I tooke at California, which ship came from the Philippines, being one of the richest of merchandize that ever passed those seas, as the king's register and merchants' accounts did shew....Which goods (for that my ships were not able to conteine the least part of them) I was inforced to set on fire." This voyage, 1586-1588, is given by Hakluyt, vol. iii, pp. 803-825.

[2] An account of this voyage, 1577-1580, was given by Nuño da Silva, a Portuguese pilot, whom Drake carried off with him, and is preserved amongst the MSS. of the Madrid Public Library: a translation of it is given by Hakluyt, vol. iii, pp. 742-8. Nuño da Silva says that Drake took away the ornaments and reliques from the church of St. Iago on the South American coast; or as Drake relates it: "We came to a small chappell which wee entred, and found therein a silver chalice, two cruets, and one altar cloth the spoyle whereof our Generall gave to M. Fletcher his minister." (R. Hakluyt, vol. iii, p. 735.)

Mr. Froude, in his essay on *England's Forgotten Worthies*, rejects the "modern theory of Drake that he was a gentleman-like pirate on a large scale, who is indebted for the place which he fills in history to the indistinct ideas of right and wrong prevailing in the unenlightened age in which he lived." Further on Mr. Froude says: "Drake, it is true, appro-

At this time it seemed fitting to the High Court and to the Bishop to send to Spain to the court of His Majesty some person of sufficient and satisfactory qualities to give an account and information of the state of affairs of the Philippine Islands in all respects, and to request that some necessary dispositions should be taken, and especially that it should be given to be understood that the High Court which had been founded might be dispensed with for the present time; for as the country was new, it was a heavy charge for all classes. The individual selected for that purpose was Padre Alonzo Sanchez, of the company of Jesus, well informed and experienced in matters of the country, and very active in business. They gave him instructions and authority on behalf of all classes, orders, and communities as to what he was to treat of and request in Spain, and of His Holiness in the Roman court where he was also to go. This padre arrived at Madrid, and after seeing His Majesty a few times (respecting those things which he thought fit to treat of), he went on to Rome, where he introduced himself as ambassador from all the estates of the Philippines, and on their behalf kissed the foot, and visited the pontiffs who were at that time, after the death of Sixtus

priated and brought home a million and a half of Spanish treasure, while England and Spain were at peace. He took that treasure because for many years the officers of the Inquisition had made free at their pleasure with the lives and goods of English merchants and seamen. ......Spain and England were at peace, but Popery and Protestantism were at war—deep, deadly, and irreconcileable."

The ideas of right and wrong were not however so indistinct in that age, for we find in De Morga an account of Blas Ruys, a Spanish adventurer, who was as patriotic, as courageous, and as unscrupulous as Drake; yet De Morga opposed his projects at the time, and in his history blames his acts. To justify Drake's buccaneering whilst Spain and England were at peace, by the fact that Popery and Protestantism were at war, is to put Protestantism into the position which the Inquisition is accused of having assumed; and how much soever history may credit the sincerity of Drake's piety, it should not on that account justify what was as much piracy then as at the present time.

the Fifth. After receiving many favours and indulgences, and many reliques, and bulls and letters for the Philippines, he returned to Spain, where he again sought for a decision as to the business which he had left set on foot when he went to Rome. His Majesty listened to what he brought from the pontiffs, and heard him favourably as to the affairs of the islands; and in private meetings the padre set forth his requests, and got the business decided very much to his satisfaction. When the despatches arrived in the Philippines it seemed beside the intention and expectations both of the bishop and the High Court, as well as of the city and inhabitants and settlers, and even detrimental to those who were in the islands; on which account they expressed their displeasure at P. Alonso Sanchez, who had remained in Spain. He negotiated that the High Court of Manila should be abolished and that a new governor should be sent, and in asking for one, he himself proposed (on account of the friendly intercourse which he had met with from him) Gomez Perez Dasmariñas, who had been corregidor of Leon, and later of Murcia, and who at that season was in the court, and named as corregidor of Logroño and Calahorra. His Majesty named him as governor and captain-general of the Philippines, and increased the salary of his office to ten thousand ducats of Castille yearly: he granted him a habit of Santiago, and a large sum towards the expenses of his voyage. Providing him with the needful despatches (both for exercising his office and for abolishing the High Court which was in Manila, and for establishing there a camp of four hundred paid soldiers with their officers at the king's expense, for the garrison and defence of the island), His Majesty commanded him to sail immediately for New Spain, in the ships which arrived in the year 1589 with the Viceroy Don Luis de Velasco, who came to take the government there.

Gomez Perez Dasmariñas left Mexico as expeditiously as

possible, and, with the ships, soldiers and captains that he required, set sail for the Philippines, whither he arrived in the month of May of the year 1590.

CHAPTER V.

Of the Government of Gomez Perez Dasmariñas; and of the Licentiate Pedro de Rojas, who at his death was elected to the government by the city of Manila, until Don Luis Dasmariñas was received instead of Gomez Perez, his father.

As soon as Gomez Perez Dasmariñas arrived at the Philippines, he was received as governor, to the general satisfaction. He abolished the Audiencia, and filled the offices of president, auditors and fiscal and other ministers of the court, by means of the Licenciate Herver del Coral, whom the Viceroy Don Luys de Velasco sent for this purpose, in virtue of a royal order which he held. The new governor commenced his rule, establishing the camp of paid soldiers, and putting into execution various matters for which he had royal orders and instructions with much heat and zeal, without excusing himself from any kind of labour, or care for his own self. The first thing which he began was to wall the town, and he took it up so much in earnest, that he left it almost completed before he died: he also built a battery on the point of Manila, where there used to be the old fort of wood, and he named it Santiago, and supplied it with some artillery; he levelled the fort of our Lady of Guidance, which his predecessor had built; he constructed with stone the cathedral church of Manila, and encouraged the inhabitants of the city to persevere in building their houses of stone, which work they had set about a few days before, the bishop having set the example in his own case. He increased the trade with China during his time, and the navigation to New Spain and despatch of vessels in that line

GOMEZ PEREZ DASMARIÑAS.

became more regular. He built some galleys for the defence of the coast, pacified the Zambales who had rebelled, and sent his son Don Luys Dasmariñas, of the habit of Alcantara, with troops into the interior of the island of Luzon, from Manila, crossing the river Ytui, and other provinces not yet seen or discovered by the Spaniards, until he came out at Cagayan. He made a cannon foundry in Manila, where, for want of expert founders, few large pieces were turned out.

In the first year of his government he sent over to New Spain the president and auditors of the High Court, which had been abolished: the licenciate Pedro de Rojas, the senior auditor remained with the governor by order of His Majesty, as lieutenant assessor in matters of justice, until a few years later, when he was named as Alcalde in Mexico.

In the time of Gomez Perez, the peace and trade which existed between the Japanese and the Spaniards began to be disturbed; for up to that ships had come for some years from the port of Nangasaqui in Japan to Manila, with flour and other goods, and had been well received and treated there; and Taicosama, the universal lord of Japan, was incited by the efforts of Farandaquiemon, a Japanese of low extraction of those that came to Manila, to write in a barbarous and arrogant manner to the governor desiring him to recognise him and send tribute, threatening to come with a fleet and troops to destroy the country.[1] And between demands and replies some years had to pass by, until at last Taico died.

[1] The substance of this letter of Taico Sama is thus given in the *Dutch Memorable Embassies:* "That since his accession to the empire of Japan, the wars and divisions which formerly agitated it had been entirely suppressed. That by the grace of their gods, everything being at peace in Japan, he was resolved to make war on the Chinese; that it depended on himself (the Governor of Manila) not to be involved in it; and that it was only necessary for him to recognise him as his sovereign, master, and lord; and that if he could not bring himself to that till after trying the fortune of war, that he should expect him on his re-

At the same time as that in which Japan gave trouble to the governor, the King of Cambodia sent him an embassy with Diego Belloso, a Portuguese, and a present of two elephants. He offered friendship and trade with his country, and begged of him assistance against Siam, which was threatening him. The governor sent him an answer and a horse, with a few emeralds and other things, leaving him hopes of assistance for another time, and thanking him for his friendship. From this took their origin the events and expeditions which were made later from Manila to the kingdoms of Siam, Camboja, and the mainland of Asia.

From the time that Gomez Perez accepted his charge in Spain, and after entering upon his government, he nourished a desire to make an expedition from Manila to conquer the fortress of Terrenate in the Moluccas, on account of the great importance of this enterprise, and from the former attempts having failed. And he was always disposing matters and making arrangements with regard to this expedition, but with such secresy that he confided it to no one; until, in the year '93, seeing himself provided with what he considered sufficient for his design, he declared it, and took measures for setting out in person with more than nine hundred Spaniards and two hundred sail, between galleys, galliots and frigates, viceroys and other craft; he left the affairs of Manila and the islands with a few troops (though not what was necessary for its defence) under the charge of Diego Ronquillo, his master of the camp, in matters of war;

turn from China, whence he would go directly to his islands to teach him who he was." The same work states that the Spanish governor was much embarrassed, and resolved to do homage and duty to the Japanese emperor, and for this purpose sent as envoy Lupus de Liano, to say that the governor doubted if this letter were really from the emperor, as the Jesuits had written him nothing on the subject. This turned the wrath of the emperor against the Jesuits, whom he then considered as spies who betrayed him. This envoy, Lupus de Liano, was two persons, Fray Juan Lobo and Capt. Llano, as stated further on by De Morga.

and in those of administration and justice under the care of the Licenciate Pedro de Roxas. The governor sent his son Don Luys Dasmariñas forward with the rest of the fleet, as his lieutenant in the office of captain-general, to the province of Pintados, whence they were to start: he himself remained in Manila making his last preparations, and armed a galley of twenty-eight benches to sail in himself. He manned it with good Chinese rowers with pay, and to gain them over more, he would not consent to chain them, and winked at some of them bearing arms. As many as forty Spaniards embarked in this galley, and some frigates and smaller vessels, in which went private individuals, sailed in company with it. They set sail from the port of Cabit, in the month of October of 1593, for the province of Pintados, where they were to join the fleet which was there waiting for them, and pursue the voyage to Maluco. On the second day of the voyage in the afternoon they arrived at the island of Caza, twenty-four leagues from Manila, close to the coast of the same island of Luzon, a place called Sulphur point, with some head wind: the galley made an effort to double this point by rowing, and not being able to advance until the wind should drop, it anchored and spread an awning, and remained there that night. Some of the vessels which came in company went in closer to shore, in sight of the galley, and there waited for it.

The governor and those who accompanied him passed the time playing on the poop till the end of the first watch, and after he had gone into his cabin to rest, the other Spaniards went to their quarters for the same purpose, leaving the usual guards in the midship gangway and in the bows and stern. The Chinese rowers three days back had agreed to rise up and seize the galley whenever they should find a favourable opportunity, from a desire to save themselves the labour of rowing on this expedition, or from coveting the money, jewels and other articles of value on board, as it seemed to them ill to lose what was offered to their hands: they had provided themselves with candles and white shirts, and had appointed some of their number as chiefs for the execution of the plan; and they carried it out that same night, in the last watch before dawn, when they perceived that the Spaniards slept. At a signal which one of them gave, at the same moment all put on their shirts, and lit their candles, and with their catans in their hands they at once attacked the guards and those that slept in the quarters and in the wales,[1] and, wounding and killing, they seized upon the galley. But few Spaniards escaped; some by swimming to land, others in the boat which was at the stern. The governor, when he heard the noise in his cabin, and perceived that the galley was dragging, and that the rabble was cutting down the awning, and was taking to the oars, hurried out carelessly, and his head being unprotected at the hatchway of the cabin, a few Chinese were watching for him there, and split his head with a catan. He fell, wounded, down the stairs into his cabin; and two servants whom he had within, carried him to his bed, where he died immediately. The same fate met the servants, who were stabbed through the hatch. The only Spaniards that remained alive in the galley were Juan de Cuellar, secretary of the governor, and Padre Montilla, of the order of St. Francis, who slept in a cabin amidship; and they stayed there without coming out; and the Chinese did not dare to go in, thinking that there were more Spaniards, until next day, when they took them out, and let them go on the coast of Ylocos, of the island of Luzon itself, in order that the natives might let them take water on shore, of which they were short.

The Spaniards who were in the other vessels, close to land, although they perceived from their ships the lights and the noise in the galley, thought it was some manœuvre that was being executed; and when afterwards they knew, after a short space, through those who escaped, swimming,

---

[1] *Arrumbadas*, planks or frames on which soldiers sleep.

what had happened, they could give no assistance, and remained quiet, as everything was lost, and they were few in number, and not in sufficient force. So they waited till morning, and when it dawned they saw that the galley had already set the mainsail, and was sailing wind astern, returning to China, and they could not follow it.

As the wind served, the galley sailed all along the coast of the island until leaving it. It took in some water at the Ylocos, and left there the secretary and the friar. It attempted to cross to China, and not being able to fetch it, brought up at the kingdom of Cochin China, where the king of Tunquin took from them what was in the galley, and two large pieces of artillery which had been embarked for the expedition to Maluco, and the royal standard, and all the jewels, money, and precious things, and left the galley to go ashore on the coast. The Chinese dispersed, and fled to different provinces. The governor, Gomez Perez, met with this disastrous death, with which the enterprise and expedition to Maluco, which he had undertaken, ceased also. Thus his government ended after he had held it for little more than three years.

Amongst other despatches which Gomez Perez Dasmariñas brought from Spain, was an order from his Majesty for naming the person whom he should judge fitting to govern in case of his death, until such time as his Majesty should name his successor. With this royal order, which he shewed to some of the more important persons of the island, he gave each one to understand that he would leave him as the person named; and especially in the case of Captain Estevan Rodriguez de Figueroa, an inhabitant of Pintados, a rich man, of merit, and one of the first conquerors. To him he shewed a nomination made in his favour, and he made use of him on all occasions, and he had to go with him to Maluco. In Manila the seizure of the galley and death of the governor became known very shortly; and with this astounding news the townspeople and the men-at-arms who had remained there, met together in the house of the licentiate Pedro de Rojas, to treat of what it was fitting to do; and first of all to elect him as governor and captain-general; and then they sent Captain Juan Ronquillo del Castillo, with other captains, in two frigates (for there was no other vessel) in pursuit of the galley; which was fruitless, for they never saw it. In like manner the governor sent to Don Luys Dasmariñas, and to the fleet and army, which was in Pintados waiting for Gomez Perez, advising them of his death, and of what had happened, and of the new election which had fallen upon him for the government, and ordered them to come with all speed to Manila, which was left very much deserted, and without the necessary precautions for anything that might occur.

This news caused much grief in the fleet, and Don Luys Dasmariñas and the Captain Estevan Rodriguez de Figueroa, each in his heart held it for certain that he was about to enter upon the government, taking it for granted that the governor had left the nomination to him; and with this hope, both together, with the best ships and crews of the fleet, came to Manila as speedily as they could, at the same time.

The licentiate Pedro de Rojas, fearing this despatch, which the governor would have left among his papers and writing boxes, which he kept in the monastery of St. Augustine of Manila, in the hands of Fray Diego Muñoz, prior and commissary of the holy office, made search for them to get them into his power; and although he took a few, yet not the despatch in question; for the prior had forestalled him, and preserved a writing box in which they understood it was to be found, until such time as Don Luys Dasmariñas should reach the city. The secretary, Juan de Cuellar, who escaped from the galley, arrived from the province of Ylocos, and he certified that a nomination for the succession to the government had been made by Gomez Perez; but he did not say in whose favour, nor amongst what papers it would be found, so that the licentiate, Pedro de Rojas, and those who were devoted to him, were very anxious.

Forty days passed in this manner, at the end of which Don Luys appeared in the bay, near the city, with Estevan Rodriguez de Figueroa and many people in his company. There he anchored without choosing to enter the city, nor disembark. He caused search to be made for the papers which had been put by in St. Augustine, and amongst them turned up the royal order and nomination of Don Luys Dasmariñas to succeed in the government. There was some one on his behalf who made it known to the regiment in the city, which changing its conduct, notwithstanding some opposition which was made by the partizans of the licentiate Rojas, called Don Luys Dasmariñas to the house of the municipality, and gave him possession of the government; and the fleet and soldiers that Don Luys brought with him did the same; so that each day brought a disappointment to the licentiate Rojas, who returned to his office of lieutenant-assessor after having governed for the above mentioned forty days.

If the death of the governor Gomez Perez Dasmariñas was unfortunate, as much for the loss of him personally[1] as for such a good opportunity having been lost for the conquest of Terrenate, the success of which expedition was held to be certain, the return of the fleet and arrival of the troops in the city was none the less a fortunate event; since not many days later (anticipating the usual time for their navigation), a quantity of ships from China came to Manila

[1] Colonel Fernando de los Rios, in a report, printed in Thevenot, vol. ii, says that he had been thirty years in the Philippines, and in all that time had only seen one governor fit for his office, and that was Gomez Perez de las Mariñas, who did more for the happiness of the people in the three years that he was there, than did the others before and after.

with many men on board and little merchandise, and seven mandarins with the insignia of their office. This gave sufficient motive for suspicion that they had had notice of the departure of the fleet to Maluco, and of the city having remained defenceless, and that on this occasion they came to attempt to take the country; from which they desisted when they found the city with more troops than ever, and they returned without shewing any particular motive which had brought them, and without any sign of consciousness being given by one side or other. Only the governor, Don Luys, was on the alert and very watchful, and took the proper arrangements, especially with respect to the Chinese and their quarters and parian.

In this year no ships came to New Spain from the Philippines, because the governor, Gomez Perez, had sent two ships before he started on the expedition to Maluco, the *San Felipe* and the *San Francisco*; but both had to take shelter in port from storms,—the *San Felipe* put into the port of Sebu, and the *San Francisco* in Manila, and they could not go out of port till the following year. In New Spain it was suspected, seeing that the ships did not arrive, that there were troubles in the islands, and persons were not wanting who affirmed to more than what did happen: at the same time (in the town of Mexico) it could not be ascertained whence the news had proceeded. This was very shortly known in Spain (by way of India), letters going through Persia to Venice, that immediately they set about naming a new governor.

In the first year of the government of Gomez Perez Dasmariñas, the want of the High Court of Justice began to be felt by many, seeing all the power placed in the hands of one person, and that there was no one to whom recourse could be had for the remedy of certain cases; and he that experienced this most was the Bishop Fray Domingo de Salazar, who had had some encounters with the governor, and met with some mortifications, which obliged him to set out for Spain, although he was very aged. The governor readily gave him leave that year, and a vessel for his journey, in order to get him at a distance from himself; but he sent at the same time, with his full powers, Fray Francisco de Ortega, of the order of St. Augustine, to court, so that he might meet whatever the bishop might allege, and defend his cause. Both arrived in Spain, and each spoke as suited his purpose. The chief thing upon which the bishop laid stress was to beg that they would again establish the High Court of Justice, and found other bishoprics in the Philippines besides that of Manila, and other things which he thought requisite for spiritual and temporal matters. In all this, Ortega contradicted him. The authority and virtue of the bishop weighed so much, that, although at first the cause which had moved him to leave his church, and come, at his age, five thousand leagues to Spain, was held to be a light one, later he was heard favourably by his Majesty and council; and all his petitions and propositions were taken into consideration, and much time was spent over them, and many consultations were held with his Majesty for him to decide upon them.

In the same year of 1593 in which Gomez Perez died in the Philippines, the council provided, after consulting with his Majesty, that the office of lieutenant-assessor in judicial causes, which had been filled by the licentiate Pedro de Rojas since the abolition of the audiencia, should be made more important than what it then was, as more convenient; and that it should have the title of lieutenant-general of the governor and captain-general; and that in matters of justice he should hear causes in appeal, which did not exceed the value of a thousand ducats of Castile; and under these circumstances the licentiate Pedro de Rojas was promoted to the place of alcalde of Mexico, and his Majesty named Dr. Antonio de Morga to take his place as lieutenant-general of the Philippines. He came to New Spain in the course of his journey out, in the beginning of the year 1594, and found that the ships had not arrived, which, as has been already said, were missing from the Philippines; but the death of Gomez Perez and the other events were not known until the month of November of the same year, when Don Juan de Velasco came in the galloon *Santiago*, which had been despatched the year before from New Spain by the Viceroy Don Luys de Velasco, with the usual succour, to the islands, and brought the news of the death of the governor, and that his son, Don Luys Dasmariñas, was in the government. Immediately men were got ready, and fresh succours, for the islands, with which, and many passengers and monks who had come from Spain, Dr. Antonio de Morga embarked in the port of Acapulco in the galloons *San Felipe* and *Santiago*, taking everything under his orders, and set sail the 22nd of March, 1595. He arrived with fair weather, and anchored in the port of Cabit the 11th of June of the same year, and entered upon his office of lieutenant-general, and began to occupy himself with its duties, and with what else was at his charge.

Whilst Don Luys Dasmariñas governed, the suspicions and fear continued with respect to Japan, and people lived in anxiety as to that, and on account of the Chinese. The governor sent his cousin, Don Fernando de Castro, to China with letters and despatches to the Viceroy of Canton and the Viceroy of Chincheo, where it was understood that there were many of the Chinese who had seized upon the galley and killed the governor, Gomez Perez. Supposing that they had gone there with it, a request was made for the guilty to be given up for punishment, and that the royal standard, artillery, and the other things which they had carried off, should be restored. This was not obtained, because, as the galley went to Cochin China, and the Chinese dispersed in so many directions, it could not be effected; though, at the end of a few days, a few of the guilty Chinese were brought from Malacca to Manila, whom the Captain-Major, Francisco de Silva de Meneses had found there. From these it was known more accurately what had passed with respect to the seizure of the galley and death of the governor, and justice was done upon them.

During the year 1594, in which Don Luys governed, a large junk came to the Philippines, in which were some Cambodians and Siamese, and a few Chinese and three Spaniards, one a Castilian, named Blas Ruyz de Hernan Gonzalez, and two Portuguese, named Pantaleon Carnero and Antonio Machado. Whilst these were in the kingdom of Cambodia and city of Chordemuco,[1] with Prauncar[2] Langara, King of Camboja, the King of Siam fell upon him with many men and elephants, took all the country, and the house and treasures of the king, who, with his wife, mother, sister, daughter and two sons which he had, fled into the upper country as far as the kingdom of Laos. The King of Siam,[3] leaving some of his captains to defend Camboja, returned to his home with the rest of his army; and what he could not carry away by land, he sent to Siam by sea in some junks. He captured the Portuguese and Castilians whom he found there, and put these three and other Cambodian prisoners of war on board this junk, with much property, and a guard of Siamese, and Chinese for sailors. When they were out at sea, the three Spaniards, aided by the Chinese, made themselves masters of the junk, and killed or took prisoners the Siamese guard. After that the Spaniards and Chinese came to blows to decide whose the

[1] Cho-da-mukha, in Siamese the place of meeting of the chief mandarins, *i. e.*, the capital.

[2] Phra Uncar.

[3] Some words are wanting or misprinted in the text, which runs:—
"Hasta el reyno de los Laos. En Siam, dexando algunos capitanes suyos en guardia de Camboja." It should be—"El Rey de Siam dexando," etc.

prize was to be, and where it was to be taken to. The three Spaniards conquered the Chinese, and, killing the greater number of them, brought the junk to Manila, with what was on board of it which was adjudged to them, and liberty was given to the Cambodian captives, and also to the Chinese who had survived from this fray.

The King of Siam having arrived at his court in the city of Odia,[1] expected the arrival of this junk, and seeing that it delayed longer than what the voyage required, feared that it had been seized or lost, and desired to send some one to bring him news or explanation of what had happened. There was a prisoner (amongst those he had brought from Cambodia), one Diego Belloso, a Portuguese, whom the King Prauncar Langara had sent to Manila, at the time that Gomez Perez Dasmariñas governed, to ask for his friendship and assistance against Siam, which was then threatening him, as has been before related: and on his return to Cambodia with the governor's answer and presents, he found that Siam had conquered and occupied the country, so that they made him prisoner, and the King of Siam took the present he brought, and carried it off with the prisoners to his own country. This Diego Belloso having been informed of the king's wishes, managed to send him word that if he were to send him on this business, as he was so well acquainted with the Archipelago, he would arrive at Manila, and bring him information of the junk; and at the same time would, in his name, establish a friendship and trade with the Spaniards, and would procure him many curiosities from Europe which were to be got at Manila, especially a coloured stone, large enough to serve as a hilt for the two-handed sword which he used; a thing the king wished for very much, on account of another smaller one which was amongst the things in the present,[2] and which,

[1] Si-Yuthia, or the Seat of Kings.
[2] To the King of Cambodia.

when he went on his elephant, he carried before him. The king agreed to this, and had a junk prepared, and sent in it a Siamese in his service, with the others necessary for the navigation, in company with Diego Belloso; and two elephants for the governor of Manila, and a quantity of benzoin, ivory and other merchandise for sale, and ordered that with the proceeds they should buy the curiosities which Belloso had mentioned. Having put out to sea they met with a storm, and the junk arrived at Malacca, where they got information that the other junk belonging to the King of Siam, which they were inquiring for, had been seized, and the Siamese guards killed, and that the Spaniards, who had left Cambodia in it as prisoners, had carried it off with all the goods on board to Manila.

With this news the King of Siam's officer grew cool as to pursuing the voyage to Manila; so much so, that against the desire of Diego Belloso, he began to discharge the goods in Malacca and to sell them, with the intention of returning immediately after to Siam. One morning this officer of Siam, named Aconsi,[1] was found dead in the junk, having gone to sleep the night before safe and sound; with which Diego Belloso made himself master of the matter, and having again collected and put the goods and elephants on board the junk, he went out of Malacca, and made the voyage to Manila. There he found Don Luys Dasmariñas governor, on account of the death of Don Gomez Perez, his father, and he gave him the present of the elephants which he brought from the king, and gave him the message with which he had been despatched, and the other goods and merchandise were offered for sale by means of another Siamese who went in the junk on account of his king's service.

Belloso met with Blas Ruyz de Hernan Gonzales and his two companions in Manila; and they all agreed together to

[1] *Id est*, the supercargo, in Chinese.

persuade the governor Don Luys to send a fleet to Cambodia, in favour of the King Langara, who was in exile and stripped of his kingdom, and that it would be easy to restore him, and at the same time in this way to gain a footing for the Spaniards on the mainland, and to settle and fortify themselves there, from which other effects would follow of greater and deeper importance. They took as supporters of their ideas with the governor the monks of the order of St. Dominic; and they easily put the matter on such a good footing (for in everything he was guided by his council), that it was decided to prepare a fleet, and send in it as many men as possible, and as head of the expedition the captain and sergeant-major, Juan Xuarez Gallinato, in a ship of middling size; and in its company two junks, one under the command of Diego Belloso, the other of Blas Ruyz de Hernan Gonzales, with a hundred and twenty Spaniards, some Japanese, and Indians of the islands, and what else was necessary.

This resolution did not seem very suitable to the greater number in the city, both on account of so many troops going away, and because the success of the expedition seemed very doubtful, as it was said that the country of Cambodia was subjected to Siam, which held it with a sufficient guard, also because nothing more was known of the matter; and above all the result of the expedition would be to gain the King of Siam as a declared enemy, whilst the governor had just received a present and a friendly embassy from him through Diego Belloso: moreover, without giving him an answer they would be taking up arms against him in favour of one who was unknown to them, and from whom the Spaniards had not received either favours or obligations. Dr. Antonio de Morga, the lieutenant-general, and with him the master of the camp, Diego Ronquillo, and other captains and persons of importance, treated of this business with the governor up to the point of requesting him in writing to desist from the expedition; but although he had no reasons to give on his side with which to satisfy them, yet being so taken with the expedition, and having the above-mentioned monks of St. Dominic of his opinion, he did not choose to change his plans, and despatched the fleet in the beginning of the year 1596 to the kingdom of Cambodia, which is usually a voyage of eight days. On the other hand, he sent away the Siamese who had come with Belloso, without giving any decided answer to the King of Siam, and sent him in return for his present some produce of the islands which seemed suitable. The Siamese, seeing that they were about to return to their kingdom, were satisfied, without hoping for any other result of their journey.

A storm overtook the fleet, on account of which, the flag-ship, which carried Juan Xuarez Gallinato and the greater number of the Spaniards, arrived in the Straits of Sinca-pura, near Malacca, where it stayed many days. The other two junks of Diego Belloso and Blas Ruyz, which carried Spaniards and some Japanese and natives of Manila, arrived with a good deal of risk at Cambodia, and went up the river Mecon, Blas Ruyz before Belloso, as far as the city of Chordemuco. There they learned that the Cambodian Mandarins had joined together against the Siamese, and had beaten them and driven them out of the kingdom; and that one of these mandarins, named Anacaparan, had got possession of the country, and governed with the title of king, though against the will of the others. It seemed to Diego Belloso and Blas Ruyz and the men of their company that they had arrived in good season for the designs which they entertained, seeing the confusion of affairs amongst the Cambodians, and the Siamese already out of the country; and encouraging themselves with the expectation that Gallinato and the flag-ship would shortly arrive, they passed several days in Chordemuco, with the good pleasure of

Anacaparan, who resided in Sistor, nine leagues distant. Although he knew of the entry of these ships, and of the people who came in them, and that many more were coming after them, and what their intentions were; and although these did not seem very suitable to his purpose, yet he dissembled with them, so as to see what time would bring. Six ships of the Chinese with goods had entered Chordemuco at the same time, and they unloaded them, and being very numerous, and at enmity with the Spaniards, they behaved towards them on various occasions with arrogance and insolence, which obliged the Spaniards, for their reputation and satisfaction of the injuries they had received, to take up arms against them. This they did, killing a great many Chinese, and taking their ships and whatever was in them; at which Anacaparan shewed his displeasure, and desired that the Chinese should take their revenge, and to assist them in it. To remedy this evil, it seemed best to the Dominican Fray Alonzo Ximenez, who was with the Spaniards, that Blas Ruyz and Diego Belloso, with fifty Spaniards and a few Japanese and Manila men, leaving the rest to guard the ships in Chordemuco, should ascend the river in small boats to Sistor to have an interview with Anacaparan, and offer him excuses and satisfaction for what had happened with the Chinese. And in order to negociate with him more easily, they made up a letter of embassy in the name of the governor of Manila, because Gallinato carried the letter which the governor had given. This stood them in little service, because Anacaparan not only did not grant them an audience, but after taking away their boats, he kept them so hard pressed in a lodging outside of the city; and threatened them so much that he would put them to death if they did not at once restore their ships and what they had taken from them to the Chinese, that they were very anxious to return to Chordemuco, and get on board their vessels for greater security, and they determined to carry that out as best they might.

Necessity and the finding themselves in such danger, gave them courage to go forth one night (though with much risk) to seek the passage for crossing the river towards the city: they crossed it with their arms in their hands at a late hour of the night, and as silently as they could, and finding themselves near the city, and their courage and resolution increasing, they entered it as far as the king's house; and setting fire to it, and to the magazines and to the other buildings which they met with, they threw the Cambodians into such confusion, that they killed a great number of them that night and the following morning, and amongst the slain was the King Anacaparan himself. They were not of opinion either to advance or to maintain their ground, so they turned back to the ships, marching in as orderly a manner as they could. A great number of Cambodians collected together with arms and some elephants, and set out in pursuit of the Spaniards, and came up with them before they reached the ships; but they defended themselves valiantly, and continued their march until they got on board without losing a Spaniard; and the Cambodians returned to their city with some killed and wounded on their side.

Diego Belloso and Blas Ruyz having got on board their ships, Captain Gallinato at this time entered by the river into Chordemuco with the flag-ship. They gave him an account of all that had happened with the Chinese and Cambodians, and of the good position in which affairs stood for continuing the enterprise; since, Anacaparan the usurper being dead, many Cambodians would immediately pass over to the side of the Spaniards in defence of the name and cry for Langara the legitimate king. And although some Cambodians came to visit the fleet, and affirmed the same things to Gallinato, and that Anacaparan was dead, and related what the Spaniards had done in Sistor, he shewed that he did not believe any of them, nor did he choose to be persuaded into it, nor that the enterprise ought to be gone on with and continued. On the contrary, he blamed the Spaniards for what they had done in his absence, and taking from them everything they had got in the way of plunder of the Chinese and Cambodians, put out to sea to sail to Manila. Belloso and Blas Ruyz persuaded him to go at least to Cochinchina, where it was said that the galley, which had been seized upon when the governor Gomez Perez was killed, had put in; and that the royal standard and artillery were there, and that he should claim them; and they offered in the meantime, whilst this business was being negociated, to go by land to the kingdom of the Laos, where the King Langara of Cambodia was living, in order to bring him back to his kingdom. Captain Gallinato consented to this, and sailed along the coast until he entered the bay of Cochinchina, where, although he was (seemingly) well received by the inhabitants, he would never disembark from his ships: and from them he sent Gregorio de Vargas to visit the King of Tunquin (who is the chief of that kingdom) to treat with him on the business of the galley and the standard and artillery. Whilst he was thus engaged, he gave permission to Blas Ruyz and Diego Belloso to go on shore and endeavour to make the journey to Laos; because, by getting them out of the way, and leaving them thus occupied, without their being able to do him an ill service in Manila respecting his coming out of Cambodia, he consented easily to what they requested.

Diego Belloso and Blas Ruyz went to the King of Sinua, son of the King of Tunquin, and begged him to favour them in their journey; and he gave them all that was necessary, so that they were well treated and served as far as the city of Alanchan,[1] the capital of the Laos kingdom, where the king of the country received them well. They

[1] Lantchang, or Lanxang, name of an ancient city in the north of Cambodia. *Pallegoix's Dictionary.*

found that Prauncar Langara, King of Cambodia, and his eldest son and daughter had died, and there survived only his son Prauncar and his stepmother, grandmother, and aunts: they related the state of affairs in Cambodia, and the arrival of the Spaniards, and death of the usurper Anacaparan. The same information was brought by a Cambodian who came from Chordemuco; and that after the death of Anacaparan, his youngest son named Chupinanu reigned; that the country was entirely divided into factions; and that there would be many who, on seeing their natural and legitimate king, would leave Chupinanu, and would come to him and obey him.

Some difficulties as to setting out from Alanchan having been overcome, by the arrival at this time in Laos from Cambodia of a mandarin named Ocuña de Chu, with ten prahus well armed with cannon, sent by order of other mandarins and grandees of Cambodia, to fetch their legitimate king, it was decided to go down to Cambodia. Prauncar and his grandmother, and aunt, and stepmother, the wife of Langara, and Diego Belloso and Blas Ruyz embarked, and all made the voyage in the above-mentioned prahus by the rivers which go from Laos to Cambodia, where they found new disturbances and insurrections of provinces; but after Prauncar arrived many came over to his side, especially two Muslim Malays who were in the kingdom with a Malay armed force and artillery and elephants—they were named Ocuña Lacasamana[1] and Cancona. Prauncar got the advantage on various occasions, and Chupinanu and his brothers and other rebels having been killed in some battles, he became master of almost all the provinces of his kingdom. He made Diego Belloso and Blas Ruyz chiefs in the affairs of war, and they always directed them until they left Prauncar on the throne; and the war being almost entirely ended, the king made Belloso and Blas Ruyz great Chofas

[1] Laksamāna, a general or admiral in Malay.

of his kingdom, and gave them two provinces and other favours, though not as many as they hoped for, or as he had offered when they were in Laos. The chief cause of this was the stepmother, and grandmother and aunt of the king, who directed him on account of his youth, and of his being addicted to wine,—more so than Langara his father. The Malay Ocuña Lacasmana had much influence with these ladies, and, envious of the valour of the Spaniards, always served them ill, and endeavoured to compass their destruction; on this account they continually had encounters with him. It must be understood that this Malay was in relations with the widow of Langara, the stepmother of the King Prauncar.

The fleet of Captain Gallinato remained in Cochin China negotiating with the King of Tunquin for the royal standard and the artillery of the galley, as has been related; because the galley was lost upon the coast, and the king had the rest in his possession. He not only did not give them up, but whilst entertaining Gallinato with good reasons, he was treating elsewhere about taking his ships and what was in them. Gallinato, having been warned of this in secret by a great lady of Cochin China who came to see him in the fleet, kept a still more careful watch than he had done hitherto, not allowing any one to go on shore. All the same he did not succeed in this with Fray Alonso Ximenez, one of the Dominican monks whom he brought with him, and who had been one of the chief promoters of this expedition: he going on shore was taken and detained there. The Cochin Chinese imagining that the fleet was off its guard, sent down some fire ships upon it; and after them some galleys and war boats to set it on fire: and on shore, which was not far off, were many people with arquebuses who molested the Spaniards. The fleet succeeded in getting out of the way of the fire, and went further from the land, and resisting the enemies' ships with artillery and musketry, sent some to the bottom; and without waiting any more, leaving behind Fray Alonso Ximenez on shore with two secular companions he had with him, it put out to sea and went out of the bay of Cochin China, making for the Philippines.

Whilst these things were happening in Camboja and Cochin China, orders had arrived from Spain from his Majesty, to conclude an agreement which Captain Estevan Rodriguez de Figueroa had made with the governor Gomez Perez Dasmariñas, under which he was to pacify and settle the island of Mindanao at his own expense, and receive the governorship of it for two lives, and other rewards. This agreement was carried out, after a few difficulties which presented themselves had been overcome; and Estevan Rodriguez got ready men and ships, and other necessaries for the enterprise, and with some galleys, galliots, frigates, viceroys, and varangayes ylapis, he set out with two hundred and fourteen Spaniards for the Isle of Mindanao in February of the same year, 1596. He took as master of the camp Captain Juan de la Xara, and some monks of the company of Jesus, for teaching, and many natives for the service of the camp and fleet.

He arrived with fair weather at the Mindanao, where the first towns he met, named Tampacan and Lumagnan, hostile to the people of Buhahayen, received him in peace and friendship, and joined his forces; they might be about six thousand men, and without delay they continued going up the river, eight leagues further, against Buhahayen, the principal town of the island, where the principal chief had fortified himself on many sides. Having arrived before the town the fleet anchored, and at once sent on shore a large part of the troops with their arms, who, before reaching the houses and fort, found in some thickets[1] which were near

[1] *Cacatal*, written also *çatatal* and *çucatal*.

the river, some of the people of Buhahayen, who came out to meet them with their campilans[1] and carazas[2] and other arms, and attacked the Spaniards in various directions. For, as the ground was swampy and thick with brushwood, they could not act in a fitting manner with the necessary concert; although the master of the camp and captains worked hard in keeping the troops together, and in encouraging them to face the natives. The governor Estevan Rodriguez de Figueroa looked at what was going on from his galley, and not being able to endure the little concert there was amongst his men, he took arms, and with three or four companions had himself put on shore. In order that he might go more expeditiously, a servant carried his helmet, and as he was crossing part of the thicket to where the fight was going on, a hostile Indian stepped out (without being seen) from one side, and with his campilan struck the governor a blow on the head, which brought him to the ground badly wounded. Those who accompanied him cut to pieces the man of Mindanao, and carried the governor to the galley. In a short time the master of the camp Juan de la Xara withdrew with his soldiers to the fleet, having left a few Spaniards killed in that encounter. The governor did not recover his senses, for the wound was very severe, and the next day he died, and the fleet after that loss and misfortune left that place and returned down the river to Tampacan, where it anchored amongst the friendly inhabitants and their towns.

The master of the camp Juan de la Xara then got himself elected by the fleet as successor to the government and enterprise, and made a fort of palms and arigues[3] close to Tampacan, with a Spanish town to which he gave the name of Murcia: and he began to dispose of everything as he chose, in order to perpetuate himself, and make himself sole

[1] Swords.   [2] Large shields.   [3] Piles.

master in this affair, without any dependence or recognition of the governor of Manila, without whose intervention and assistance this enterprise could not be pursued further.

CHAPTER VI.

Of the Government of Don Francisco Tello; and of the second establishment of the Audiencia of Manila; and of the things that happened during the period of this government.

The Governor Don Luys Dasmariñas was expecting news of Captain Juan Xuarez Gallinato, and of the Governor Estevan Rodriguez de Figueroa, respecting the voyage which each had made in the beginning of this year, ninety-six, to Cambodia and to Mindanao; when advices reached Manila in the month of June that there were two ships from the passage of the Espiritu Santo, within amongst the islands, and that there came in them, sent from Spain as new governor, Don Francisco Tello de Guzman, knight of the habit of Santiago, a native of Seville, treasurer of the House of Commerce with the Indies. He entered Manila in the first days of July, and was received at the Government House. At the same time it was known that there remained in New Spain the Archbishop-elect of Manila, Fray Ygnacio de Santivañez of the order of St. Francis, a native of Santivañez in the province of Burgos; for the Bishop Fray Domingo de Salazar had died in Madrid; and that Fray Miguel de Benavides, native of Carrion, a Dominican monk, was bishop-elect of the city of Segovia in the province of Cagagan; he had gone to Spain as the companion of the Bishop Fray Domingo de Salazar. It was also known that there had remained behind in Mexico the bishop-elect of the city of the most holy name of Jesus, Fray Pedro de Agurto, of the order of St. Augustine, a native of Mexico: and these two bishops (with another for the city of Caceres

in the province of Camarines, who was not yet named) had
been added to the Philippines, and given as suffragans to
the Archbishop of Manila,[1] at the instance of the Bishop
Fray Domingo, at the same time that the High Court of
Justice of Manila, which had been abolished, was again to
be established, with other matters, in which he had taken
part at Court.

A short time after Don Francisco Tello entered upon the
government, news was brought of the death of Estevan
Rodrigues de Figueroa in Mindanao, by the brother Gaspar
Gomez, of the Company of Jesus, who brought the body for
burial in the college of Manila, the patronage of which was
his. Juan de la Xara wrote word how he had remained in
the government, and had settled in Tampacan, and that he
meditated continuing the pacification and conquest of the
island, as it should seem to him convenient, and asking for
succours of men and other things to be sent to him. It was
understood that he intended to make an ill use of the government,
without observing due subordination to the governor
of the Philippines, and to deprive the heirs of Estevan
Rodriguez of what belonged to them from this source: also,
that in order to make himself safer in this respect, he was
sending confidantes of his to the town of Arevalo in Oton,
where Estevan Rodriguez had left his wife Doña Ana de
Osseguera and two little daughters, and his house and property,
to persuade that lady to marry him. As these intentions
appeared to be very prejudicial in many respects, they
took into consideration how to find a remedy; but in order
not to disturb the affairs of Mindanao, it was let alone for
the present, until time should show what course ought to be
followed. And so it happened; for Juan de la Xara having
left the camp and settlements of Mindanao, and come hurriedly
to Oton to negotiate his marriage personally (though

[1] The episcopal staff of the Philippines still consists only of the archbishop and three bishops.

the widow of Estevan Rodriguez had never been favourable to it), Don Francisco Tello sent to arrest him, and he was brought to Manila, where he died whilst his affair was under investigation.

After de la Xara had been put in prison Don Francisco Tello at once sent Captain Toribio de Miranda to Mindanao with despatches to take the command of the camp, and govern the settlements until some one should continue the carrying out of that enterprise by agreement. When he arrived at Mindanao, and the soldiers saw that the machinations of Juan de la Xara were defeated, and that he remained in prison at Manila and would not return, they obeyed Toribio de Miranda, and the orders which he brought.

In Manila the governor considered with much attention the measures to be taken for continuing the war; for, as the island of Mindanao was so near the other islands that were already settled, and in the island itself there were some provinces that had submitted and were settled with Spanish magistrates, such as the river of Butuan, and Dapitan, and Caragan, it was desirable to pacify the whole island and reduce it to submission to his Majesty. The royal property had been spent, and nothing was left for further expense, and Estevan Rodriguez had bound himself by a formal writing to carry on the war at his own expense until entirely completed, in conformity with the conditions of the agreement. The guardian of his daughters and heirs brought the matter before the Court, and excused himself from this obligation on account of the death of Estevan Rodriguez; and, in order not to lose time, since what had been commenced had to be continued in one way or other, the governor decided on following it up, giving out of the royal exchequer what was requisite either on account of the exchequer or of the heirs of Estevan Rodriguez, if such should be according to law. The governor then looked out for a person to go to Mindanao, and selected Don Juan Ronquillo, general of the galleys, and gave him what seemed the necessary succour of men and other things. So he arrived at Mindanao, and took the command of the fleet and camp of Spaniards which he found in Tampacan : he confirmed the peace and friendship established with the chiefs and their people of Tampacan and Lumaguan : he restored and set in order the Spanish town and fort, and began to equip himself for the war with the people of Buhahayen. He made a few expeditions to their lands and forts, in which he passed many days without any notable result, as these enemies were many in number and good soldiers, with plenty of firearms and artillery in a strong position, and many other fortifications in the interior of the country, amongst which they passed from one to another whenever it suited them, without receiving any hurt, and greatly harassing the Spaniards, who were little used to such swampy country. The Spaniards, moreover, were short of provisions, and in the country they were not to be got on account of the war, as there were a great many people in camp both of Spaniards and natives, as servants and boatmen ; and it was not easy to go and come at all times from one part to another to get the necessary supplies.

As Don Juan Ronquillo saw that the war was advancing very slowly, and that little advantage was derived from it, and the camp was suffering, having made a report, he sent despatches with speed to the governor Don Francisco Tello, giving him an account of the state of affairs, and that it would be better to remove the camp from the river of Mindanao, not to let it perish, and that a garrison might be put in the island itself in the port of Caldera, which might be left fortified, so as not to turn their backs entirely on the enterprise ; and in order to maintain their friends, the people of Tampacan and Lumaguan, in their hostility to those of Buhahayen : and he proposed that the fleet and rest of the camp should return to Manila, if he gave him permission for that, and requested that instructions should be sent him with all speed. Upon the governor Don Francisco Tello receiving this despatch, he resolved to order Don Juan Ronquillo that, the state of affairs being such as he had reported, and seeing that the camp could not be sustained, nor the war continued advantageously, he should withdraw with all the camp from the river of Mindanao, after first making a great effort to chastise the enemy in Buhahayen; and then burn the Spanish town and fort, and go to Caldera and fortify it, and leave in it a sufficient garrison, with artillery, boats, and provisions for its service and maintenance; and that he should come to Manila with the rest of the forces, explaining to their friends in Tampacan that the Spaniards would shortly return to the river, better provided, and in greater numbers.

Silonga, and other chief men of Buhahayen, did not neglect its defence; since, amongst other measures, they had sent a chief to Terrenate, begging assistance against the Spaniards who had brought war into their homes. Upon this the King of Terrenate sent a fleet of many caracoas and other boats to Mindanao, with cachils[1] and valiant soldiers, and a quantity of small artillery, rather more than a thousand fighting men in all, to oblige the Spaniards to raise their camp and go away (if they could not succeed in doing more). In Buhahayen they had news and advices that this fleet was coming for their defence and protection, and they got ready and prepared to fall upon the Spaniards, who also had heard the same news, and were not off their guard. On this account more care was taken by them of their principal fort, and they reduced the number of men in other smaller forts in the river Buquil, and other posts, mouths and arms of the same

[1] Chiefs. *Ketchil*, Malay word signifying little, young; hence a young man of distinction, a son or brother of the Molucca princes: in Amboina it is the designation of the heir-apparent. *Marsden's Dict.*

river, which enabled them the better to garrison the fort
and armed galleys, and other smaller craft, in order to
make use of them for the attack of the enemies whom they
expected. The enemy entered gallantly with all his vessels
and men as far as the Spanish fort, and attacked and
assaulted it to enter it with all vigour and speed. Those
within resisted valiantly, and the Spaniards outside who
were on the river in the galleys assisted them in such
manner, that together, with artillery and firearms, and at
times coming to close combat with swords and campilans,
they made a great destruction and desolation amongst the
men of Terrenate, and of Buhahayen, who had joined to
assist them. Killing and wounding a great number of
them, they took almost all the caracoas and boats which
they had brought, so that very few escaped by flight; and
the Spaniards followed them up and burned them, capturing
many prisoners, and spoils and weapons of the enemy.
After this, with as much speed as they could, they turned
against the town and forts of the people of Buhahayen,
succeeding so well against some of them, that the enemy,
finding himself hard pressed and with no one to assist him,
sent messengers and proposals of peace to Don Juan Ronquillo. These ended in their making recognition and submission, and establishing friendship with the people of
Tampacan, their ancient enemies; and to strengthen this
more, it was corroborated by the marriage of the greatest
Chief and Lord of Buhahayen with the daughter of another of
Tampacan, named Dongonlibor.[1] In this manner the war was
apparently ended; for now provisions were to be had; and
the Spaniards (with few precautions) crossed and went about
the whole country. Buhahayen promised at once to dismantle all the forts, which was one of the conditions of

[1] In the Malay annals there is a princess named Dáun-libar, the
broad leaf.

peace. So the Spaniards returned to their fort and settlement of Tampacan, from which Don Juan Ronquillo immediately sent news to the governor Don Francisco Tello; he advised him of the change of circumstances which had happened, and in accordance with the state of the enterprise, he begged him to issue fresh instructions as to his conduct, because he would wait without making any change, notwithstanding the arrival of the answer which he expected to his first despatches, since now the times were different; and, having changed so much for the better, the governor's decision would also be a different one.

The governor Don Francisco Tello had replied to the first despatch of Don Juan Ronquillo in the sense which has been above related. When the second despatch arrived with the good news of the events in Mindanao, as it was feared that the men in the camp (who had always shown a desire to return to Manila, and little disposition for the hardships of war), would return to Manila on the arrival of the first order; and that they would obey that, and abandon the expedition which was in such a satisfactory state, and the abandonment of the river now would be ill-timed; the governor immediately sent with speed and by various roads a second order for them to stop in Mindanao without paying attention to the first order, and carry on the business, and he would shortly send them what was necessary for the future.

It appears that this message travelled slowly, for the first having arrived, it was executed without any further delay, the camp raised, and the country abandoned. They gave as a reason to the people of Buhahayen who had been their enemies, that the governor of Manila had sent to summon them; and to their friends of Tampacan they said that, for their security, they would leave people in Caldera, and that they would send them assistance from Manila. For which reason, these remained as sad and disconsolate as the people of Buhahayen were well pleased. After that, they burned their fort and town, and as speedily as possible embarked all the forces, and went out of the river, going to Caldera, twenty-four leagues lower down on the way to Manila. Having put into port, a fortress was built, in which they left a garrison of a hundred Spaniards, with some artillery and provisions, and boats for its service.

At this juncture, the second order of the governor to Don Juan Ronquillo arrived, to which he replied that he had already left and was in Caldera, and could not return to the river. Without further delay, he came with the rest of the fleet to Manila, by the provinces of Oton and Panay. The governor, being informed of his arrival before he entered the city, sent to arrest him on the road, and proceeded against him by law for having brought away the camp and army from the river of Mindanao, and for not waiting for the orders, which he should have expected according to the turn which things had taken. Don Juan Ronquillo was set at liberty on showing a private letter from the governor, which he had sent him separately with the first instructions, ordering him in any case to come to Manila with all his forces, because he wanted them for other necessities of the islands; and Don Juan said that on the strength of that letter he had not waited for second instructions.

The Captain and Sergeant-major Gallinato crossed over with the flagship of his fleet from Cochin China to Manila, where he related and gave an account to Don Francisco Tello, whom he now found in the government, of what had happened in his expedition, and how Blas Ruyz and Diego Belloso had gone by land from Cochin China to Laos in search of Langara King of Cambodia: by their absence he avoided calumny in this matter of leaving Cambodia; although there were not wanting many of those that came with him who spoke with regret of the opportunity which he had lost, by not showing himself and staying in Cambodia, in such a good conjuncture; and they even asserted that had he done so, everything would have been effected which had been looked forward to in that kingdom.

The other ship of his convoy, to which his fleet had been reduced, of which he had made the ensign Luys Ortiz the commander, was not able to pursue the voyage, and put into Malacca for shelter from the storms. Some Spaniards remained there, and with the remainder of the crew he was able to sail some months later, and return to Manila.

At this same time, and at the beginning of Don Francisco Tello's government, two Indian chiefs of the province of Cagayan, the principal one named Magalat, were detained in Manila, because they and their kinsmen, and others who followed their party and way of thinking, had several times raised up the people of that province, and it had cost no slight trouble to reduce them to submission, and they had frequently killed Spaniards, and done other injuries to the peaceable natives and to their crops. Magalat was the captain and head of these men; and as he and a brother of his and some other Indians were in Manila, without being able to leave it, that province was more secure.

Some Dominican monks who had to go to the city of Segovia, capital of the province, where they were charged with teaching, being moved with pity, persuaded the governor to give to them Magalat and his brother, that they might return to their homes. They importuned him so much about this that he granted it. When these two reached Cagayan, they went further up the country by the river of Lobo, and they again raised all the country, and with the help of other chief men of Tubigarao and other towns, they so stirred up the country that it was not possible to pass through it, or to go a step beyond the city. Magalat was the head of these enemies, and he committed cruel murders and injuries upon his own country people, if they would not rise against the Spaniards. This reached such a point that it became necessary for the governor to send the master of the camp Pedro de Chaves from Manila with troops, carefully to set about remedying the evil: and, although with great difficulties, he had such good luck that he laid hands on several chiefs of the insurgents, upon whom he executed justice and public punishment: and, as for Magalat himself, he caused him to be killed in his own house and estate in which he had fortified himself, by the hand of his own Indians, because they offered to do it for a reward which was given them; for in any other manner it seemed impossible, and if Magalat had not died it would have been impossible to end the war in many years: so the province remained quiet, and peace established.

In April of the year 1595, the Commander Alvaro de Mendaña de Neira went out from Callao of Lima in Peru, to people the islands of Solomon, which he had discovered many years before in the South Sea,[1] and he had named the principal one the island of St. Christopher. He took with him four ships: two large ones, a flagship, and an admiral's ship, and a frigate, and a galliot, with four hundred men in all, and his wife Doña Ysabel Barreto, and three brothers-in-law. In the voyage he discovered other islands, at which he did not stop, and not finding those he had before discovered,[2] and the admiral's ship having been lost, for it did not again appear, he anchored with the other ships at an island of negroes, close to New Guinea, to which he gave the name of St. Cruz; and there he settled, to the small satisfaction of his people. The commander-in-chief and two of his brothers-in-law, and many of his people died there. Doña Ysabel Barreto removed the settlement on account of

[1] This first voyage was in the year 1568.
[2] From this it is clear that it was generally known that Mendaña did not reach the Solomon Islands in his second voyage; yet, as those islands were the object of his expedition, the mutilated printed account of his second voyage, translated by De Brosses, would easily have received the title of *Descubrimiento de las islas de Solomon*. See Preface.

the sickness and want, and put her remaining people on board the flagship, frigate, and galley, and whilst they were sailing to the Philippines the frigate and the galliot disappeared in another direction. The flagship entered the river of Butuan in the island of Mindanao, and reached Manila with great labour, and scarcity of provisions. There Doña Ysabel Barreto married Don Fernando de Castro, and returned in his ship, the San Geronymo, to New Spain in the year 1596. The events of that voyage have been touched very lightly, as it will be to the purpose to set down here the narrative of this voyage which Pedro Fernandez de Quiros signed with his name, which is as follows:—

Narrative of the Voyage of the Adelantado Alvaro de Mendaña de Neira for the Discovery of the Islands of Solomon.

On Friday the ninth of April, of the year 1595, the Commander-in-chief Alvaro de Mendaña set sail with his fleet to go and subject and people the western islands of the South Sea, from the port of the Callao of Lima, which is in twelve degrees and a half south latitude, passing by the valleys of Santa, Truxillo and Saña, and collecting men and provisions, he went to Paita, where he took in water, and made a list of four hundred persons, more or less, with his four vessels, two large and two small. He left this port (which is five degrees higher than the said part), steering west-south-west, making for the islands of his discovery: he took as master of the camp Pedro Merino Manrique, and as admiral his brother-in-law Lope de la Vega, and as chief pilot, Pedro Fernandez de Quiros; and he sailed on this course to the altitude of nine degrees and a-half, from which point he sailed west and to the point south-west to fourteen degrees, where he changed his course to west and the point north-west; and having reached by this course fully ten degrees of latitude, on Friday, twenty-first of July, we sighted an island, to which the general gave the name of Madalena, and from a port in it there came forth about seventy canoes, in each of which came three men, in some more in others less. Others came swimming, and others on logs: they were more than four hundred Indians, white, and of very agreeable appearance, tall and strong, large limbed, and so well made that they had greatly the advantage over us; with handsome teeth, eyes and mouth, hands and feet, and most beautiful flowing hair, and many of them very fair. Amongst them were most beautiful youths; they were entirely naked, without covering on any part, and all had their bodies, legs, and arms, and hands, and some of them their faces, marked after the manner of the Bisayas here: and indeed, for savage people, naked and of so little reason, at sight of them there was much cause to praise God who created them. Let this not be taken for exaggeration, for so it is. These people called us to go to their port, and they called to them from our flag-ship, and they went on board of her, a matter of forty of them: and we appeared to be men of less than the usual stature by the side of them: and amongst them there came one who was understood to be a palm taller than the tallest man of our fleet, although we had in the fleet men of more than regulation height. The general gave there to some of them shirts and other things, which they received with much pleasure, and danced after their fashion, and called to the others. The general was put out of temper at the liberties they took, because they were great thieves; and he ordered a cannon to be fired to frighten them: when they heard it they took to swimming, and all seized their arms, and sounding a conch, they threw a few stones, and threatened with their lances, for they had no other arms. From the ship they fired at them with arquebuses, and killed five or six, and they remained there. As our fleet sailed on we discovered three other islands. This island may be six leagues round;[1] we passed by it on the south side; this is high, precipitous towards the sea, with rocky ravines, in which the Indians dwell. There seemed to be many inhabitants in it, for we saw them on the rocks and beach; so we went on making for the other three islands. The first, to which was given the name of San Pedro, will be ten leagues from Magdalena, and runs with it northward and to the point north-west: it will have three leagues circuit. It is an island beautiful to look at, with much wood and fair fields: we did not know whether it was inhabited, for we did not come close to it. To the southeast of it, about five leagues off, is another, which the general named Dominica; it is very fair to look at, and seemed thickly inhabited: it may have about fifteen leagues circumference; and to the south of this, and a matter of little more than a league off, is another island, which may be eight leagues round, which received the name of Santa Christina; and our fleet passed through the channel between this and the other island. For all that we saw of these islands is clear sailing; and on the west side of Sta. Christina a good port was found, in which the fleet anchored. These Indians did not come before me like the others, but some very beautiful women were seen: I did not see them, but persons who had an opinion in the matter affirmed to me that there were as beautiful women as in Lima, but white, and not so tall; and in Lima there are some very pretty. What was seen in the way of victuals in that port was pigs and hens, sweet canes, very good plantains, cocos, a fruit which grows on high trees; each is as large as a large fir cone; it is very good to eat; much of it was eaten—green, roasted and boiled, and when ripened it is indeed so sweet and good a fruit to my way of thinking, that I know no other which has the advantage of it: there is hardly anything in it to throw away, unless a little husk.

[1] *De box, boxear*, to go round: hence, to box the compass.

There was another fruit, like chestnuts in savour, but much larger than six chestnuts together: a good deal of that was eaten, roast and boiled; and some nuts with a very hard shell, which were very oily, and many of them were eaten: some suspect that they brought on looseness. We also saw pumpkins of Castille sown in the ground. There is a pretty waterfall close to the beach of very good water; it comes out of a rock, at the height of two men: its volume may be of the thickness of four or five fingers, and then, close to it, a stream of water, and the vessels supplied themselves from it. The Indians went off to the mountains and rocks, in which they fortified themselves, and tried to do mischief by rolling stones and hurling them, but they never wounded any one, for the master of the camp stopped their advance by placing outposts. The Indians of this island, on seeing a negro of ours, made signs towards the south, to say that in that direction there were men like him, and that they went there to fight, and that the others had arrows, and that these went in large canoes which they possess. As there was no interpreter, nor much curiosity to learn more, the matter remained thus; but in my opinion, this is not possible for Indians so isolated, unless there is a chain (of islands), because their boats and customs in other matters do not show that these people had come there from any great distance.

This port is in nine degrees and a half (south) latitude. The commander-in-chief ordered three crosses to be set up in it; and, on Saturday 5th of August, to weigh anchor and set sail, making for the west, to the south-west, or north-west, a matter of four hundred leagues. Sunday, the 20th of August, we saw four low islands, with sandy beaches, full of very many palms and woods, and on the south-east side; towards the north, a great sand-bank. All four may have a circuit of twelve leagues. We did not know whether they were inhabited, because we did not go close to them. This year all seemed timid: I say this with rage. They are in ten degrees and three-quarters latitude, and were named after St. Bernard, having been discovered on his day. Henceforward we began to meet with south-easterly winds, which appear to predominate here. With these we continued sailing to the above-mentioned points, never rising above eleven or going below ten leagues, until Tuesday, 29th of August, when we discovered a round islet, which might be a league round, all surrounded by reefs. We tried to land on it, and could not find where to do so, in order to get wood and water for the admiral's ship, of which it had run very short; it was given the name of Solitary Island; it is in ten degrees and two-thirds, and will be one thousand five hundred and thirty-five leagues from Lima. From this place we went on navigating, with the before-mentioned orders, and a variety of opinions were given: some saying that we did not know where we were going, and other things which did not fail to cause grief. It was God's pleasure, that on the eve of our Lady in September, at midnight, we saw an island, which might have a circuit of from ninety to a hundred leagues, and it lies about east south-east and west north-west, and will be a thousand eight hundred leagues from Lima. The whole of it was very full of woods, reaching to the highest ridges, and where it was not cleared for the Indians to sow, in all the rest not a span of earth was to be seen. The ships came to anchor in the northern part of the island, in ten degrees latitude. To the north of this port, about seven leagues off, is a volcano, with a very well shaped hill, from the top of which and from other parts issued much fire. The volcano is lofty and may have a circumference of three leagues; it is precipitous on the side of the sea, and all bare, and without any part where a landing can be effected; it rumbles within frequently and loudly like thunder. To the north-east of this volcano there are some small islets which are inhabited, and a great quantity

of shoals; there is a distance of seven or eight leagues to
these islets, and the shoals run to the north-west; and the
person who went to see said that they were numerous.
Around the great island there were some small islands: all
of them, and the great one (when it was circumnavigated)
were found to be inhabited; and within sight of this great
island, to the south-east of it, there was seen another island
of no great size: this must be the link with others. After
putting into port in the great island of Santa Cruz; for this
was the name given it, the commander-in-chief ordered
Captain Don Lorenzo, brother of his wife, to go with the
frigate to seek the Admiral's ship, which disappeared on the
night in which we saw the island, respecting which I make
no favourable conjecture; it was sought for this and two
other times, and was not found, but only the shoals which I
have mentioned. What was seen in the way of victuals in
this port consisted of pigs, hens, plantains, sweet canes,
one, two, or three kinds of roots like sweet potatoes, which
they eat roast and boiled, and make biscuit with it, *buyos*,
two kinds of good almonds, and two kinds of pine nuts,
wood-pigeons, doves, ducks, grey and white herons, swal-
lows, potherbs,[1] pumpkins of Castille, the fruit which I mentioned in the first islands, and chestnuts and nuts. There
is a very strongly scented sweet basil, and coloured flowers,
which at this port they keep in the gardens, and two other
species of another sort also coloured. There is another fruit
on high trees, like pippins for their good smell and savour.
There is a great quantity of ginger which grows there without its being cultivated, and much yerba chiquilite, with
which they make indigo. There are agave trees, and a
great deal of sagia, and many cocoa nuts. Marble was seen,
and pearl shells, and large snail shells like those which are
brought here from China. There is a very copious spring,
and five or six other rivers, though not very large. The
settlement was established close to this spring. The In-

[1] *Muchos bledos*, blites.

dians attempted to defend themselves, and as the arquebuse tells at a distance, seeing the evil effects, they did not defend themselves much, but on the contrary gave some of what they possessed. In this matter of going for provisions there were a few things happened, which were not very good treatment of the Indians, for they killed the Indian who was our best friend, and the lord of that island; his name was Malope; and two or three others, who were also friendly. Of the whole island no more was seen than a matter of three leagues around the camp. The people of this island are black: they have small canoes made of one tree,[1] in which they go about their villages, and other very large canoes with which they go out to sea. On Sunday, the eighth October, the commander-in-chief ordered the master of the camp to be killed by stabbing, and they killed Tomas de Ampuero in the same manner, and they cut off the head of the ensign Juan de Buitrago; and he wished to put to death two other friends of the master of the camp: but he left them alone, because we entreated him to do so. The cause of this was public, because they wished to go away from the country and abandon it, and there must have been other reasons, but I am unacquainted with them. What I saw was much dissoluteness and shamelessness, and more than enough improper conduct. On the eighteenth of October the commander-in-chief died: on the seventeenth there had been a total eclipse of the moon.[2]

---

[1] *De un palo*, or, with one mast.
[2] Pingré's translation of the *Descubrimiento de las islas de Salomon* says, p. 41,—"On the 17th October there was a total eclipse of the moon: this luminary, on rising above the horizon, was already totally eclipsed. Mendaña, by his will, which he signed with difficulty, named as lady governor of the fleet his wife Doña Isabella de Barreto." And in a note, he says that he calculated this eclipse by the tables of Halley: the immersion must have happened at Paris at 19 hours 6 minutes, and the moon had already been risen since 5 or 6 minutes; so that the isle of Sta. Cruz would be at least 13h. 2m. west of Paris, which would

On the second of November his brother-in-law, Don Lorenzo, who had succeeded as captain-general, died; and seven or eight days before, the priest Antonio de Serpa; and on the eighth November the vicar Juan de Espinosa. There was great sickness amongst our people, and as there was little care for want of an apothecary and doctor, many of them died; and they begged the lady governor, Doña Ysabel Barreto, to take them out of the country. One and all agreed to embark; and, trusting ourselves to the mercy of God, we left this port on Saturday the eighteenth of the said month, in a westerly direction to the south-west point, making for the island of St. Christopher; or more exactly in search of it, to see if it or the admiral's ship could be fallen in with, for so the lady governor commanded. We sailed two days and saw nothing; and at the request of all the people, who cried out that we were taking them to destruction, she ordered me to shape the course from this town to Manila, from a port in ten degrees and a half, from which I came steering to north-west, to avoid meeting islands on the way, for the ill prepared we were to go amongst them, with the crews so sick that there died whilst we were sailing some fifty persons, and there in the island forty persons, a little more or less. We made our course, short of provisions, navigating five degrees south and as many in north latitude. We met many impediments and calms, and in fully six degrees north latitude saw an island, which seemed to have a circumference of twenty-five leagues, thickly wooded, and inhabited by very many people, like those of the Ladrones, for we saw them in canoes which came out to us. From the south-east to the north and then to south-west it is surrounded by large reefs. On its western side, about four leagues off, there are some low islets: we

make it 184 degrees 30 minutes longitude, or at most 190 degrees, allowing for the Spaniards not having perceived the eclipse before sunset."

found no place to anchor, though we tried; for the galliot and frigate which sailed with our ship had disappeared some days back.[1] From this place we came by the said course to latitude thirteen degrees and three quarters, and in two days that we sailed west in this latitude we sighted Serpana[2] and Guan in the Ladrones, and we passed between the two and did not anchor, from not having ropes to lower and recover the boat. This day was the third of January of 1596, and on the fourteenth of the said month we saw the cape of Espiritu Santo, and on the fifteenth anchored in the bay of Cobos. We arrived there in such a state that only the goodness of God could bring us thither, for human strength and resources were not enough to reach to a tenth of the way. Here we arrived so dismantled, and the men so thin and worn out, that it was the most pitiable sight that could be seen, with only nine or ten pitchers of water. In this bay of Cobos the ship and crew were set to rights as much as was possible, and on Tuesday, second of February, we left that port and bay, and on the tenth of the same month we anchored in this port of Cabite, etc.

Besides the desire which I have to serve your Honour, that which moves me to leave this brief narrative with your

[1] The *Descubrimiento de las Islas de Salomon* says:—"The frigate was found cast away on the coast with all the crew dead. The galliot touched at Mindanao, in 10 degrees, where the crew landed on the islet of Camaniguin; and while wandering on the shore, and dying of hunger, met with some Indians, who conducted them to a hospital of the Jesuits. The corregidor of the place sent five men of this ship prisoners to Manila, upon the complaint of their captain, whom they had wished to hang. He wrote to Don Antonio de Morga the following letter: 'A Spanish galliot has arrived here, commanded by a captain, who is as strange a man as the things which he relates. He pretends to have belonged to the expedition of General Don Alvaro de Mendaña, who left Peru for the Solomon isles, and that the fleet consisted of four ships. You will perhaps have the means of knowing what the fact is. The soldiers who were prisoners declared that the galliot had separated from the general only because the captain had chosen to follow another route.
[2] Isle of Seypan.

Honour is, that an account may remain (if perchance God should dispose of my life, or anything else should arise, or I or she that I take with me should be missing),[1] and that it may give light, which may be a business of great service to God and to the king our sovereign. May your Honour be pleased to accept the good will to serve you which I retain; and if God make me return to this port, there will be an opportunity to set it forth better: and at the same time will your Honour forgive my being so short, for time is in fault for being so with me. I beg you to keep it secret, for man does not know what time brings; for looking at it rightly, it is fit that the first islands remain concealed, until His Majesty be informed and order whatever may be most for his service: for as they are placed, taking a middle position between Peru, New Spain and this country, the English, on knowing it, might settle in them, and do much mischief in this sea. And consider me as the faithful servant of your Honour, whom may God preserve many years, with much satisfaction and increase of dignity, etc.

Your servant,

PEDRO FERNANDEZ DE QUIROS.

To the Dr. Antonio de Morga, Lieutenant-general of His Majesty of the Philippines.

[1] "*Que yo, ó la que llevo faltemos.*" The astronomer Pingré is rather severe (in a note, p. 46) upon the President de Brosses, and upon the editors of the Holland edition of the French collection of voyages, for a prolix note respecting Doña Beatrix, whom they suppose to have been the wife of Lope de Vega, Mendaña's second in command, who was lost during the voyage; she returned, they say, with Doña Ysabel de Barreto, to America. M. Pingré urges that there was no such person in the fleet as Doña Beatrix, or else that she and Doña Ysabel were the same person; and he is of opinion that the person who wrote down the name of Beatrix in one part of the narrative instead of Ysabel, probably had his mind full of some other Beatrix altogether foreign to the narrative. However, as Doña Ysabel de Barreto was married again to Don Fernando de Castro, and returned to America with him in his ship, it is

Don Francisco Tello, when he entered upon his government in the year '96, found the ship *San Geronymo* (in which Don Fernando de Castro and Doña Ysabel Barreto his wife returned to New Spain) getting ready in the port of Cabite: the galloon *San Felipe* was likewise ready for sea, to make the voyage to New Spain with the produce of the Philippines: and as soon as the governor Don Francisco Tello had assumed the government, both ships were despatched, and set sail. Although the *San Geronymo* went last out of port, it made the voyage and reached New Spain at the end of the year of '96. The ship *San Felipe*, which was large and heavily laden with merchandise and passengers, and had for commander and general Don Mathia de Landecho, met with many storms during the voyage; so that in one of these it became necessary to lighten the ship of much of the cargo, and the rudder was lost in thirty-seven degrees of latitude, at six hundred leagues from the Philippines, and a hundred and fifty from Japan. Seeing themselves unable to repair the loss and continue the voyage, it was proposed to make for the Philippines, and they began that navigation, changing the course which they had followed. In this again the greatest difficulties and labours presented themselves: they frequently saw themselves on the point of being lost, for the seas were very high, and as the ship had no rudder, the rigging and few sails she carried were so violently shaken that everything was shattered, and they could not hold her on her course; and she was so often taken aback, that she was in great danger of foundering, and all hope of reaching the Philippines was lost. It was found that the nearest land was Japan, but not so near that the ship could reach it, or venture near its coast, which is very wild, and was un-

hardly probable that Quiros would have spoken of her in the above terms; so that the lady referred to in the text by Quiros may perhaps be Doña Beatrix.

known and had not been seen by them: and even should they have the good fortune to reach it, they did not know how they would be received by the Japanese. Here arose the confusion and diversity of opinions of the people on board the ship; some said the course they were making for Manila ought not to be altered, although it was accompanied by the great peril and discomfort which they were experiencing: others, that it would be great rashness to do so, and that since Japan was much nearer, that they should go to it, making for the port of Nangasaqui, whence there was trade to the Philippines, and where they would meet with shelter, and the means of repairing the ship, and continuing their voyage from that point. This opinion prevailed, for some monks who were on board embraced it, and the remainder conformed to it, on the assurance of the pilots that they would in a short time take the ship in to Japan. So they altered the course for that country, and at the end of six days discovered the coast and country of Japan, in a province called Toza; and although they made every effort by day to reach the land, at night, when they struck the sails, the currents carried them away from it. Many boats[1] came out to the ship from a port called Hurando, and persuaded by the king of that province, who assured them of harbour, tackle and repairs, they put the ship into port: having first sounded and reconnoitred the entry, and ascertained that there was water enough. The Japanese, who were infidels, and did it with malice, took the ship in tow with their boats into the port, and led and guided her on to a shoal, and as there was not much water on it, the ship touched and grounded on it: so that it became necessary to unload the ship, and take out all the cargo on shore close to the town, in a spot staked round which was given them for that purpose. The Japanese gave the Spaniards at the time a good reception, but with

[1] *Funcas.* Query funny *Etonice*.

respect to repairing the ship and going out of port again, they gave them to understand that this could not be done without license and permission from Taicosama, lord of Japan, who was in his court at Miaco, a hundred leagues from the port. The General Don Matia de Landecho, and those in his company, resolved, in order not to lose time, to send his ambassadors to the court, with a good present of valuable things from the ship to Taicosama, to entreat him to give orders for despatching them. They sent Christoval de Mercado with this message, and three other Spaniards; also Fray Juan, *Pobre*, a Franciscan, and Fray Juan Tamayo, of the order of St. Augustine, who had come on board the ship: they were to treat this business with Taico, and avail themselves of the Franciscan fathers who were in Miaco; for these had gone formerly from the Philippines as ambassadors, to settle the affairs of Japan with Manila, and they were staying at the court, with a permanent house and hospital, and (being winked at by Taico) making a few Christians, though with much opposition on the part of the monks of the company of Jesus, who are in the kingdom of Japan; as they said that other friars could not meddle or occupy themselves with the conversion of Japan, on account of apostolic briefs and royal letters. The King of Hurando, although in appearance he was friendly and gave a good reception to the Spaniards who were in his port, yet he took great care that they and the merchandise should be ready at hand; and he at once gave notice at court that a foreigner's ship had been lost there, foreigners whom they called Nambajies,[1] and who had brought great riches. Upon which Taicosama, having become covetous, and desiring to

---

[1] *Nambaji*, a monk. Kœmpfer, vol. ii, p. 12, says that Nembuds Koo are devout fraternities who chant the Namanda, which is an abridgment of Nama Amida Budsu, "Great Amida help us;" and at p. 198 he says that Dai-Nembudzsui are persons specially devoted to the worship of Amida.

make himself master of them, sent Ximonojo, one of his favourites and councillors, to Hurando; he, on his arrival, took possession of all the property, and imprisoned the Spaniards within a palisade under a guard, obliging them to give up whatever they had got, and had hidden away, under pain of death. Having executed this with much rigour, he returned to the court, after giving leave to the general and others of his suite to go to Miaco. The ambassadors who had been despatched at first with the present (although it was accepted) could not see Taico, nor negotiate anything available, notwithstanding that the Padre Fray Pedro Baptista, prelate of the Franciscan monks who were at Miaco, set on foot many plans for remedying the injury which was being done to the Spaniards. This only served to increase the evil, because the favourites, seeing Taico so set upon the riches of the ship, and so distant from listening to anything on the subject of the restitution of them, not only did not ask him to do so, on the contrary to make the matter easier, and in order to profit by the time and opportunity, being infidels, and abhorring the monks who made Christians in the court; they set Taicosama against them; telling him that the monks and the people of the ship all belonged to one sovereign, and were conquerors of the kingdoms of others; and that they did this by first sending in their monks, and entering later after them with arms, and that this was what they intended doing in Japan. They supported themselves in this statement by the fact that, when the confidante who went to take possession of the property in the ship was at Hurando, Francisco de Landa, the pilot of the ship, had shewn him the charts of navigation, and in them all that had been discovered by Spain and the other kingdoms, and what His Majesty possessed; and amongst these possessions Peru and New Spain: and on the confidante asking him how they had gained those very distant kingdoms, the pilot replied that first the monks had entered and preached their religion, and the military forces following after them had subjected those countries. It is indeed true that this pilot imprudently gave these reasons, which Ximonojo noted well, and committed to memory in order to repeat them to Taicosama on a good occasion, as he did on this.[1]

From all these things together, and from the instance with which the monks begged Taico to give the merchandise to the Spaniards, the result was that he was at last thoroughly irritated, and like a barbarous tyrant, and so avaricious, he gave orders to crucify all of them, and the rest of the monks who preached the religion of Namban in his kingdoms. Five monks who were in the house at Miaco were immediately seized, and another of those of the ship *San Felipe*, who had joined them, and all their Japanese preachers and teachers; and it was understood that this persecution would be extended to the rest of the monks and other Christians in Japan, so that all were in great fear and confusion. But Taicosama later became more moderate;

[1] The Dutch account of *Memorable Embassies of the United Provinces to the Emperors of Japan*, printed in 1649, and translated into French by Jacob de Meurs, and printed at Amsterdam in 1680, states that Taicosama died on the 16th September, 1598, and relates the above conversation of the pilot a little more fully, as the second reason for the persecution of the Christians by Daifusama, successor of Taicosama. It states that a Spanish vessel having anchored in one of the Japanese ports (it does not mention when), a Japanese gentleman named Yemondone went to see it, and was received by the pilot, who spoke as related by De Morga. It adds that Yemondone informed the emperor, who praised the policy of his predecessor, who had banished the Papists in 1587; and that the same time the emperor was informed that a Spanish pilot had been surprised sounding the ports of Japan, and no doubts remained to the Japanese that the Spaniards intended to invade them. It is probable that Yemondone is the same person as Ximonojo of De Morga, as the Dutch account gives five reasons for the persecution of the Christians on the authority of the Jesuit Hazard. Ximonojo may be intended for Siomio, a title given by Kœmpfer. i, p. 70, as inferior to that of Dainio.

for, allowing himself to be entreated, he declared that there should only be crucified those monks who had been found in the house at Miaco, and the Japanese preachers and teachers their companions who had been arrested; and that all the others, and the Spaniards of the ship, might be allowed to return to Manila. The execution was committed to Fonzanbrandono, brother of Taracabadono, governor of Nangasaki: he took out of the house of the Franciscan monks at Miaco all that were there, on bullock waggons, with a numerous guard, to wit: Fray Pedro Baptista, Fray Martin de Aguirre, Fray Felipe de las Casas, Fray Gonzalo, Fray Francisco Blanco, and Fray Francisco de San Miguel, and twenty-six Japanese preachers and teachers, with two boys in the service of the friars: and he cut off their right ears, and led them about the streets of Miaco, and through the cities of Fugimen, Usaca and Sacai, to the great grief and regret of all the Christians who saw them suffer. The sentence and cause of their martyrdom was carried hanging on a spear, written on a tablet in Chinese letters, and it was as follows:—

Sentence of the Combaco, lord of Japan, against the barefooted friars and their teachers, whom he caused to be martyred in Nangasaqui.

Forasmuch as these men came from the Luzons, from the island of Manila, with the title of ambassadors, and were allowed to remain in the city of Miaco, and preached the faith of the Christians, which I in former years rigorously prohibited;[1] I order that they be executed, together with the Japanese who became of their religion, so these twenty-

---

[1] According to the Dutch *Memorable Embassies*, an embassy of four Franciscans and a Jesuit had an audience of Taico Sama in 1583, and received permission to establish themselves at Miaco on condition of not converting any Japanese: according to De Morga this date should be 1593, as the governor Gomez Perez Dasmariñas, who received Taicosama's summons, only arrived at Manila in 1590; and the Dutch account says that Taicosama became emperor in 1584.

four shall be crucified in the city of Nangasaqui; and whereas I again prohibit anew from this time forward the said religion, let all hear this : and I order that it be put in execution, and if anyone should dare to break this order, that he be punished with all his family. Done on the first of Echo and second of the moon.

In this manner these saints were taken to Nangasaqui, and upon a hill, which was in sight of the town and gate, sown with wheat, and close to a house and hospital named St. Lazarus, which these monks had founded in Nangasaqui when they left the Philippines, they were all crucified in a row, the friars in the middle, and the others on either side of them, on high crosses, with iron staples at their throats, hands and feet, and long sharp iron lances passed through their sides, from below upwards crossways: so that they gave up their souls to their Creator, for whom they died with much valour, on the fifth of February, day of Sta. Agueda, of the year 1597. They left behind them in that ploughed field, and through it in the whole of that kingdom, a great sowing of seed, watered with their blood; from which we hope to gather the abundant fruit of a numerous conversion to the Holy Catholic faith. Before these saints were put upon the crosses, they wrote to Dr. Antonio de Morga, a letter to Manila, by the hand of Fray Martin de Aguirre, which is word for word as follows:—

To Dr. Morga, Lieutenant of the Governor of Manila, whom may God preserve in Manila.

Farewell, Doctor! farewell, for our Lord, in his mercy, not looking at my sins, has been pleased to unite me to a company of twenty-four servants of God, who die for love of Him; of whom six of us are friars of St. Francis, and eighteen Japanese. With the hope that many more will go by the same way, may your worship receive the last farewell and the last embrace of all this company, for we all acknowledge the favour which you have shown to the affairs of this conversion; and now, in taking leave, we beg you (and I especially) to take up as a business of your own the favouring of this Christian body; as you are a father, and favouring all things which may present themselves for the mission of monks to this conversion, so may your worship find one to favour you and intercede for you before God, in time of need. Farewell, sir! and give my last adieu to the Lady Doña Juana, whom may God preserve, etc. From the road to execution, twenty-eighth of January of 1597.

This king's appetite has been much increased by what he robbed from the San Felipe, and they say that next year he will go to Luzon, and that he does not go this year, being taken up with the Coreans; and that for this purpose he intends to take the islands of Lequios[1] and Hermosa,[2] to throw people thence into Cagayan, and from thence take Manila, if God does not first put a stop to his advance. Your worship will see to what is necessary and fitting. Fray Martin de la Ascencion.

The bodies of the martyrs, although they were guarded by the Japanese for many days, were removed by bits (particularly those of the friars) from the crosses as relics by the Christians of the place; they, with much veneration, distributed them, and they are now throughout Christendom, without forgetting the staples and wood of the crosses.

Two other friars of the same company, who were out of the house at the time of the arrest, did not suffer this martyrdom; one named Fray Geronymo de Jesus, hid himself and got into the interior of the country, so as not to have to leave it; the other, named Fray Agustin Rodriguez, was taken in by the Fathers of the company, and they sent him away by the way of Macan. General Don Mathia and the Spaniards of the ship left Japan stripped and without equipments, they

---

[1] Lu Tchu.   [2] Formosa.

embarked at Nangasaki and went to Manila, in different ships, of those which make that voyage on account of the Portuguese and Japanese; and the first news of this event was received through them in the month of May of the year ninety-seven; it caused much grief and sadness on account of the death of the holy monks, and the disturbances which were to be expected in the future in the affairs of Japan and the Philippines; and for the loss of the galloon and property which were going in it to New Spain; for its value was more than a million, so that the Spaniards were much impoverished. In considering what it became them to do under the circumstances, it was ultimately decided, in order not to abandon the matter, that a person should be sent to Japan as messenger with letters from the Governor to Taicosama, to represent to him the regret which he felt at what he had done in taking the ship and merchandise from the Spaniards, and killing the monks, and to beg him to repair it as much as possible, by restoring the property of the Spaniards, and the artillery, tackle, and other things that remained of the ship, and the bodies of the monks whom he had crucified, and providing for the future in such manner that the Spaniards should not be so treated in his kingdom.

The Governor despatched Captain Don Luis Navarrete Fajardo with this message to Japan, and with a present of some jewels of gold and silver, swords, and valuable stuffs, for Taicosama; also an elephant well caparisoned, and with a silk covering, with its nairs in the same livery, which was a thing which had not been seen yet in Japan; in order that, conformably to the usage of that kingdom, the envoy might make a present to Taico, when he acquitted himself of his embassy; because otherwise it is not usual either to send one nor to receive it. Don Luys de Navarrete having arrived at Nangasaki, Taicosama sent from the Court with much readiness for the ambassador and present sent to him from Luzon, which he wished to see, particularly the elephant, which he was much delighted with. He heard the embassy, and gave it a reply with much ostentation and state; he excused himself with respect to the death of the monks, upon whom he laid the blame, since, though he had prohibited them from making Christians or teaching their religion, they had broken his commands in his very Court, making no account of them. Likewise the taking the ship and its merchandise, which entered the port of Hurando of the province of Toza, had been a justifiable thing according to the law of Japan, because all ships which are lost on its coast belong to the king, with their merchandise.[1] But he regretted the whole matter, and would give the merchandise if he had not distributed it; and as to the monks, that could not now be remedied; and rather he would beg the Governor of Manila not to send him such persons, for he had again made laws forbidding the making of Christians under pain of death; and he would give up to him whatever had remained of the bodies of the monks. With respect to peace and amity with the Luzon Islands and the Spaniards, he would be greatly pleased with it, and for his part would endeavour to secure it, and would give orders that if another ship from Manila should come to his kingdom it should be received and treated well. With this reply, and a letter to the same effect for the governor, Taicosama despatched and granted leave to depart to Don Luys Navarrete, giving him to take to the governor a present of lances and arms, and catans of great merit and estimation amongst the Japanese. So Don Luys left Miaco and came to Nangasaki, whence he sent word to the Governor Don Francisco by the first ship which sailed for Manila, of what he had negotiated, which, as he died there of illness, was brought later by another person to Manila. Taiçosama remained satisfied with the reply which he gave to the ambassador, without, indeed, having

---

[1] Like our early law and that of other European nations.

done any of the things which had been asked of him; for that reply was more a semblance and compliments, than a desire for friendship with the Spaniards; and he boasted and gave out arrogantly, and his favourites said in the same manner, that that present and message which the Spaniards had sent, was from the fear they had of him, and as a recognition of tribute and lordship, in order that he should not destroy them, as he had on other occasions threatened them in former years, when Gomez Perez Dasmariñas governed; on which occasion also they had then answered and sent a present with Padre Fray Juan Lobo, of the order of St. Dominic, and Captain Llanos.

Faranda Quiemon, a Japanese, sought for war against Manila, and the confidantes who assisted him were not negligent in entreating Taico not to lose the opportunity which offered for conquering it, for it would be easy as there were few Spaniards in it, and Faranda Quiemon assured him of success, as a man who knew the country and its resources. They made such instances, that Taico gave him the enterprise and some succours, and other assistance towards it. He began to equip himself, and to collect Chinese vessels to go on the expedition: which he was never able to carry out, because he was a man who was personally low and mean, and had neither qualities nor sufficient resources for the enterprise, and his protectors did not choose to furnish them to him; so that his preparations were prolonged until the matter fell through with the death of Taico, and his own, as will be related later. In Manila news constantly arrived that a fleet was being prepared in Japan, and that Faranda was the person who was doing it all, so that they lived with a natural anxiety, as the enemy was proud and powerful, and notwithstanding that there was a full intention on the part of the city and valour to resist him. For all that, the governor and the city never chose to show (in public that they were aware and knew that Taico was about to change, in order not to bring on war, and give a motive to the other side to hasten it; they trusted to time for a remedy, and disposed the affairs of the city in readiness for what might happen, and sent to Japan all the Japanese who were settled in Manila (and they were not a few), and those who came in trading ships, taking charge of their arms on their arrival until they again left the country; and endeavouring to cause them to remain as short a time as possible in the islands, but giving them in all other respects a good reception. As it was understood that Taico was thinking of taking the island of Formosa, which is on the Chinese coast, and very near to Luzon, on the way to Japan, a large well-provisioned island, in order to make of it a rallying point for his fleet, and carry on from it war with Manila with greater convenience; the governor despatched two ships of the fleet, commanded by Don Juan de Zamudio, to reconnoitre this island and all its ports, and the state in which it was, in order to take possession of it first: or, at least, should there not be means or time for that to give advice in China to the Viceroys of the provinces of Canton and Chincheo, so that they, as ancient enemies of Japan, might prevent their entry into it, which was so injurious to all of them. With these measures and precautions the business was prolonged for some days, although in this matter of the expedition to the island of Formosa, nothing else was carried into effect besides giving warning to Great China of the designs of Japan.

After a few days, during which Fray Alonso Ximenez was imprisoned in Cochin China, where Captain Juan Xuarez Gallinato had left him, the King of Tunquin and the King of Sinua gave him leave to go away to Manila, and he got a passage by Macan, in Portuguese ships. He not only did not arrive wearied by the voyage and labours and imprisonment which he had undergone, but on the contrary with renewed health and spirits, he proposed that the expedition to Cambodia should again be set on foot; although there was little news of the good state of affairs in that kingdom, and of the restoration of Prauncar, he, accompanied by other friars of his order, as they had so much influence with Don Luys Dasmariñas, who at this time was already out of the government of Manila, persuaded him, and brought him round to offer to undertake to make this expedition again, in person, and at the cost of his own property, from which would follow good effects, for the service of God and of his majesty.[1] Don Luys spoke of the matter to the governor, Don Francisco Tello, and offered to bear all the expense. The taking a resolution was put off until some news should be received from Cambodia, and the only information possessed was, that Blas Ruyz and Diego Belloso had gone to Laos from Cochin China, having there left Captain Gallinato with his ships.

The people of Tampacan lost courage so much from the departure of Don Juan Ronquillo with the camp from the river of Mindanao,[2] and the spirits of the people of Buhahayen rose, so that notwithstanding the friendship that had been made, and the obedience promised, they began to declare themselves as enemies, and the state of affairs was again disturbed, so that not only they did not dismantle their forts as they had promised, but even they repaired them, and committed other excesses against the people of Tampacan, their neighbours, and they would altogether have broken out into open war, if they had not feared that the Spaniards would return with more decided intentions, and a greater number of men, as it was with this intention that they had left the garrison in Caldera; and thus they let matters go, neither de-

[1] This Fray Alonso Ximenez and his historian give a fresh proof of the veracity of the "imprudent" pilot who explained to the Japanese how such large kingdoms had been conquered. Modern practice has substituted "the supply of the markets" for the phrase "the service of God and of His Majesty."

[2] M. Gayangos informs me that there is in the Archives of the Indies at Seville a letter from D. Juan Ronquillo to De Morga, dated 1597, in which he describes his expedition to the isle of Mindanao.

claring themselves as revolted, nor acting as friends towards the people of Tampacan, and other allies of the Spaniards.

Near the island of Mindanao there is an island named Jolo, not very large, but thickly inhabited, it may have three thousand men, with their own king and lord; all of them are Mussulmans. When the Governor Francisco de Sande went on the expedition to Borneo, he sent Captain Estevan Rodriguez de Figueroa to Jolo, and he entered there, and brought over the inhabitants to submission to his majesty, as was noted further back; these were committed to Captain Pedro de Osseguera during his life, and after his death to Don Pedro de Osseguera, his son and successor. For some years he went on asking and receiving as tribute whatever they chose to give him, which was of small amount, without pressing upon them more heavily, so as not to upset the arrangement altogether: and when Don Juan Ronquillo was in the camp in Mindanao, the Jolo people, seeing the affairs of the Spaniards in a flourishing condition, shewed a desire to enjoy peace and to pay their tributes; but on seeing the departure of the Spaniards, they again grew cool. Captain Juan Pacho, who, in the absence of Don Juan Ronquillo, remained as chief of the garrison at Caldera, had sent a few soldiers to barter for wax, the people of Jolo ill-treated them, and killed two of them; and Juan Pacho desiring to chastise this excess of the Jolo people, went there in person with a few boats and thirty soldiers, and landed. A great number of Jolo men came down from the king's town, which is on a high and strongly fortified hill, and attacked the Spaniards; and as they were very numerous, and the Spaniards were unable to make use of their arquebuses, from the occurrence at the time of a heavy rainfall, they were routed, with the death of their Captain Juan Pacho, and twenty more of their companions, and the rest wounded, and taking to flight, they embarked in their vessels, and returned to Caldera.

This event caused much regret in Manila, especially on

account of the reputation which had been lost by it, both among the Jolo people themselves, and among the people of Mindanao, their neighbours. Although it was held to be necessary to repair this disgrace, and send and chastise the Jolo men; yet, as this had to be done with vigour, and at that time there was not a sufficient force, it was deferred for a better opportunity; only Captain Villagra, with a few soldiers, was sent immediately as head of the garrison at Caldera. When they arrived, they passed the time quietly until their provisions were running short, and the garrison suffered; and with this little support which the people of Tampacan felt, knowing that there were Spaniards in the island, they sustained themselves and passed the time, hoping for the arrival of more Spaniards, as Don Juan had said and promised them, and for chastisement and revenge on the people of Jolo.

Whilst the affairs of the Philippines were in this state, in the month of May of 1598, there arrived at Manila ships from New Spain; which brought despatches ordering the re-establishment of the royal court of justice of the Philippines which had been abolished in a former year. The president named and appointed to it was Don Francisco Tello, who governed the country; and the auditors, Dr. Antonio de Morga; and the licentiates, Cristoval Telles Almazan, and Alvaro Rodriguez Zambrano, and the Fiscal, the licentiate Geronymo de Salazar, with the rest of the officials of the court. In the same ship arrived the Archbishop Fray Ignacio de Santivañez, who enjoyed the archbishopric but for a short time, for he died in the month of August of the same year, of dysentery; there arrived likewise the Bishop of Sebu, Fray Pedro de Agurto. On the eighth day of May of this year, 1598, the royal seal of the High court of justice was received. It was brought from the monastery of St. Augustine to the Cathedral Church upon a horse caparisoned with cloth of gold and crimson, under a canopy of the same cloth; its staves of office were borne by the city magistrates, with their robes of crimson velvet, lined with cloth of white silver, and doublets and breeches of the same material. He who held the office of alguazil mayor, clothed in cloth of gold without a cloak, led the horse on the right hand side, upon which the seal was placed in a case of cloth of gold, with a covering of brocade; and the president and auditors went, all on foot and bareheaded, around the horse. In front there went a large procession of the whole city, dressed in costly and gay clothes; and behind followed all the camp and men-at-arms, with their drums and standards, their arms in their hands, and the captains and officers at their posts, and the master of the camp in front of them with his staff. The streets and windows were richly adorned with many hangings and ornaments, and many triumphal arches; and enlivened by the music of minstrels, trumpets and other instruments. When the seal reached the door of the Cathedral church of Manila, the Archbishop in pontifical robes came out to receive it, with the cross, and the chapter and clergy of the church; and having lowered the case in which it went, from the horse, the president under the canopy put it into the hands of the Archbishop, and went into the church with the auditors, whilst the singers in the chapel began the *Te Deum Laudamus*. They arrived at the great altar, upon the steps of which there was a place prepared with brocade upon which the case with the seal was placed, and whilst all knelt the Archbishop sung some orisons to the Holy Ghost, and also for the health and good government of the king our sovereign. The president then again took the case with the seal, and with the same order and music with which it had been brought in, it was taken out of the church, and again placed upon the horse; and, the Archbishop and clergy remaining at the door of the cathedral, the cortege continued on its way to the royal buildings; where in an apartment well fitted up, under a canopy of crimson velvet, with the royal arms embroidered on it, and on a table covered with brocade, and its cushions of the same stuff, the before-named case with the seal inside of it, was placed and left, and covered over with a cloth of crimson cloth of gold. There was publicly read the royal order for the establishment of the court, and the nominations of the president and of the auditors and fiscal, and they received obedience, and the usual oaths were taken from them. The president then went out to the hall of the court, where the seats and platform were dressed out, with a canopy for the royal arms. There the president, auditors, and fiscal sat down and received the ministers and officials of the court, and its ordinances were read out in the presence of as many of the city and people as could find room in the hall. With this an end was made that day of the foundation of the High court of Justice; and from that time forward it continued in the exercise of its functions, having under its charge and administration all the civil and criminal suits and causes of its district: which consists of all the Philippine Islands and mainland of China, discovered or to be discovered; and under the charge of the president, as governor, was all the business relating to the government according to the royal laws, ordinances, and special orders, which were brought before and despatched by the High court.

A few days after the Chancery of the Philippines had been established in the city of Manila, there arrived news of what had happened in the kingdom of Cambodia after the coming of Prauncar (son and successor of Prauncar Langara, who died in the Laos country), in company with Diego Belloso and Blas Ruyz de Hernan Gonzalez, and of his victories and restoration to his kingdom, as has been before related, by letters from the King Prauncar for the Governor Don Francisco Tello, and for Dr. Antonio de Morga, signed by his hand, and with his seal of coloured ink, written in Castilian, that they might be better understood; and as they were all in the same sense, it seems fit to put in this place the letter which the King Prauncar wrote to Dr. Antonio de Morga, which is word for word as follows:—

Prauncar, King of Cambodia, salutes Dr. Antonio de Morga, and sends this letter with much love and satisfaction.

I Prauncar, King of Camboja, an abundant country, I the sole lord of it the great, I have a great love for Dr. Antonio de Morga, and cannot separate him from my thoughts, because I have learned from the Captain Chofa Don Blas Castile that he with his good heart took part, and assisted the Governor of Luzon,[1] in sending to this country the Captain Chofa Don Blas Castile, and the Captain Chofa Don Diego Portugal, and soldiers in search of the King Prauncar my father. They did not find him, and the two chofas and soldiers killed Anacaparan, who was the only great man. And then they went to Cochin China with the ships, and the two chofas went to the Laos in search of the king of this country, and they brought me to my kingdom, in which I now am, and through them; and the two chofas, and other Spaniards who have come, have assisted me to pacify that which I now possess. I understand that all this has happened to me through the Doctor having an affection for this country, and for this I will endeavour that Dr. Antonio de Morga may always love me, like my father Prauncar, and assist me now, in order that monks may come, and be with the two chofas, and with the other Spaniards and Christians who are in my kingdom; for I will build them churches, and will give them leave and per-

[1] The reader will remember that De Morga stated at p. 46 that he and others had opposed the expedition to Cambodia, and had sent in to the governor a minute against it. De Morga does not seem to have had a very favourable opinion of the two adventurers Don Diego Belloso and Don Blas Ruyz, and leaves it to be suspected that Diego Belloso had put a troublesome Siamese colleague of his out of the way. (See p. 45.) Further on he expresses a doubt whether their designs were consistent with the obligations of conscience.

mission to make Christians all the Cambodians who may wish to become it: and I will give them people to serve them, and I will foster them as did formerly the King Prauncar my father. And I will assist Dr. Antonio de Morga with everything of this country which may be of use to him. To the two chofas I have given the lands which I had promised them; to Captain Don Blas Castile the province of Tran; and to Captain Chofa Don Diego Portugal the province of Bapano; which provinces I grant and concede to them for the services which they have rendered me, and in payment of the property which they have spent in my service, in order that they may possess and enjoy them, and use them at their will, like their own property, whilst they are in my service.

Blas Ruyz de Hernan Gonzales wrote to Dr. Morga, together with the King's letter, another long one, in which he gives an account of all the events of his expeditions, which is that which follows:—

To Dr. Antonio de Morga, Lieutenant of the Governor of the Filipine isles of Luzon, in the city of Manila, whom may our Lord preserve. From Camboia.

Of that which happened in this kingdom of Cambodia, since I entered it, until the captain took away the fleet, your worship will already have had news, although in various modes, according as it suited each one to speak, in order to gild his own business; some according to their bent and opinion, and others according to their passion. Notwithstanding that it has been already seen by many persons, and clearly known, I undertake to give you the best relation I can, as to a person who can weld them all together, and attribute to each circumstance the weight which it may possess or deserve; together with an account of all the rest of what happened to Captain Diego Belloso and to me in the journey to Laos, and the vicissitudes and wars which there have been in this kingdom since we have been in it until now, and the actual state of affairs. And as Spaniards have been mixed up in all these affairs, it will give you some satisfaction to know the method and retirement with which I have lived in this kingdom, ever since I arrived from Manila, sustaining the soldiers and other people whom I brought at my expense in my ship, keeping them in a state of discipline and honour, without consenting to their straggling; possessing no credentials, because those which the governor was to have given me, Gallinato carried them. And of that which happened with the Chinese, wherefore and how, I do not treat of, because the Padre Fray Alonso Ximenez and the Padre Fray Diego were present at some of these affairs, and others heard of them, and they will have given you an account of all that, together with the war with the usurper, and the manner in which Gallinato abandoned this kingdom, when the business was already done; and if it had been followed up, half the kingdom would at this day belong to His Majesty, with just grounds, and the whole of it governed by Spaniards and in their power,[1] and it might be that the king would be a Christian with the greater part of his people. In the matter of the Chinese, which is what most requires explanation, I only say to you, consider the kingdom which we came to assist, and that the Chinese had no more rights in it than we had; and that we had to endeavour to gain re-

---

[1] Blas Ruyz is a very frank adventurer, and seems to have no misgivings, not only as to the piratical nature of his proceedings, but as to his personal baseness and ingratitude in seeking to despoil a sovereign from whom he had received many favours. It will be seen further on that his immoral propositions were rejected by the jurists and theologians of Manila. It would be desirable to know if Gallinato acted from greater scrupulousness, or only from timidity, as Blas Ruyz insinuates. Gallinato was frequently employed later, and was very highly approved of for his valour, zeal, discretion and tact by Andrea Furtado de Mendoza, the Portuguese commander-in-chief, at a siege of Ternate.

putation, and not to lose it, for we came in a warlike fashion, and it was the first time that an armed force of Spaniards entered the mainland, was it well to suffer, from people as infamous as they, disgrace and outrages, contempt and public affronts, before all these pagan communities? And they went further, inveighing against us to the usurping king so that he might kill us; telling him of us many evil and infamous things to induce him to what they entreated of him; and above all to be so impudent as to kill Spaniards, and disarm them, and go forth to spear them in the streets, all which I endured with much patience, not to disturb the country by breaking with them. Until one day they designedly sought to kill some in their Parian, having already wounded them and shamefully treated them, the numbers being very unequal; and coming out at this noise, they drew up in the open ground with many warlike instruments, summoning us to battle with insults and contemptuous expressions. Having reached this term, what reputation remained to us had we retired? They having obtained the advantage, since after attacking and killing many of of them, what security had we in this tyrannised kingdom, which in nothing showed itself friendly to us, and with one ship only, which at that time was grounded, with the artillery and provisions on shore; and they with six ships, and many row-boats, which fight with one or two guns, and many men, both those of the ships, and those who live in the port. Was it fitting, after war had broken out, to leave them with all their resources, whilst we were without ours? If they should deprive us of our lives, what reputation would Spaniards leave behind them in these kingdoms? For which reason, I held it to be better to make ourselves their masters, rather than be at their mercy or at that of the king; so, to insure our lives, we were obliged to take their ships, and strengthen ourselves in them, since they began the war. After this was done, Padre Fray Alonso

Ximenez was of opinion, and we also, that by presenting ourselves to the king, and giving him the embassage, and some presents, and disculpating ourselves in the matter, it would turn out well; and that if he were peaceably disposed, and our persons in safety, either in a fort or under his word and safe conduct, we would give up to them their ships and property, and this was written out and signed. In order to go and do this, a letter was written in the name of the governor of Manila, and we went to give it nine leagues off in the place where the king was living, leaving the ships guarded. When he had got us there, he took away from us the boats in which we had gone, and would not receive the letter, which went under the forms of an embassy, nor listen to our speech, unless we first gave up the ships; he then immediately began to prepare arms, and call in many people, with the intention, if we would not give up the ships, of killing us, or of putting us by force in such extremities as to make us give them up, and after they were given up, make an end of us all, without trouble or risk to his own people; because he would in nothing trust to us, for we were going to assist and search for him whom he had dispossessed. All this was related to us by some Christians that were amongst them, especially by a young man of mixed race, who had come from Malacca, and lived with them, and knew the language. Therefore, taking into consideration that we were already divided, and that if we gave up the ships, it would be easy for them to take ours by means of them, and kill those who had remained in them, and afterwards us who were in that place; and that if we waited until people were collected, and attacked us, they might easily kill us, we determined to seek a remedy, rather by attacking than by waiting to be attacked, and to endeavour to rejoin our own men, and ensure the safety of our lives, or end them fighting. So we made an attack, and our good fortune was such that we killed the king in the battle, and we withdrew to our ships, with infinite labour, but without losing a single Spaniard, and without permitting the sack of his house, that it might not be said that we had done it to rob him. At this juncture the captain and sergeant-major, our commander, arrived, and found fault with, and reduced to nothing what we had accomplished, and ridiculed what we and some of the Cambodians said, that we had killed the usurper. All he did was, to collect all the gold and silver which some soldiers had taken in these affairs, and all that was good in the ships, and then set fire to them; and draw up statements against us, dispossessing us of our ships and commands, causing suspicion and distrust; and he gave orders to quit the kingdom, without listening to many Cambodians, who came to speak to us when we went on shore, and who said that we should build a fortress, as they before had a legitimate king, and he who now ruled had made him fly to the Laos, and so they had not got a king; and that wherever they obtained most shade, thither they would flock, and that we should follow up the war. Neither did the captain admit from us any opinion which we gave, when we told him that the usurper held in arrest a relation of the lawful king, a man of much good fortune, and that we should go and rescue him, and he would raise men in favour of the legitimate king, and that with his favour we should come to possess the kingdom, and then we would go and fetch the king. To all this he refused to listen, and so abandoned the kingdom, and this great opportunity was lost. We only obtained from him when out at sea, by much entreaty, that we should go to Cochin China to make inquiries about the galley; since they had wished to send from Manila to make them: and I offered to go to the Laos, by land at my expense, in search of the King of Cambodia, as I knew that that was the road to go by. So we went, and as soon as we arrived he despatched us, Captain Diego Belloso and me, to the Laos, and Captain

Gregorio de Vargas to Tunquin. Meantime he held an auction of whatever was good of what was in the (*Chinese*) ships, and of the rest of what he had taken from the soldiers, among them, although they were all without a real, and ordered everything to be bought up for himself for whatever he thought proper. The king of Sinoa, a province of Cochin China, equipped us for the road to Lao, with a very good outfit, giving us an embassage for that country, and people to accompany us on the road. So we went all the way well provided for, being always well attended to and respected, and much looked at, as something never seen before in those kingdoms. We were all laid up on the road, but in all that, we were assisted by the affection which the people shewed to us, and the good reception which we met with from all. Thus we arrived at Lanchan, the capital of the kingdom, and where the king resides. It is a kingdom of great extent, but thinly inhabited, because it has been frequently devastated by Pegu. It contains mines of gold, silver, copper, iron, brass,[1] tin. It possesses silk, benzoin, lac, brasil, wax, ivory, grapes, many elephants, and horses larger than those of China. It borders on the east side with Cochin China, and on the north-east and north with China and Tartary, from whence come the sheep and asses which I saw when I was there; it has a large exportation of its merchandise by means of them. On the west and south-west it touches Pegu and Siam; and on the south and south-east Cambodia and Champan. It is a rich country, and everything costs much which comes from abroad. Before we arrived at Lanchan there had arrived from Cambodia a cousin of the king who had fled, who, on the death of the usurper, had come away in fear lest the son who now governed should kill him. This person had related what we had done in Cambodia, on which account the King of Lao gave us a great re-

[1] *Laton.* Blas Ruyz probably did not know that this was a composite metal.

ception, and held us in high esteem, praising the deed, and showing amazement at the small number who had done it. When we arrived the old king of Cambodia was already dead, with his daughter and eldest son; there remained only his younger son, and his mother, aunt, and grandmother, who were greatly rejoiced at what we had done and at our coming; and from that time forward they were more attended to. Before we had arrived at the city we met with an ambassador, whom Anacaparan, the usurping king, had sent from Cambodia before we had arrived there, to see what was going on there, with the excuse and pretext of asking for the old queen, the stepmother of Prauncar, the deceased king, who, he said, was a sister of his father: and the king of Lao was sending her, and on account of our arrival, and the certainty of his death, he ordered her to return, and the ambassador fled to Cambodia, in a boat down the river, from fear of being killed. Then we gave our embassage, and asked for the heir of the kingdom, to take him to the ships and from thence put him in his own country. It was answered that now he could not any more go alone, and that they could not give him, especially in order to go through a foreign kingdom, and by such rough roads and seas. The youth wished to go, and his mothers would not consent to it. At length it was determined that we should return to the fleet, and take it to Cambodia, and that from thence we should send them notice, and then they would send him with many people. The mothers gave me letters for Manila, with large promises on the part of the kingdom, if the Spaniards would return to Cambodia to pacify it and restore it to them. The king of Lao gave another embassage, by which he asked for friendship, and requesting that the fleet should return to Cambodia; and should Gallinato not choose to return, that he would give assistance by land with large forces, and they should be confided to the heir of the country. With this we took leave, and departed to Cochin China. While these things were taking place, the following happened in Cambodia. As soon as the fleet left, the death of Anacaparan was published, and when this news reached Chupinaqueo, the kinsman of the lawful king, who was imprisoned, he escaped from prison, and caused a province to rise up in arms, and collected its inhabitants, and raising a cry for Prauncar, the legitimate king, came in search of us with as much as six thousand men, to effect a junction with us, and make war on the sons of the usurper, who were now governing: and as he did not find us in Chordemuco, in the place where the ships had been lying, he sent boats as far as the bar to seek us; and as he did not find us, he took all the Chinese and other people who lived there, and returned to the province where he had levied his forces, and fortified himself there. At this time there arrived the people who were in Champan, who had gone there to take it, and the commander of the camp, named Ocuña, of Chu; he took sides with the sons of the usurper, and caused one of them to be set up as king, the second one, named Chupinanu, because he was the most warlike. For which reason the elder, named Chupinanon, and those of his party were discontented, and so there never was peace between them. After that they went out together with the camp, which had come from Champan in pursuit of Chupinaqueo; and he went out to meet them with many of his people, and they fought many days; but at length it was his fate to be conquered, and killed with much cruelty. So Chupinanu remained for the time as king, and the camp was disbanded, each man going to his home. At this time a ship came from Malacca with an embassy, and in it some Spaniards looking for us, and many Japanese. Chupinanu wished to kill them all, but, seeing that they came as an embassy and from Malacca, at once let them alone. On account of the cruelties which he exercised among his people, a large province, named Tele, rose in insurrection, crying out for liberty; and set up a new king, and came against Chupinanu, and conquered and routed him, taking from him a great number of elephants and artillery, and sacked his city. In this battle the greater part of the Spaniards and Japanese who had come from Malacca were killed. Chupinanu retreated with all his brothers, who were six, to another province, always accompanied by Ocuña of Chu; and there they sought counsel, and collected people, and called two Malays, heads of all the other people, in whom he confided much, and at the death of Chupinaqueo, when the camp was broken up, they had gone to the lands of which they were the magistrates. And in order that what follows may be understood, I will mention who they were. At the time this kingdom was ravaged by Siam, these two went to Champan, and took with them many Malays of their own people, and many others, Cambodians; and because the ruler of Champan did not do them as much honour as they desired, they seized upon his city, whilst he was not in it; and they fortified themselves in it, and afterwards they sacked it, and returned to this kingdom, bringing all the artillery and many people captives and prisoners. When they arrived here the usurper Anacaparan was ruling, and each praising what the other had done, he received them with friendship, and they gave him all the artillery which they had brought, and other things; and he gave them lands for their maintenance, and made them great mandarins. These Malays made it easy for him to take Champan, and offered to seize its king, and as he is a great enemy of Cambodia from a long time back, forces were at once prepared, and Ocuña of Chu sent as commander: and when we killed Anacaparan, these were in Champan; and on account of his death, returned as I said. These having presented themselves before the new king Chupinanu, with all their Malays, it was at once resolved to go against the insurgent people of Tele. At this time arrived from Lao the ambassador, who had fled when we arrived at Lanchan, and he related how we had remained there, and that we were going to ask for the legitimate heir of Cambodia, in order to convey him to the ships, and bring him in them to his kingdom; and that the king of Cochin China was giving his aid in this matter, and that we had entered Lao with that report, also that the king of Lao wished to send him with large forces by the river and by land, and us and the Cochin Chinese by sea, and that we were to join in Cambodia and make war, and inflict severe chastisement upon whoever would not obey. So when the new king and his friends heard this news they grew fearful, it made each one look out for himself. After some days had passed a report came from the bar that four Spanish ships had entered the river with many galleys from Cochin China. This report, either was a vision which some one had seen, or it was feigned and fictitions, for to this day we have not cleared it up: at any rate, hearing this news, all that the ambassador who fled had told them was confirmed to them as truth. So the mandarins of Cambodia taking into consideration the war which they now had with the people of Tele, and the new one which was impending over them with Spaniards, Cochin Chinese, and Laos, resolved to depose the new king, and to obey the king who was coming from Lao. For this purpose they communicated with the two Malays, and together they attacked the king and his brothers, and turned them out of the State; and both the two elder brothers fled each one separately to the province where he imagined he would find the greatest number of friends. The mandarins, having done this, ordered a fleet of rowboats to start on the way to Lao to receive their king, who, they said, was already coming: Ocuña of Chu went for this with two of his sons. They also sent other boats to the bar to receive the Spaniards, and to agree with them in a friendly manner, and for this purpose they sent some Spaniards who had remained in the country: and they settled that two

Cambodian mandarins and the two Malays should remain as governors to preserve the kingdom. The Spaniards went to the bar, and, as they found nothing, they returned. Ocuña of Chu went on the way to Lao, and, seeing that he did not meet his king nor hear any news of him, he resolved to go as far as Lanchan to seek for him; and pursued his journey with some difficulties on account of hunger, having left the kingdom unprovided, and the journey being long. For which reason some of his men ran away; but at last he arrived, with ten prahus mounting artillery. He disturbed all the kingdom of the Laos, as it was supposed he came for a warlike purpose, and they abandoned their villages and property and went to the mountains; but, on seeing that he came with peaceable intent, they became quieted. When he arrived we were already on the road to Cochin China; and, on account of his coming, the king sent to order us to return immediately to Lanchan. The king (*of Lao*), on being acquainted with what was passing in Cambodia, despatched many vessels by sea and troops by land, and sent the king to Cambodia, and despatched me to Cochin China, to carry the news of what was going on, and to take the ships to Cambodia: and then on the road I heard the news of the battle which our forces had fought, and I returned with the king to Cambodia. When we came to the first village of the kingdom, we knew from the spies who had gone on before, that, as the news of the ships had not been true, and Ocuña of Chu delayed so much, the provinces to which the two brothers had betaken themselves, had set them up as kings, and they were fighting with one another; and that the people of Tele had come to fight with the governors, and that they had become divided amongst themselves, and every man obeyed whomsoever he liked best. But that Ocuña Lacasamana, the head man of the Malays, had the greatest force of artillery and prahus, and that a Japanese junk had come, which was the one which was in Cochin China when our fleet was there, and that it was with Chupinanu. In the place where this news was received the land and sea forces were collected together, and it was found that there were few men to enter the country for war: so they made a fort there and sent to Lao to ask for more troops. In the meantime they despatched secret letters to probe the hearts of the great men. The people of Lao delayed, and the answers to the letters did not arrive, and they did not feel very secure where they were, and were deliberating upon returning to Lao, but at this juncture news arrived from Ocuña Lacasamana, one of the Malays who was in his own land and fortified, and he said that he was on his side (*of the lawful king*), although he had given obedience to Chupinanu, but that that was feigned, seeing that the king had delayed, and that when he entered the country he would pass over to his side. Then came a message from another Cambodian governor, saying that though he had obeyed Chupinanu, yet if the king would come to where he was, he would fall upon Chupinanu, and would dispossess him or kill him, and that to do this he had got four thousand men with whom he had fortified himself on a hill. He sent a relation of his with this message: all put confidence in this man, and we set out at once for that place, and when he knew that the king was coming he attacked the other and routed him, afterwards he came out to receive us; and so we entered, and that province was at once given up to us, and several others. Chupinanu withdrew to some mountains, and immediately the two Malays joined us, each with his forces, the Japanese also came in. The king then gave orders to pursue Chupinanu, until he was taken and killed. He then captured another who was judge in another province, and put him to death. War then began against the eldest (*of the brothers*), and against the people of Tele, who also would not obey. At this time arrived a vessel from Malacca, in which came fourteen Spaniards of the men of our fleet, who had put in to Malacca,

and the king was much pleased with them, and did them
great honours, and held them in high estimation, knowing
that they were of those who had killed the usurper; and
they were loved and respected in an extraordinary degree
by all the kingdom. Captain Diego Belloso wished to subject them to obedience to him in virtue of an old document
which he had from Malacca: this I forbade, alleging that
the right of this jurisdiction ought to be from Manila, since
from that place proceeded the restoration of this kingdom,
and that these men were Castilians, and had nothing to say
to his document, nor to Malacca. The king answered, for
this business came before him, that he did not wish to interfere between the two, in these matters. Some of those who
had come followed his opinion, and others mine: and thus
we have gone on till now, and this was the cause of my not
asking the king for a fort, to secure our personal safety,
which would have been a footing for some business, and that
which I will relate later would not have happened to us.
After their arrival, the king sent an embassage to Cochin
China, with a Spaniard and a Cambodian, to look for Padre
Fray Alonso Ximenez and some Spaniards, who, as we
heard, had remained there. The ruler of Champan arrested
them, and they have not returned. The wars continued,
and wherever we the Spaniards and Japanese went, and
whatever we attacked, by the assistance of God we gained
the day; and wherever we did not go, there were always
losses, so that we won great reputation, and were loved by
our friends and feared by the enemy. Whilst we were
making an incursion, Ocuña of Chu wished to revolt: he
now was named Mambaray, which is the highest title of the
kingdom; one of the headmen of the Malays, named Cancona, was supporting him in this. The king sent to call
me, and order me to take with me the Spaniards of my
party, and ordered Diego Belloso to stay with him, for both
of us were heads, and still are, in any war in which any of

us are engaged. I came at his bidding, and he related to me how those people wished to kill him and deprive him of the kingdom, that I might give him a remedy. The Mambaray was the person who governed the kingdom, and as the king was a youth and yielded to wine, he made little account of him, and thought to be king himself. At last I and the Spaniards killed him, and after that they caught his sons and killed them. After that the capture of the Malay Cancona was undertaken and he was killed, and there was security from this danger by means of the Spaniards. We then returned to the war, and I learned that another grandee, who was head of a province, wished to rise up, and go over to the side of Chupinanon; I seized him and killed him, putting him on his trial. With all this the king and kingdom loved us very much, and that province was pacified, and returned to the king. At this time a vessel arrived from Siam, which was going with an embassy to Manila, and put in here. There came in it Padre Fray Pedro Custodio, and some Portuguese. The king was much delighted at the arrival of the priest, and wished to set up a church for him. We all joined together, and followed up the war, and again reduced many provinces to submission to the king, and left Chupinanon withdrawn into some mountains, and the war almost ended. At this time many Laos came, commanded by a relation of their king, for up to this time they had done nothing, and had not uttered a sound. I do not know whether it was from envy at seeing us so advanced in favour with the king, and the people of the king, or whether they had settled the matter before in their own country, but they killed a Spaniard on a slight motive; and when we asked the king for justice in this matter, he ordered his mandarins to judge the case. Meanwhile, we sent to call the Japanese who were carrying on the war in another part, in order, if justice were not done, to take vengeance on the Laos. The Laos, either fearful of this, or having the design of making an end of us, fell upon our houses at night, so that they killed the priest and some of the Spaniards who had come with him, and who were sick, and they killed some of the Japanese, for their anger was directed against all. The rest of us escaped, and got on board the Japanese vessel, and there we defended ourselves until the Japanese arrived. The Laos made a fort and strengthened themselves in it; they might be six thousand in number, and they sent to tell the king, that they would not agree to any act of justice which he might order to be carried out. The king felt much regret for the deaths they had caused, and for the disrespect with which they treated him; but in order not to come to a rupture with their king, he would not give us forces with which to attack them, although we requested it several times, and we did not do it ourselves, having been left without arms. The king sent word of this affair to Lao, and we remained for the time stripped, without property, without arms, and without justice or revenge, and very much discontented with the king, although he was continually sending us excuses, saying that if the King of Lao did not do justice in the matter, that he would do it, and on that account he would not let them go away from his country, and he sent us food and some clothes and arms. At this time a ship was sent with an embassage to Malacca, in which we all wished to go away, but neither the king nor his mothers would consent to Diego Belloso or I going away. Some went away in it, and others returned to Siam, others remained with us; and from that time forward the king made us more presents than ever. The Japanese took to their ship, and would not any longer continue the war. The enemy, having learned that we were in confusion, collected large forces, and regained much undefended country. The king requested the Laos to go to the wars, since they had thrown into confusion those who defended his country. They went and lost the first battle, and returned completely defeated, leaving many killed and wounded. Chupinanon followed up the victory, and came within sight of where the king was, with a river between them. Here the king made little account of the Laos, and persuaded us and the Japanese again to take up arms and defend him. By this time we had all replaced our arms and ammunition, and with much entreaty from him and his mothers, we went to the war, to succour a fortress which Chupinanon was besieging: we won two battles and made him retire, regaining all that he had just gained, and other lands which had remained in those parts, taking much rice from the enemy, and provisions, with which the king's men recruited themselves, for they suffered from want, and we went into quarters. This we did, I and the Spaniards and Japanese on my part, and Diego Belloso and his men went to Tele and killed its king, and won part of the province, and returned. At this time a Portuguese ship with merchandise arrived from Macao, on which account, and seeing what we had done, the Laos were filled with great fear, and without leave from the king, they went away in boats to their country. Upon which we had recourse to the king to request him not to let them go without doing justice, if he did not wish to break the friendship between him and Luzon and Malaca. He replied that he did not dare to detain them, but that if we wished to go after them, he would give us people secretly, if we ventured to fight with them; and so we settled ourselves all in ten prahus, and followed them. And as they had gone forward a good deal, and with fear, we could not reach them till after many days: for that reason Belloso turned back with some Spaniards and Japanese. I followed with great difficulty, on account of the strong currents, for in parts we dragged the prahus with ropes, although with few people, until I came up with several of them and took from them their prahus and property, by which we all got compensation, and gained still more in reputation: at present we have higher repute than ever any nation had in foreign kingdoms. We are much loved by the king and his men, and by the inhabitants, and much feared by the strangers, and so we receive great respect in all parts of the kingdom. The king has given to Captain Diego Belloso and to me the highest titles of grandees of his kingdom, that we may be more respected and feared, and better obeyed. Two provinces, the best in kingdom, are put down to our names, and will be made over to us as soon as the affairs of the war are grown quiet, and parliaments have been held to take the oaths to the king, which has not yet been done. Meantime we make use of other people whom the king orders to be given to us. As possessing entire power of management and command in the kingdom, there is no one to be found beside Ocuña Lacasamana, the head of the Malays, whom the king likes, because he has large forces, and because he requires him for the wars on hand. The Spaniards have some encounters with his people, for which reason we hold aloof from one another. I have related to you these wars and affairs so minutely, in order that it may be seen whether His Majesty has any right, with justification and justice, to take possession of some part of this kingdom; since his forces killed the man who was in quiet possession of it, and the heir of the kingdom, who was driven away where he had lost the hope of ever again possessing it, has since returned to conquer it through His Majesty's vassals, and they have guarded and defended his person from his enemies. For to hope that he will give it up voluntarily, that will never be, because, on the contrary, he fears having many Spaniards in his country, although he loves them, because he is in dread lest they should deprive him of his kingdom, for he sees that this only requires the will to do it; and some of our enemies impress this upon him, especially the Mussulmans. I beg and supplicate you to take part in this matter, since you can do so much in it, in order that we may not lose our hold on this country, since so much has been done in it, and its affairs have been brought to such a satisfactory state; and it is of such great importance to hold a fortress on the mainland, since it is a beginning of great things. For if a well-prepared expedition should come, and the king see a large force in this country, even though he should be ill-disposed, he would have to do what he would know is justice. I say this, for his mother, aunt, and grandmother, who are the persons who command and govern, for he only does as they tell him: he is a boy, and is overcome with wine oftener than his father, and he only thinks of sports and hunting, and cares nothing for the kingdom. For this, if he should see that there are many Spaniards, and that no one can injure them, he will do whatever they wish, because (as I say) he loves them: the opposite party, moreover, will not venture to contradict. And if perchance there should at present be so few people in the Philippines, that it is not possible to send any great number, let at least some come, as many as possible, in company with priests, so as not to lose this jurisdiction, and our share in anything; because Diego Belloso sent to Malacca to ask for friars and men and documents, so as by that means to be the chief justice of this country, and to make over this jurisdiction to Malacca. And since this kingdom has been restored by the Philippines, do not you permit that it should have been tilled for others to gather the fruit. And if some soldiers should come, and from being few in number, and their not being feared, the Cambodians should not give them wherewithal to maintain themselves, I will do here whatever you bid me (which is reasonable), and until more come I could manage that the Cambodians should give it, however much against their inclination. And let them come tied down with good documents, so that as the country is wide and remote, they may not wish to avail themselves of licence; for the not possessing means of discipline and restriction was the cause of what happened to us with the Laos. I have despatched this vessel with much labour, as little is given to the king for nothing, and as there were many opposing persons who were preventing it; for it is clear that the mandarins, whether native or foreign, cannot like that there should be persons in the kingdom to command them; and as I am poor, for up to this time I have lived by war and its profits, I have maintained myself, as the king also is very poor, by the many wars. The Spaniard who goes is a very good soldier, and poor, and to enable him to go I have assisted him from my indigence. Will your worship be pleased to assist him and the Cambodian, in order that the Cambodian may become acquainted with some of the grandeur of His Majesty. I should rejoice to be the bearer of this, to give you a long account of these affairs and of other notable things, and of the fertility of these kingdoms; but neither the king nor his mothers have allowed me to go, as the bearer will relate these and other matters, and you may believe him, as a person dispassionate in all respects, who has now come from Macao. On account of the many wars, the king has not got many things to send to you. He sends two ivory tusks, and a slave, will you excuse him, and the next year he will send many things, if the pacification of his country is accomplished, for he still has much to do in it. I have spoken to him and urged him to send to Manila to ask for soldiers to complete the pacification of the country: his mothers would not have it on any account. I imagine, for certain, that they act thus, not to promise them lands for their maintenance, or in order that they may not take them. But when they were in Lao, they promised very wide lands; but if what is done is not sufficient to provide for them, let the mercy of God suffice. At the time of sending this embassage, Diego Belloso and I told the king that if he did not give us the lands which he had promised us, we wished to go to Luzon, because we had not now got wherewithal to maintain ourselves. With respect to this, much took place, but at last he gave them to us, and so it is stated in the embassage; but he gave them with the charge that we had to hold them in his service and obedience. By this means I shall have more resources for the service of your worship. With the expenses which I paid in that city (*Manila*) I spent what I had got, and in maintaining men in this kingdom; for that I took the silver of the ship's boys who were in my ship, and although I paid them with some which was found in the (*Chinese*) ships, Gallinato would not consent to it, but, on the contrary, took it all for himself; and in Malacca they made me pay it out of the property which was on board my ship, and did not consent that they should be paid out of the prizes, since the war was considered a just one:[1] for this reason I am now without any property. So I am without the means of serving you, as I am bound to do, and as I should have desired. Recollecting your very curious armoury, I send a bottle and a little flask of ivory, will you forgive the trifle, for next year I promise something better, and do you send and command anything for your service it will be a great favour to me: and will you do me the favour to shield and protect my affairs, so that by your fervour they may obtain some approbation. Trusting to this, may our Lord preserve your worship, and give you increase in your dignity, as this servant of yours desires in his affairs. From Camboja twentieth of July of 1598, the servant of your worship,

BLAS RUYZ DE HERNAN GONZALES.

With this despatch and news which came from Cambodia it was understood in Manila how good a result had been ob-

---

[1] The more correct reading would seem to be, since the war was *not* considered a just one.

tained from Diego Belloso and Blas Ruys having remained behind in that country; and Don Luis Dasmariñas was more encouraged in the enterprise which he had proposed; he treated of it with more warmth, and since difficulties were raised as to the justification with which an entrance could be made into Cambodia with armed forces (for anything else than to favour, and complete the setting upon his throne of Prauncar, and to leave priests with him) he said on his behalf, that having accomplished the above, he would, with the necessary permission of the king of Cambodia himself, pass on to the nighbouring kingdom of Champan, and would take possession of it for his majesty, turning out of it a usurper who lorded over it, a common enemy of all those kingdoms, and who from a fortress which he had close to the sea, sallied out against all navigators, and robbed them, and made them prisoners: and he had committed many other crimes, murders and robberies, on the Portuguese and on other nations who were obliged to pass his coasts in their trade and voyages to China, Macao, and Japan, and other kingdoms, respecting which sufficient information and reports had been given. On account of these reports the theologians and jurists considered as established the justification of war against this ruler of Champan, and the conquest of his country: and that this position was of no less importance for the Spaniards than Cambodia.

The Governor and President Don Francisco Tello held a consultation with the Audiencia, and with other persons, monks, and captains, as to what, in their opinion, it was most fitting to do in this matter, and it was resolved: that, since Don Luys offered to make this expedition at his own expense, with those persons who might choose to follow him in it, this offer should be carried out. Accordingly an agreement was made with him in the above-mentioned sense, he taking people at his expense, with commission and provision from the governor for the affairs of government and the war, and instructions from the high court of justice for the administration of justice; and they set about preparing ships and people and provisions in order to sail as shortly as possible.

At this time the governor, Don Francisco Tello, despatched Don Juan de Zamudio with a ship of middle size to Great China to obtain from the Viceroy of Canton leave for the Spaniards to communicate and trade with his province; and to fetch saltpetre and metals which were wanted for the royal magazines of Manila. Don Juan performed his voyage with fair weather, and having stationed himself off the coast of Canton, he sent some persons of his company to the city with despatches to the Tuton, who is the same as the Viceroy. He, after hearing of the arrival of the Spaniards, and the cause of it, listened to them, and gave them a good reception. The Portuguese, who reside in Macao, near the city of Canton itself, took many steps and busied themselves with the Viceroy and the Conchifu, and other mandarins, to get them not to admit the Castilians of Manila into their country, alleging against them that they were pirates and men of evil deeds, and that they seized upon kingdoms and provinces wherever they came; and they told them so many things, that it would have been sufficient to destroy them if the viceroy and mandarins had not looked at the matter dispassionately, for they knew that it was enmity and open hostility which moved the Portuguese, also the desire that the Castilians should not have any trade with China, for their own interests. The affair went so far that, being brought before a court of law, silence was imposed upon the Portuguese of Macao, with severe corporal punishments; and to the Castilians was given and assigned a port on the coast, named the Pinal, twelve leagues from the city of Canton, to which they might at that time and always come and anchor, and make a settlement of their own, with chapas[1] and provisions sufficient for it. Upon which Don

[1] Chops, edicts.

Juan de Zamudio entered the Pinal with his ship, and was very well provided there with every necessary by the Chinese, and at moderate prices: the Spaniards went backwards and forwards by the river to Canton in lorchas and champans to do their business. Those days in which they were detained in the said port they were always well received and lodged in the city in houses within the walls, going about the streets freely and with arms, a new and very special thing in China with respect to foreigners, at which the Portuguese (who are not so treated) were so much amazed and envious that they endeavoured by every means to prevent it, even going so far as to come by night in boats from Macao to the Pinal to set fire to the ship of the Castilians, which did not succeed, because, as they were heard, the necessary resistance was made; and ever after a good watch was kept in the ship, until it went away from there, after ending its business, much to the satisfaction of the Chinese, and with chapas and documents which were given for the future. The ship arrived at Manila in the beginning of the year 1599.

After Don Luys Dasmariñas had equipped two ships of middling size and a galliot, with two hundred men in his company who chose to follow him in this enterprise of Cambodia, taken from those who were going about Manila without pay, and had collected the necessary munitions and provisions, and had got in his company Fray Alonso Ximenez, Fray Diego Aduarte, of the order of St. Dominic, and Fray Juan Bautista, a Franciscan, and some Japanese and Indians natives of Manila: he set sail with the fleet from the bay in the middle of the month of July of the year '98. He met some contrary weather, the season of south-westerly gales having set in, but the desire to accomplish his voyage and lose no time and get out of Manila, which was the greatest difficulty, made him pay no attention to the weather; he thought that having put to sea, he would be able to pass the time on the coast, in the port of Bolinao.

This scheme did not turn out as well as Don Luys had imagined, for as soon as this fleet of three ships went out of the bay, it was so hard pressed by the weather, that it was unable to fetch the port of Bolinao, neither could it hold the sea, and the flag-ship taking in water, the ships returned to the mouth of the bay, opposite Miraveles, where they were detained for some days to refit. They again went out, the weather having grown calmer, but it again beat them so much that the ships separated from one another, and the galliot which was the weakest, with great labour made the port of Cagayan, and entered by the bar of Camalayuga to the city of Segovia, at the head of the isle of Luzon, opposite to great China, very much distressed and in great extremity; there the chief alcalde of that province gave it the necessary provisions and tackle. Captain Luis Ortiz, who commanded this galliot with twenty-five Spaniards and some Indians, used good speed in getting ready for sea, and again went out from that port in search of the fleet which he had to follow, according to his instructions, making for the bar of the river of Cambodia, whither they were going directly. He had hardly gone out of Cagayan, when the admiral's ship entered the same port, in the same distress as the galliot had been in: and she also was detained there some days to refit. She went out again to seek for the flag-ship and galliot: the flag-ship (being a ship of greater strength) kept out at sea with difficulty, and as the storm lasted long, she was obliged to run before it, making for China; and the wind was always so steady, that without being able to make anything in the direction of the voyage, it had to arrive with very high seas and cloudy weather at the coast of China, at some small uninhabited islands below Macao. There it was several times exposed to shipwreck, every day lightening herself of part of the cargo. The admiral's ship, after refitting and leaving Cagayan, made the same voyage with the same storm, and came to anchor near the flag-ship, where she was lost with some persons, and without saving any of the cargo. The flag-ship made shift to take in the people who escaped from the admiral's ship, and although she held on for some days, at length she grounded near the coast, and began to make so much water, that with that and the heavy seas that struck her on the broadside, she went to pieces. The boat was already lost, and they were obliged, in order to save the men before the ship entirely broke up, to make rafts and frames of spars and planks, on which Don Luis and the monks and the people came ashore, as many as a hundred and twenty Spaniards; and they brought away from the ship a few things of those of most value, and their arms, and the most manageable pieces of artillery, abandoning the rest as lost: all of them were soaked, and in such a wretched condition, that some Chinese who came to the coast (from some towns which were in the neighbourhood), both from feeling compassion for their loss and on account of some things which they gave them of what they had brought off from the wreck, provided them with victuals and with a country vessel of small burden, in which they might get away from that place and make for Macan and Canton, which were not far off.

Don Luis and his people, having arrived in sight of Macao, sent two soldiers of his company in Chinese vessels to the city and settlement of the Portuguese, giving them notice of their arrival and of their hardships, so that they might give them assistance, and two others to Canton, to beg of the viceroy or Tuton his assistance and favour to enable them to equip themselves, and leave China to pursue their voyage. The people of Macan, and their captain-major, Don Pablo de Portugal, received the Castilians so ill, that he put them in prison, and would not allow them to return to Don Luys, and sent to tell Don Luys to go away from the coast immediately, as they would treat them no less ill; and as the Portuguese knew that Captain Hernando de los Rios and another person his companion had gone to Canton for the same business, they at once sent two Portuguese of their council and regiment, to oppose their entry into China, saying that they were robbers and pirates, and people of evil actions, as they had before said of Don Juan de Zamudio, who at this season was in the port of Pinal with his ship, as has been already related.

Captain Hernando de los Rios and his companion met in Canton with the ensign, Domingo de Artacho, and other companions belonging to the ship of Don Juan, and being informed of the disaster of Don Luis' fleet, and how it had been cast away near there, they united together and defended themselves against the calumnies and pretensions of the Portuguese. So that as the chief difficulty had been already overcome in the matter of Don Juan, and the viceroy and mandarins were informed that all were from Manila, and who Don Luis Dasmariñas was, and that he was going with his fleet to Cambodia, they received him with the same goodwill as they had received Juan de Zamudio; and they gave him permission to enter with him into the port of Pinal, where both met together, with much regret for the loss of Don Luis Dasmariñas, and much satisfaction at finding there Don Juan de Zamudio with his people, who provided them with some of the things they stood in need of. With his assistance Don Luys at once bought a strong junk of middle size, in which he put himself with some of his people, and the artillery and property which had remained to him, and enjoyed the same conveniences as the Spaniards of Don Juan de Zamudio's ship had in that port. His intention was to remain there until, with the advices which he would send to Manila, they should send him ships, and the rest of what was requisite to prosecute his voyage thence to Cambodia, with respect to which Don Luys never chose to shew himself discouraged or as having given it up.

Don Juan de Zamudio went out of Pinal, leaving Don

Luys Dasmariñas and his people in that port, in the beginning of the year '99, and he reached Manila within twelve days. Don Luys sent after him the ensign Francisco Rodriguez, with three companions, to Manila in a small champan, to beg from the governor and his supporters succour and assistance in the extremities in which he found himself, and a ship, and what was necessary for continuing the expedition upon which he had set out. In Manila the disaster of Don Luis Dasmariñas, and the condition to which he was reduced, was heard of both from Don Juan de Zamudio and from the ensign Francisco Rodriguez (who arrived just after him at Manila); and seeing that it was impossible for him to continue his voyage to Cambodia, and that there was neither property nor substance with which to equip him again, nor time for it, a middle-sized ship was at once bought for him, and with the same ensign Francisco Rodriguez, and some soldiers in his company whom he commanded, and with provisions and other things, this ship was despatched from Manila to Pinal, with an order sent by Don Francisco Tello to Don Luys to embark with his people and come to the Philippines, without for the time thinking of the expedition to Cambodia, or of anything else.

Captain Hernando de los Rios, who attended to Don Luis' business in Canton, wrote a letter at this time to Dr. Antonio de Morga; and that what happened in this respect may be better understood, it is here given word for word:

Colonel Fernando de los Rios,[1] to Dr. Antonio de Morga, of His Majesty's Council, and his Auditor in the Royal Audiencia and Chancery of the Philippines, whom may our Lord preserve, in Manila.

The hardships which have fallen upon us within the short

[1] This officer wrote a memorial to the king on the state of the Philippine Islands, published in Thevenot, vol. ii, from which it appears that he was sent to Spain in 1605 by the inhabitants of the Philippines to represent their wants, and that he had returned to Manila in 1610.

space which there has been since our departure from Manila have been so many, that, if an account were to be given of all of them to your worship, it would weary you, especially as the short time in which Don Juan is to depart does not allow of it. And because he will give an entire narrative of everything, I will only relate that which has happened to us since our arrival in this country, for the Lord has been pleased to undo our intentions, which were to wait in Bolinao till the bad weather, which we were experiencing, had passed. And in sight of the port a storm overtook us, and placed us in imminent peril; and we were forced to come to this kingdom of China, where we expected that at least the Portuguese would allow us to refit our ship. As it was the Lord's will that we should lose it, we have suffered hardships enough, for hardly anything was saved, and I lost my property, and some portion of what belonged to other men, because at the time I was not present, for the day before my commander had ordered me to go out in search of refreshments with a pilot of the coast, which is vilely laid down in the charts, so that we did not know where we were; and I could not return to the ship on account of the wind which sprung up. For which reason I was obliged to go Canton, where the Sangleys,[1] who conveyed me, and those who left the ship with me, raised the accusation against us of having killed three Sangleys; and if we had not found there the ensign, Domingo de Artacho, and Marcos de la Cueva, who were pleading against the Portuguese, we should have passed a very ill time of it. God was pleased that, by His favour, we settled the pleadings in the Court; although without proofs, and without taking our depositions, they condemned us in fifty taes of silver. There we learned that, for a month and a half, they had been defending themselves against the

[1] Chinamen. Chinese traders, from *hiang* and *ley*, travelling merchants. Mallat, vol. i, p. 38.

Portuguese, who, as soon as they had arrived, went about saying that they were robbers and rebels, and people who seized upon the kingdoms in which they entered, and other things not worth while writing. Finally, all their measures, good and evil—and, indeed, very evil—did not profit them, since, by means of great assiduity and much silver, that was negotiated which they had never imagined, which was, the opening of a port in this country, where the Castilians could always come in security, and that they might be lodged in Canton, which had never been done in the case of the Portuguese, on which account they are, or very shortly will be, exceedingly vexed. Besides, silence was imposed upon them, although this was not part (*of the negotiation*), in order that by other means they should not attempt to do all the injury possible, according as the Sangleys tell us, who were among the Portuguese. They so abhor the name of Castilians, that it is not possible to express it, unless it be experienced as we have experienced it for our sins: since they placed us in great extremity, as Don Juan will well relate; since, when our commander wrote to them that he had been wrecked and was dying of hunger amongst infidels and in great peril, and that he was not coming to trade, but was going on the service of His Majesty, the courtesy which they showed him was to seize his messengers, and up to the present time they have kept them in a dungeon.[1] And latterly, whilst we have been in this port, with the hardships and difficulties which Don Juan will relate, and they such near neighbours, not only do they leave us to suffer, but, if there are any well-intentioned persons, they have prohibited their communicating with us,

---

[1] These violent disputes between the Portuguese and Spaniards, even whilst they were fellow-subjects of Philip II, shew how much strife and bloodshed was averted by the intervention and arbitration of Pope Alexander the Sixth, who imposed peace between them by what is known as his demarcation. See p. 11.

or giving us anything, not only under temporal, but also spiritual penalties. In truth, to reflect upon this cruelty, and still more to experience it as we are doing, exhausts all patience. May God give it to us, and a remedy through His mercy, because these infidels are the people who have the natural light more corrupted than any others that are in this world; and so to deal with them it requires angels, and not men. Since there are historians of what goes on in those parts, I will not detain myself with this matter. I only say, in order that it may be understood in what a country we are, that it is the true kingdom of the devil, and where it appears that he governs with full command; and so each Sangley appears to have got him inside himself, for there is no malice or deceit which they do not attempt. The government, although it appears good in externals, and with all its good order and method with respect to its maintenance, yet, when experienced in practice, it is all a scheme of the devil. Although here they do not rob or publicly plunder foreigners, they do it worse by other methods. Señor Don Juan has laboured much, and certainly gratitude is due to him, for he has done a thing so difficult that the Portuguese say only the devil or he could have done it. Though, indeed, it has cost him, as I have heard, at the rate of seven thousand dollars, and the risk to which he has been exposed, for the Portuguese endeavoured to burn him in his ship; and though their schemes turned out to be ineffectual, the Portuguese feel a bitterness which cannot be told at our coming here to traffic, for the notable injury they receive thereby. Although the truth is, all things well considered, if this business were established on a footing of fair agreement, they, on the contrary, would gain; because they would dispose of a thousand things which they have got, and the greater part, especially the poor, would be repaid by selling the work of their hands, and what they receive from India, which they always get a very good price for; and with respect to raising the price for them of merchandize, if it was once established, and if the Sangleys understood that ships would come every year, they would bring down much more merchandize; so much the more, that Canton possesses so much that there is over and above enough for as many more as are here, as has been seen by the eye. I am a witness that, if they wish to load a ship with only one kind of goods, even be it needles, they may do it. The more so, that the greater part of what they use are not the kinds which we buy. The chief staple is raw silk. So I conceive that to follow this up would be much to the interest of Manila for the reasons which present themselves to me. The first is that, if orders were given for a ship to come of sufficient bulk to be able to employ the gross[1] of the money of Manila, much more and better goods would be bought with much less money, and of the kinds of goods which are most profitable: since after all we should save what the people of Chincheo gain with us, which is much.

The second reason is that Manila would be provided with everything necessary, because there is in this city of Canton as much as can be desired.

The third is that by this means would be avoided the excessive commerce of the Sangleys in Manila, who do the mischief which your worship knows, and even that which we do not know of: and they are people who, the less they are admitted, the better it will be for us in all respects; and so it will not be necessary that there should be more of them than the number required for the service of the republic, neither would they raise the price of provisions, nor traverse what remains of the country, as they now do, and many pernicious sins would be avoided which they commit, and teach to the natives: and although it seems that there would be some

[1] Gruesa.

difficulty in establishing this, and in smoothing down the Portuguese, it might be accomplished.

The fourth is that the purchases going from here would reach Manila about Christmas, and each one would put his property in his house, would prepare and arrange it, and then, even should the ships from Castile come early, no loss would be suffered as now, when, if they arrive before the purchases, the merchandise rises a hundred per cent.

The fifth is that the ships might take in cargo during the whole of May, and take advantage of the first south-westerly winds, which sometimes set in by the middle of June or before: and going out at that time they run less risk, and would arrive more than a month, or even two months, earlier at New Spain; then they can leave that country in January and come here by April without any danger, which, if they come late, follows them amongst these islands, as we know.

The sixth is that many inconveniences would be avoided at the time of the purchase, such as there are, which your worship is aware of, and for the inhabitants it would be less trouble. Also, with respect to the expense and the distribution of it, (it is certain) it would be arranged better, not to allow the money of Mexico to be employed, nor that of companies: for only to prevent this rigorously would be sufficient to make Manila prosper in a short time; because if only the inhabitants alone were to send their bought property already invested for traffic, it is certain that they would have to employ all the machinery of the money of the people of Mexico, in the goods which should go from here; I say of Manila, if they do not allow them to purchase in Manila; and less merchandise going from here, and there being more buyers there, the property would be worth double.[1] This is easily seen, and if, as your traders have

[1] This sixth reason is very obscure. The colonel seems to wish to prove too much; it might be better to send a ship to purchase in China, and better not to have Chinese traders in Manila, but it is not likely

begun to remedy this matter, they carry it on with rigour much further, Manila must prosper greatly; since by not sending other produce to New Spain, but only that of Manila, and principally purchasing in this country (*Canton*), there would be all the prosperity which could be desired. If we look at the benefit and favour which his Majesty confers upon us in this matter, we should esteem it much more than it is esteemed; but I believe that we shall have to weep for it, when perchance it is taken from us. Could anyone say against this which I have said, about coming here to purchase, that his Majesty would be defrauded of the customs dues and duties which the Sangleys now pay, and of the tributes which they give; all this has a remedy, since with only the freights his Majesty would save much more, and by buying munitions here, and other things which he stands in need of for preserving this country, at twice as cheap and abundant, and not subject to their bringing them when they please, and at other times they leave us without them, as they now do every year, since they oblige us to go and fetch them. In the matter of the tribute I believe that his Majesty would be better served if there were no Sangleys, than by receiving the tribute; and by this it might be, if the Lord ordered it, that a door should be opened for the preaching of the Gospel and conversion of the people, which his Majesty so much desires, and which is the principal matter which he seeks to attain. And after all things require a beginning, and the road would be opened, although at present it appear to be shut, since, if it is hoped that the Portuguese will endeavour to accomplish this, I do not know when they will do it, since in so long a period as they have settled here they have not attempted it. Even the Sangleys themselves

that limiting the trade to one yearly ship would increase the prosperity of Manila; and if Chinese goods are made to cost double in Manila, though good for the shippers, it can hardly be good for the people of Manila.

say it, that they began like ourselves, and at first they came and went away, later two sick men remained, another year they built four houses, and so they went on increasing. And to do likewise, I know that there is no other difficulty than that which they cause. To return to the Portuguese opposition, it is something amazing; for not only are they vexed at our coming here, but also that we should go to Cambodia or to Siam: they say that those are their districts, and I do not know why they give them that name, since it is very much the reverse, and rather it is because we have indolently suffered them to seize upon what belonged to us, which is out near the Straits of Malacca, which enters within the line of demarcation, and falls to the crown of Castile: as I would give them fully to understand if an opportunity offered. It will be seen in the history of the Indies, in the chapter one hundred and two, before and after; how at their request his Holiness drew the said line, from three hundred and seventy leagues more to the west of the islands of Cape Verde, which were called the Hesperian Isles, and the hundred and eighty degrees of longitude which fell to them terminate and conclude, as I have said, near the above-mentioned Straits. All the rest belongs to us; and all the more, since we are under one king, how is it allowed that they forbid us all our trade? Why do they shut up Maluco, Siam, Cambodia, Cochin China, China, and all the rest of this Archipelago? What then are we to do, if they wish to seize upon all, for certain, this is very far from reasonable. I have written at length on this matter to express my feelings. Of the fertility and nature of the country, and of its greatness, I do not write to you until we depart; then I will endeavour to write very fully and to mark out the coasts, for nothing is put down correctly.

It is the best coast of all that has been discovered, and the most convenient for galleys: if God should ordain that they should come this way, I have already spied out where

the king keeps his treasure. It is a very rich country, and
the city of Canton is very well supplied, though in respect
to edifices there is nothing to be said, for the whole city has
few of any importance, according to what I was told by a
Theatine Sangley, with whom I had much pleasure in talking, though I was only able to do so for one afternoon; he
was a man of good understanding and demeanour, and they
say he is a scholar. He related to me that in Paquien,[1]
where the king is, and in Lanquien,[2] the fathers of the
company have got three houses in their tranquil possession,
and there are seven fathers, amongst whom there is one
called Padre Rizio,[3] companion of Padre Rugero, who went
to Rome: he is a very good mathematician, and he has
corrected their calendars, which contained many errors and
false opinions, as also in the fabric of the world, which they
considered to be flat. He made them a globe and a sphere,
and with this and the good arguments and reasons which
they give them, they are esteemed as people come down
from heaven. He says that there is in those parts a very
great disposition towards conversion, if there were ministers;
and there foreigners are not looked upon as strange, as in
this city.[4] He says that the people are very sincere and
reasonable, and so they call those here barbarous. He
says that Lanquien is in the latitude of Toledo, which is
thirty degrees and two-thirds, and from there to Paquien it
takes as long as twenty-five days on the road, which natu-

[1] Pekin.
[2] Probably Nankin: that city is however in nearly 32° latitude, and
Toledo is in nearly 40°, not in 30° and two-thirds, as stated further on.
[3] The Jesuits established themselves in Canton in 1583: Matthew
Ricci reached Pekin in 1595, but was obliged by an accidental excitement among the Chinese to withdraw to Nankin. In 1600 he was enabled to go again with presents to the emperor: he died May 11, 1610.
Col. Yule, *Cathay and the Way Thither*, p. 536.
[4] This shows that the greater disinclination to foreigners which prevails at Canton is not modern.

rally must be in more than fifty degrees. This brother comes every year for the stipend which those here give them for these three houses: they are now expecting a great friend of theirs, who is to be the second person near the king. All this country can be travelled in by water, and on this account it is so well supplied with everything, because things are brought by the rivers without its being necessary to load a beast, which is the most wonderful thing.[1]

He who should wish to paint China without having seen it, let him paint a very flat country of rivers and towns, without a span of ground which they suffer to lie idle. I could wish to have more time to relate some of the things of China, which I have noted, and informed myself about with especial care, and if God please, I will be the messenger. The affairs of Cambodia are in a good state, and we should arrive at a good time, if our Lord is willing, that we leave this place prosperously. The king sent a ship at the end of August to Manila to ask for assistance, I do not know whether it will have arrived, or if it will have turned back to put into port, for it left very late. Blas Ruys sent fifty pieces of *caman guian*. The king, according to what they tell us, has given and committed to him nine thousand vassals, and as many to Belloso.

We for our part remain at present with the necessities which Don Juan Zamudio[2] will tell you of. I entreat your worship to succour us, since it is of such importance. I kiss the hands many times of my lady Doña Juana, and our Lord preserve you many years with the prosperity and tranquillity which your servants desire for you. From the port of Pinal, frozen with cold, the twenty-third of December of ninety-eight. [1598.]

[1] *Que es la mayor grandeza.*
[2] This name is generally printed Camudio, the cedilla under the C appears to have been omitted.

If my brother should come before I return, I entreat you, since it is so natural to you to do good to all (especially those of that country), to let him receive that which your worship has always done for me.

FERNANDO DE LOS RIOS, *Colonel.*

After Don Juan de Zamudio had gone out of the Pinal, where Don Luis Dasmariñas remained with his junk, waiting for the succour which he hoped for from Manila, and which he had requested through Don Juan and the ensign Francisco Rodriguez; it seemed to Don Luis that several days had passed, and that the answer was overdue, and that his people were suffering there great want and cold; so he attempted to go out to sea with the junk, steering for Manila. This the weather did not admit of, neither was the vessel large enough with the people that he had on board for crossing; so he passed the time near the port, where the Portuguese of Macan again sent him many messages and requisitions to leave the coast immediately, advising him that they would seize him and the men of his company, and would send them to India, and that they would be punished severely. Don Luys always answered them, that his arrival was not for their detriment or to offend them, but only for the service of God and His Majesty on the way to Cambodia, that he had been shipwrecked and had suffered great hardships and travail; among which the severest had been owing to the Portuguese of Macan themselves, vassals of His Majesty; and he was waiting for assistance from Manila, in order to be able to return thither, and he begged and required them to assist and favour him, and to set at liberty the two Castilians whom they had taken from him and imprisoned; and that if besides all this they should seek to do him any injury or insult, he would defend himself as he could, protesting against any losses which might result to them, which would lie at their door. From that time forward Don Luis Dasmariñas was always very watchful on board his ship, keeping the arms in readiness, and the artillery loaded, on his guard day and night. And he was not mistaken, for the people of Macan resolved to come out and seize him; and with this intention, the captain-major himself, with some lateen rigged boats and other craft, and men armed with javelins, guns and artillery, came one day when they thought the Castilians would be off their guard, and fell upon Don Luys Dasmariñas. He, suspecting what was about to happen, held himself with his arms in readiness, and seeing that the Portuguese fleet was attacking him, began to open fire upon them with muskets, arquebuses, and a few pieces of artillery, with such rapidity, that he caused a great loss to the enemy, and to the ship which carried the captain-major; one of whose pages who stood behind him, and other persons were killed. The Portuguese vessels then retired, and desisted, beaten back by Don Luis, who did not choose to follow them, but remained on the watch; and as they did not venture to return to attack him, but made for Macan, Don Luis Dasmariñas put into the port of Pinal, where he thought he should be in greater security. There he remained until Captain Francisco Rodriguez arrived with a ship from Manila, and joined Don Luis, and having distributed their men between the two ships, they made some purchases with what this last ship had brought from Manila in the city of Macan itself; for the Portuguese for the sake of their interests supplied them and sold to them, though with some fear of their magistrates. They returned to Manila leaving in Pinal a few persons dead of sickness, and among them was Fray Alonso Ximenez, who had been the principal promoter of this enterprise. His companion, Fray Diego Aduarte, did not choose to return to Manila, and went to Macan, and thence to Goa, to go on to Spain. Don Luis returned with both ships to Manila, and the expedition of Don Luis to Cambodia, and the undertaking of that enterprise on his part, remained in this state.

It has been already related how the galliot, one of the ships under the command of Don Luis Dasmariñas, in which Luis Ortiz and twenty five Spaniards sailed, after having put into Cagayan and refitted there, had again left the port, with moderate weather, in search of the fleet. This ship, although it was so little fit to resist storms at sea, yet God permitted it to weather those which it met without being lost. Making its way along the coast of Cochin China and Champan, within the shoals of Aynao, it reached the bar of Cambodia, and, expecting to find within all or some of the ships of its convoy, it went up the river as far as the city of Chordemuco, where it found Diego Belloso and Blas Ruyz de Hernan Gonzalez, with some Castilians who had joined him, and other Portuguese who had come from Malaca, with whose assistance many battles had been won in favour of King Prauncar, who was restored to his kingdom, although some of the provinces were not entirely pacified. There the people of the galliot heard that neither Don Luis Dasmariñas, nor any one else of his fleet, had reached Cambodia; and they related that Don Luis was coming in person, with a large force of ships, men, arms, and some monks, for that which he had always desired in that kingdom, and that he would not be long in coming, and that this galliot and her men belonged to his fleet. Blas Ruyz and the Castilians rejoiced much at such opportune news: it seemed to him that everything was turning out well for him, and that this time, according to the state to which affairs had now reached, they would accomplish and establish all that they pretended to. Diego Belloso and his partisans, although they did not show their regret, were not so satisfied, for they much preferred that the happy termination of this expedition and its rewards should be for the Portuguese and the government of India; upon which matter they had had some differences and encounters with Blas Ruyz; but as they saw the affair in this conjuncture, they conformed to the times and circumstances. All joined together, Portuguese and Castilians, and informed Prauncar and his mandarins of the arrival of the ensign, Luis Ortiz, with his galliot and companions, and they were a portion of a good fleet, which would come shortly, in which was Don Luis Dasmariñas in person, with monks and people to assist and serve him, in conformity with what he had written to Manila a few months ago to ask for. The king showed satisfaction, and some of his mandarins also, who liked the Spaniards, and knew the benefits which they had received from them up to that time; and understanding that this would turn out such as it was represented to them. But the king's stepmother, and other mandarins who acted with her, especially Ocuña Lacasmana, the Malay Mussulman, were vexed at the coming of the Spaniards, and were of opinion that they, as valiant men, and being so many and so enterprising, as they already knew, would become masters of all, or at least would take what was best; and they wished to be alone to deal with the king, Prauncar, and so their aversion to the affairs of the Spaniards became known to be as great as the feelings of Prauncar were, on the contrary, favourable to them. He at once ordered the Spaniards and their ship to be placed close to the city, at the place which Blas Ruyz and Diego Belloso occupied.

Before Don Luis Dasmariñas went out from Manila with his fleet, Captain Juan de Mendoza Gamboa had proposed to the governor, Don Francisco Tello, to give him leave to go to the kingdom of Siam, with a ship of middle size, to effect some barter; and for the greater security of his voyage and business, he asked the governor to give him letters to the King of Siam, giving him to understand that he sent him as his ambassador and envoy to continue the

peace and amity and the commerce which Juan Tello de
Aguirre had treated of with Siam the year before. In
order to give greater facilities for the granting his request,
he offered, as Don Luis Dasmariñas (who was on the way to
Cambodia) had left in Manila some munitions and other
things of use to his fleet for another opportunity, to take
these stores on board his vessel, and make his voyage by
way of Cambodia, where he supposed he should find Don
Luis Dasmariñas, and he would there deliver them to him.
The governor thought both of these proposals well timed,
and having given him the necessary despatches, Juan de
Mendoza went out of Manila in his ship, taking, as pilot,
Juan Martinez de Chave, who had been the pilot of Juan
Tello when he went to Siam, and some sailors and Indians
of the country in his company, and a quantity of *siguey*
and other goods to barter, and the ammunition and stores
which he was to convey to Don Luis. Fray Joan Maldonado
and a companion, Dominican monks, embarked with him:
he was a grave and learned man, and a very intimate friend
of Don Luis Dasmariñas, whom his Order were pleased to
send to him for the sake of his companionship. They went
out of Manila, without knowing of the shipwreck of Don
Luis, two months after he had set sail, and, crossing
over the shoals, they shortly arrived at the bar of Camboja,
and went up to the Court, where they found the galliot
belonging to the fleet, and learned that the other ships had
not arrived. They were well received by the king, and
lodged with Diego Belloso, Blas Ruyz, and Luiz Ortiz and
his companions. They passed the time together, and
would not let Joan de Mendoza leave Camboja with his ship
until something was heard of Don Luis Dasmariñas. Some
days later they heard, through Chinese ships and by other
ways, that he had remained there, preparing to prosecute
his journey; and although this event caused them regret,
there remained the hope that, in a short time, he would
come to Cambodia, with the two ships of his fleet.

At this same time a man of mixed race, son of a Portuguese and a Japanese woman, who lived in Japan, named Govea, who had a junk, which he kept in the port of Nangasaki, collected some companions of mixed race, and some Japanese and Portuguese, in order to go out to the coasts of China, Champan, and Cambodia, for their adventures, and to barter, but principally to lay hold on what they might fall in with at sea. A Castilian embarked with him, who had remained in Nangasaki from the time of the loss of the galleon San Felipe, which was going to New Spain in the year ninety-six. He was named Don Antonio Malaver, and had been a soldier of Italy, and had come over from New Spain to the Philippines as captain and serjeant-major of the troops which Dr. Antonio de Morga brought that year in the fleet from New Spain to Manila. Don Antonio Malaver, who had not wished to return to the Philippines, intending to return by that way to India and Spain, and thinking that on the road there might fall to him some part of the ill-gotten gains of the voyage, embarked with Govea and his company. Having run down the coast, and heard some news of the entry of the Spaniards into Cambodia, he persuaded Govea to enter the river of Cambodia, where they would most likely find the Spaniards, and, affairs in such a conjuncture, that they might take some effective action in this kingdom, and thrive more than at sea. After going up the river to Chordemuco they joined with the Castilians and Portuguese, and were received into their company and reckoned with them; and as they all of them severally (and they were a considerable number) saw the delay of Don Luis Dasmariñas, they set up as their head Fray Joan Maldonado and Diego Belloso and Blas Ruyz. They began (on their own account) to treat with King Prauncar,[1] of their establishment and convenience,

[1] After forging a letter of credentials from the governor, this next step of setting up a plenipotentiary of their own was a natural one on the

and to ask for lands to be given them and rice for their maintenance, and other things which had been promised, because they had not derived the benefit and profit which they required from what had been given to Belloso and Blas Ruyz. Although the king gave them good hopes with respect to everything, he brought nothing to a conclusion, his stepmother and the mandarins of her party impeding it, for they desired to see the Spaniards clear out of the kingdom; and they were every day more encouraged in this by the delay of Don Luis Dasmariñas. In this way the Spaniards wasted time in going and coming between their quarters and the city to negotiate with the king, with whose answers and conversations they were sometimes satisfied, and at others not quite so much so.

Near the Spaniards' own quarters, Ocuña Lacasamana had his, with his Malays; and as Muslims so opposed in religion and pretensions, there was not a very neighbourly feeling between the two parties. And on one occasion there occurred a dispute between the Spaniards and Malays, and both sides had many of their men severely wounded, amongst them the Ensign Luys Ortiz, commander of the galliot, had both legs run through, and was in much danger: at which the King Prauncar shewed his regret, but he did not venture to inflict chastisement or make reparation for these injuries. Affairs were much inflamed, and the Malay very ill-disposed to the Spaniards, and one day that Fray Joan Maldonado, Diego Belloso, and Blas Ruyz were in the city, and had left Luys de Villafañe in command of the quarters, on account of Luys Ortiz being laid up with his wounds and illness, another dispute arose in the quarters with the Malays. Taking this opportunity, Luys de Villafañe determined, with a few Spaniards who followed him, to unite with Govea and his

part of the adventurers. The course they were now going to follow was in direct opposition to that which had been enjoined on the real plenipotentiary Don Luis Dasmariñas.

men, and fall upon the Malays, and their quarters and the goods they possessed, and sack them: moved by their anger and still more so by their covetousness, they carried this out, and having killed many Malays, and taken from them much property, they took to their own quarters and fortified themselves there and in the Japanese ship. The king was much vexed, and his mandarins also, and no less Fray Joan Maldonado, and Belloso, and Blas Ruyz, who were in Chordemuco; but far more Ocuña Lacasamana, at the sight of the injury and affront done to him, and at the breaking of the peace and agreement, which had so lately been established with reference to the former disputes. Although Fray Joan Maldonado, Belloso, and Blas Ruyz went at once to the quarters to remedy the affair, they found it so complicated, and so much excitement, that not even King Prauncar, who wished to intervene, could arrange it; and he advised the Spaniards to look to their personal safety, as he saw their party fallen, and in much peril, without his being able to remedy it. Fray Joan Maldonado and his companion, although they faced the business in company with Diego Belloso and Blas Ruyz, at the same time betook themselves to the ship of Joan de Mendoza for greater security, and some Spaniards did the same. Diego Belloso and the rest with Blas Ruyz relying on the friendship of the king, and the services they had rendered in the country, remained in it, though with the greatest watchfulness and precautions for their safety that they could take.

The Malay Lacasamana, with his people and the mandarins his partisans, and the support which the king's stepmother afforded him, did not lose any more time, nor the opportunity which he held in his hands, and at one blow, both by sea and by land, attacked the Castilians, Portuguese, and Japanese; and finding them separated, although some made as much resistance as they could, he made an end of all of them, and amongst them of Diego Belloso and Blas Ruyz de

Hernan Gonzales; and burned their quarters and vessels, excepting that of Joan de Mendoza, who, fearing the danger, went away down the river, making for the sea, and defended himself from some prahus which followed him. He took with him Fray Juan Maldonado and his companion, and some few Spaniards: on shore there only remained alive a Franciscan friar with five Indians of Manila, and a Castilian named Juan Dias, whom the king caused to be hid with much care in the country, regretting much the death of the Spaniards: and, although he advised the friar not to come out in public until the Malays were appeased, this friar thinking that he could escape from their fury, came out with two of the Manila men, to fly from the kingdom, when they were found and killed like the rest. Juan Dias and three Manila men remained many days in concealment, and the king supported them until after other events they were able to show themselves. In this manner the cause of the Spaniards in Cambodia came to an end, and so entirely thrown down, that the Malay and his partisans remained complete masters, treating the affairs of the kingdom with such little respect for the King Prauncar, that finally they killed him also: upon which there was a fresh insurrection, and the provinces were disturbed, each one taking what he could get, and there was more confusion and disturbance than what there had been before.

The garrison of Spaniards which remained in Caldera when Don Juan Ronquillo raised the camp from the river of Mindanao, was under the command of Captain Villagra, on account of the death of Captain Juan Pacho in Jolo; and it was suffering from shortness of provisions, for neither the people of the river could give them to the Spaniards, nor would the Jolo men supply them, as war was declared between them. So they urged the governor Don Francisco Tello to succour the garrison with provisions, soldiers and munitions, or to give them orders to withdraw to

Manila (which was what they most desired), since there they did not obtain any other result than that of suffering hunger, and of being shut up in that fort, without having any place in which to seek for sustenance. The governor, seeing the urgency of the case, and finding himself with a very small sum of money in the royal treasury, from which to supply that garrison and maintain it; and for the same reason the punishment was deferred which ought to be inflicted on the Jolo men, for the outrages which they had committed against Spaniards, and for their revolt; and that to renew what had been done in Mindanao would be a long business, was inclined to avoid the care and trouble of maintaining and supplying the garrison of Caldera. And in order to do so with a decent excuse, he submitted it for consultation to the High Court, and to other persons of understanding, requesting them to give their opinion, at the same time letting them know his desire and giving some reasons with which he hoped to persuade them to give an answer in conformity with his desire. The High Court advised him not to remove or raise the garrison of Caldera, but on the contrary to maintain and succour it, and that as shortly as possible the affairs of Jolo and Mindanao should be attended to, even though it should be by taking what was required for that from some other part; this being the major necessity, and the one it was most necessary to attend to in the islands, both for the sake of pacifying those provinces as for that of restraining them, lest they should be encouraged by seeing the Spaniards withdraw from all of them, and should venture still further, and come down to make captures amongst the Pintados, and carry the war to the very doors of the Spaniards. Notwithstanding this reply, the governor resolved to raise and remove the garrison, and sent orders to Captain Villagra to burn the fort of Caldera immediately, and withdraw with all the people and ships that he had with him, and come to Manila.

This was speedily executed, for the captain and soldiers of the garrison hoped for nothing else than to dismantle it and come away. When the Jolo men saw the Spaniards abandon the country, they were persuaded that they would not return again to Mindanao, and that they had not sufficient forces for it, and they gained fresh spirits and courage, to join with the people of Buhahayen on the river, and to arm a number of caracoas and other craft, to make an expedition against the coast of Pintados, to plunder and make captives. The people of Tampacan lost all hopes of being again assisted by the Spaniards, and of their return to the river, since they had also abandoned the fort of Caldera and left the country; and in order to avoid war and the injuries which they would suffer from their neighbours the people of Buhahayen, they made an agreement and united with them, and all turned their arms against the Spaniards, promising to themselves that they would make many incursions into their country and gain much plunder. So they got their fleet ready and appointed two chiefs as heads of it, of those who lived on the river of Mindanao, named Sali and Silonga: and in the month of July of the year '99, in the season of the south-westerly winds, they left the river of Mindanao, making for the islands of Oton and Panay and the neighbouring isles, with fifty caracoas, and in them more than three thousand fighting men, with arquebuses, campilans, carasas, and other arms with handles, and many pieces of artillery. Passing by the island of Negros, they went to the river of Panay, and going as far as its principal town, five leagues up the river, where there was an alcalde mayor and some Spaniards, they sacked and set fire to the houses and churches, and took prisoners many Christian natives, men, women and children, committing many murders, cruelties and injuries upon them, and following them in boats more than ten leagues up the river, without leaving anything standing. For the alcalde mayor and those who could took flight towards the mountains in the inner part of the country, and so the enemy had greater opportunity to do what he pleased. They went out of the river of Panay with their fleet loaded with the property which they had pillaged, and with Christian captives, and burned all the boats that there were in the river before leaving. They did the same in the other islands and villages which they passed by, and then returned to Mindanao, without being attacked by any one, with much gold and property, and more than eight hundred captives, besides those they left slain. In Mindanao they divided the spoil, and remained agreed to get ready a larger fleet for next year, and return to make war with more preparation.

This daring attack of the Mindanaos did a very great injury to the islands of the Pintados, as much by what they did there, as by the fear and terror which the islanders felt for them, since they were in the power of the Spaniards, who kept them subject and tributary, and disarmed, so that they neither protected them from their enemies nor left them the means to defend themselves, as they used to do when there were no Spaniards in the country: in consequence of this, many towns of peaceable and subject Indians rose up and withdrew to the Tingues,[1] not choosing to come down to where they had their houses, and magistrates, and the Spaniards, amongst whom they were distributed.[2] They had, as they said daily, the desire to rise up in rebellion, all of them, but, by means of some promises and presents from proprietors and monks, they were appeased and brought back again, with much regret and vexation at the injuries they had received. And although these injuries were felt with regret in Manila, and still more those which were expected from the enemy in future, as the governor was ill provided with ships and the rest of what was needful for defence, nothing more was done than to regret them, and set them to the account of

---

[1] In the interior.   [2] Encomenderos.

the injury which had been suffered, by raising the camp of the river of Mindanao, and dismantling the fort of Caldera.[1]

As soon as the weather allowed of it, the Mindanao and Jolo men returned with a large fleet of more than seventy vessels, well armed with more than four thousand fighting men, with the same chiefs, Silonga and Sali, and other chiefs of Mindanao and Jolo, against the same islands of Pintados, with the determination to take and sack the Spanish town of Arevalo, which was built in Oton. Captain Juan Garcia de Sierra, chief alcalde of that province, having heard of their setting out, and of the design entertained by the enemy, attended to what was most necessary, and collected in the town all the Spaniards who resided there and in the district, and shut himself up in it with all of them, repairing, as well as he could, a wooden fort which it possessed, into which he gathered the women and property; and with the Spaniards, who might be seventy men, with their arquebuses, he waited for the enemy. The enemy, who wished to attack the river of Panay another time, passed by the island of Negros to the town of Arevalo, anchored there close to the native town, and landed one thousand five hundred men with arquebuses, campilans, and carasas; and, without stopping anywhere, made for the Spanish town, which was the object of their attack. The Spaniards, divided into troops, came out to meet them, firing upon the enemy, and attacked them so suddenly that they forced them to turn their backs and return to embark in their caracoas, and in such confusion that many Mindanao men were killed before they could embark. Captain Juan Garcia de Sierra, who went on horseback, pursued the enemy so closely to the water's edge, that, cutting off the legs of his mare with campilans, they brought him to the

[1] See Appendix II for the subsequent history of Mindanao, and the fort of Caldera.

ground and killed him. The enemy embarked with great loss of men, and halted in the island of Guimaraez, which is in sight of the town, and there mustered their people, the wounded and killed, who were not few, and amongst them one of the principal chiefs and head men. They made a great show of grief and regret, and made for Mindanao, sounding their bells and *tifas*, without stopping any more at Pintados, carrying away from this expedition little profit or gain, and much loss and injury to their people and reputation, which, when they arrived at Jolo and Mindanao, they felt much more deeply. To remedy this event, they proposed to return at the first monsoon against Pintados with more ships and men, and this they agreed upon.

When treating further back of the affairs of Japan, an account was given of the loss of the ship San Felipe in Hurando, in the province of Toza; and of the martyrdom of the barefooted Franciscan monks in Nangasaki,[1] and of the departure of the Spaniards and monks who had remained there, with the exception of Fray Geronymo of Jesus, who, changing his habit, concealed himself in the interior of the country; and how after Taicosama had given an answer to the Governor of Manila, through his ambassador, Don Luis Navarrete, excusing himself for what had happened, he had been moved, at the persuasion of Faranda Quiemon and his supporters, to send a fleet against Manila, and had provided Faranda with rice and other provisions in order to despatch him, and he had begun to prepare the fleet, and had not managed to bring it to the point which he had promised, so that the affair had been deferred, and had so remained. That which happened afterwards was, that Taicosama fell ill in Miaco of a severe illness, of which he died; although it gave him an opportunity to dispose of his succession and of the government of the kingdom, and that the empire should be continued to an only son of his of ten

[1] These are the Japanese martyrs who were canonised by H. H. Pius IX on the 8th June, 1862.

years old. For which purpose he fixed his choice on the greatest Tono, lord, in Japan, named Yeyasudono,[1] lord of Quanto, which are some provinces in the north, who had sons and grandsons, and more influence and power in Japan than any other in the kingdom. He called him to court, and said to him that he wished to marry his son with his grandaughter, the daughter of his eldest son, and for him to succeed to the empire. He celebrated the marriage, and left the government of Japan till such time as his son should be older, to Yeyasudono, in partnership with Guenifiun, Fungen, Ximonojo, and Xicoraju, his great confidantes and councillors, through whose hands and names the affairs of his administration had passed for some years, in order that all together should continue to administer them after his death, until his son was of age to govern in person: whom he left named and accepted by the kingdom as his successor and supreme lord of Japan. Taicosama having died in the year 1599,[1] the five governors put his son in custody under a guard in the fortress of Usaca, with the service and state due to his person, and they remained in Miaco governing, which they were occupied with for some time, so that the pretensions of Faranda Quiemon to make an expedition against Manila ceased altogether, and were not again talked of. As the affairs of Japan are never settled, but have always proceeded with disturbances, they could not last for any long period in the state in which Taico left them, for, with the new government and the arrival at court and in other provinces of Japan of the Tonos, lords, captains, and soldiers, whom the Combaco during his lifetime had occupied (in order to divert them from the affairs of the kingdom) in wars with Coray and the King of China, the Japanese began to be in a state of disunion and disturbance, so that the four governors entertained suspicions

[1] The *Dutch Memorable Embassies* call the Regent Ongoschio, and state that Taicosama died of dysentery Sept. 16, 1598, at the age of sixty-four, having reigned fifteen years.

and differences with Yeyasudono, fearing, from his manner
of governing and from his proceedings, that he was preparing, as he was so powerful, to take for himself the
empire, excluding and taking no account of the son of
Taico, married to his grandaughter. This flame burned
still higher, for many Tonos and lords of the kingdom felt
in the same manner in this respect; and, now either from
a desire for the succession of the son of Taico, or because
they wished to see matters in disorder, so that each one
might profit by it, and this was the most likely, and not
affection for Taicosama, who, as an usurper, had been more
feared than loved. These persons persuaded the governors
to face Yeyasudono, and check his designs. Thus excited,
they opposed him so thoroughly, that they entirely declared
themselves, and it suited Yeyasudono to leave the kingdom
of Miaco, and go to his kingdom of Quanto, to put himself
in safety, and return with large forces to Court to be
obeyed. The governors, seeing what was intended, were
not negligent, and collected men, and formed a camp of
two hundred thousand fighting men: with these united
most of the Tonos of Japan and its lords, Christians and
Gentiles, and the less number remained among the partisans
of Yeyasudono, who came down as speedily as he could
from Quanto, in search of the governors and their army, to
give them battle with a hundred thousand men, but good
troops, of his own kingdom. The two armies joined, and a
battle was fought on equal terms, in the course of which
various things happened which made the event doubtful
until many people passed over from the side of the
governors to that of Yeyasudono, and the improvement of
his affairs was perceptible, and victory declared in his
favour. Many having been killed, and many lords, those
who remained, for few escaped, fell into the hands of
Yeyasudono, and amongst them the four governors.
Having destroyed the greater number of the Tonos, and

deprived others of their lordships and provinces, and reappointed everything anew amongst persons devoted to his party, he ordered a special execution of the governors (after returning to court, triumphant over his enemies, and in possession of the whole kingdom), by having them crucified and their ears cut off, and he had them carried through the streets of the principal cities of Usaca, Sacay, Fugimen, and Miaco, in carts, until they died on the crosses, with other tortures. As these were the men by whose counsel and artifices Taico a few years before had done the same thing to the barefooted friars whom he martyred, it may be understood that God chose to punish them in this world also with the same rigour.

Thus Yeyasudono remained in the supreme government of Japan, as Taico had held it, without taking out the son whom he left from the fortress of Usaca; on the contrary, he set more guards over him; and changing his name, as is the custom of the rulers of Japan, he called himself Daifusama for greater dignity.

Fray Geronymo of Jesus, companion of the martyrs, who remained hid in Japan on account of the persecution by the tyrant Taicosama, passed the time in the interior of the country amongst the Christians, with his habit changed, so that, although he was carefully searched for, they were not able to discover him; until after Taicosama was dead, and Daifu had made himself master of the government, when he came to Miaco, and received an order to make himself known to a servant of Dayfu, and to tell him many things of the Philippines and of the King of Spain, and of his kingdoms and provinces, particularly of those which he possessed in New Spain and Peru, from which the Philippines depended, and with which they had correspondence, and how good it would be for Dayfu to possess the friendship and have dealings with the Spaniards. This servant had an opportunity to repeat all these things to Dayfu, who for some

L

time had desired to have the trade which the Portuguese had established in Nangasaki, in his own kingdom of Quanto, to give it more importance, as he was its natural sovereign, and it seemed to him that it might be arranged by means of what Fray Geronymo related; so he had him brought before him, and, asking him who he was, the friar related how he had remained in Japan after the martyrdom of his companions; that he was a monk, and of those whom the governor of Manila had sent, during the life of Taico Sama, to treat of peace and amity with the Spaniards, and they had suffered, as was well known, after converting Christians, and had established some hospitals and houses at Court, and in other cities of Japan, to cure the sick, and perform other works of piety, without pretending to any reward or advantage other than the service of God, and the teaching souls in that kingdom the faith and path by which they had to save themselves, and the service of their neighbours. In this, and in works of charity, especially to the poor, as he and those of his order made profession, they lived without seeking or holding any goods or property upon earth, and maintained themselves only with the alms which were given them for that purpose. After this, he related to him who the King of Spain was, and of his being a Christian, and what great kingdoms and states he possessed in all parts of the world, and that New Spain, Peru, the Philippines, and India, were his, and that he governed all this, and maintained the faith of our Lord Jesus Christ, true God, who created the universe. The friar explained to him other things relating to the Christian religion, as well as he could, and said that, if he wished for the friendship of His Majesty, and of his vassals in Manila, he would be able to assist in establishing it with them, and with the Viceroys of New Spain and Peru, which would be very useful and profitable to him and all his kingdoms and provinces of Japan.

This last matter, of the friendship and trade of the Spaniards, on account of the profit and benefit which might be obtained from it, was more to the taste of Dayfusama than what he had heard of their religion; and though he did not reject it, nor say anything about it, yet at this interview, and in others with Fray Geronymo (who now had appeared in public with his religious habit, by permission of Dayfusama, who gave him what was required for his maintenance), Dayfusama only treated of friendship with the governor of Manila, and of the Spaniards coming from there with their ships and goods every year to Quanto, where they would have a port and established trade, and that the Japanese should sail thence to New Spain, where they were to have the same amity and trade; and on hearing that the voyage was long, and that it required Spanish ships in which to perform it, he proposed that the governor of Manila should send masters and workmen to build them, and that, in the said kingdom and principal port of Quanto, which it has been said is in the northern part of Japan, a country of mountains, abounding in mines of silver, which gave no profit, because there was no one who knew how to work them. Fray Geronymo and the companions whom he might prefer amongst the Spaniards who came there, should have their house and dwelling, like as those monks of the company of Jesus had theirs with the Portuguese in Nangasaki. Fray Geronymo, who desired by whatever means offered, to restore the cause of his monks, and the conversion of Japan by his labour, as he had begun during the lifetime of the martyrs, and this end only moved him, did not doubt that he could once and several times facilitate the desires of Daifusama, and assured him that they would certainly be realised by his means, and that in nothing was there any difficulty to impede this; upon which Dayfu showed himself favourable, and more well affected towards the affairs of Manila than his predecessor Taico had been, and he assured that he would give a good reception to the Spaniards in Japan, and that their ships which should come there in distress, or in any other way, should by his orders be equipped and refitted with all they wanted, and he would not consent to any Japanese going out to plunder or commit any injury in the coasts of the Philippines. And because he learned that in that year six ships of Japanese corsairs had gone out of the island of Zazuma[1] and other ports of the lower kingdoms, which had captured and plundered two Chinese vessels which were entering Manila with their merchandise, and had done other mischief on its coast; he immediately ordered them to be sought for in their kingdom, and more than four hundred men having been taken prisoners, he caused them to be crucified. He also ordered that for the future the ships that went each year from Nangasaki to Manila with flour and other goods, should not be so many in number, but only as many as were sufficient for the supply of Manila, with the permission and good pleasure of its governor, so that they should not cause loss or injury to that place.

As Daifu pressed Fray Geronymo every day more with respect to what he had taken upon himself, Fray Geronymo told him that he had already written, and would write again, about those matters to the governor and the Royal Audiencia of Manila; and he entreated of Dayfu, that a servant and person of his house should be the bearer of these letters and message, so that they might go with more credit and authority. Dayfu approved of this, and despatched them with Captain Chiquiro, a pagan Japanese and one of his servants, who carried a present of various weapons to the governor, and the letters of Fray Geronymo, without any special letter from Dayfu, only that Fray Geronymo said that he wrote in the name of Dayfu; and he made much entreaty and explained the better state which the affairs of peace and

[1] Satsuma.

amity were in between Japan and the Philippines, and gave an account of what Dayfu promised and assured; and that to establish this more securely, he had promised him that the Spaniards should go with their ships of trade to Quanto; and that the governor was to send masters and workmen to build ships for navigation between Japan and New Spain, and that there was to be trade and friendship with the Viceroy of that country, and that Dayfu had already given him leave for monks to come to Japan to make Christians, and found churches and monasteries, and he had given him a good site for one in Miaco, where he was staying, and it would be the same in the other parts and towns of Japan, where they pleased. This, Fray Geronymo added to what Daifu had offered, and he said it with artifice and cunning, in order to move the monks of the Philippines so that all of them should more eagerly undertake to push the business with the governor and the High Court, so that they should agree to all this with greater facility, not to lose what Fray Geronymo said he had obtained.

During the same government of Don Francisco Tello, in the year 1600, towards the end of October, a ship arrived from the province of Camarines, bringing news, that two ships had entered and anchored in one of its bays in the northern part, twenty leagues from the mouth of the channel and Cape of Espiritu Santo: they were a flag-ship and admiral's-ship well provided with artillery, with foreign crews, who had, as friends of the Spaniards, requested and obtained by barter from the natives, rice and other provisions of which they were short; immediately after, they weighed and went out, making for the channel and entered it, having left a few feigned letters for the governor Don Francisco Tello, to say that they were friends, and came with the permission of His Majesty to Manila for their trade. From this, and from a negro, who throwing himself into the sea, escaped from these ships to the island of Capul, and through an Englishman[1] whom the natives arrested on shore, it was understood that these ships were from Holland, whence they had sailed, in company with three other ships, with patents and documents from Count Maurice of Nassau, who was named Prince of Orange, to make prizes in the Indies: and that they had entered the South Sea by the Straits of Magellan, and of the five ships three had disappeared, and these two, the flag-ship and admiral's-ship, had run along the coast of Chili, and there taken two vessels, and having turned away from the coast of Lima, had put out to sea and made their voyage without stopping anywhere, shaping their course for the Philippines, where they had entered with the intention of plundering what they might fall in with: and they were informed that a galloon named *Santo Tomas* was expected from New Spain with the money for the merchandise of the cargoes of two years, which had been sent from Manila to New Spain; also that within a few days merchant ships would begin to arrive from China, from which they could fill their hands. They knew that there were no galleys or armed ships in that season which could attack them, and they determined to come to the mouth of the bay of Manila, and pass the time there, supplying themselves with the provisions and refreshments which would enter the city: and this they carried out. In the flag-ship named *Maurice* there went as commander Oliver de Nort of Amstradam, with a hundred men, and twenty-four pieces of brass[2] cannon; this ship was one of those which a few years before was with the Count of Leste at the taking of the city of Cadiz.[3] In the admiral's ship, named *Concordia*, there was as captain Lambert Viesman of Rotterdam, with forty men and ten pieces of artillery. When these ships

[1] This man was John Calleway of London, a musician, as stated in Van Noort's account.
[2] *Bronze de cuchara.*
[3] In 1596 an English fleet sacked Cadiz.

were seen on the coast of Chili, the Viceroy Don Luis de Velasco, who governed Peru, sent to seek and pursue them, along the coast of Peru and New Spain as far as California, a fleet well supplied with artillery and brilliant soldiers, which sailed from the Callao of Lima, under the command of Don Juan de Velasco; they were unable to find the enemy, as he had left the coast and taken sea room, pursuing his voyage to the Philippines: and in a storm which overtook the Peru fleet whilst returning from California, its flag-ship was lost, with all hands, for it never again appeared.

The governor, Don Francisco Tello, seeing that this corsair was making incursions among the islands, according to advices from some captains and soldiers, whom he had sent by land along the coasts of the isle of Luzon that they might prevent his throwing men on shore and doing injury to the towns; and hearing of other small light boats which the enemy had within sight, considered how to remedy this extremity, which seemed on this occasion to be very difficult, both because he found himself without any kind of rowing barges or ships with high bulwarks with which to put out to sea, and also because he had but little soldiery in the camp, for the greater part of it had been taken away by Captain and Sergeant-major Juan Xuarez Gallinato, and was with him in the province of Pintados, with galleys and galliots, and other craft occupied in defending the inhabitants from the vessels of the Mindanao and Xolo men, who continually made descents to plunder them; and he was preparing for the expedition to Jolo, which it was intended should be made in the first monsoon, for it could no longer be deferred. The governor, finding himself hard pressed on this occasion, and that the Dutch enemy was able to inflict great injury and make many prizes, and go off with them, leaving the country ruined, summoned the High Court and communicated the state of affairs, and requested the auditors to assist him

in person, as might be fitting. It was settled what ought
to be done, which was, to put the port of Cabit, which was
inside the bay, in a state of defence, so that the enemy
should not make himself master of it, and of the magazines,
artillery and stocks for the ships; at the same time at once
to use diligence in arming a few ships with which to put to
sea, and present some front to the enemy (if no more could
be done), so that he should not be so thoroughly established
in the country, and should go away from the islands; since,
finding everything so defenceless and without resistance, it
was natural that he would remain until he had carried out
his designs. The execution of this was committed to Dr.
Antonio de Morga, and the licentiate Telles de Almazan
was charged with remaining in the city, together with the
governor president, for its defence; and from thence he was
to provide and supply the port of Cabit and Dr. Antonio de
Morga with what he might require for what was under his
charge. Dr. de Morga went out of Manila the same day,
which was the last day of October of the year six hundred,
with some soldiers and munitions; and he put it in a state
of defence with a hundred and fifty men well armed, hackbut men and musketeers, who always guarded the port day
and night from their guard-houses and posts, and in the
points that required it. He collected the ships that were
in port close to the town, as near as possible to the building
yard, where a lateen-rigged vessel[1] was building, and a ship
of Sebu, and another a small vessel[2] belonging to some
Portuguese, which had come from Malacca with merchandise.
For the defence of these he put in position on the beach
twelve pieces of brass cannon[3] of middling size, and two of
greater range, which were placed on a point at the entrance
of the port; the fire of all these defended the port, and the

[1] Galizabra.   [2] Patache.
[3] *De artilleria de bronce de cuchara:* the cuchara appears to have been
a ladle with which the charge of powder was placed in the gun.

ships in it. On the beach further on, a rampart was made with wood and planking, filled in with earth, behind which, if the enemy should enter, the soldiers would cover and defend themselves with their artillery. The auditor having thus put this port in a state of defence, set about completing the ship on the stocks (although much work was wanting to it), to launch it, and fit it with sails, and at the same time he caused the ship of Sebu to be refitted; and, looking after these works, he hurried them so much that within thirty days he hoisted the yards on the galizabra and on the ship of Sebu, and furnished them with artillery, putting on board of each eleven guns of middling and larger size, which were sent to him from Manila, besides those which were in the port.

The corsair came to the mouth of the bay, which is eight leagues from the port of Cabit; he did not venture to make a dash into the port, as he had thought of doing, for he had heard from some Sangley men who went out to sea in champans that it was already defended, but he was not informed that they were arming to come out against him, nor that there was any preparation or forces at that season for this purpose, and so he allowed himself to remain at the mouth of the bay, both ships and their boats moving about, changing from one side to the other on various days, and seizing the small vessels which came in to the city with provisions, without any of them escaping him, and anchoring at night under the shelter of the land; all this at a distance of four leagues from the mouth of the bay, without going further away, so as to be nearer at hand for the opportunities which might offer.

Dr. Antonio de Morga kept a few small and light vessels within sight of the enemy, under the shelter of the land, which every day brought him news of the place in which the enemy was anchored, and of what he was doing, which was to have quietly stationed himself, placing his guard every day towards evening on the deck with drums and banners, and firing his musketry, so that the forces which the corsair carried were estimated, and the larger and best portion of them were in the flagship, which was a good and handy ship. The auditor also took measures that no champan or other vessel should go out of the bay, so that the corsair should not get information of what was going on; and when affairs were at this point, he informed the governor of what had been done, and that if he thought fit the Portuguese vessel might also be armed, to go out in company with the two ships, the galizabra and the *Sant Antonio* of Sebu, and that he had laid an embargo on it, and equipped it for that purpose. Ammunition, and some provisions of rice and fish were provided for the two ships, and it remained to equip them with sailors and fighting men to go out in them: of these there was but little supply, the sailors hid themselves and feigned sickness, and one and all shewed themselves ill inclined to go out to an affair of more risk and peril than of personal profit: captains and private soldiers of the city, who were not receiving pay or rations from the king, and who were able to go on the expedition, did not offer themselves to the governor for it, and if any one were ready to do so, he dissembled until he should know who was to go as commander of this fleet: for, although some army captains might have taken the command, the governor was not inclined to give it them in charge, nor would the others have chosen to go under their orders, for each one presumed, and claimed for himself, that he could be the leader, and that no other neighbour of theirs was to give them orders. The governor was prevented from going out in person, and he saw that all the townspeople shewed the intention that if Dr. Antonio de Morga went out with the fleet they would go with him, and would not take account of the difficulties which presented themselves. The governor having heard of the desire of those who were able to embark, and that by other means he would not be able to effect what was sought for, and seeing that the deferring the matter was each day a very great detriment to it, he summoned the Auditor to the city and set the business before him; and, in order that he should not excuse himself from it, he issued an act, which he then caused to be notified to him by the secretary of the government, ordering him on behalf of His Majesty to embark and go as general and chief of the fleet to search and pursue the corsair, because otherwise, according to the state in which affairs were, they could not meet with the result which was most suitable. As it appeared to the Auditor, that if he omitted to do this, blame would be cast upon him for having allowed to pass so pressing an occasion for the service of God and of His Majesty, and for the good of the whole country, and that the affairs of war had been under his charge, and he had managed them by sea and land; and it might be reckoned ill against him if he turned his back on this conjuncture, which sought him of itself, especially as the governor made out documents for this, to cover his responsibility: so he obeyed what was ordered him by the act of the governor, which, with his reply, was word for word as follows:—

Act of the Governor Don Francisco Tello, and Reply of Dr. Antonio de Morga.

In the city of Manila, the first of December of one thousand six hundred years, the lord Don Francisco Tello, knight of the order of Santiago, governor and captain general of these Philippine islands, and President of the Royal High Court of Justice which resides in it, said: Whereas, two ships of the English[1] enemy have come to these islands, after con-

[1] Here and in another document English has been put by mistake for Dutch.

sultation and in concert with the High Court, it was proposed to fit out armed ships to go out against them, and for this purpose it was agreed that Dr. Antonio de Morga should go to the port of Cabit to direct the fitting out and equipment of the said armed ships and the defence of that port, as it appears by the act and resolution which was passed upon that matter, in the book of the affairs of the administration of this present year, to which reference is made. And, in execution of the said resolution, he has until now attended to the defence of the port, and to the fitting out and equipment of the said fleet, which consists of the ship *San Diego*[1] of Sebu, and the galloon *San Bartolome*, which he caused to be finished on the stocks and launched in the sea, and a small vessel which came from the city of Malacca; and a galliot and other smaller boats, which have been fitted out with the care and diligence which he has used in this business. The said fleet is in such good condition, that very shortly it may set sail; nevertheless, the said enemy is near this city, on the coast of the island of Miraveles. As many captains, gentlemen and persons of importance of this republic have understood that the said auditor would make this expedition, they have offered to go and serve in it (at their own expense) in his company the king our sovereign; and great preparation of men and provisions has been made with this intention, which expedition would fall to the ground and be undone if the said auditor were not to proceed with this fleet in pursuit of the aforesaid enemy, and it would not obtain the result which is expected of it, so much for the service of God our Lord, and for the good of this country; the more so, as the said auditor is experienced in the business of war, and has been at other times general of the forces of His Majesty, and by his nomination; and has been lieutenant of the captain general for some years in this kingdom, of which he has given a

[1] In other passages this ship is named *San Antonio*.

good account, and he is well looked up to and loved by the men of war, and is the person who is most fitting, according to the state of affairs, and other just considerations which bear upon it, so that this expedition may have a result and not be undone; or at the least be not deferred with loss and prejudice. For all this, the governor has ordered and orders the said auditor, that since he has fostered this business, and by his own exertions has put it on the good footing in which it is, and all the people who are not on the pay list (who are many) are prepared to go for his sake, that with all possible speed he shall prepare himself to go as general and commander of the said fleet in search of the enemy, for which the necessary documents and instructions will be given him; because thus it is expedient for the service of the king our sovereign, on whose behalf I command him to do this and fulfil it, giving him for this, during the time which he may occupy with it, as President of the Royal High Court of Justice, leave of absence, and exoneration from attending to the business of the said High Court; which he gave formally to make the said absence, and so he issued it, ordered, and signed with his name, DON FRANCISCO TELLO: before me, GASPAR DE AZEBO.

In the city of Manila, the first of December of one thousand six hundred years, I, the secretary of the government, notified the act above-contained to Dr. Antonio de Morga, Auditor of this Royal High Court, who said:[1] That from the first day of the month of November ultimate he has occupied himself, by commission from the Royal High Court of these islands, in all which the said act mentions,

[1] The Governor-President of the High Court and Dr. Antonio de Morga, carried the traditions of the law court into their new career at sea, for our author's instructions, which are drawn up like a legal document, were served upon him like a writ, the secretary indorses a memorandum of the service, and then follows the return of De Morga to the citation.

and in the execution of it he has done the utmost which has been within his power, and the expedition is on the good footing and condition which is known; and that if it is for its good result, and for what is expected from it, his person and fortune are at the disposition and convenience of the service of the king our sovereign; he is ready to employ it all for it, and to do what has been ordered and commanded him by the said president; and so he has no other will or desire than for what might be for the service of God, and of His Majesty; upon which may your lordship order and direct what may be found to be most expedient, and so he will fulfil it, and he has signed it with his name,

DOCTOR ANTONIO DE MORGA.
GASPAR DE AZEBO.

Dr. Antonio de Morga, without asking or taking anything from the king's exchequer, provided himself with all that was requisite for the expedition; and assisted several necessitous soldiers, who came to offer themselves, besides many other persons of importance who did so likewise; so that within eight days more, there was already a sufficient quantity of people for the expedition, together with abundance of provisions, arms, and marine stores; and all embarked. What with adventurers, and the paid soldiers whom the governor gave to the auditor of those whom he had in the camp, with Captain Augustin de Urdiales, there were enough to arm both ships, each carrying about a hundred fighting men, without reckoning gunners, sailors, and shipboys; for of these there was a less supply than what was needed. The governor appointed as admiral[1] of this fleet, Captain Juan de Alcega, an old soldier, and experienced in these islands; and as captain of the paid soldiers who were to go in the admiral's ship, Juan Tello y Aguirre; and as sergeant-major of the fleet, Don Pedro Tello his kinsman;

[1] Second in command.

and he appointed the other officers and employments, and gave the nomination and title of general of the fleet to Dr. Antonio de Morga, and the instructions as to what he was to do in the course of the voyage and expedition, closed and sealed, with orders not to open them until he had got out to sea, outside of the bay of Manila, which were as follows.

Instructions of the Governor, for Doctor Antonio de Morga.

That which Doctor Antonio de Morga, auditor of the Royal High Court of Law of these Philippine Islands, and captain-general of the fleet which is going to seek the English enemy, has to do, is the following :—

Firstly, as there is information that the English enemy, against whom this fleet has been prepared, is in the cove of Maryuma, and if perchance he should have notice of our fleet, he might take to flight, without its being possible to attack him; it is ordered, that the fleet go out with the greatest speed possible, in search of him, in order to join and fight him until he be taken or sunk; by the favour of our Lord.

Item, in fighting with the said enemy, as well with artillery, as by boarding, (for this should be attempted with all the care and diligence that may be), as the weather may best admit of: if the enemy should take to flight in sight of the fleet, it will follow him until the desired result is obtained.

Item, if at the time the fleet goes out to the said enemy, he should have absented himself from this coast, and there should be news of his having gone along it to any other of these islands, the fleet will seek him and pursue him until it has taken or sunk him; and if the enemy have left these islands, it will follow him as far as it can, for in this it is left to its discretion, so that the object be attained.

Item, forasmuch as in a council of war held on the second day of the present month and year, by the master of the camp, and some captains who were present, they gave their opinion, that if there was no certain information of the course and direction which the enemy had taken, the fleet should follow the coast of Ilocos, steering for the straits of Singapore, by which it is supposed the enemy would have to pass to continue his voyage: notwithstanding the said council of war, if it should happen that the general should have no information of which course the enemy has made, in that case he will do what he thinks most expedient, as one who is present at the circumstance; and as the enemy and the occasion may suggest to him; endeavouring to attain the object of our desire, which is, to reach and destroy the enemy.

Item, if the fleet should fall in with any other of the enemy's corsairs, or others, going about these islands, or which should have come out of them doing them injury, whether English, Japanese, Terrenates or Mindanaos, or of any other nation, it will endeavour to chastise or attack them in such manner that in this also (if it should happen) some good effect should be made.

Item, if the enemy is captured (as is hoped with the favour of God our Lord), the people will be preserved alive, and the fleet will bring the ships with it.

Item, the spoil which may be found in the said ships, will be divided and distributed in the manner usual on such occasions amongst those who gain the victory.

Item, good care must be taken that the people on board the fleet be peaceable and well disciplined; and with respect to this, let that be followed which is usual on similar occasions.

Item, let there be good order with respect to the provisions and munitions carried by the fleet, and the expenditure of both with much moderation; more especially if the fleet goes to a distance from these islands.

Item, if perchance, after closing with the aforesaid enemy,

or following after him, he should go away from these islands, and the object having been accomplished, the fleet will endeavour to return as shortly as possible to the islands; and if the weather do not allow of its returning until the setting in of the monsoon, it will endeavour to keep together, and the fleet is to be provided and refitted with everything necessary on account of his Majesty, so that it may perform its voyage with the greatest celerity and safety possible. Done in the city of Manila, the tenth of December, of the year one thousand six hundred.

Don Francisco Tello.
By order of the Governor and Captain-General,
Gaspar de Azebo.

The auditor with all his people went to the port, and he put them on board the two ships, taking as flagship the *Sant Antonio* of Sebu, on account of its being more roomy for the supplementary men whom he was taking with him, and left the Portuguese vessel because the Governor had taken off the embargo, to allow the Portuguese to return to Malacca without losing time. He equipped two caracoas for the service of the fleet, with Indian crews, and two Spaniards to direct them. They went out of the port of Cabit, and set sail (after having confessed and communicated), on the twelfth of December, 1600, taking as chief pilot Alonzo Gomez, and on board the flagship Padre Diego de Santiago, with a lay brother of the company of Jesus, and Fray Francisco de Valdes of the order of St. Augustine; and on board the admiral's ship Fray Juan Gutierrez, with another companion of the same order, for whatever might occur requiring their ministry.

The same day both ships of this fleet came to anchor at night close to the town and anchorage of the island of Miraveles, in the mouth of the bay; and as soon as it was daybreak, a rowboat[1] put out from shore, in which came the sentinels, whom the auditor had sent the day before hurriedly to get him certain information of where the corsair was. They told him that when the fleet came out of the port at Cabit, the enemy had weighed also from where he was anchored on the side of the Friar's port, and had crossed with both ships, taking their boats inboard to the other side in the open sea, and they had seen him anchor after nightfall in front of the point of Balcitegui, where he had remained. With this information the auditor understood (that it was possible) that the corsair had news of the fleet which was getting ready, and of its coming out, and that he had weighed from where he was at anchor, and since he had taken his boats aboard, he was going out to sea to get out of the way of the fleet. He at once sent the same news to the admiral, and opened the governor's instructions, and seeing that they ordered him to seek the enemy (with all diligence) and pursue him, and endeavour to fight with him, he was of opinion that he should shorten the work before him and not lose time, nor let the enemy get further off. Agreeably to this, the fleet spent this day of Sta. Lucia, the thirteenth of December, in making bulwark nettings, preparing the artillery, getting ready the arms, distributing the men to quarters, and preparing to fight next day, on which it was expected they would fall in with the corsair. The auditor sent special instructions in writing to the admiral of what he was to do and observe for his part, principally that on finding themselves with the enemy, both ships were to board and fight the corsair's flagship, which was the ship in which he carried all his forces, and other things which will be understood from the instructions which were given to the admiral, which were as follows:—

[1] Barangay.

Instructions of Doctor Morga for the Admiral Juan de Alcega.

The order which is to be observed by Captain Juan de Alcega, Admiral of this fleet of the King our Sovereign, in the course of this voyage and navigation, is the following:

Firstly, because the object with which this armament has been made, is to look for and pursue the English ships, which at present have entered among these islands, of which there is information that they are near these parts, and in conformity to the instructions given by the governor and captain-general of these islands, they are to be sought for and pursued with all care and diligence, wheresoever they may be able to be met with, in order to close with the aforesaid enemies, take them or send them to the bottom. Care must be taken that the admiral's ship go well prepared, and the sailors, soldiers and gunners all in readiness, so as to be able on their side to effect the above-mentioned object on this occasion.

Moreover, the admiral's ship will follow the flagship of this fleet to leeward of her (unless it were necessary to go to windward for the navigation of the ship or to overhaul the enemy), and attention will be paid to the smaller vessels which accompany this fleet, that they do not remain behind nor fall off; this without prejudice to the navigation and voyage, and keeping close company with the flagship, which is what is of most importance.

Item, if there is an opportunity to close with the enemy, the admiral will endeavour to do so, together with the flagship, or without her, in case the flagship should be to leeward, or in a position not to be able to do this so quickly, for the flagship will endeavour with all speed and diligence to come to the admiral's assistance on any occasion.

Item, if the enemy is found with the two ships which he

possesses, an attempt is to be made to enter and board the flagship, which is the ship in which he carries his chief strength, and the flagship of this fleet will do the same. But in case the enemy's flagship should not be within reach, and his admiral's ship should be in a position to be brought into action, this will be attempted.

Item, whenever this fleet attacks the enemy and boards him, it must be contrived that both ships, the flag-ship and admiral's ship, should both board on the same side, and if this cannot be done, care shall be taken that the artillery and musketry do not hit our own ships and men, and that in this as much care and attention be bestowed as possible.

Item, on boarding the enemy, it must be endeavoured to grapple with him, and cut down his sails, so as that he should not cast off, and before throwing men aboard of him, make sure of the harpings and deck of the enemy, sweeping them and clearing them so that it be with the least risk possible to our men.

In the course of this navigation in search of the enemy, no muskets nor arquebuses are to be fired nor drums beaten until after discovering him, nor will any artillery be fired, because it must be managed to catch the enemy at anchor, and that he be not warned of the fleet which is in pursuit of him.

If the admiral's ship were in any extremity, so as to require assistance, she will fire a gun from the side on which the flag-ship may be, which will be a signal for assistance; and notice is given that the flag-ship will do likewise in case of being in a similar extremity.

Item, if the flag-ship should hoist a flag on the shrouds, it will be a signal for a summons to a council of war, or other matter important to the admiral, who will come to the flag-ship with the boat which may be most convenient.

Item, of the two caracoas which go with this fleet, one of them will go close to the admiral's ship, as near as possible for its service and requirements.

Item, care will be taken that the munitions and provisions be expended by reckoning, and with as much economy as well may be, on account of the distance to which this voyage may be prolonged.

Item, an endeavour must be made for all these vessels to sail in company, and no fixed point for rendezvous is named, in case of any of the ships parting company on account of a storm or other necessity, because the designs of the enemy and the course which he will follow are not known. Only it is to be noted that all have to go in search and pursuit of him, until chasing him out (if no more can be effected) from all these islands, and leaving them free and assured against the said enemy; thus taking information of the course followed by the enemy, it will be the most certain method for the ship which should part company to follow that course, in order to rejoin the fleet.

Item, inasmuch as the governor and captain general of these islands gave the charge of captain of infantry to Captain Juan Tello y Aguirre (who is on board the admiral's ship), with respect to the men whom I should appoint under him, I appoint them by this present. The troops of infantry receiving pay who are embarked on board the admiral's ship, during the time they are so, and that this expedition lasts; which men the admiral will make over to the said Juan Tello y Aguirre, that, as their captain, he may hold them under his command, rule and discipline them.

All this is what has to be observed and attended to (for the present) in pursuance of this voyage, and I give it as instructions to the said admiral, and other persons whom it concerns, in conformity with those which I hold from the governor and captain general of these isles, and in faith of it, I have signed it with my name, on board the flag-ship, off the island of Miraveles, Wednesday, thirteenth of December of one thousand six hundred years.

Doctor Antonio de Morga.

At the same time the auditor sent to inform the admiral that the fleet would weigh anchor from where it was a little after midnight, and would go out of the bay to sea, setting as much sail as possible, so that at dawn it should be off the point of Baleitigui, to windward of where the enemy had anchored on Tuesday night, as the sentinels had stated.

At the hour appointed, both vessels, the flag-ship and admiral's ship, weighed from Miraveles, and, the wind serving them, though light, they sailed the rest of the night, making for Baleitigui, without the two caracoa tenders having been able to follow them, the sea being ruffled by a fresh north-west wind, so they crossed to the other side by the inner part of the bay, under shelter of the island; and when day broke both ships found themselves off the point, and discovered, at a league to leeward and seaward, the two corsair ships at anchor; which, as soon as they recognised our ships, and that they carried captain's and admiral's flags at their gaffs, weighed anchor and set sail from where they were (after the flag-ship had reinforced herself with a boatful of men taken from her consort, which put out to sea), and the flag-ship remained hove to, firing a few pieces at long range at our fleet. Our flag-ship, which could not answer him with artillery, because the ports were closed, and the ship hauling on the starboard tack, determined to close with the enemy, and grappled with his flag-ship on the port side, sweeping and clearing his decks of the men that stood upon them, and threw upon them a banner and thirty soldiers, and a few sailors, who took possession of the poop, castle and cabin, and captured their colours at the gaff and poop, and the standard which floated at the stern of white, blue, and orange colours with the arms of Count Maurice. The mainmast and mizen were stripped of all the rigging and sails,[1] and a large barge was

[1] This is confirmed by the plate given in the Dutchman's account, where the main-shrouds are represented as cut away. See plate.

taken which he carried at the stern. The enemy, who had retreated in the bows below the harpings, seeing two ships fall upon him with such resolution, sent (as surrendering) to ask the auditor for terms, and whilst an answer was being given him, and whilst the Admiral Juan de Alcega, in obedience to the instructions which the auditor had given him the day before, should have boarded at the same time as the flag-ship and have grappled, as he thought that that business was already accomplished, and that the corsair's consort was getting away, and that it would be well to capture her: leaving the flag-ships, he followed astern of Lambert Viesman, crowding sail, and chased him until he came up with him. Oliver de Nort, who saw that he was alone, and with a better ship and artillery than what the auditor had, did not wait any longer for the answer to the terms which he had at first asked for, and began to fight again with musketry and artillery. The combat was so obstinate and hardly fought by both sides, that it lasted more than six hours between the two flag-ships, with many killed on both sides; but the corsair had the worst of it all the time, for of all his men there did not remain alive more than fifteen, and those much damaged and knocked to pieces. Ultimately the corsair's ship caught fire, and the flame rose high by the mizenmast and part of the poop. It was necessary for the auditor, not to risk his own ship, to call back the banner and men which he had in the enemy's ship, and cast loose and separate from her, as he did, and found that his ship, from the force of the artillery during so long a fight (being a slightly built ship), had a large opening in the bows, and was making so much water, that she could not overcome the leak, and was going down. The corsair seeing his opponent's work, and that he was unable to follow him, made haste with his few remaining men to put out the fire on board his ship, and having quenched it, he took to flight with the foremast

which had remained; and, damaged in all parts, stripped
of rigging and without a crew, he reached Borneo and
Sunda, where he was seen so harassed and distressed, that
it seemed impossible for him to navigate or go on any further without being cast away. The flagship of the Spaniards, which was fully occupied in attempting to find a
remedy in the extremity to which she was reduced, could
not be assisted, being alone and so far from land, so that she
sunk and went down in so very short a time that the men
could neither disembarass themselves of their arms, nor
provide themselves with anything which could save them.
The auditor did not abandon the ship, although some soldiers got possession of the boat which was carried at the
stern to save themselves in it, and told him to get into it,
after which they made off and went away, so that others
should not take it from them. When the ship sunk, the
auditor went on swimming for four hours, with the flag of
the poop and standard of the enemy, which he carried about
him, and at last reached land at an uninhabited island two
leagues from there, very small, named Fortuna, where also
some of the people of the ship arrived in safety, of those
who had most strength to sustain themselves in the sea.
Others perished and were drowned, who had not disarmed
themselves, and this difficulty overtook them when they were
exhausted by the long fight with the enemy. Those who died
on this occasion were fifty of all sorts, and the most important were the Captains Don Francisco de Mendoza, Gregorio de Vargas, Francisco Rodriguez, Gaspar de los Rios,
killed fighting with the enemy; and drowned in the sea,
the Captains Don Juan de Zamudio, Augustin de Urdiales,
Don Pedro Tello, Don Gabriel Maldonado, Don Cristoval
de Heredia, Don Luis de Belver, Don Alonzo Lozano, Domingo de Arrieta, Melchoir de Figueroa, the chief pilot
Alonzo Gomez, the padre Fray Diego de Santiago, and the
brother his companion. The admiral, Juan de Alcega,

having come up with Lambert Viesman, a little after midday, captured him with little resistance; and although later he saw pass by at a short distance the ship of Oliver de Nort, making off and very much battered, he did not follow him, and without stopping any more he returned with his ship to Miraveles, leaving the prize with some of his own men whom he had put on board to follow him. Neither did he seek for his flagship, nor take any other steps, supposing that if any unfortunate event had happened, blame might be imputed to him for leaving the flagship alone with the corsair, and having gone after Lambert Viesman, without orders from the auditor, and in disobedience of the orders which he had given him in writing; and fearing that if he joined him after the loss that ill would befall him. The auditor found his ship's boat at the islet of Fortuna, together with the boat of the corsair, and a caracoa which arrived there, and when it was night he took away in these boats the wounded and people who had escaped, so that on the following day he got them ashore in Luzon, at the bar of Anazibu, in the province of Balayan, thirty leagues from Manila, where he equipped and supplied them as shortly as he could. Besides that, he explored the coast and islands of the district with swift boats, seeking for the admiral's ship and the captured corsair. This prize was carried into Manila, with twenty-five men alive and the admiral, ten pieces of artillery, and a quantity of wine, oil, cloth, linen, arms and other goods which were on board. The governor caused the admiral and Dutchmen of his company to be executed with the garotte,[1] and this was the end of this ex-

---

[1] *A el almirante y Olandeses de su compañia, hizo dar garrote el governador*: from this phrase, the governor seems to have ordered this execution of his own authority, without trial or the intervention of the High Court; it is unfortunate that the author omits to state the ground of their execution. Since the independence of Holland was not recognised by Spain till 1609, it was most probably because these Dutchmen were

pedition; and thus ceased the injury which it was understood that the corsair would effect in these seas, if he had been allowed to remain in them with the object he sought, although so much to the detriment of the Spaniards by the loss of the flagship, which would not have happened if the order had been observed which the auditor had given.

The governor, Don Francisco Tello, gave a certificate of this event to the auditor, which is as follows :—

Certificate of the Governor Don Francisco Tello, of that which happened in the expedition against the Dutch corsair.

Don Francisco Tello, knight of the habit of Santiago, Governor and Captain-General in these Philippine Islands, and President of the High Court and Royal Chancery, which resides in them, etc., etc.

I certify to the gentlemen who may see this present, that in the past year of one thousand six hundred, a squadron of Dutch armed ships under the command of Oliver de Nort, after passing through the Straits of Magellan to the South Sea, arrived at these islands in the month of October of the aforesaid year, with two armed ships, and entered amongst the islands, effecting some captures and losses, and at length stationed itself off the entrance of the bay of this city of Manila, with the design of laying in wait for the ships and merchandise which were coming from China, and for the galloon Santo Tomas which was expected from New Spain, with the silver of two years belonging to the merchants of this kingdom. By a decision of the said Royal High Court of the thirty-first of October of the said year, Doctor Antonio de Morga, the senior auditor of this High Court, was commissioned and charged to go at once

---

rebels. If the ground was that they were pirates, the Dutchmen's own account of their burning villages, etc., where there were no Spaniards, is more damaging to themselves than the statements of De Morga, and enough to make them out to have been *hostes humani generis*.

to the port of Cabit, and place and hold it in a state of defence; and to prepare and equip a fleet to go out against the said corsair. In this business the auditor occupied himself in person with much care and diligence, fortifying and defending the said port, and he completed on the stocks, and launched into the sea a middle-sized ship, and armed and equipped another belonging to private persons which was in the port; and on both he set the yards and rigging in the space of forty days. And in order that the expedition might be made with more speed, and to obtain a larger supply of men used to war, and of what was most necessary, I ordained and appointed (for, according to the state of affairs at the time, they could not be managed by any other person), the said anditor on the first of December of the same year to go out with the fleet as its general to seek the enemy, and fight with him till he should be destroyed, and to drive him out of these islands; which the auditor did, and accomplished in this manner. On the twelfth day of the said month of December he set sail with the two ships of his fleet from the port of Cabit, and on the fourteenth of the same month, at dawn, he sighted the corsair outside of the bay of this city, off the point of Baleitigui, with his two ships, flagship and admiral's ship, and he followed them till he got close to them; and the two fleets having got ready for action, they engaged each other, and the said auditor in his flagship with much gallantry and resolution attacked the flagship of the corsair and boarded her (for she was a large and strong ship with much artillery and many fighting men), and he at once threw on board of her a standard of infantry with thirty arquebuseers and a few volunteers and sailors, who took possession of the stern castle and cabin, and the flags that were flying; these men at the end of the action retreated to our ship, on account of the strong fire which at last began to rage on board of the enemy; and so the action and fight was carried on by both sides, and lasted more than six hours, with much artillery, musketry and arquebuses that were fired from all parts. In another direction the enemy's consort, which was under the command of Lambert Viesman, was conquered and captured, with the crew, artillery, and other things on board of her. The two flagships, having cast loose and separated on account of the fire which had sprung up, and our ship taking in much water at the bows, the enemy took to flight with only the foremast which remained, with almost all his men killed, having lost his boat, and the standard and flags on the gaff and poop, stripped of his yards, sails and rigging, and the ship leaking in many parts, he ran before the wind, and it has been understood from various accounts which have been received, that he passed by Borneo with only fifteen or sixteen men alive, and most of them crippled and wounded, and a few days later he was entirely lost close to the Sunda. The same auditor, with the men in his company, underwent much labour and danger; because, besides some persons of importance who died fighting, on account of the ship having a large leak in the bows, as has been said (from being a weak ship and not built for armament, and unable to stop or overcome the water which poured in), she went down the same day, when part of the people on board were drowned from being wearied with fighting and not having got rid of their arms; and the auditor, who never would leave the ship, nor abandon her, when she sank, took to the water with the rest of the people and saved himself by swimming, carrying with him some of the enemy's colours, to an uninhabited island named Fortun, two leagues from where the action was; and the next day, in a few small boats which he found, he brought away the people from there and put them in safety on the land of this island. In all which circumstances the auditor has proceeded with much diligence and valour, exposing himself to all the risks of the battle, and afterwards of the sea, without their having been given him before or since in recompense of these services, salary or expenses, or any other advantage; on the contrary, he furnished and spent out of his own property all that was necessary for his equipment in the expedition, and assisted some volunteer soldiers who went in it. Of the prize property which was won in the corsair admiral's ship which was carried into this city, he would not have, nor did he take away anything; on the contrary, the portion of it which might have belonged to him, he ceded it and passed it over to the king our sovereign, and to his royal exchequer. In this manner the end and intent which was aimed at was followed out, of destroying and finishing the said corsair, as much to the service of God and of his Majesty as for the good of this kingdom. As all the above-mentioned facts are established more at length by acts, depositions, and other inquiries which have been made with respect to this expedition; and at the request of the said Doctor Antonio de Morga I have given him this present signed with my name, and sealed with the seal of my arms, which is done in Manila, the twenty-fourth day of the month of August, of the year one thousand six hundred and one.

DON FRANCISCO TELLO.

[*Note.*—The corsair was not made an end of, for Oliver de Nort returned to Rotterdam in safety, through the misconduct of Juan de Alcega, who besides disobeying his orders in the first instance to board the Dutch flag-ship, subsequently let her go past him without pursuing her when she was disabled by De Morga's ship. Our author's statements on the whole agree with those of his antagonist, as will be seen by the following Dutch account of the voyage of Oliver van Noort and of his action with the auditor, taken from the *Recueil des voyages qui ont servi à l'établissement et aux progrès de la Compagnie des Indes orientales, formée dans les Provinces-Unies des Païs Bas. Seconde Edition, reveue par l'Autheur et considérablement augmentée. A Amsterdam. Aux depens d'Estienne Roger, marchand libraire, chez qui l'on trouve un assortiment général de musique.* M.DCC.XVI. Tome ii, p. 1.[1]

[2] "A certain number of inhabitants of the United Provinces, named Peter van Beveren, Huyg Gerritz, John Benninck, and some others, having in the year 1598 formed a company for commerce, treated with Oliver de Noort, a a native of Utregt, to take the conduct of their ships. Their design was that he should pass through the Straits of Magellan, and traffic on the coasts of America, in the South Sea, named by the Spaniards *Mar del Sur*, and go all round the globe, if he was able to do so."

With this object they equipped two ships, one named the *Maurice*, and the other *Henry Frederick*, and two yachts named the *Concord* and the *Hope*, which all together were manned by 248 men of all ages. Oliver de Noort, captain general of this little fleet, embarked in the *Maurice* as admiral. James Claasz, of Ulpendam, commanded the *Henry Frederick* as vice-admiral. Peter de Lint had the command of the yacht *Concord*, and John Huidecooper that of the *Hope*.

All these crews having gone to Rotterdam, by order of the Council of Admiralty of that town, at the request which was made to it to that effect by the company which fitted out the expedition, they were assembled on the 28th of June, 1598, and the naval regulations, named Artykel-brief,[3]

---

[1] This work is by De Constantin, as appears from a dedicatory epistle to *Monseigneur de Chamillart, Controleur Général des Finances*. There is another edition, Rouen, 1725, *Chez Jean Baptiste Machel, le jeune*. A very abridged account of Oliver van Noort's voyage, in English, is contained in John Hamilton Moore's *Complete Collection of Voyages*, vol. i, pp. 45-47; also in Robert Kerr's *Voyages*, vol. x, pp. 112-129.

[2] The paragraphs between inverted commas are translated, the rest is abridged.

[3] This statement, with the other above, that they were to traffic on the coasts of America seems to exclude the idea that they were duly commissioned by letters patent to take prizes; further on a letter given by De Morga states that Van Noort was forbidden to attack any one.

were read to them, so that they should conform to it. These regulations had before been submitted to Prince Maurice, who had approved and confirmed them, and all the men of the crews took an oath to observe them.

"The 13th of September, 1598, the two ships *Maurice* and *Concord* went out of the port of Goerée, and the *Henry Frederick* and the *Hope* having joined them from Amsterdam, they sailed together for Plymouth, where an English pilot, who had sailed in these distant regions with Thomas Candish, was to pick up his baggage which he had left there. The 21st they went out of Plymouth with a fresh north-east wind."

* * * * * *

The Dutch fleet arrived at Prince's Island on the 10th December, 1598, and at Rio de Janeiro on the 9th February, 1599; at both these places they got into difficulties and skirmishes with the Portuguese. On the 3rd June they landed their sick on the small island of Sta. Clara; in a fortnight all were cured of the scurvy except five who died. On the 17th of December, 1598, the council of war had condemned Hans Volkerts of Heligoland, a pilot, to be deserted, and this was executed; he was abandoned on the shore of the mainland near Prince's Island: on the 18th of June, 1599, John Claasz, a gunner, and Girard Willemsz Prins, a gunner, were condemned to be deserted. On the 21st June, the Dutch left Sta. Clara, after burning the *Concord*, which leaked. The name of the *Hope* was changed to that of *Concord*; and James Jansz Huydecooper, captain of the *Hope*, having died on the 5th October, 1599, Peter Lint, captain of the old *Concord*, was appointed to the *Hope*, now named *Concord*. On the 5th November, 1599, they attempted the passage of the Straits of Magellan, having spent fourteen months on the voyage there, and already lost nearly a hundred men. They did not get through the Straits, however, till the 29th February of 1600. At the entrance of the Straits the vice-admiral, James Claasz, refused to obey orders, and said he had as much authority as the commander-in-chief. On the 28th December a court-martial was assembled on board the *Maurice*, and the vice-admiral put in arrest, and three weeks given him to prepare his defence. Lambert Biesman, first clerk, was provisionally appointed vice-admiral. The 2nd of January, 1600, the crews were still 151 men: on the 8th a boat from the *Maurice* went to the shore in the straits, and was attacked by savages, and had two men killed; the ships advanced but slowly, and were at times driven back. On the 24th January the vice-admiral was brought before the court-martial for his defence; he was found guilty, and condemned to be deserted in the Straits of Magellan. On the 26th, in execution of the sentence, he was put ashore, with a little bread and wine, and the prospect of dying of hunger or of being eaten by the savages.

"After the execution, the admiral ordered general prayers in all the ships, and that all should be exhorted to profit by this example, and to do their duty well. Captain Peter de Lint was made vice-admiral, and in his stead Lambert Biesman was made captain of the *Concord*."

On the 27th February the ships again set sail with a favourable wind, and got out of the Straits on the 29th February; on the 8th March the crews of the three ships mustered 147; on the 14th the vice-admiral's ship had disappeared; on the 21st they sighted land of the continent of Chili. On the 24th they saw a vessel, which at first they took for their vice-admiral's ship; making her out to be a Spaniard, they chased her, and on the 26th she was captured by the *Concord*. The prize was named the *Buen Jesus*, of sixty tons, and carried flour and other provisions. On the 28th March the Dutch entered the port of St. Iago in boats, and carried off the ship *Los Picos*, of one hundred and sixty tons, and burned some other small vessels. On the 5th

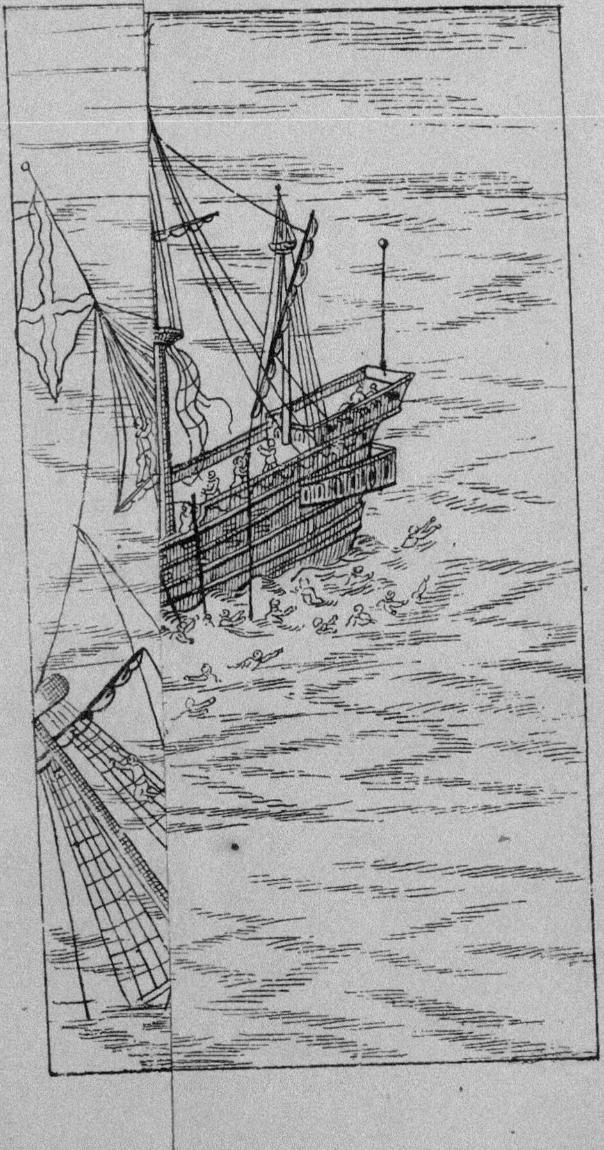

Folio 67. 25

L'admiral, estant surmonté s'en allant au fondts a nostre veue

April, Oliver de Noort set at liberty the captain of the *Buen Jesus*, named Don Francisco de Ibarra, and his crew; he retained the pilot named Juan de Sant Aval, and two negro slaves, and two ship-boys of mixed race. On the 6th, James Dircksz of Leiden, a sailor, was condemned and shot for stealing the bread of some other sailors, and a jar of oil from the hold. On the 7th, the Dutch burned the prize *Los Picos*: half the cargo of tallow was still on board. "On the 25th April, Nicolas Pietersz, the master of the prize *Buen Jesus*, came on board the admiral to tell him that one of the negroes whom he had detained, named Manuel, had declared to him that in that same ship there had been three barrels full of gold, that he had assisted in taking them on board, and that during the night of the chase Captain Francisco de Ibarra had had them cast into the sea for the Dutch not to profit by them. Upon receipt of this news the admiral had the pilot examined again, and the other negro named Sebastian; at first they denied it, but being put to torture, they acknowledged all. They said that there were fifty-two small cases, containing each four arrobas, full of gold, and besides, five hundred bars of gold, weighing eight, ten, and twelve pounds, so that altogether there was 10,200 lbs. of gold; and that the captain had so scrupulously cast all in the sea, that when they told him that there was still a little more concealed in the hold, he had it brought out and thrown away, so that not a piece should remain. The admiral did not fail to search the vessel again all over, but nothing was found, except in the pilot's hose, where there was a little bag with just a pound of gold."

As the Dutch had heard from the Spanish pilot of three ships of war from Lima that were looking after them, they made sail for the Philippines, with the intention of touching at the Ladrones, and seeking the island of Buena Vista or Guam in thirteen degrees north latitude. "On the 30th of June of the same year, 1600, the admiral and council of

April, Oliver de Noort set at liberty the captain of the *Buen Jesus*, named Don Francisco de Ibarra, and his crew; he retained the pilot named Juan de Sant Aval, and two negro slaves, and two ship-boys of mixed race. On the 6th, James Dircksz of Leiden, a sailor, was condemned and shot for stealing the bread of some other sailors, and a jar of oil from the hold. On the 7th, the Dutch burned the prize *Los Picos*: half the cargo of tallow was still on board. "On the 25th April, Nicolas Pietersz, the master of the prize *Buen Jesus*, came on board the admiral to tell him that one of the negroes whom he had detained, named Manuel, had declared to him that in that same ship there had been three barrels full of gold, that he had assisted in taking them on board, and that during the night of the chase Captain Francisco de Ibarra had had them cast into the sea for the Dutch not to profit by them. Upon receipt of this news the admiral had the pilot examined again, and the other negro named Sebastian; at first they denied it, but being put to torture, they acknowledged all. They said that there were fifty-two small cases, containing each four arrobas, full of gold, and besides, five hundred bars of gold, weighing eight, ten, and twelve pounds, so that altogether there was 10,200 lbs. of gold; and that the captain had so scrupulously cast all in the sea, that when they told him that there was still a little more concealed in the hold, he had it brought out and thrown away, so that not a piece should remain. The admiral did not fail to search the vessel again all over, but nothing was found, except in the pilot's hose, where there was a little bag with just a pound of gold."

As the Dutch had heard from the Spanish pilot of three ships of war from Lima that were looking after them, they made sail for the Philippines, with the intention of touching at the Ladrones, and seeking the island of Buena Vista or Guam in thirteen degrees north latitude. "On the 30th of June of the same year, 1600, the admiral and council of war resolved to have the Spanish pilot thrown into the sea, because, although he ate in the admiral's cabin and was very civilly treated, he had gone as far as to say, in the presence of some of the crew, that he had been poisoned; a malignant imagination, which he had conceived because he had found himself ill. He even had the impudence to maintain this imposition in presence of all the officers. Besides this, he had not only sought to escape himself, but had solicited the negroes and ship-boys to do the same." On the 15th August the prize *Buen Jesus* was abandoned, as it was very leaky. * * *

On the 14th October they sighted land of the Philippines, which they believed to be the Cape of Espiritu Santo: on the 16th, while they were at anchor off the coast, a canoe came off with a Spaniard on board; he did not venture to come very near, so the Dutch hoisted Spanish colours and dressed up a sailor as a monk, when he took courage and came on board, where the admiral received him well, and told him that they were French who had a commission from the King of Spain to go to Manila, but that the length of the voyage had put them in want of refreshments; he also said that their pilot was dead, and that was why they had entered that bay without knowing where they were. The Spaniard, whose name was Enrique Nuñez, told them they were in a bay called La Bahia, seven or eight leagues to the north of the Straits of Manila; and he ordered the Indians to fetch them rice, fowls and pigs, which they did, but would only take money in payment. On the 17th October another Spaniard came with a halbard; he was named Francisco Rodriguez, and was sergeant of all the district. Most of the Indians were naked; some were clothed with a linen dress, others in Spanish fashion with doublets and hose. "They are weak people, and have no arms, so that the Spaniards easily master them. They pay a tribute of three reals, that is a little less than three florins of Holland, a head, both men and women, of more than twenty years of age. There are very few Spaniards in each district; they have a priest for each, whom the inhabitants hold in great veneration, so much so, that it is only for want of priests if they do not hold all these islands in servitude, for there are even places where there are neither priests nor Spaniards, and nevertheless they cause the tribute to be paid there."

In the afternoon the admiral dismissed Enrique Nuñez and made him a respectable present, because they had obtained much fresh provisions through him: a sailor named James Lock, who spoke good Spanish, was ordered to go with him on shore. Every one in this country believed that these ships had a commission from the King of Spain, and without this belief the people would not have shown such good will.

"On the 18th October they saw a Spanish captain and a priest come off to the ships. The captain had leave to come on board, but the priest remained in the canoe. After the first compliments, he asked the admiral to show him his commission, because it was forbidden them to trade with strangers. The general showed him the commission which he held from Prince Maurice, which caused him great astonishment, for he had thought these two ships from Acapulco, a port of New Spain.

"As James Lock was still on shore, the general sent back one of the Spaniards with a letter, by which he asked for him to be sent back, failing which he would carry off in his stead the captain who was with him, and who was named Rodrigo Arias Xiron. Next day the priest came back, and asked of the admiral an assurance in writing to set free the captain as soon as Lock was restored to him; this was done, and some presents were also given to the captain."

After that time no more provisions were supplied: the Dutch had taken on board two Indians who were well known at Capul. The 20th, at dawn, they made for the

Manila straits. On the 21st the *Concord* found a Spanish vessel with twenty-five measures of rice and seven hundred fowls; the crew had abandoned it and fled. They unloaded it and sunk it: the Indian pilot said it belonged to a Spaniard, who was to take in some planks and go on to Manila. The 24th they entered the Manila straits, and came near the isle of Capul, and anchored off a sandy bay and village to the west of the island. On the morning of the 25th they saw that the inhabitants of the village had run away. "On the 27th, as no one appeared, the admiral sent some men on shore, and fired at the houses with large cannon to frighten the inhabitants. At the noise a Chinaman came from another village to the Dutch, who took him to the admiral. They could not understand him, but he made signs that he would bring provisions; and a present was given him, and he was promised money for anything he brought. The sailors who had gone on shore left there one of their number, named John Calleway, of London, a musician and player on instruments. They did not know how he had separated from them, and suspected that the Indians had attacked him on seeing him far from the others: one of the Indian pilots was also detained. The following night the other pilot, who had been taken in La Bahia, jumped into the water and escaped, in spite of the good treatment he had received from the admiral. He was named Francisco Tello, from the name of the governor of Manila, who had presented him at baptism. For the Spaniards act in that manner in that country: they pay some honour to the Indians when it costs them nothing, and give them even some small commission to win them over.

"On the 28th the admiral landed with thirty-two men and caused several villages to be set on fire,[1] whose inhabitants had run away with their property, so that nothing was found there, and no Indian made his appearance." * * *

[1] See note, p. 169.

"The night of the 22nd October the negro Manuel, who was on board the *Concord*, got down into the boat and escaped, contrary to all the promises which he had made of remaining in the service of the Dutch. The admiral then had the other negro, named Sebastian, examined, who owned that he had been acquainted with the design of his comrade, and that he had had the same intention, but that he had not thought the opportunity which Manuel had availed himself of sufficiently safe.

"The admiral, seeing the ingratitude of these negroes, and that all the good treatment practised towards them was of no use, and that they were always disposed and ready to betray the Dutch, ordered Sebastian's brains to be blown out with an arquebuse, so as not to be again exposed to his treasons. Before dying, he again said that all that the Spanish pilot and he had before declared respecting the gold which had been in the prize *Buen Jesus* was true.

"The 31st October part of the crew went again on shore to seek for victuals: they found in a certain place more than thirty measures of rice, but they saw no one. Every one had run away to hide in the woods. They then again burned four villages, each of fifty or sixty houses."

On the 1st November the two Dutch ships again sailed for Manila: on the 5th they saw a canoe and sent a boat to fetch it; it contained nine Indians, two of whom they kept to show them the way to Manila, the rest were let go.

"Letters were found in their possession, with an authorisation from the governor, under the seal of the King of Spain, which were addressed to a priest who lived in a place named Bovillan, sixty leagues from Manila. The contents of these letters were to the effect that complaints had been made to the governor on the subject of certain Spaniards who had much ill-treated the Indians; and the governor gave orders to the priest to take informations on these acts, and to transfer the guilty to Manila at the king's expense."

On the 6th November, after remaining for some days sheltered behind an island four leagues from Capul, on account of contrary winds and calms, they captured a boat which ran on shore, and the men escaped into the woods: this boat carried four Spaniards and some Indians, and was taking half a barrel of powder, a quantity of balls and pieces of iron: the admiral unloaded the boat and had it sunk. One of the Spaniards came, and, on the promise of the Dutch not to hurt him, let himself be taken on board: from him they learned that the boat was going to Soubon to go to make war on the Moluccas, whose people had been plundering some of the Philippines. On the 7th they saw a Chinese vessel of 100 or 120 tons, which they call a champan: the master of it, a Chinese of Canton, had learned Portuguese at Malacca, and was of great assistance to the Dutch; he informed them that there were two large ships of New Spain and a little Flemish vessel bought from people of Malacca anchored at Cabite, the port of Manila, two leagues from it; that this port was defended by two forts, but that they then had neither cannon nor soldiers. He also said that the houses of Manila were very crowded, that the town was surrounded by a rampart. More than 15,000 Chinese live outside. Every year four hundred ships come from Chincheo in China with silks and other goods, and take silver coin in return; they came between Christmas and Easter. Also two ships were expected in November from Japan, with iron, flour and other victuals: there was a little island called Maravilla, about fifteen leagues from the town, with a good anchorage. From there it would be easy to reconnoitre the country.

On the 9th November the two ships weighed, and on the 11th they anchored half a league off an island named Banklingle. On the 15th, as they were still at anchor, they discovered two boats going to Manila with their cargoes as tribute. This adventure supplied them with two hundred and fifty fowls and fifty pigs, for which the admiral gave the Indians a few pieces of cloth and a letter to the governor of Manila, saying he would come and visit him. On the 16th they again set sail, and captured two canoes with thirty pigs and one hundred fowls going to Manila: the Indians were set free, and charged with another letter to the governor begging him not to take it ill that they carried off his tributes, because the Lord had need of them. The 21st the wind was so contrary that the two ships had to return to Banklingle: here they took another Chinese champan, quite new; the crew had escaped to the woods. During the night the champan, which had been taken before on the 7th, and in which James Thuniz had been put as pilot with five other Dutchmen and five Chinese, set sail; the crew called out to ask the admiral if they were to steer south. The admiral sent to tell them to stop and cast anchor again. It is not known what became of that champan, for it was not seen again: the Chinese were suspected of having cut the Dutchmen's throats and of having carried off the vessel. The master and pilot of the champan, who had been all this time detained on board the admiral's ship, made as much noise as if the Dutch had been the cause of this loss; they complained bitterly, and bore with impatience the loss of their champan and merchandise, protesting that they knew nothing of what had happened. * * *

On the 24th the ships came to the bay of Manila, and could not fetch the island Mirabilis, and anchored on the west side of the bay, behind a point twelve leagues from the town.

On the 3rd December, 1600, the admiral's ship was at anchor, and the *Concord* under sail: she discovered a large ship and captured her, and brought the captain and some of the chief men of the crew aboard of the admiral. It was one of the Japanese ships which the Chinese master had said was coming. The admiral received the Japanese captain well, his name was Jamasta Cristissamundo: the admiral asked him for some provisions, on which he sent twenty-nine baskets of flour, eight baskets of fish, some hams and a wooden anchor with its cable. The admiral gave him three muskets and some pieces of stuff: he also asked for a passport and flag, and the admiral gave him one in the name of Prince Maurice. In acknowledgment the captain gave him a Japanese boy of eight years old: he then made for Manila.

On the 9th the *Concord* brought in a boat loaded with wine, which the Spanish crew had abandoned: the wine tasted like the spirits made from a kind of cocoa nut; the wine was divided between the two ships, and the boat sunk: more boats with fowls and rice were captured.

"The morning of the 14th December, which was a Thursday, when they had their topmasts struck, they saw two sail come out of the straits of Manila, they took them at first for frigates; but as they approached it was seen that they were large ships, and it was known that they came to challenge. At once the topmasts were raised, and the artillery and other arms were got in readiness to receive them.

"The Manila admiral, who had taken the van, came within range of the cannon of the Dutch; and after that these had discharged their broadside, he came and grappled with the Dutch ship, and part of his crew sprung on board of her, with a furious mien, carrying shields and gilded helmets, and all sorts of armour; they shouted frightfully, 'Amayna Perros, Amayna,' that is to say, 'Strike dogs, strike your sails and flag.'

"The Dutch then went down below the deck, and the Spaniards thought they were already masters of the ship, the more so, that they were seven or eight to one. But they saw themselves all at once so ill treated with blows of pikes and musketry, that their fury was not long in slacking.

Indeed, there were soon several of them stretched dead upon the deck.

"However the Spanish vice-admiral was also bearing down upon the Dutch admiral, but there is much probability that he thought that his countrymen had already gained the mastery, for he went off in chase of the yacht, which had set her topsails and had gone to leeward of the admiral.

"The Manila admiral remained all day grappled with the Dutchman, because his anchor was fast in the cordage[1] before the mast of the latter, and the anchor tore the deck[1] in several places, which left the Dutch crew much exposed. Meantime the Spaniards frequently discharged their broadsides at them, and the others did not fail to answer them. But at last the Dutch began to slacken their fire, seeing that there were already a great many of them wounded.

"The admiral having perceived this slackness, went below the deck, and threatened his crew to set fire to the powder if they did not fight with redoubled ardour. This threat had its effect: they regained courage, and there were even some wounded men who got up and returned to the fight.

"On the other side the enemy was not less disheartened, and part of his men had abandoned the Dutch ship. There were close by two Chinese champans full of people, but they did not venture to come any nearer on account of the cannon. So the Spanish crew, instead of continuing their attack, only made efforts to cast loose, in doing which they had very great difficulty.

"However, the Dutch kept discharging their heavy guns upon the ship: at last the Manila admiral got away, and a little while after he was seen to sink, which he did so fast that he went down almost in the twinkling of an eye, and disappeared entirely, masts and all. Then the Spaniards were to be seen trying to prolong their life by swimming

[1] *Pont de cordes* and *ce pont*. This should probably be bulwarks and not deck.

and crying out *Misericordia,* seeming to be about two hundred, besides those who were already drowned or killed.

"The Dutch squared their fore yard, for their main yard had been cut down and their shrouds cut away. But what alarmed them most was the fire, which, from the continual discharges which they had made, had caught between decks, so much so that they had reason to fear that all would be burned. They succeeded, however, in extinguishing it, and then they rendered their prayers of thanksgiving to God, who had delivered them from so many dangers.

"When they saw themselves out of danger they lay to, to repair damages, passing amongst many of their enemies who were still swimming, and whose heads, which appeared above water, they pushed under whenever they could reach them.[1] Two dead bodies of Spaniards had remained on board: upon one of them was found a small silver box, in which were little papers full of recommendations and devotions to various Saints, men and women, to obtain their protection in perils.

"On the side of the Dutch there were seven men killed and twenty-six wounded, so that on board the admiral there remained only forty-eight persons, both of wounded and sound. When they got the ship under sail, they saw the Manila vice-admiral and the yacht *Concord* at more than two leagues off; and they thought the Spaniards had got possession of her, because it seemed to them that her flag was down, and that the Manila flag was still flying. Besides, they did not consider it possible for the yacht, which no longer had more than twenty-five men of the crew, including ship-boys, and which was a weak ship, to resist such a ship, which was fully of six hundred tons burden.

---

[1] See note, p. 169, and the plate taken from Oliver van Noort's voyage, in Dutch, the edition of Rotterdam, by Jan van Waesberghen ende by Cornelis Claessz tot Amstelredam, anno 1602, Bib. Imp. Paris, O $\frac{1200}{A}$. This feat is similar to that performed in those seas more recently with Terry's breech-loading rifle.

"The two Spanish ships had each crews of about five hundred men, both of that nation and Indians, and ten pieces of cannon. They were the same ships which go every year from Manila to Mexico, laden with silk and other rich merchandise. They had been armed to drive away the Dutch from these coasts, where they will not permit any foreign nation to come and traffic, and a crowd of Indians had been employed in them, who, having been instructed by the Spaniards, knew well how to handle a musket and other arms. The governor of Manila and of all the Philippines was named Don Francisco Tello de Meneses.

"The admiral having saved himself by his valour and by that of his men, made his course towards the island of Borneo, which is one hundred and eighty leagues from Manila, to refresh his crew there and refit his ship, which was in nowise in condition to sustain an attack from the Spanish vice-admiral, or to disengage the yacht."

On the 16th December they ran along the island of Boluton at five leagues from the coast: on the 26th they put into a bay of Borneo, and left it on the 5th January, 1601: by the 10th February they got through the straits between Java and Baly, passed near the Cape of Good Hope on the 24th April, and returned to Rotterdam about midday of August 26, 1601, after a voyage of three years.]^[1]

---

[1] This voyage of the first Dutch circumnavigator was popular in Holland, as appears from the numerous editions of it, the following list of which is taken from a *Mémoire Bibliographique sur les voyages des navigateurs Néerlandais*, by Tiele, published by F. Muller of Amsterdam, 1867. One copy of 1602 with the plates was priced at eighty florins.

1. Extract of Kort Verhael reyse by ...... Olivier van Noort, Rotterdam, Jan van Waesberghe, 1601, 4to, oblong. (Mr. Lenox of New York has a copy of this.)

2. Beschryvinghe van de Voyagie om den geheelen Werelt Cloot, ghedaen door Olivier van Noort van Utrecht, Generael over vier schepen, etc. Rotterdam Jan v. Waesbergen, and Amsterdam Cornelis

In the same year, 1600, two ships loaded with merchandise left Manila for New Spain; the flag-ship was the Sta. Margarita, whose commander was Juan Martinez de Guillestigui, who the year before had arrived with this command; and the ship *San Geronymo*, under Don Fernando de Castro. Both met with storms in the voyage, in thirty-eight degrees latitude and six hundred leagues from the Philippines, and suffered great hardships: at the end of nine months that they had been at sea, many persons having died, and much merchandise lost and thrown overboard, the *San Geronymo* put in to the Philippines, off the islands of the Catenduans, outside the channel of Espiritu Santo, and there was wrecked, the crews having been saved. The flag-ship *Sta. Margarita*, after the death of the commander and most of the crew, reached the Ladrone islands, and anchored at Zarpana, where the natives, who came out to the ship, and saw it so solitary and battered, entered within, and took possession of it, and of the goods and property which the ship carried: they took with them to their towns the few people whom they found on board alive; some they killed, and others they kept in various villages, maintaining them and giving them good treatment. The Indians carried the gold chains and other things of the ship hung round their

Classz, 4to, oblong, twenty-five plates. No date given. This edition is supposed to be the second.

3. Another edition, same title, 1602, 4to, oblong, same plates.

4. Another edition, 1602, 4to, oblong, same plates. (This or the third edition in Dutch is in the Bib. Imp., Paris. German type.)

5. Another in Dutch, 4to, oblong, 1618, same plates. (Roman type, two copies of this edition are in the Bib. Royale, Brussels.)

6. An abridgment and some additions: no date.

7. Edition of 1648, title printed, not engraved like the earlier.

8. 1649; 9. 1650; 10. 1652; 11. 1663; 12. 1684; 13. 1708; 14. 1764. There were two French editions, folio, 1602 and 1610: this accounts, perhaps, for the subject of the plate being engraved upon it in French in the Dutch editions. Van Noort was born at Utrecht in 1568, and died after 1611.

necks, and they suspended them to the trees, and put them in their houses, like people who did not understand the use of them.

In May of 1601 the galloon *Santo Tomas* arrived at the Philippines from New Spain, with passengers and soldiers and the return proceeds of the merchandise which had been overdue and deferred in Mexico. The licentiate Don Antonio de Ribera Maldonado came as commander of the ship, and to be auditor in Manila. A small vessel sailed in company with them from the port of Acapulco, but being unable to sail as much as the *Santo Tomas*, after a few days voyage, it remained behind. When they arrived off the Ladrone Islands some native boats came off to the ship, as their custom is, and brought them five Spaniards of the crew of the *Sta. Margarita*, which had been lost there the year before, from whom the news of that wreck was learned, and also that as many as twenty-six Spaniards had remained alive in the towns of those islands, and that if they would stop two days with the ship the natives would bring them.

The monks and people who came in his company tried to persuade the commander to wait in that place, since the weather was calm, to fetch away these men from the islands, where they had now been for a year; and some more spirited persons offered to go themselves ashore to seek for them, either in the galloon's boat or in the Indian boats: this the commander would not allow of, as he thought time would be lost, and his navigation exposed to risk. Without leave from the commander, Friar Juan, a poor lay brother, who came as head of some barefooted Franciscan friars who were on board the ship going to the Philippines, jumped into one of the Ladrone vessels, and the Indians carried him on shore to the island of Guan, where he remained with the Spaniards whom he found. The galloon *Santo Tomas* without any more delay pursued her voyage, to the great grief and regret of the Spaniards on shore at seeing themselves left amongst those barbarians; some of them died there later of illness and other fatigues. The galloon arrived at the Philippines, making for the cape of Espiritu Santo and harbour of Capul, at the conjunction of the moon, and a change of weather, and the land so covered with thick clouds that it could not be seen till the ship was close upon it, nor did the pilots or sailors know it, nor the part in which they were; and, running in the direction of the Catenduans, they entered a bay, called Catamban, twenty leagues from the channel, where they found themselves embayed, and so much wind and sea astern of them, that the galloon went upon some rocks near the land, where it was very near being lost that night with all hands. As soon as it was day the commander went on shore in the boat, and had the ship made fast to some rocks; and as the weather did not improve, and the ship was now in greater danger of being lost, and the cables with which she was made fast would give way, he determined to discharge the cargo there as quickly as might be with the boat. They at once set about this, and brought away all the people, the silver, and much of the goods and property, until, with country boats, the Spaniards and Indians of that province carried it all to Manila, a distance of eighty leagues, partly by sea and the rest by land: they left the ship, which was new and very handsome, there cast away, without being able to derive any profit from it.

The daring and audacity of the Mindanao and Jolo men in making incursions with their fleets into the islands of Pintados, had reached such a pitch that it was now expected they would come as far as Manila, plundering and inflicting losses; so that, in order to restrain them, the governor Don Francisco Tello determined, in the beginning of the year 1602 (deriving strength from weakness), that the expedition to Jolo should be made without further delay to chastise and subdue it, by means of the forces and men whom Captain and Sergeant-major Juan Xuarez Gallinato held in Sebu and the Pintados: and by sending him some more men, ships and provisions, with the necessary documents and instructions, for him to enter the island, chastise its king and inhabitants, and pacify and reduce it to obedience to His Majesty. By this means, until there should be an opportunity for going to the affair of Mindanao, which lies very near Jolo, the audacity of the enemy would be checked, and bringing the war into his country he would not come forth to inflict loss. Captain Gallinato went off to this expedition with two hundred Spanish soldiers, ships, artillery, and the provisions that were required for four months, which it was thought the expedition might last, and with Indians as crews for the ship, and for other matters of service that might occur. Having arrived at Jolo, and at the bar of the river of this island, which is two leagues from the principal town and dwellings of the king, he landed his men, the artillery, and the provisions that were needed, leaving his ships with a sufficient guard. The islanders were all in the town and dwellings of the king, which are on a very high hill above some cliffs, which have two roads for ascending them by such narrow paths and ways, that people can only go by them following one another in single file. And they had fortified the whole, and palisaded it with palms and other logs, and placed many small cannon, and collected within provisions and water for their maintenance, with a supply of arquebuses and arms, and without any women or children, for they had taken them out of the island, and had requested succour from the people of Mindanao, Borneo and Terrenate; and they expected it, as they had had notice of the fleet which was preparing against them in Pintados. Gallinato determined to place his camp close to the town before this succour should arrive, and to assault the fort, having quartered himself at a distance of half a league, in a plain close to the ascent. He sent some messages to the king by interpreters, and to the chief men of the island, calling on them to surrender, and that they would thus be acting in the best way for themselves. Whilst he was waiting for the answer, he fortified his quarters in that spot, entrenching himself wherever it was necessary, and placing his artillery so as to be of use to him, and keeping his men in readiness for whatever might occur. An answer was returned with deceptive and feigned phrases, making excuses for the excesses they had committed, and for not then doing what was asked of them, putting him off with hopes that they would do it later; all this with the object of detaining him in that spot (which is very sickly) until the rains should set in, and that they should have consumed their provisions, and the succour which they expected should arrive. After this answer, as it seemed to them that with it the Spaniards were more careless, a large crowd of people came down in a great hurry from the fort with arquebuses, and arms with handles, campilans and carazas; they might be more than a thousand men, and together they attacked and assaulted the quarters and camp of the Spaniards. This could not be done with sufficient secresy for the Spaniards not to see it, and have time, before they arrived, to put themselves in readiness to receive them; as they did, for they let them all come together in a body as far as within the quarters and trenches, and when they had discharged their firearms, then the Spaniards gave them a discharge, first with the artillery and then with the arquebuses, which, killing a great number, made them turn back in flight to the fort. The Spaniards continued in pursuit of them, wounding and killing, as far as half way up the ridge; for as beyond that the paths were so narrow and craggy, they retreated before the quantity of light pieces which were discharged from the heights, and the large stones which were sent rolling down upon them, and returned to their quarters. For several other days efforts were made to ascend to the fort, but nothing was effected; upon which Gallinato, judging that the war would be much drawn out, from what had been seen of it, built two forts, one where he kept his ships for the defence of them and of the port; and the other half a league further on, in a suitable place, in which they could take refuge and communicate with the camp. They were of wood and fascines, armed with the artillery they had brought, and the Spaniards shut themselves in them; and from time to time they sallied out, making incursions as far as the enemy's fort, in which he was always shut up, without ever choosing to come down or to yield: and he was convinced that the Spaniards could not remain long in the island. Gallinato saw that the rains were fast setting in, and his men were getting sickly, and his provisions running short, and that he had not accomplished what he had intended, and that it could not be done with the resources which remained to him, and that the enemy from Mindanao, with other allies of theirs, declared that they were going to drive the Spaniards out of Jolo; so he sent advices of all that had happened to the governor of Manila, with a description of the island and fort, and the difficulties which the enterprise presented, by means of Captain Pedro Coleto de Morales, in a swift vessel, towards the end of May 1602,[1] in order to obtain instructions as to what he was to do, and succours of more men and provisions, which were needed; and he charged him to return speedily with the answer.

When, in the kingdom of Cambodia, the Mussulman Ocuña Lacasamana and his partisans killed Diego Belloso and Blas Ruyz de Hernan Gonzalez, and the Castilians and Portuguese in their company, it was related that Juan de Mendoza Gamboa in his ship, with Padre Fray Juan Maldonado and his companion, Don Antonio Malaver, Luys de Villafañe and other Spaniards who escaped by embarking in

[1] A.H. Zilhijjeh, 1010.

this ship, went away down the river towards the sea, defending themselves against some prahus of Cambodians and Malays, who pursued them until they got outside the bar. Juan de Mendoza performed his voyage along the coast to Siam, where his principal business was; and, having arrived at the bar, he ascended the river to the city of Odia,[1] the court of the king, who received the letter and embassage of the governor Don Francisco Tello, though with less state and courtesy than Juan de Mendoza would have wished.

He then set about the business of his merchandise, and was so stingy in the matter of making some presents and gifts to the king and his favourites that he had great difficulties in bargaining for what he wanted, and the king was even inclined to take from him the artillery in his ship, having got a longing for it. Juan de Mendoza fearing this, sunk it in the river with buoys, in a place where he could again get it up when he should have to depart: and he left in the ship, for appearances, only one iron gun and some light cannon. There was in Odia a Dominican Portuguese monk, who since two years back resided in that court, administering the Portuguese who busied themselves there in trade: amongst them were some whom the king had brought out of Camboja and Pigu, in his wars with both kingdoms. These and other Portuguese had had some disturbances in the city with Siamese, and had killed a servant of the king, who, as he was little inclined to pardon, had roasted some of the delinquents; and as to the rest of them, and the monk, he did not allow them to go out of the city, nor from the kingdom, although they had asked his permission, and pressed for leave to go away. Seeing themselves without liberty and less well treated than they had used to be, and threatened with danger every day, they settled with Fray Juan Maldonado that, when his ship should depart, they

[1] This name means the court, which was then higher up the river than Bangkok.

should be secretly embarked and taken out of the kingdom. He undertook this; and now that Juan de Mendoza had concluded his business, although not as he had desired, because the king did not give him an answer for the governor, and put it off, and his merchandise had not made much profit, he determined upon the advice of Fray Juan Maldonado to get up his artillery some night, and depart with all speed down the river, and that the same night the Portuguese friar and his companions, who might be twelve men, should come out of the city secretly, and wait on the river eight leagues from there in an appointed place, where he would take them on board. This was executed, and the king, on hearing of the departure of Juan de Mendoza with his ship, without his leave or dismissal, and that he was taking away the monk and the Portuguese whom he was keeping at his court, was so indignant that he sent forty prahus with artillery and many soldiers in pursuit, to capture them and bring them back to the court, or to kill them. Although Juan de Mendoza made all the haste he could to descend the river, as it was a ship without oars and the sails did not always serve, and the distance was more than seventy leagues, the Siamese overtook him in the river. Juan de Mendoza put himself in defence when they drew near, and with his artillery and musketry hit them so hard that they feared to board him: notwithstanding they came up several times, and managed to enter, and threw in artificial fire, which gave the Spaniards much work, for the fight lasted more than eight days day and night, until they had arrived near the bar, when, to prevent the ship escaping them, all the prahus, which had remained from the past engagements, attacked together, and made the last effort in their power. Although the Siamese could not carry out their intentions, and got the worst of it in the number of killed and wounded, the Spaniards did not fail to suffer great loss; for there died in the fight the pilot Juan Martinez de Chave, the companion of the friar Juan Maldonado, and eight other Spaniards; and Fray Juan Maldonado was badly wounded with the ball of a small cannon, which broke his arm, and the captain Juan de Mendoza got some dangerous wounds. Upon this the Siamese returned up the river, and the ship went out to sea much battered, and the weather not very favourable for crossing by the shoals to Manila, nor for Malacca, which lay nearer to them; so they shaped their course for Cochin China, where they put in and joined a Portuguese ship which was there, and waited for her to make her voyage to Malacca, to sail in her company. There Fray Juan Maldonado and the captain Juan de Mendoza grew worse of their wounds, and both died. Fray Juan Maldonado left a letter, written a few days before his death, for his prelate and order of St. Dominic, in the Philippines, giving them an account of his journeys and labours, and the occasion of his death, informing them of the quality and substance of the affairs of Cambodia, to which he had been sent, and of the slight foundation and motives that there were for giving themselves so much trouble about that undertaking, and the slight utility that could be hoped for from it; and he charged it upon their consciences not again to become the instruments for returning to Cambodia.[1] The ship and its cargo went to Malacca, and there all was sold by the intervention of the judge for the deceased; and some of the Castilians who remained alive came to Manila sick, poor and necessitous after the hardships which they had undergone.

The affairs of Maluco each day assumed a worse appearance, because the ruler of Terrenate was making war openly

[1] Death allowed the poor friar to speak openly: he had perhaps now discovered that Diego Belloso and Ruyz Blas thought more of themselves than of the service of God, or even of that of His Majesty. It will be remembered that those adventurers made use of the Dominican monks to promote their objects and obtain the governor's consent to their expedition to Cambodia. See pages 46, 52, 87.

upon his neighbour of Tidore, and upon the Portuguese with him; and he had admitted some ships which had come to Terrenate from the islands[1] of Holland and Zealand by way of India, for their trade: and by means of them he had sent an embassage to England and to the Prince of Orange, respecting peace, trade and commerce with the English and Dutch: to this he had received a favourable answer, and he expected shortly a fleet of many ships from England, and from the islands, by whose favour he expected to do great things against Tidore and the Philippines. Meantime, he had got in Terrenate some Flemings and Englishmen, who had remained as pledges, with a factor who busied himself with the purchase of cloves: these people had brought many good weapons for this trade, so that the island of Terrenate was very full and well supplied with them. The King of Tidore and the captain major wrote every year to the governor of the Philippines, giving him information of what was going on, so that it might be remedied in time, and succour sent to them: and once there came to Manila Cachil Cota, brother of the King of Tidore, a great soldier, and one of the most famous of all Maluco; they always received men, provisions and some munitions: what they most desired was that an expedition should be sent opportunely against Terrenate, before the English or Dutch came with the fleet they were expecting: this could not be done without an order from His Majesty, and much preparation and appliances for a similar enterprise. The same message was always sent from Tidore, and ultimately, during this government of Don Francisco Tello, Captain Marcos Dias de Febra returned with this request, and brought letters to the governor and to the High Court from the king and from the captain major Ruy Gonzales de Sequeira, relating

[1] It is not to be supposed that our author was ignorant of Dutch geography: 'islands' is an Arabic idiom, as in that language Spain is usually called *jezirah*, an island.

what was going on, and the necessity that existed at least to send succour to Tidore. The king wrote especially about this to Dr. Antonio de Morga (with whom he used to correspond) the letter which follows, written in the Portuguese language, and signed in his own.

To Doctor Morga, in the Philippine Islands, from the King of Tidore.

I rejoiced exceedingly at a letter from your worship, written on the eighth of November last, by which I particularly understood your great sincerity in recollecting me and my affairs, for which may God reward you with long life and prosperity for the service of the King, my lord. For I understand that he keeps you in these islands with the intention of increasing your state, which I am not unaware is the same thing as a remedy for this island and fortress of Tidore. I have written to the governor, and to the High Court about the succour which I beg for, since I have asked so often, as it is so necessary to bring it; for by this the injury may be checked, which later may cost much to the King our lord. Do you favour me in this, or at least for what may be necessary for this fortress, for it will render a great service to God, and to the King, my lord. God preserve your worship with life for many years. From this island of Tidore to day eighth of March of 1601.

THE KING OF TIDORE.

The bearer of this, who is Marcos Dias, will give your worship a flaggon, with a little bottle of Moorish brass workmanship. I send this that your worship may remember this your friend.

Marcos Dias returned to Tidore in the first monsoon at the beginning of the year six hundred and two, with an answer to his embassage, and the succour which it requested of provisions, munitions, and a few soldiers, with which he was satisfied, until there was an opportunity to make with due preparation the expedition from Manila to Terrenate, as was desired.

CHAPTER VII.

Of the Government of Don Pedro de Acuña, Governor and President of the Philippines; and of that which happened in his time, until he died in June of the year 1606, after having returned to Manila from Maluco, having accomplished the conquest of the isles subject to the King of Terrenate.

In the month of May of six hundred and two, four ships arrived at Manila from New Spain, with a new Governor and President of the High Court, named Don Pedro de Acuña, Knight of the Order of St. John, Commander of Salamanca, who had just been Governor of Cartagena, on the main land. He was received into the government with much satisfaction on the part of all the country, for the necessity which was felt of some one who should be as experienced in warlike matters as vigilant and careful in administration. Don Francisco Tello, his predecesor, who waited for his successor, had to remain in Manila until the following year of 1603, when, in the month of April, he died of a sudden illness. The new governor, seeing that affairs were in such extremities and required setting up, and so little substance in the royal exchequer for doing it, thought his lot was not so good as he had imagined when he was appointed; for the state of affairs obliged him to risk part of his reputation, without being able to remedy them in as short a time as was expedient. He took courage as far as was possible, and omitted no personal labour wherever it was required. He began with what was to be done inside Manila and its neighbourhood; putting galleys and other vessels on the stocks, which were very much wanted to defend the seas, which were full of enemies and corsairs from other islands, especially people of Mindanao. He proposed going at once to visit the provinces of Pintados in person, in order sooner to remedy the necessities of that part, which was what caused most anxiety, and he was obliged to defer it for some months in order to attend to the affairs of Japan and Jolo, and of the ships which were to sail to New Spain, for all happened at the same time, and had to be provided for.

Chiquiro, the Japanese, having arrived at Manila, gave his message and present to the governor, Don Pedro de Acuña, who had only been a few days in the government; the business was at once entered upon, and the answer to be returned gave much matter for reflection how it was to be framed most expediently; since, although it was held to be an advantage and of great profit to possess the friendship of Dayfusama, and a matter of necessity to secure and establish it, even should it be by overcoming some difficulties, and although the navigation and commerce with Quanto did not altogether suit the Spaniards, nevertheless his desire should be satisfied by sending him a ship with some merchandize; but that the rest, concerning trade and friendship with New Spain, and the sending of masters and workmen to build ships in Japan, for that navigation which Dayfu was so urgent about, and which Fray Geronymo had assured him would be done, was a grave matter, and impossible of being put in execution, as being very injurious and prejudicial to the Philippines, because their chief security with regard to Japan is that the Japanese have no ships and do not know how to navigate, and on the occasions on which they have entertained the design of coming against Manila it has fallen through on account of this impediment, and to send them master builders and workmen, to build for them and teach them to build Spanish ships, would be to give to them those arms which they were in want of for the destruction of the Spaniards, and the navigation of the Japanese to New Spain, and their making long sea voyages would be very inexpedient;[1] and both affairs were of great import and consideration, and such that the governor could not resolve them (neither could it be done in Manila) without an account being given of them to His Majesty, and his viceroy of New Spain, whom they so much concerned. In order to take a course in this business, and not to retard the return of the Japanese officer with his answer, a moderate present was sent to Daifu by the same ship which had come, consisting of Spanish articles in return for those the Japanese had brought, and he was to tell him of the good will with which the governor accepted the friendly disposition shown towards him by Daifu, and the peace and amity with the Spaniards, and all the rest of what he was doing in their behalf; and he, the governor, would keep and observe the same conduct on his part, and that he would send this same year a Spanish ship with merchandise to Quanto, in conformity to the desire expressed, and that shortly. With respect to the navigation which he wished to make to New Spain,

[1] These considerations were very narrow, and contrary to the international obligations of mutual assistance incurred by the Spaniards by their trading with Japan; such treatment of Japan furnished that country with an additional motive for secluding itself and declining relations, the benefits of which were so one-sided: however, the Spaniards themselves may have felt this only nine years later, for, according to the *Dutch Memorable Embassies*, part i, p. 163, a large Spanish ship, commanded by Don Rodrigo de Riduera, came from Mexico to Wormgouw, near Yeddo, in August of 1611; these Spaniards were requesting permission from the Japanese emperor to sound the Japanese ports, because the Manila ships were frequently lost on the voyage to New Spain, for want of knowledge of those ports. "Moreover, these same Spaniards requested permission to build ships in Japan, because, both in New Spain and in the Philippines, there was a scarcity of timber fit for ships, and also of good workmen."

In the Philippines there was no scarcity of timber, so that the statement to that effect was either an error of the Dutch author, or a pretext on the part of the Spaniards.

and that for that purpose master shipwrights should be sent
to him to construct ships for that voyage, it was an affair
which, although the governor would endeavour to effect it,
and to give him satisfaction in all respects, it was not within
his power to decide without first rendering an account of it
to His Majesty, and to his viceroy in New Spain, because
he had neither power nor authority over matters outside his
government of the Philippines, but that he would immediately write and treat of this matter, and he hoped it would
be there settled satisfactorily, and that until the answer returned from Spain, which perforce would be a delay of three
years on account of the distance, Daifu would forbear with
patience, since more was not in his power, neither could he
do anything else. [A message was sent to Fray Geronymo
de Jesus][1] to satisfy Daifu with the best words he could find
to entertain him, but not to embarrass himself with him
from that time forward by promising to facilitate for him
such affairs as these. With this despatch the Japanese
Chiquiro departed with his ship, which was so unfortunate
in the voyage that it was wrecked off the head of the
island Hermosa, without either the ship or the people being
saved; it was not till a long time later that news of this
was received in Japan or in Manila.

Upon the receipt of the letters of Fray Geronymo de
Jesus, relating the changes which had taken place in Japan,
and the permission which he said he held from Daifu to
make Christians and build churches, not only the barefooted
friars of St. Francis, but others of the orders of St. Dominic
and St. Augustine put themselves in motion to go over to
Japan, and lose no time, and each one hurried to the

---

[1] I have supplied these words, which seem to have been omitted either here or at the beginning of the message to Daifusama; for it was Fray Geronymo and not Chiquiro who had made these promises of master shipwrights, and the governor of Manila could give instructions to the friar but not to the Japanese officer.

Japanese ships and captains that were at the time in Manila, and had come with flour and were then going back, to beg of them to take them; especially the order of St. Dominic sent four monks to the kingdom of Zazuma, with Fray Francisco de Morales, prior of Manila, at their head, in a ship which was going to that island and province, saying that its king had sent to call them—for this province only had not yet made submission to Daifusama. The order of St. Augustine sent two monks to the kingdom of Firando, in a ship belonging to that port, and as their head, Fray Diego de Guevara, prior of Manila, having understood that they would be well received by the king of that province. The order of St. Francis sent, in the ships which were going to Nangasaki, Fray Augustin Rodriguez, who had been before in Japan in company with the martyrs, and a lay friar to go to Miaco, to be companions to Fray Geronymo de Jesus. Although some difficulties occurred in the mind of the governor with respect to these monks leaving Manila, and their going to Japan in such a hurry, yet from the urgent instances which all used with him, they did not have the effect of preventing his giving them leave to depart. The friars arrived at the provinces for which they set out, and were received in them, though with more coolness than they had been led to expect, and they had fewer commodities for their maintenance than what they required; whilst in the affairs of the conversion, in which they had imagined that they were going at once to produce a great effect, there was less disposition than they had hoped, for very few Japanese became Christians; and in truth the kings and tonos of those provinces entertained them rather for the purpose of opening in their country, by means of them, trade and commerce with the Spaniards, which they desired for their interests, than for the sake of the religion, to which they were not inclined.

The governor, Don Pedro de Acuña, in fulfilment of what

he had written, that he would send a ship to Quanto, equipped and at once sent out to sea a middle-sized ship, named *Santiago el menor*, with a captain and the requisite officers and crew, and some goods of coloured woods, horns of deer, raw silk, and other things. This ship sailed with orders to go to Quanto, where it would find barefooted Franciscan friars, and sell its goods, and it was to come back with the return produce, and with the permission of Daifusama, to Manila; in this manner all that seemed necessary in the affairs of Japan, in the state they then were in, was attended to and provided for.

Daifusama, sovereign of Japan, who was waiting for his servant Chiquiro, whom he had sent to Manila with Fray Geronymo's letters, pressed him so much respecting the affairs he had at heart, and of which he had treated with him, that the friar, the better to satisfy him, and seeing that Chiquiro delayed his return, and that few arguments availed to satisfy him, asked permission to go in person to Manila, where he would treat and settle these affairs with the governor by word of mouth, and would bring him an answer; and he added that he left in the court Fray Augustin Rodriguez, and another companion, who had then already come to him, as pledges of his return. The king granted it to him, and gave him an outfit, with which Fray Geronymo shortly came to Manila, where he learned of the despatch which Chiquiro had taken with him, and began to treat of his business with the governor, Don Pedro de Acuña, saying that Chiquiro had not arrived in Japan, which caused it to be suspected that he had been lost. The governor's ship not being able to double the head of Japan in order to pass to the Northern district, put into the port of Firando, where the Augustine monks had established themselves a short time back, and anchored there. The captain sent advices thence to Miaco, of how he had not been able to get on to Quanto, with letters for the monks, and the present that was to be given to Daifu. The friars, the companions of Fray Geronymo, gave him the presents which had come for him, and told him that the governor had sent that ship at his disposition and orders, and that the weather had not permitted it to go to Quanto. Daifusama accepted it, though he did not show that he was convinced by what they told him, but rather that these were compliments to entertain him, and gave orders at once that the ship should effect its barter, and should return with some things which he sent to the governor, and that thenceforward it should go to Quanto, as it had been promised him; and with this the ship returned to Manila.

Fray Geronymo de Jesus arrived in so short a time at the Philippines, as has been related, that he had an opportunity to treat with the governor Don Pedro de Acuña of the business he had been charged with; and it was promised that ships should continue to be sent to Quanto to keep Daifusama contented. Fray Geronimo then returned to Japan carrying with him a good present from the governor of a rich Venetian mirror of a large size, glass, clothes of Castile, honey, some large China jars,[1] and other things which it was known would be to the taste of Daifu. The friar, on his arrival, was well received by Daifu: he gave him to understand the message he brought, and how his servant Chiquiro had been well despatched by the new governor, and nothing else could have happened to him than a shipwreck, since he had not turned up in so long a time; and he presented the things he had brought, with which Daifu was much pleased.

When the governor first entered upon his office, he found upon the stocks at Cabit two large ships, which were being finished in order to perform the voyage that year to New Spain. One, belonging to Don Luys Dasmariñas, which, by an agreement which had been made with Don Francisco

[1] Tibor.

Tello, the ex-governor, was to go with a cargo of merchandise; and the other, the *Espiritu Santo*, which had been built by Juan Tello de Aguirre and other townsmen of Manila, and it was to perform the voyage with the goods of that year, on account of the builders, the galloon remaining, after arriving in New Spain, as the property of His Majesty, according to an agreement and contract made with the same governor Don Francisco Tello. Don Pedro de Acuña made so much haste in preparing both ships for sea, that he sent them out of port with their cargoes in the first days of July of the said year of 1602, Don Lope de Ulloa going as general in the *Espiritu Santo*, and Don Pedro Flores, in command of the *Jesus-Maria*. Both ships went on their voyage, and in thirty-eight degrees encountered such great storms, that they were several times on the point of being lost, and they lightened themselves of much of the merchandise which they carried. The ship *Jesus-Maria* put in to Manila with difficulty, having been for more than forty days among the Ladrone Islands, without being able to pass them, during which time it had an opportunity of recovering all the Spaniards who remained alive of those who had been left with the ship *Sta. Margarita;* and among them Fray Juan, indigent friar, who had jumped into a boat of the natives out of the galloon *Sto. Tomas*, when it passed by there the year before. Five other Spaniards were in other islands of these Ladrone Islands, who were not able to come, though measures were taken to get them brought. The natives brought Fray Juan in their own boat to the ship, and the others also, with much affection and friendliness, and after they had been treated on board the ship, which they entered without fear, and had received iron and other presents, they went away crying and shewing much regret for losing the Spaniards. The ship *Espiritu Santo*, with the same difficulties, put into Japan, being unable to do anything else, having cut away her mainmast, and entered a port of Firando, twenty leagues from the place were the Augustine monks had established themselves on their arrival the same year from Manila, and where also the ship had put in which was going to Quanto. The port had good anchorage, but the entry and going out of it were very difficult, because it was a channel with many windings, with cliffs and high mountains on either hand, and as the Japanese with their boats towed and conducted the ship to bring it in, there was less difficulty. When it was within they set a Japanese guard over it, and those who went on shore were not permitted to return to the ship; the provisions which they supplied to them were not all that were necessary nor at proper prices, on which account, and much soldiery having come into the port from all the district, and the general having been asked to give up the sails, which he always excused himself from doing, he feared that they wished to take the ship and the merchandise, as had been done at Hurando, in the case of the ship *San Felipe*, in the year ninety-six. He was suspicious, and from that time forward watched with more attention, without leaving the ship or permitting his men to leave her, or that any of the merchandise should be discharged. Together with this he despatched to Miaco his brother, Don Alonso de Ulloa, with Don Antonio Maldonado, as bearers of a reasonable present to Daifusama, and to ask him to grant them leave and equipment to go out of that port again; these performed their journey by land. Meantime in the ship they suffered much molestation from the Japanese of the port and their captains, for they were not satisfied with the presents which they gave them to keep them in good humour, but they also took by force what they saw, and gave to understand that the whole was theirs, and that soon they would have it in their power. Fray Diego de Guevara, an Augustin, who was prelate in Firando, came to the ship, and told the general that he had put into a bad port of infidels and bad men, who would take his ship and plunder it, and that he should try if he could get it out of there, and take it to Firando, where he resided, and meanwhile watch and guard as best he might. When the friar was returning to his house with some pieces of silk, which they gave him in the ship for his new church and monastery in Firando, the Japanese did not leave him anything, and took it away, saying that all was theirs, and he went without them. There were on shore as many as a dozen and a half of Spaniards belonging to the ship, who were detained without liberty, and who had no opportunity of returning on board; and although the general gave them notice, as he had taken the resolution to get out of the port as he could, to make an effort to come to the ship, they could not all of them do so, only four or five of them. So, without waiting any longer, having turned out of the ship the Japanese guard that were on board, set the foretopsail and spritsail, loaded the artillery, and arms in hand, one morning he got the ship in readiness to weigh, and the anchor apeak. The Japanese rowed about the channel of the entrance of the port with many boats and arquebusiers, stretching across it a thick cable made of slender canes, and they made it fast on both sides, so that the ship should not go out. The general sent to reconnoitre what they were doing in a small boat with six hackbut men, who, having come near, were attacked by some boats of Japanese who came to take them; but, defending themselves with their arquebuses, they got back to the ship, and told the general that they were closing the outlet of the port with a cable; and this being looked upon as a bad sign, the ship was at once steered against the cable to break it, and a negro, to whom the general promised his liberty, offered to go with a large chopper lowered over the bows to cut the cable when the ship reached it.

The channel was cleared of the boats which were in it with artillery and arquebuse discharges, and on reaching the cable, what with the force with which the ship went, and the good use which the negro made of his chopper, the cable parted, and the ship passed through it. There remained to get through the many turns which the channel made before opening into the sea; it seemed impossible for a ship to get through them which was going out in haste, but God permitted it to pass through all, as though each turn had its breeze on purpose. The Japanese, who had come up in greater numbers, with their arquebuses, to the rocks and cliffs wherever the ship passed within range, did not neglect to molest her with many volleys, by which they killed one Spaniard in the ship and wounded others; the ship did the same, and with the artillery hit some of the Japanese, who, not being able to prevent the ship going out, remained without her. The general seeing himself out at sea, free from the past danger, and that a light north wind was beginning to blow, thought it best to venture to make the voyage to Manila, rather than seek and enter another Japanese port, and having set a jury mast[1] instead of the mainmast, and the North wind growing fresher every day, in twelve days he crossed over to Luzon, by Cape Bojeador, and came off the mouth of the Bay of Manila, where he found the ship *Jesus-Maria*, which also came in distress by the channel of Capul; and the two ships in company, as they had gone out of the port of Cabit five months before, returned to put in there in distress, with much loss and damage to the exchequer.

Don Alonso de Ulloa and Don Francisco Maldonado, who, while this was going on in the port where they had left the ship *Espiritu Santo*, had arrived at Miaco, gave their embassage and present to Daifusama, who, on being informed who they were, and of the entry of their ship into

[1] *Una cabria*, sheers.

Japan, and that they were from Manila, received them well, and in a very short time despatched them, and gave them chapas (passports) to the effect that the tonos and governors of provinces, where the ship had put in, should let it and its people go away freely, and that they might occupy themselves with refitting it, and obtain all that was requisite, and that all that had been taken from them, whether in a small or a large quantity, should be restored to them.

Whilst this despatch was preparing, news arrived at Miaco of the ship having gone out of port, and of the encounter which had ensued thereupon with the Japanese, of which they again complained to Daifu. He showed his regret at the departure of the ship and at the inconvenience to it, and at the excesses of the Japanese, and issued new chapas for the restitution of all the property, and a catan from his own hand, with which justice should be executed upon those[1] who had been guilty in this matter, and ordered that the Spaniards should be set at liberty, who had remained in the port, and that their property should be restored to them. With this dispatch the Spaniards left the port, and recovered what had been taken from them. The ambassadors and the others returned to Manila in the first vessels which sailed, carrying with them eight chapas of the same tenour from Daifusama, ordering that in whatever ports of Japan Manila ships might arrive they should be treated and received well, without any offence being done to them thenceforward. When they arrived at Manila they delivered these edicts to the governor, who gives them to the ships which go to New Spain, for what might happen to them in the voyage.

At the same time that the governor, Don Pedro de Acuña, entered upon the government, the captain and

[1] From contemporary descriptions of Japan, it is probable, as the emperor sent a sword of his own, that the guilty would execute justice upon themselves and perform *hara-kiri*.

sergeant-major, Pedro Cotelo de Morales, arrived from Jolo, with the message and advices of Juan Xuarez Gallinato respecting the state of affairs of that island, whither he had gone with an armament in the beginning of the same year; and the governor, desiring, on account of the importance of the affair, to make as great an effort as possible, determined to send him provisions and succours of some soldiers, which was done as soon as could be, and an order was sent to him to do his utmost at least to chastise the enemy, even if he could do nothing of greater importance, and according as the business might allow of an opportunity, he should go to do the same in the river of Mindanao, returning by Pintados. When this despatch reached Jolo, Gallinato was already so worn out, and his men so sickly, that the fresh troops that were brought only served to enable them to get out of the place; and, without undertaking anything else, he raised the camp, set fire to the forts which he had built, and embarked and came to Pintados, leaving the people of Jolo and their neighbours of Mindanao in greater spirits and disposition to come to Pintados, and the inner parts of the island, as they did do.

The governor, without delaying longer in Manila, went away with little preparation, in a galliot, with other small boats, to the island of Panay and town of Arevalo, to see with his own eyes what their necessities were, in order to remedy them. He left the affairs of war in Manila under the charge, during his absence, of the licentiate, Don Antonio de Ribera, auditor of the High Court.

As soon as the governor left Manila, the auditor had plenty to occupy him; for a squadron of thirty caracoas, and other vessels of Mindanao, entered among the islands, making prizes, as far as Luzon and its coasts, and having captured some vessels which came from Sebu to Manila, they made prisoners ten Spaniards, and amongst them a woman and a priest, and Captain Martin de Mandia, and they carried them off with them. They entered into Cali-laya, burned the church, and carried off many persons of all conditions amongst the natives into captivity. Thence they went to the town of Valayan to do the same thing, and the auditor having got news of the enemy in Manila, had already put it in a state of defence, with fifty Spaniards and a captain, and some vessels, which was the cause of their not venturing to enter into the town or into its bay; but they crossed over to Mindoro, and in its principal town led captive a large number of men, women, and children of the natives, taking from them their gold and their property, and burning their houses and the church, where they made prisoner the prebendary Corral, the priest of that parish. So they filled their vessels, and others which they took there with captives, gold and property, and moved about the port of Mindoro as leisurely as if they were in their own country, though it was only twenty-four leagues from Manila. Captain Martin de Mendia, prisoner of these corsairs, offered for himself, and for the other Spaniards who were made captive, that if they let him go to Manila he would fetch the ransom of all of them, and would go with it, or would send it within six months to the river of Mindanao, and if not, that he would return to put himself in their power. The chief who came as head of the armament acceded to this, with certain pacts and conditions, and made the other captives write, so that what was agreed upon should be fulfilled, and with that let him leave his fleet; he came to the city, and at his relation the auditor sent ships and munitions, and more soldiers to Valayan than what there were in that place, with orders to go out without delay in pursuit of the enemy, and they would find him in Mindoro. The Captain, Gaspar Perez, who was charged with this in Valayan, did not start as quickly as was requisite in order to find the enemy in Mindoro, for when he arrived they had gone out of that port six days before, returning to Mindanao laden with vessels and spoils. He went in their pursuit somewhat leisurely, and the enemy having put in with his fleet into the river of a small uninhabited island, to get wood and water, there passed by at this moment the governor, Don Pedro de Acuña, who was hastily returning to Manila from the town of Arevalo, where he had heard of the incursion of this corsair; he passed by so close to the mouth of this river, in two small champans, and a viceroy,[1] and so few people, that it was a wonder he was not seen and captured by the enemy. He was informed of the enemies stopping there by a boat with natives which came out escaping; and the governor having met Gaspar Perez a little later, made him make more haste, and gave him some of the people he had with him, to guide him to where they had left the corsairs the day before. They went to attack them, and the corsairs by means of sentinels whom they had now placed outside of the river in the sea, knew the fleet was coming, and went out of the river in haste and took to flight, lightening themselves by throwing into the sea goods and captives, so as to run more swiftly. The caracoas that belonged to the first and second in command of the Mindanao men looked up the vessels which were remaining behind, making them lighten themselves, and row with all the force they had of paddles[2] and sails. The fleet of the Spaniards, which consisted of heavier ships, could not make such an effort as to overtake them all, also because the enemy stood out into the offing without fear of the high sea that was running, like one who is flying, though some of the vessels of Gaspar Perez being swifter, got among the enemy's ships, and sunk some caracoas and took two; the rest escaped, though with great danger of being lost. The fleet returned, without having effected anything else, to Manila, where the governor had already arrived, with much regret and vexation at things having reached the pitch

[1] *Virey*, a kind of vessel.
[2] *Buzeyes*.

that these enemies, who had never ventured to come out of their houses, should be so proud, and emboldened to come up to the very gates of the city, inflicting so many losses and injuries.

Some years back, his Majesty had commanded that Portuguese India should prepare a fleet for the taking of the fortress of Terrenate, in Maluco, which was in possession of a Mussulman, who had usurpingly risen and made himself master of it, and driven out the Portuguese that were in it. The necessary preparation for this expedition was made (in India) of ships, munitions, and people; and a hidalgo, named Andrea Furtado de Mendoza, was chosen as general of this expedition : he was a soldier of experience in the affairs of India, who had gained victories of much name and fame, by sea and land in those parts, and latterly had gained a very notable one at Jabanapatan. He came out of Goa, with six galloons of the kingdom, and fourteen galliots and fustas, and other craft, with fifteen hundred fighting men, provisions and munitions for the armament. From the storms which he encountered before reaching Amboino, the fleet was so dispersed that the galleys and fustas could not hold on with the galloons nor follow them, and only three galleys and fustas reached Amboino in company with the galloons, and the other ships put into Goa and other fortresses along that course. The isle of Amboino was in revolt, and the fort which the Portuguese held there in great straits, so that it seemed fit to Andrea Furtado de Mendoza, while his fleet was collecting, and the galliots and other vessels which had been dispersed in the voyage, and while succour was coming, which he had sent to ask for from the fortress of Malacca, to detain himself at Amboino, (which is eighty leagues from Maluco) to pacify the island, and some towns of the district, and reduce them to submission to the crown of Portugal. In this he was occupied for more than six months, having had encounters with the enemy and the rebels, in which he always came out victorious, and he obtained the result which he had aimed at, leaving everything reduced and pacified. But seeing that his ships did not come, neither did the succour which he had sent for from Malacca arrive, and that it became obligatory upon him to go to Terrenate, which was the principal cause of his having been despatched, for which expedition he had a less number of men than what was necessary, and the greater part of his munitions and provisions being expended, he determined on sending to the governor of the Philippines, to inform him of his arrival with an armament, and of what he had done at Amboino, and how he had to go against Terrenate, and that on account of part of his ships having been dispersed and separated from him, and his having been detained some months in those undertakings, he had fewer soldiers than he could have desired, and was in want of several things, especially provisions, and he entreated the governor, since this affair was so important, and so much for the service of his Majesty, and that so large a sum had been spent on it out of the exchequer of the crown of Portugal, to favour and succour him by sending him provisions and munitions, and some Castilians for the enterprise, and if all this was in Terrenate by January of six hundred and three, when he would be before that fortress, the succour would reach him in very good time. He sent this message with his letters to the governor and to the High Court, by padre Andre Pereira, a Jesuit, and Captain Antonio Fogoza, who accompanied him, in a despatch boat from Amboino. In Manila they found the governor, Don Pedro de Acuña, and entered upon the business with him, availing themselves of the High Court and religious orders, and telling great things of their Portuguese fleet and the brilliant soldiers who came in it, and of the valour and renown of their general in all that he had undertaken, and certifying with that the good result of the assault on Terrenate on this occasion, especially if they got from Manila the succour and assistance for which they had come, and which it was just that they should give to them, since it was given from the Philippines whenever the king of Tidore and captain major of that fortress asked for it, and his Majesty had so commanded, and with the more reason and foundation on such an occasion as this.

Although Don Pedro de Acuña, from the time he had been appointed to the government, had the desire and intention of making an expedition against Terrenate, and whilst he was passing through Mexico had spoken of this affair with those who in that place had some knowledge of Maluco, and he had sent from New Spain to the court of his Majesty, to the Jesuit brother Gaspar Gomez, who had been many years in Manila and in Maluco in the time of the governor Gomez Perez Dasmariñas, to ask him to speak to his Majesty on his behalf of this affair, and he had hopes that he should make this expedition, nevertheless it seemed to him necessary to accede (without declaring his own desires,) to that which Andrea Furtado begged for, and giving him greater advantages, both for the importance of the thing itself, and also that by giving it so much assistance the general and his messengers should not give as an excuse, if they did not meet with success, that they asked the governor of the Philippines for aid and succour, and that he had not given it them, and that it should not be understood that he had omitted to do so because he himself was intending to make the expedition. Don Pedro de Acuña consulted with the High Court upon the matter, and it was of opinion that he should send to the Portuguese fleet, by the time which they had named, the aforesaid succours, with more than had been asked for. This having been resolved upon, it was put in execution, to the great satisfaction of Padre Andrea Pereira and Captain Antonio Fogaza, who in the end of the year 1602 went away despatched from the

Philippines, taking in company with them the ship *Sta. Potenciana*, and three large frigates, with a hundred and fifty well armed Spanish soldiers, ten thousand fanegas of rice, one thousand five hundred jars of palm wine, two hundred salted cows, twenty cases of sardines, conserves and medicines, fifty hundredweight of powder, cannon balls and bullets, cordage and other munitions, all under the command of the captain and sergeant-major, Juan Xuarez Gallinato, who had by this time come from Jolo, and was in Pintados, with orders and instructions as to what he had to do, which was to conduct that succour to Terrenate, to the armament of Portugal which he would find there, and to be at the orders and in obedience to its general. He made his voyage thither in fifteen days, and anchored in the port of Talangame, of the island of Terrenate, two leagues from the fortress; he found there Andrea Furtado de Mendoza, with his galloons at anchor, who was waiting for what was being sent him from Manila, at which he and all his people rejoiced greatly.

In the month of March of this year of 1603, there entered into the bay of Manila a ship from Great China, in which, as the sentinels announced, there came three great mandarins, with their insignia as such, and they came out of the ship and entered the city with their suite. They went straight, in chairs carried on men's shoulders, very curiously made of ivory and fine woods and gilding, to the royal buildings of the High Court, where the governor was waiting for them with a large suite of captains, and soldiers throughout the house and in the streets where they had to pass. When they arrived at the doors of the royal buildings, they were set down from their chairs, and entered on foot, leaving in the street their banners, equipage, lances, and other insignia of much state which they had brought; and went as far as a large hall, well fitted up, where the governor received them standing up, the mandarins making many low bows and courtesies after their fashion, and the governor answering them in his. They told him, by means of the interpreters,[1] that the king had sent them, with a Chinaman whom they had brought with them in chains, to see with their own eyes an island of gold, which he had informed their king was named Cabit, and was close to Manila, which was in the possession of no one; and that he had asked the king for a quantity of ships, and that he would bring them back laden with gold; and if it was not as he had stated, let them punish him with death: and they had come to ascertain the truth of the matter and to inform their king of it. The governor replied to them in few words beyond giving them a welcome, and inviting them to rest in two houses which had been prepared for them within the city, where they and their people could lodge, and that their business would be talked of later. Upon this they went out again from the royal buildings, and at the door mounted their chairs on the shoulders of their servants, who wore coloured clothes, and they were carried to their lodgings, where the governor ordered them to be abundantly provided with whatever they required for their maintenance during the time of their stay.

The arrival of these mandarins seemed suspicious, and that they came with a different intention from that which they announced, because, for people of so much understanding as the Chinese possess, to say that the king sent them on this business, seemed to be a fiction;[2] and amongst the Chinese themselves, who came to Manila about the same time with eight merchant ships, and those who were established in the city, it was said that these mandarins came to see the country and its condition, because the king wished to break off relations with the Spaniards, and to

[1] *Naguatatos*, according to Caballero's dictionary an American word.
[2] It probably was only a pretext; yet the prevalent idea in Europe at that time of an Eldorado was not less extravagant.

send a large fleet before the year was out, with a hundred thousand men, to take the country.

The governor and High Court were of opinion that they should be watchful in guarding the city, and that these mandarins should be handsomely treated, but that they should not go outside of the city, nor be allowed to administer justice (as they were beginning to do among the Sangley men), at which they felt some regret: they were desired to treat of their business, and then return shortly to China, without the Spaniards letting themselves appear conscious or suspicious of anything else than what the mandarins gave out. The mandarins had another interview with the governor, and he said to them more clearly, and making rather a joke of their coming, that it caused amazement that their king should have believed what that Chinaman they had got with them had said; and that even had there been in truth any such gold in the Philippines, the Spaniards would let it be carried away, the country belonging as it did to His Majesty. The mandarins replied that they understood well what the governor explained to them, but that their king had bid them come, and they were bound to obey him, and bring him an answer, and that having done their business, they had fulfilled their duty and would return. The governor, to shorten the matter, sent the mandarins with their prisoner and servants to Cabit, which is the port, two leagues from the city, where they were received with many discharges of artillery, which were fired at the time they disembarked, at which they shewed much fear and timidity; and when they landed they asked the prisoner if that was the island of which he had spoken to the king: he answered that it was. They asked him where was the gold: he replied that all that they saw there was gold, and that he would make it good with his king. They put other questions to him, and he always made the same answers, and all was taken down in writing, in the presence of some Spanish captains who were there with private interpreters; and when the mandarins had ordered a basketful of earth to be taken from the ground, to carry it to the King of China; and when they had eaten and rested, they returned the same day to Manila with the prisoner. The interpreters said that this prisoner had said, when hard pressed by the mandarins to answer to the purpose the questions they put to him, that what he had meant to say to the King of China was, that there was much gold and wealth in the possession of the Spaniards and natives of Manila, and that if a fleet and men were given him, he offered, as a man who had been in Luzon and knew the country, to take it, and bring back the ships laden with gold and riches. This, together with what the Chinese had said at first, seemed of much importance, especially so to Don Fray Miguel de Benavides, archbishop-elect of Manila, who knew the language, and that it went much further than what the mandarins had implied. The archbishop, therefore, and other monks, warned the governor and the city, publicly and secretly, to look to its defence, because they held it as certain that a fleet from China would shortly come against it. The governor at once despatched the mandarins and put them on board their ship with their prisoner, having given them a few presents of silver and other articles, with which they were pleased. Although, according to the opinion of the greater number of the townspeople, the coming of the Chinese against the country was a thing very contrary to reason, yet the governor began in a covered manner to make preparation of ships and other things for the purpose of defence; and he hastened to complete considerable repairs which he had begun to make in the fort of Santiago, at the point of the river, constructing a wall with its buttresses in the inner part which looks to the parade, of much strength for the defence of the fort.

At the end of April of this year 1603, the eve of St.

Philip and St. James, fire broke out in a small house of reeds[1] occupied by some Indians and negroes of the hospital for the natives of the city, at three in the afternoon, and reached other houses so quickly, and driven by a rather fresh wind so that it could not be got under, it burned houses of wood and stone, including the monastery of St. Dominic, the house and church of the royal hospital of the Spaniards, and the royal magazines, without leaving an edifice standing amongst them. Fourteen persons, Spaniards, Indians, and negroes, were killed in this fire, and among them the licenciate Sauz, canon of the cathedral; two hundred and sixty houses were burned in all, with much property that they contained; and it was understood that the loss and damage amounted to more than a million.

Ocuña Lacasamana, the Malay Mussulman, assisted by the mandarins of Cambodia, and his partisans, and by the stepmother of the King Prauncar, had killed and put an end to Blas Ruyz de Hernan Gonzales and Diego Belloso, and the Castilians and Portuguese and Japanese of their party who were in the kingdom, and his audacity had reached such a pitch, that at last he also killed the king himself, through which the kingdom became divided into factions, and there were greater disturbances than ever had been before: God permitting it, both for His just judgments and because Prauncar could not be deserving to enjoy the good fortune he had obtained in being restored to the throne of his father, since he had lost it together with his life; neither did Blas Ruyz de Hernan Gonzales and Diego Belloso, and their companions deserve to enjoy the fruits of the labour of their expeditions and victories, since these were changed into a disastrous and cruel death when it appeared that they held them most secure and assured to them; for perhaps their designs and pretensions were not so adjusted to the obligations of conscience as they ought to have been:

[1] *Zacate*; hence *zacatal*, a place of reeds, a thicket.

neither did God choose that the Malay should remain unpunished.

When this Malay understood that he was about to get the best position in the kingdom of Cambodia, after having killed the Castilians and Portuguese and their captains, and the natural and legitimate king who had favoured them, he found himself more deceived than he had imagined, because the disorders and insurrections of provinces induced some powerful mandarins, who held for and sustained the soundest party, to join together and revenge the death of king Prauncar with arms. So they turned them against Ocuña Lacasamana and his Malays, and giving battle to him on different occasions, they conquered and routed him. So much so, that the Malay was obliged to escape by flight, with the rest of his men who survived, from Cambodia, and go over to the kingdom of Champa, conterminous to it, with the design of disturbing it, and making war on the usurper who possessed it, and of making himself master of the whole, or of such part of it as he could. Neither did this turn out well for him, because although he brought war into the country, and the disturbances which he caused in Champa gave a great deal of trouble to the usurper and his partisans, at last he was routed and killed, and ended by paying in person miserably for his sins.

The mandarins of Cambodia seeing themselves free from the Malay, and the kingdom still in a disturbed state as he had left it, and without any male heir descending from Prauncar Langara, who died in the Laos country, turned their eyes to a brother of his, whom the king of Siam had taken prisoner and carried off with him in the war which he waged with Langara, and whom he kept in the city of Odia, as it seemed to them that this person had the best right by legitimate succession to the kingdom of Cambodia. They sent an embassy to Siam requesting him to come and reign, and to the king of Siam, who held him captive, to ask him to allow it. The king thought well of it, and with some arrangements and agreements which he made with his prisoner, he gave him his liberty, and six thousand soldiers to serve and accompany him. With these he came to Cambodia at once, and was received readily in Sistor and other provinces, and established in the kingdom, and from these provinces he went on reducing and pacifying the more distant ones.

This new king of Camboja, who from being a captive of the king of Siam, came to reign through such extraordinary events, and such various accidents, (for whom God held this good fortune reserved, and reserves other things of greater estimation if he know how to continue in the future that which he has begun to do) caused search to be made for Juan Diaz, the Castilian soldier who had remained out of the company of Blas Ruyz de Hernan Gonzales; and ordered him to go to Manila, and tell the governor from him how he was in possession of the kingdom, and what had happened with regard to the death of the Spaniards, and of his nephew Prauncar, who had not been in any way to blame for it; and that he recognised the friendship which Langara, his brother, and Langara's son had experienced from the Spaniards during their difficulties, and how well disposed he was to continue in friendship and relations with them; and that he again requested, if it pleased the governor, that he would send some monks and Castilians to be present at his court, and make Christians of those who might wish to become it.

Juan Diaz arrived at Manila with this message and embassage, and many promises, and finding Don Pedro de Acuña in the government, he explained to him the business. The governor was of opinion that it would be well not to close the door upon the preaching of the Holy Gospel in Camboja, which in this manner God had again opened, and he agreed to do what the king asked of him. In the beginning of the year 1603 he sent a frigate to Cambodia with four Dominician monks, at the head of whom was Fray Yñigo de Santa Maria, Prior of Manila, and five soldiers for their company; amongst them was the same Juan Diaz. They were to give the king the answer to his message in confirmation of the peace and amity which he desired, and according to the disposition they might find, the monks were to remain at his court, and send word what they thought of the situation. This frigate reached Cambodia, with a fair wind, in ten days' voyage, and the monks and soldiers in their company having gone up to Chordemuco, the king received them with much satisfaction. Immediately he built them a church and gave them rice for their maintenance, and liberty to preach and make Christians. As this seemed to the monks the work of Heaven, and that many labourers might be employed in it, they at once sent word to Manila of their good reception and condition by the same frigate, having asked the king's permission for it to return to Manila. The king gave it, and the supplies required for the voyage, and at the same time sent a servant of his with a present of ivory tusks and benzoin and other rarities for the governor, with a letter from himself, thanking him for what he had done, and asking him for more monks and Castilians. Fray Yñigo de Santa Maria, with another companion, embarked in this frigate, to come and give a better narrative of what he had met with; he died of illness during the voyage; his companion and those who sailed in the frigate reached Manila in May of 1603, and gave an account of what had happened in Cambodia.

About the end of the same month of May two ships arrived at Manila from New Spain, commanded by General Don Diego de Zamudio, with the ordinary succours for the Philippines. News was brought that Fray Diego de Soria, of the order of St. Dominic, bishop of Cagayan, had remained in Mexico, and that he was bringing the Bulls and pallium for the archbishop elect of Manila, and for Fray Baltasar de Covarrubias, of the order of St. Augustine, bishop of Camarines, on account of the death of Fray Francisco de Ortega. In the same ships were two auditors for the High Court of Manila, the licentiate, Andres de Alcaraz and Manuel de Madrid y Luna.

The captain and sergeant-major, Juan Xuarez Gallinato, with the ship *Sta. Potenciana* and troops which she carried to Maluco to succour the Portuguese armament which Andrea Furtado de Mendoza brought against the fortress of Terrenate, found those forces in the port of Talangame; as soon as this succour arrived, Andrea Furtado put on shore the Portuguese and Castilian forces, with six pieces of cannon, and marched with them along the shore in the direction of the fortress to plant a battery. He spent two days in arriving before the fortress, and getting through some passes and gullies which the enemy had fortified. Having arrived at the principal fortress, there was hard work to plant the artillery, for the enemy sallied out frequently against the camp and impeded it. Once they reached the doors of the very quarters, and would have done great damage there had not the Castilians, who were nearer to the entrance, prevented them, and pressed the Muslims so much, that some of them being killed, they turned back and shut themselves up in the fortress; at the same time five pieces were planted within range of it. The enemy, who had as many men as were necessary for the defence, and much artillery and munitions, inflicted much loss on the camp, whilst the cannon in battery produced no effect of any importance, being ill supplied with powder and munitions. So that what Gallinato and his people had heard on joining the Portuguese fleet, of the small supplies and equipments which Andrea Furtado had brought for so great an enterprise, was seen and experienced in a short time. That they might not all perish,

Andrea Furtado, after taking the opinions of all the officers of his camp and fleet, withdrew his artillery and camp to the port of Talangame. He embarked his people in his galloons, and made sail for the islands and fortresses of Amboino and Banda, where he had been at first, taking for the supply of his fleet those provisions which Gallinato had brought to him; and he gave him leave to return to Manila with the Castilians; this he did, in company with Ruy Gonzales de Sequeira, captain-major of the fortress of Tidore, who had just ceased holding that post, and who, in another ship, left that fortress with his family and merchandise; and they arrived in the beginning of the month of July of this year 1603, bringing a letter from the General Andrea Furtado to the governor Don Pedro de Acuña, which was as follows:—

Letter which the General Andrea Furtado de Mendoza wrote to Don Pedro de Acuña from Terrenate, on the 25th March, 1603.

There are no misfortunes in the world, however great they may be, that some benefit is not obtained from them. From all those which I have undergone in this expedition—and they are infinite—the result to me has been to know the zeal and spirit which your lordship displays in the service of His Majesty, for which I envy you and hold you as my master; and affirm that what I should most value in this life is that your lordship might hold me in the like estimation; and that as to some one particularly belonging to yourself, you should command me in what is for your service.

The succour which your lordship sent me arrived in time, the Divine favour permitting it, for that it was which gave this fleet to His Majesty, and the lives of all those who this day preserve them; and by what has happened in this expedition His Majesty will understand how much he owes to your lordship, and how little he owes to the captain of Malaca; for he was, in a measure, cause that the service of His Majesty has not been performed. When the succour which your lordship sent me arrived, this fleet was without any ammunition, as it was two years since we had left Goa, and it was all spent and expended on the occasions which had presented themselves. This being understood, that it may not be imagined that through neglect of mine the service of His Majesty was not performed, I disembarked on the shore, which I got possession of, the enemy losing many of his men, and I established the last trenches at a hundred paces from the enemy's fortress; I had landed five heavy battering cannon, and in ten days battering a large piece of the rampart was in ruins, in the part where all his forces were. During these days all the powder that was in the fleet was expended, nothing remaining with which to load its artillery even once; and if it should happen to me (of which I have no doubt) to meet any squadron of the Dutch, I shall be bound to fight with them; this was the principal cause of my raising the siege, after pressing the enemy severely both by hunger, and having during the course of the war killed many of his captains and soldiers. From this your lordship will judge of the state I was in of vexation and grief. God be praised for all, since He has been so pleased, and may He permit that the principal enemies in these parts may become vassals of His Majesty.

I depart to Amboino to see if I find succour there, and should I find sufficient, and if there is no urgent necessity in other parts of the South which oblige me to go to its assistance, I shall return to this enterprise, and will send full news of it to your lordship; and if I do not find there the succour which I hope for, I must go to Malaca to refit, and in whatever place I may be, I will always send notice to your lordship. I write to His Majesty, and am giving him a long account of the affairs of this enterprise, pointing out to him that it cannot be accomplished, nor maintained in future time unless it is done by the orders of your lordship,

and succoured and reinforced from the government of the
Philippines, seeing that India is so far, and that it cannot
be succoured thence in less than two years' time. Your
lordship should advise His Majesty in conformity with this,
so that he may be disabused in this particular of Maluco;
and I trust in God that I shall be a soldier of your lordship.

I do not know with what words to thank your lordship
or enhance the many favours which you have conferred upon
me; which have all been set forth to me both by Antonio
de Brito Fogaza and Tomas de Araux, my servant. These
are things which can neither be recompensed nor paid for,
except by risking life, honour and property in whatever
occasions may present themselves for your lordship's service;
and should they present themselves it will be seen that I
am not ungrateful for the favours I have received; the chief
of which, and that which I most valued, was your lordship's
sending me Juan Xuarez Gallinato with this succour, and
Sr. Don Tomas de Acuña, with the other captains and
soldiers: for to point out to your lordship the deserts of
each would be never to come to an end.

Juan Xuarez Gallinato is a person of whom your lordship should make much account on all occasions that may
offer, for he deserves it in all respects. In this expedition
and enterprise he conducted himself so satisfactorily—with
such zeal and discretion, that it was clear that he had been
sent by your lordship, and had served under the banner of
such distinguished captains, so that I shall greatly rejoice
to know that your lordship (on account of the services which
he has rendered to His Majesty in these parts, and to me),
has shown him many favours. That which I have judged to
be most worthy of being remembered of this expedition, is
that in the course of this war the proverb of the old Portuguese women has been broken, and between Spaniards and
Portuguese there has not been one angry word spoken,
both eating together at the same board; but this your lord-

ship must attribute to your own good fortune, and to the understanding and experience of Juan Xuarez Gallinato.

Sr. Don Tomas [de Acuña] conducted himself in the war not like a gentleman of his age, but like an old soldier, full of experience. Your lordship should make much of this relation, for I trust that you will be another father to him.

The sergeant-major conducted himself in this war as a good soldier, and he is a man whom your lordship should esteem, for I give my word for it that the Manilas do not contain a better soldier than him; and I shall esteem it highly if your lordship honour him, and do him especial favours on my account. Captain Villagra fulfilled his duty well, and so did Don Luys; in short, all without exception, soldiers, great and small, behaved so well in this enterprise, and on this account I remain under such obligations to them, that I would wish to see myself now before His Majesty, so as not to leave his feet until he had filled them all with honours and gratifications, since they so well deserve them. In conformity with this I shall always feel especial pleasure if your lordship confer honours and favours upon them all in general. Our Lord preserve your lordship for many years as I, your servant, desire. From the port of Talangame, in the island of Terrenate, twenty-fifth of March of 1603.

ANDREA FURTADO DE MENDOZA.

On the tenth of [July of][1] the same year the ships *Espiritu Santo* and *Jesus-Maria* went out of the port of Cabit, following two other smaller vessels which had cleared out fifteen days before, with the merchandise of the Philippines, to make the voyage to New Spain. The general of these ships was Don Lope de Ulloa, and in the admiral's ship, named *Espiritu Santo*, Doctor Antonio de Morga, went away from the islands to fill the place of Alcalde of the court of Mexico. Before going out of the bay, a violent

[1] The mouth is omitted in the text.

head-wind met both ships, and from three in the afternoon till the morning of the next day (although they were anchored with two thick cables, under shelter of the land, and the topmasts struck) they went on dragging with the heavy seas and wind upon the coast, with thick weather, and grounded upon it, in Pampanga, ten leagues from Manila. The bad weather lasted three other consecutive days; so much so that it was thought impossible that these ships could get out and perform the voyage, the season being now much advanced, and the ships very large and heavily laden, and they were much imbedded in the sand. Advices were at once sent by land to Manila, from whence they brought some Chinese ships, and cables and anchors, and with great exertions, which were used in this matter, both ships, each one separately, were fitted with tackle and cordage, which they made fast to the poop, waiting for the spring tide, and by force of capstans and of men, they got out the ships, dragging them by the sterns, for more than a league through a bank of sand, into which they had entered until they got them afloat on the day of St. Magdalen, the twenty-second of July. They at once set sail again, the ships having received no injury, and making no water; and performed the voyage and navigation to New Spain with light and insufficient winds. A violent gale from the south-south-west, with heavy showers, hail and cold, overtook the ship *Espiritu Santo*, on the tenth of November, in forty-two degrees latitude, and in sight of land, upon which the wind was driving: the ship was several times nearly lost upon it, and was in great distress, the rigging rent, and the crew worn out with the voyage and cold. The storm lasted till the twenty-second of November, and on that day in the morning, whilst the ship was in the trough of the sea, with topmasts struck, a waterspout of water and hail came upon it, with much darkness; and a thunderbolt struck the ship amidships, descending the mainmast: it killed three men, and wounded and crippled eight other persons, and entered the hatches, opening the main hatch with a blaze, showing the interior of the ship.[1] Another thunderbolt fell down the same mast amongst all the people, and stunned sixteen persons, some of whom were speechless and senseless for all that day: it went out again at the pump-dale. The following day the wind shifted to north-north-east, when the ship set sail and coasted the land with plenty of wind, till the nineteenth of December, when it made the port of Acapulco, finding in it the two smaller vessels which had sailed first from Manila. Three days later General Don Lope de Ulloa entered the same port of Acapulco, with the ship *Jesus-Maria*, having encountered the same storms as the ship *Espiritu Santo;* and since they had parted company, on leaving the channel of Capul of the Philippines, they had not seen one another again in all the voyage.

The same year of 1603, the governor, Don Pedro de Acuña, sent the ship *Santiago* from Manila to Japan, with merchandise, and orders to make its voyage to Quanto, to satisfy the desire and will of Daifusama: four monks, the most important of their order in Manila, were embarked in that ship for Japan, news having been received of the death of Fray Geronymo de Jesus; these were Fray Diego de Bermeo, who had been provincial, Fray Alonso de la Madre de Dios, Fray Luys Sotelo, and another companion.

When the ships *Jesus-Maria* and *Espiritu Santo* had sailed for New Spain, and the *Santiago* with the four monks for Japan, there remained the affair which had been started by the coming of the Mandarins from China, and more opportunity for attending to it, for finding themselves unoccupied by other business, they had nothing to do but put themselves on their guard against the Sangleys, and busy themselves with their suspicions that these people would cause mischief in some unexpected manner: this the Archbishop and some monks gave assurance of, and

[1] This passage is very obscure.

spoke of it in public and in secret. At this season there were a great many Chinese in Manila and its neighbourhood; some of them were baptized Christians in the villages of Baibai and Minondoc, on the other side of the river opposite the city, and the rest of them, pagans, were occupied and dwelling in these same villages, and in the shops of the Parian in the city, as merchants, and exercising all other employments; the greater number of them were fishermen, quarrymen, coal dealers, carriers, masons, and day-labourers. There was always more security with regard to the merchants, as they were a better sort of people, and much interested in behalf of their property : in respect of the others there was not so much, although they were Christians, because as they were poor and covetous people, they would be inclined to any meanness. It was always understood, however, that they would with great difficulty make any change or move, unless a powerful fleet came from China, upon which they could rely. Every day conversation went on increasing upon this subject, and with it suspicion, because some of the Chinese themselves, both pagans and Christians, in order to show themselves to be friends of the Spaniards, and free from all blame, gave notice that in a short time there was to be an insurrection, and said other things to the same purpose, which although they always appeared to the governor to be fictions, and the exaggerations of that nation, were not credited by him, yet neither was he so careless of them as not to watch and provide himself without ostentation for whatever might occur: and he endeavoured to keep a good guard in the city, and the soldiery well armed, and at the same time the principal Chinese merchants satisfied and in good humour, giving security to their lives and properties. The natives of Pampanga and other provinces of the district were ordered to supply the city with rice and provisions, and to come to its assistance with their persons and arms whenever it should be necessary.

He took the same steps with some Japanese who were in the city; as all this was done with some publicity, for it could not be in secret where so many were concerned, one and all became convinced that the occasion was certain to arise, and even many now desired it, to see the game begun, and have an opportunity to lay their hands on something. From this time forward they began to persecute the Sangley men by word and deed, both in the city and in the country districts, where they lived scattered about; the natives, Japanese, and soldiers in the country districts, depriving them of their property and subjecting them to other ill-treatment, and calling them dogs of traitors, and saying that they knew they intended to rise, but that first they would kill them all, and in a very short time; that the governor was making preparations for that purpose. This alone was sufficient motive for the Chinese to find themselves in the necessity of doing what they had not thought of doing.[1] Some more cunning and avaricious undertook to raise the spirits of the others, and set themselves up as heads, telling them that their perdition was certain in consequence of the determination which they saw the Spaniards had taken, unless they anticipated them, for they were so many in number that it would not be difficult for them to fall upon the city and take it, and kill the Spaniards and take their property, and become masters of the country, with the assistance and succour which would come at once from China when the good beginning which had been given to the business should be known there. They added, that to carry this out effectually it would be well to make a fort and quarters in some secret and strong place not far from the city, where their people could join together and take shelter, and where they could collect arms and provisions for the war, and which

[1] This observation of De Morga's may be applied to other cases where a like timidity and openly expressed suspicions have driven an opposite party, or one belonging to another race, into acts of violence.

at the least would serve to secure their lives from the injury which was expected from the Spaniards. It was understood that the principal promoter of these things was a Christian Sangley, who had been very long in the country, named Juan Bautista de Vera, a rich man much favoured by the Spaniards, feared and respected by the Sangleys, and who had been many times their governor, and had many godchildren and dependents, for he had become very much of a Spaniard and high-spirited. This man, with cunning and duplicity, did not go out of the city at this time, nor out of the houses of the Spaniards, to give them less cause of suspicion of himself; and from that place, by means of his confidants, he pushed on the business, and to make himself more certain of the result, and to know the number of people of his nation whom he had ready, and to keep a list of them, he had ordered his friends with dissimulation to bring him each of them a needle, which he feigned that he wanted for a certain work which he had to do; and he went on putting these into a little box, out of which he took them, and found that there were enough people for the purpose which he designed. The building of this fort or quarters was then at once begun, a little more than half a league from the town of Tondo, a hidden place between some lakes and marshes; they put in it some rice and other provisions, and some arms of little importance, and the Sangleys began to collect there, particularly the poor people, common men, and day labourers; for those of the Parian and officials, although they had been solicited to do the same, would not take that resolution, and remained quiet, taking care of their houses and property. Every day the disquiet of the Sangleys went on increasing, for this and the information given to the governor and to the Spaniards kept them in a greater state of anxiety and excitement, and caused them now to talk more publicly of the affair. The Sangleys seeing that their business was being discovered, and that delay might be very prejudicial to them, although they had agreed that the rising should be on St. Andrew's day, the last day of November, determined to anticipate it, and to lose no more time, and on Friday, the 3rd of October, the eve of St. Francis, they collected together very hastily in the before-mentioned fort, so that when the night had set in there were in it two thousand men. Juan Bautista de Vera, acting the part of a good robber, being the chief and leader of the treason, came at once to the city and told the governor that the Sangleys were in insurrection, and that they were collecting together on the other side of the river: he was at once arrested, put under a guard and in confinement, being suspected of his evil designs, and afterwards was executed. The governor ordered the troops of the country and city to be called out without sound of drum, and for all to be under arms. Night had hardly set in when Don Luis Dasmariñas, who lived close to the monastery and church of Mindoc on the other side of the river, came in great haste to the city to inform the governor that there was a revolution amongst the Sangleys, and to ask him for twenty soldiers to go over to the other side to guard the before-named monastery. Cristoval de Axqueta, sergeant-major of the camp, passed over with these men, in company with Don Luis; and every hour the noise increased during the silence of the night, which the Sangleys made as they assembled together, sounding horns and other instruments of their fashion. Don Luys remained guarding the monastery with the people whom he brought from Manila, into which he had gathered many women and children of the Christian Sangleys along with the monks. The sergeant-major then returned to the city, giving an account of what was going on. The drums beat to arms, because the noise and clamour of the Sangleys, who had come out to set fire to some houses in the country, was so great that it seemed that they were levelling them. They first burned a country-house of stone belonging to Captain

Estevan de Marquina, where he was with his wife and children, without any one escaping, except a little girl, who remained wounded and hidden in a thicket. From there they went on to the town of Laguio on the bank of the river and burned it, killing a few of the Indian inhabitants, for the rest came flying to the city; where the gates were already shut and all the people with arms in their hands leaning over the walls, and in other convenient posts, for whatever might occur, till dawn. The enemy, who now had a greater number of men, withdrew to his fort, to sally out thence again with more power. Don Luys Dasmariñas, who was on guard at the church and monastery of Minondoc, expecting every hour that the enemy was going to fall upon him, sent to the governor to ask for more men; and he sent him some paid soldiers and inhabitants of the city, under the captains Don Tomas Bravo de Acuña, his nephew, and Juan de Alcega, Pedro de Arzeo, and Gaspar Perez, by whose advice and opinion he was to be guided on this occasion. In the city all was confusion, clamour, and outcry, particularly among the Indian women and children who came to seek safety in it; and although to make sure of the Sangleys of the Parian, their merchants were invited to place themselves in the city with their property, they did not venture to do so, for they had always understood that the enemy, with the power of numbers he possessed, would take the city and massacre the Spaniards, and all would be in danger, so they preferred to remain in their Parian in order to join the party which should get the best of it. Don Luys Dasmariñas, with the succour which the governor sent him, being of opinion that it was expedient to seek the enemy at once, before they finished collecting together and swelling their numbers, left seventy soldiers under Gaspar Perez in Minondoc, and with the rest of the troops, who might be a hundred and forty men of the best of the hackbutteers, he went to the town of Tondo to fortify himself in the church, which was of stone, where he arrived at eleven o'clock in the morning. The Chinese had the same intention, and fifteen hundred of them arrived at the same place and time. A skirmish took place between both parties to gain possession of the monastery, which lasted one hour; and Gaspar Perez, with the men who had remained in Minondoc, came up to succour the Spaniards. The enemy retreated to his fort with the loss of five hundred men, and Gaspar Perez returned to his post, where also remained Pedro de Arzeo. Don Luys Dasmariñas, stimulated by this fortunate engagement, determined to go forward at once with the men he had with him in pursuit of the enemy, in the greatest heat of the sun, and without resting his men. He sent the ensign Luys de Ybarren to reconnoitre, and he brought news that the enemy was in great numbers and not far off. Although Juan de Alcega and others begged Don Luys to make a halt and rest his troops, and wait for an order from the governor as to what he was to do; the desire which he felt not to lose this opportunity was so great that, calling upon his men to follow him with hard and provocative words, he went forward until he reached a swamp. Having got out of this they suddenly entered a savannah where the enemy was, who, on seeing the Spaniards, all together with cudgels and some catans, and a few arms on handles, surrounded them on all sides. Don Luys and his men, unable to retreat, fought valiantly, killing many Sangleys, but at last, as these were so many, they cut all the Spaniards to pieces, without any more escaping than four badly wounded, who brought the news to Manila. This event was of great importance to the Sangleys, both because so many soldiers died in this place, and of the best of the Spaniards, and also on account of the arms which they took from them, and which they were short of, so that they flattered themselves that the accomplishment of their design was more certain and secure. The following day, the fifth of October, they sent the heads of Don Luys, Don Tomas, and of Juan de Alcega, and of other captains to the Parian, telling the Sangleys that since they had killed the best men in Manila, they should rise and join with them, and unless they did so, they would come over at once and kill them. The confusion and grief of the Spaniards in the city was so great, that it prevented their making the preparations and using the assiduity which the business required; but the necessity in which they saw themselves, and the spirit of the governor and his officers, made every one keep to his post, under arms, upon the walls, and having to the best of their ability manned the gates of the town towards the Parian and Dilao, and all that front by which the enemy might make an attack, they put a piece of artillery over each gate, with their best men, amongst whom there were monks of all the orders. This day, Sunday, the enemy finding themselves in high spirits with the victory of the day before, and their army increased with more men who had flocked to them, came against the city, burning and destroying all that they passed, and crossed the river, for there was no vessel with which to oppose them, as all the vessels were in the provinces of Pintados. The enemy entered the Parian, and with much fury attacked the city gate, from which they were driven back with the fire from the arquebuses and muskets, and the loss of many Sangley men; they then went to the church of Dilao, and from thence, with the same determination, brought up some scaling ladders to the gate and wall, which was lower, and met with the same resistance and loss; upon which they retreated with much loss to the Parian and to Dilao towards night. The Spaniards spent all the night in guarding the walls and preparing themselves for the next day; and the enemy, in the Parian and Dilao, were making carts, screens, ladders, fire machines, and other inventions, by which to get close to the wall and assault it, and burn the gates, and set fire to everything. The following day (Monday) at daybreak, the Sangley men collected together with these warlike implements, and putting their best men and the best armed in front, they attacked the wall with great courage and determination; the artillery dismounted the machines they were bringing up, and so much resistance was made and loss inflicted that they again withdrew to the Parian and Dilao. Juan Xuarez Gallinato, with some soldiers and a troop of Japanese, sallied out of the Dilao gate, against the Sangleys; they arrived as far as the church, and the Sangley men turning round upon them, the Japanese got into confusion, and were the cause of all having to retreat and take shelter behind the walls, the Sangleys following them as far as that.

At this juncture Captain Don Luys de Velasco entered Manila, coming from Pintados, with a good caracoa, into which a few arquebuseers were put, and others in boats under its protection, which by the river got up to the Parian and Dilao, and harassed the enemy who was there established, both that day and the two following days, so much so that they made them evacuate those posts: these vessels set fire to the Parian, and burned it entirely, and pursued the enemy wherever they were able to do so. The Sangleys seeing that their cause was declining, and that they could not effect the object which they had aimed at, determined to withdraw from before the city, having lost more than four thousand men, and to send word to China, so that they might send them assistance; and, in order to maintain themselves, they decided on dividing their forces into three bands in different districts, one to go to the Tingues of Passic, the others to those of Ayombon, and another to the lagoon of Bay and San Pablo, and Abatangas. On the Wednesday they entirely abandoned the city, and divided as has been said, marched into the interior of the country. Don Luys de Velasco, by the river, and some soldiers and armed Indians, who from all quarters came up to the succour of Manila, with some Spaniards who guided them, and the monks their teachers, followed in pursuit of them, exhausting them in such a manner that they killed and put an end to those who were going to the Tingues of Passic and to Ayonbon; the greater number and mass of the Chinese passed to the lagoon of Bay and the mountains of San Pablo, and to Batangas, where they thought themselves more secure; they burned the villages and churches, and all that they found in their path, and fortified themselves in those places. Don Luys de Velasco continued in pursuit of them with seventy soldiers, every day killing many of their people, and on one occasion Don Luys followed up the enemy so closely, that he was killed and ten soldiers of his company, and the enemy again fortified themselves in San Pablo and Batangas, with the hope of being able to maintain themselves there until the assistance from China should arrive.

The governor fearing this mischief, and desirous of making an end of the enemy, and that the country should become entirely tranquil, sent the captain and sergeant-major, Cristoval de Axqueta Menchaca, with some forces to seek the enemy and make an end of him. He set out with two hundred Spaniards, soldiers and adventurers, three hundred Japanese, and fifteen hundred Indians, Pampangos, and Tagals, on the twentieth of October, and took such skilful measures that he found the Sangleys fortified in San Pablo and Batangas, and with little or no loss of his own men, he fought with them and killed and massacred them all, without any of them escaping, except two hundred whom he brought alive to Manila for the galleys. He was occupied in this twenty days, and this put an end to the war. There remained in Manila but very few merchants, who had been well advised enough to place themselves and their property with the Spaniards inside the city, which, when the war began, did not contain seven hundred Spaniards who could bear arms.

When the war was at an end the want and difficulties of the city began; because as there were no Sangleys, who exercised various arts, and brought all the provisions, neither was any food to be found to eat, nor shoes to wear, not even for very excessive prices. The native Indians are very far from fulfilling these offices, and even have much forgotten husbandry, the rearing of fowls, flocks, cotton, and weaving robes, as they used to do in the time of their paganism, and for a long time after that the country had been conquered.[1] In addition to this it was understood that, after the revolution which had just been gone through, the ships and merchandise of China would not come to the islands; and above all, they lived not without fear and apprehension that instead of them an armament would come against Manila to avenge the death of the Sangleys. All this together weighed down the spirits of the Spaniards, and after having despatched this news by way of India to the Court of Spain, by Fray Diego de Guevara, prior of the monastery of St. Augustine of Manila, who, from various circumstances which happened to him in India, Persia, and Italy, through which he travelled, could not reach Madrid until two years had elapsed; they also at once despatched Captain Marco de la Cueva, accompanied by Fray Luys Gandullo, a Dominican, to the city of Macao in China, where the Portuguese reside, with letters for the captain-major and the chamber of that city, advising them of the insurrection of the Sangleys, and of the result of the war, in order that if they heard any rumour of an armament in China, they might send information of it. At the same time, they carried letters from the governor for the Tutons, Aytaos, and visitors of the provinces of Canton and Chincheo, giving an account of the outbreak of the Chinese, which obliged the Spaniards to kill them. Marcos de la Cueva and Fray Luys Gandullo

[1] See Appendix II with reference to the Chinese in the Philippines, and the textile fabrics of the Philippine islanders.

having arrived at Macao, they found that there was no news of any armament, but that everything was quiet; although the insurrection and much of what had happened was already known through some Sangleys who had come in champans, flying from Manila on that occasion. In Chincheo it was at once known that these Spaniards were at Macao, and the captains Guansan Sinu and Guachan, very rich men accustomed to trade with Manila, came to look for them, and having informed themselves of the truth of what had happened, they received the letters directed to the Mandarins to take and deliver them; and they encouraged other merchants and ships of Chincheo to go to Manila that year, for they did not venture to do so, which was very beneficial, for by their means a great part of the want from which Manila was suffering was supplied. Having despatched this business, Marcos de la Cueva supplied himself with some gunpowder, saltpetre, and lead for the magazines, and, leaving Macao, sailed to Manila, where he entered in the month of May, to the general satisfaction of the city at the news which he brought, which they shortly began to see confirmed by the arrival of thirteen ships with provisions and merchandise from China.

In this year 1603, when the month of June had set in, two ships were sent from Manila to Spain, under the command of Don Diego de Mendoza, whom the Viceroy, the Marquis of Montesclaros, had sent that year with the ordinary succours for the islands; the flagship was *Nuestra Señora de los Remedios*, and the admiral's ship *Sant Antonio*.

Many rich persons of Manila, terrified by the experience of the past troubles, embarked in these ships with their families and property for New Spain, especially in the admiral's ship, with the greatest quantity of wealth that has left the Philippines. Both ships met with such violent storms in the voyage—in thirty-four degrees latitude—before passing Japan, that the flagship put in in distress into Manila, dismasted, and having suffered great losses by throwing cargo overboard, and the admiral's ship was swallowed up by the sea, without any person on board being saved. This was one of the great losses and calamities which the Philippines underwent after those that had passed.

The rest of this year, and the year sixteen hundred and five, until the despatching of the ships to go to Castile, were spent by the governor in restoring the city, and providing it with supplies and munitions, with the special object and care that the determination, which he expected from the Court, to make the expedition to Maluco, (and of which he had received advices and promises) should not find him unprepared, so as to cause him to defer that expedition. In this he acted with great judgment and foresight, for at this same time the master of the camp, Juan de Esquivel, had arrived from Spain, with six hundred soldiers at Mexico, where more men were enrolled, and great preparations made of munitions, supplies, money and arms; which the viceroy, by order of His Majesty, sent from New Spain in March of this year [1605] to the governor for him to go to Maluco, all which arrived safely and in good time at Manila.

A little while after the ships for New Spain had left Manila, and those which the viceroy had despatched from that country had arrived, the archbishop, Don Fray Miguel de Benavides, died of a long illness, and his body was buried with the general prayers and acclamation of the city.[1]

About the same time during this year ships continued coming from China with goods, and through their principal captains Don Pedro de Acuña received three letters of the same tenour, copied into Castilian,[2] from the Tuton, the Haytao, and the Visitor general of the province of Chincheo,

[1] In 1605, this was the last year mentioned. This archbishop seems to have been a principal cause of the disturbances and massacre of the Chinese, by taking a leading part in exciting suspicion against them.

[2] *Trasuntadas.*

respecting the affair of the insurrection which the Sangleys had made, and their chastisement, which said thus:

Letter from the Visitor of Chincheo in China; written for Don Pedro de Acuña, governor of the Philippines.

To the great captain general of Luzon.

Having known that the Chinese who went to buy and sell in the kingdom of Luzon have been killed by the Spaniards, I have inquired into the cause of these deaths, and have prayed the king to do justice upon all who have been the cause of so great evil, that a remedy may be provided for the future, and that the merchants may have peace and tranquillity. In former years, before I came here as Visitor, a Sangley named Tioneg, with three Mandarins, by the permission of the king of China, went to Luzon, to Cabit to seek for gold and silver, which was all a deception, for neither gold nor silver was found; and on this account I prayed him to chastise this deceiver Tioneg, in order that it might be known and understood what righteous justice is done in China. It was in the time of the ex-viceroy and eunuch when Tioneg and his companion, named Yang lion, told the aforesaid falsehood, and I afterwards prayed the king to cause to be transferred all the documents of the affair of Tioneg, and to give orders to bring the said Tioneg, with the process, before himself; and I myself saw the said documents, and perceived that all which the said Tioneg had spoken was a falsehood. And I wrote to the king, saying that through the lies which Tioneg had spoken, the Castilians had suspected that we intended to make war upon them, and that on this account they had killed more than thirty thousand Chinese in Luzon: and the King did that which I entreated of him, and so punished the said Yang lion, ordering him to be killed, and he ordered Tioneg's head to be cut off, and set up in a cage; and the Chinese people who died in Luzon were not to blame. And I with others, we treated of this matter with the king, that he might decide what his will was in this and in another business—which was that two English ships had arrived near these coasts of Chincheo, a very dangerous thing for China, so that the king might see what he had to do in these two so serious matters. Also we wrote to the king that he should order the two Sangleys to be punished, and after having written the above-named matters to the king, he answered us, saying, for what purpose had the English ships come to China? if perchance they were coming to plunder, that they should at once send them thence to Luzon; and that they should tell the people of Luzon not to give credit to knaves and lying people of the Chinese, and that the two Sangleys should at once be put to death who had shown the port to the English: and with regard to the rest of what we had written to him, that our will and pleasure should be done. After having received this (*we send*) our messages to the governor of Luzon, that his lordship may know the greatness of the king of China and of the kingdom, for he is so great that he governs all that the moon and sun shine upon, and also that the governor of Luzon may know by how much reason and judgment this so great kingdom is governed, which kingdom no one for a long time back has ventured to insult, and although the Japanese have attempted to disturb Coria, which belongs to the government of China, they have not been able to effect it, but on the contrary, have been driven out of it, and Coria has remained in great peace and tranquillity, as the people of Luzon know very well by report.

Last year, after that we learned that through the lie of Tioneg, so many Chinese had been killed in Luzon, many of us mandarins collected together to concert in representing to the king that he should avenge himself for so many deaths, and we said that the country of Luzon is a miserable country of little importance, and that in old times it was the abode only of devils and serpents, and that from so great a number of Sangleys having for some years back gone to trade with the Castilians, it has become so much ennobled; in which country the said Sangleys have laboured so much, raising the walls, building houses and tilling gardens, and in other works of much advantage to the Castilians; and these things being so, why have not the Castilians held this in consideration, nor been grateful for these good works, instead of having with such great cruelty killed so many people: and although we wrote two or three times to the king respecting what has been mentioned, he answered us, having been angered on account of the above-mentioned events, saying that for three reasons it was not expedient to take revenge nor make war on Luzon. The first, because the Castilians, for a long time and until now, are friends of the Chinese; the second reason was because it could not be known whether the Castilians or the Chinese would obtain the victory; and the third and last reason, because the people whom the Castilians had killed were vile people, and ungrateful to China, to their country, fathers, and friends, since so many years had passed that they did not return to China; which people, the king says, he did not hold in much value for the above-mentioned reasons; and he only commanded the viceroy, the eunuch, and me, to write this letter by this ambassador, in order that the people of Luzon may know that the king of China has a great heart, great long-suffering, and much clemency; since he has not commanded to make war on the people of Luzon, and well may his rectitude be perceived since also he has punished the lie of Tioneg; and since the Spaniards are wise and discreet persons, how do they not feel grief at having killed so many people, and repent themselves of it, and entertain kindliness of heart towards the Chinese who have remained? because if the Castilians have a good heart towards the Chinese, and the Sangleys return who have survived from the war, and the money which is owing be paid, and the property which has been taken from the Sangleys, there will be friendship between that kingdom and this, and each year there will be trading ships; and if not, the king will not give leave for trading ships to go; on the contrary, he will order the construction of a thousand ships of war, with soldiers and the kinsmen of the slain, and with the other nations and kingdoms which pay tribute to China; and without sparing anyone they will make war, and afterwards the kingdom of Luzon will be given to those people who pay tribute to China. The letter of the visitor general was written on the twelfth of the second month.

Which according to our reckoning is March of the twenty-third year of the realm of Vandel. That of the eunuch[1] was written on the sixteenth of the said month and year; and that of the viceroy on the twenty-second of it.

The governor answered these letters, by the same messengers, civilly and authoritatively, giving explanations of the event, and justifications of the Spaniards, and offering to renew amity and trade with the Chinese, and to restore to their owners the goods and property which had remained in Manila, and that liberty would be given in due time to the prisoners whom he had got in the galleys, whom it was intended to make use of first for the expedition to Maluco, which was in preparation.

The entrance into Japan of the barefooted Franciscan monks, and of the Dominicians and Augustine friars continued in various provinces, both in the Castilian ship itself, which this year was sent to the kingdom of Quanto, as well as in other Japanese ships which came to Manila with their silver and flour to trade; this with the permission and license of Daifu, now named Cubosama; who this year sent by a servant of his certain arms and presents to the governor, in return for

[1] The Arab travellers of the ninth century mention that eunuchs were employed in China, especially for the collection of the revenue, and that they were called *thoucam*.

others which the governor had sent to him, and answered his letter by the following letter.

Letter of Daifusama, Sovereign of Japan, to the Governor Don Pedro de Acuña, in the year one thousand six hundred and five.

I have received two from your lordship, and all the gifts and presents according to the list, and amongst those which I have received, I was greatly pleased with the wine made of grapes. In former years your lordship requested leave for six ships to go (*to Japan*) and last year leave for four, which petitions I always granted; but this has given me great displeasure, that amongst the four ships which your lordship asks leave for, one should be that of Antonio, who set out on his voyage without my orders, which was to act with great licence, and with contempt of me. Would perchance the ship which your lordship wishes to send to Japan be sent without my permission? Besides this, your lordship and others have frequently made representations to me about the sects in Japan, and many losses have been suffered in that respect: this, not even I can grant it, because this region is named Xincoco, which means dedicated to the idols, which from the time of our ancestors until now have been honoured with the highest praise, and their deeds I alone cannot undo or destroy. For which reason it is by no means expedient that your faith should be promulgated or preached in Japan, and if your lordship desire to maintain friendship with these realms of Japan and with me, do that which I desire, and that which is not my pleasure never do it. Lastly, many have told me that many Japanese, bad and perverse men, who go to that kingdom (of the Philippines) and remain there many years, afterwards return to Japan. This is a cause of great displeasure to me, and so from this time forward will your lordship not permit any of the Japanese to come in the ships which come here; and in the other matters will your lordship endeavour to act with counsel and judgment, and in such manner that henceforward they should not be to my displeasure.

As that which the governor most desired was to make the expedition to Terrenate, in Maluco, and that this should take place shortly, before the enemy grew more powerful than what he was, for he had news that the Dutch, who had got possession of the island and fortress of Amboino, had done the same in the island of Tidore, and driven out the Portuguese who were settled in them, and had introduced themselves into Terrenate, and set up a factory for the clove trade. So when the despatches for this enterprise arrived from Spain in June of 1605, and the troops and supplies which at the same time were brought from New Spain by the master of the camp, Juan de Esquivel, the governor spent the remainder of the year in getting ready the ships, men, and provisions which he thought necessary for the undertaking, and leaving in Manila what was requisite for its defence, and he set out, in the beginning of the year 1606, for the provinces of Pintados, where the fleet was collecting.

On the fifteenth day of February, the fleet was prepared and in order; it consisted of five ships, four galleys with poop lanterns, three galliots, four champans, three funeas, two English launches, two brigantines, a flat-bottomed boat for artillery, and thirteen tall frigates of lofty bulwarks, with one thousand three hundred Spaniards, regular soldiers, captains and officers, men hired for the expedition, and adventurers. Amongst these forces were some Portuguese captains and soldiers, with the captain-major of Tidore, who had been in that island when the Dutch gained possession of it; they had now come from Malacca to go on this expedition. There were also four hundred pioneers, Indians, Tagals, and Pampangos of Manila, who came at their own expense with their officers and arms to serve; and a quantity of artillery of all kinds, munitions, warlike implements and supplies for nine months. Don Pedro de Acuña sailed with all this armament from the point of Hilohilo, near the town of Arevalo, in the island of Panay, and coasting along the isle of Mindanao, put into the port of Caldera, to take in water, wood, and other things which were wanted.

The governor went on board the galley *Santiago*, taking under his immediate command the other galleys and rowing vessels. The ship *Jesus-Maria* was flagship to the other ships, and carried the master of the camp, Juan de Esquivel; Captain and Sergeant-major Cristoval de Azcueta Menchaca was vice-admiral of the fleet. When the fleet had done what it required in Caldera it weighed from that port; and on setting sail, the flagship, which was a heavy ship, could not fetch her way, and the currents cast her on shore in such a manner that she went on the beach, where she was lost; the people, artillery, and part of the munitions and stores which she carried, were saved. After setting fire to the ship, and taking from her all the iron-work and bolts which they could, to prevent the Mindanaos availing themselves of them, the fleet continued its voyage; the galleys coasting along the isle of Mindanao, and the ships and other craft standing out to sea, making their course, all of them, for the port of Talangame, of the isle of Terrenate. The ships, though with some impediments, first sighted the isles of Maluco; and having been recognised by a large Dutch ship, with good artillery, which was anchored in Terrenate, this ship fired a few heavy pieces at our ships, and after that retreated within the port, where it fortified itself under shelter of the land, with its artillery and crew and the Terrenate men. The master of the camp passed on with the ships to the island of Tidore, where he was well received by the Muslim chiefs and cachils, because the king was absent, having gone to be married in the island of Bachan. There the master of the camp found four Dutch factors who traded for cloves; from them he got information to the effect that the ship that was at Terrenate was from Holland—one of those that had come out from Amboino—and had taken possession of Tidore, and driven out the Portuguese, and that it was taking in cloves; and was expecting other ships of its convoy, because they had made friendship and treaties with Tidore and Terrenate to obtain support for themselves against the Castilians and Portuguese. The master of the camp at once sent to call the king of Tidore, whilst he there refreshed his ships and crews, and made gabions and other implements required in war; and waited for Don Pedro de Acuña, who, with his galleys, by the fault of the pilots, had fallen off thirty leagues to leeward of the isle of Terrenate, as far as the isle of Celebes, or, as it is otherwise named, Mateo. Reconnoitring this island, he returned to Terrenate, and passing in sight of Talangame, he discovered the Dutch ship. He wished to reconnoitre her; but seeing that her artillery struck the galleys, and that the master of the camp was not there, he went on to Tidore, where he found him, to the great satisfaction of all, and there they passed the rest of the month of March. At this time the king of Tidore came with twelve well-armed caracoas, and showed satisfaction at the arrival of the governor, to whom he made many complaints of the tyranny and subjection under which he was held by the Sultan Zayde, king of Terrenate, by the assistance of the Dutch. He promised to go and serve His Majesty in person, and, with six hundred Tidore men, in the fleet. Don Pedro accepted, and made presents to him; and without delaying any longer in Tidore, nor occupying himself about the ship which was in Talangame, he considered the chief business about which he had come. He sailed on the last day of March, making for Terrenate; that day he anchored in a cove between the town and port, and the king of Tidore did the same with his caracoas. That same night the Dutch ship weighed and went to Amboino. The following day, the first of April, at day-break, they landed the men with some labour, with the design that they should march by the beach, which was a very straight and narrow pass, as far as the fortress, in order to plant the artillery with which they were to batter it. As it appeared to the governor that harm would ensue from the narrowness and insufficiency of the pass, he sent up to the higher ground a number of pioneers to open another road for the rest of the army to go by, and to cause a diversion to the enemy in several parts. By this measure the camp was brought close to the walls, though a great number of Terrenate men had sallied out to prevent it. The out-posts of the camp were under the charge of Juan Xuarez Gallinato, with the captains Juan de Cuevas, Don Rodrigo de Mendoza, Pasqual de Alarcon, Juan de Cervantes, Captain Vergara, Cristoval de Villagra, with their companies. The other captains were stationed with the main body of the army; and Captain Delgado had command of the rear-guard, the master of the camp attending to all parts. The army arrived under fire of the enemy's artillery, which opened fire hurriedly. The governor went out to see how the army was formed, and leaving it posted, returned to the fleet to have the battering guns brought up, and refreshments for the soldiers. Between the army and the walls there were some high trees, in which the enemy had posted some sentinels, who could look over all the field; they were driven out, and our sentinels were placed there, and from this high position they could give notice of what passed in the fortress. Captain Vergara, and after him Don Rodrigo de Mendoza, and Alarcon, sallied out to reconnoitre the wall, the rampart of Our Lady,[1] and

[1] The Malays could not have given it this name, so that either the Spaniards must have given it the name to distinguish it, or have so named it after *mariam*, the Malay name for a cannon, the origin of which is unknown, and which may have misled the Spaniards. Unless

the pieces which it had on the ground; and a low wall of stone without mortar, which ran as far as the mountain, where there was a bulwark, at which it terminated, which they call that of Cachiltulo, and which was armed with pieces of artillery, and many wall-pieces, musketeers, arquebusers, and men with pikes and other arms of their fashion, lining the wall for its defence. When they had seen all and reconnoitred it, though not without loss, for the enemy had killed six soldiers with their artillery, and wounded with a musket-shot Ensign Juan de la Rambla in the knee, they returned to the brigade. It was a little more than mid-day when an elevated position was discovered towards the bulwark of Cachiltulo, from which it was possible to harass the enemy and drive him from the wall. Orders were given to Captain Cuevas to occupy it with twenty-five musketeers. Having done this, the enemy sent out a body of men to prevent it. A skirmish was engaged, and the Muslims turned, retreating to their wall. Cuevas followed them, and pressed them so closely that he stood in need of assistance. The watchmen in the trees gave information of what was going on, and the Captains Don Rodrigo de Mendoza, Alarcon, Cervantes, and Vergara, came to their relief with halbards and lances brought to the charge,[1] and followed the enemy so quickly and with such resolution that they entered over the walls behind them, though with some of their men wounded; and Captain Cervantes was thrown back down from the wall and his legs broken, of which he died.[2] Captain Don Rodrigo de Mendoza, following the enemy, who was retreating, ran along the inner side of the wall as far as the cavalier of Our Lady; and Vergara in the

the strong point or key of a fortification was at that period dedicated to Our Lady.

[1] *Picas volantes.*

[2] If this captain was a relation of the great Cervantes, the fact of Don Quixote having been published only the year before, and not having obtained immediate celebrity, would account for De Morga's omitting to state that such was the fact.

other direction, along the face of the wall leading to the bulwark of Cachiltulo, going forward as far as the mountain. By this time all the forces had rushed up to the wall, and helping each other they climbed over it, and entered the place in all directions, with the loss of some soldiers killed and wounded. The troops were detained by a trench which was further on than the fort of Our Lady, for the enemy had withdrawn into a shed[1] fortified with much musketry and arquebuses, and four field-pieces. They fired their arquebuses and muskets at the Spaniards, and discharged at them darts hardened in the fire, and *bacacaes* of their fashion. The Spaniards rushed at the shed; and a Dutch artilleryman, trying to fire a large swivel-gun, with which he would have done much harm, being confused, could not succeed in firing it, and threw away the linstock on the ground, and turned his back and fled. Following him, the enemy did the same, and abandoned the shed, flying in different directions. Those who could, embarked with the king and some of his wives, and Dutchmen in a caracoa, and four flat boats which they kept ready equipped near the fort of the king, into which Captain Vergara entered shortly after and found it quite empty. Don Rodrigo de Mendoza and Villagra followed the enemy a long distance towards the mountain, killing many of their men; so that, at two in the afternoon, the town and fortress of Terrenate was completely captured; and over it the banners and standards of Spain were now hoisted, without its having been necessary, as had been expected, to batter the walls, and at so little cost to the Spaniards. Their killed were fifteen men, and the wounded twenty more. All the town was reconnoitred, and its extremities, as far as a small fort named Limataen, with two pieces of artillery, and two others which were close to the mosque on the side of the sea. The pillage of the place was not of much importance, because they had already taken

---

[1] *Jacal* and *xacal*, a shed or hut. *Caballero's Dict.*

away what was of most value, and the women and children to the island of the 'Moor,' where the king went in his flight, and shut himself up in a fortress which he had there. Some country goods were found, and a large quantity of cloves; and in the Dutch factory two thousand ducats, some cloths, linen pieces, and many arms; and in various places good Portuguese and Dutch artillery, and many wall-pieces and munitions which were taken for His Majesty. A guard was set over what had been won; and with some guns which were brought up from the fleet the place was put in a state of defence, the governor having given orders and provided for the rest as was most expedient.

Cachil Amuxa, the principal chief of Terrenate, nephew of the king, with other Cachils came to make peace with the governor, saying that he and all the people of Terrenate wished to become vassals of His Majesty, and that they would have given in their submission to him a long time before, if their king had not prevented it; for as a proud man, and fond of his own opinion, although he had been advised to give the fort up to His Majesty, and make himself subject to him, he had never chosen to do so, having been always encouraged and inspirited by the success which he had met with on other occasions: this had been the cause of his now finding himself in the wretched condition in which he was, and he offered to induce the king to come from the fortress of the Moor, if security for his life were given him. Don Pedro de Acuña received this Muslim well, and Pablo de Lima, a Portuguese, one of those whom the Dutch had turned out of Tidore, a man of importance and well known to the king, having volunteered to go in his company, he despatched them with a written safe conduct, as follows:

Safe Conduct of Don Pedro de Acuña, for the King of Terrenate.

I, Don Pedro de Acuña, governor and captain general and president of the Philippine islands, and general of this army and fleet, say, that under the signature of my name, I give security for his life, to the King of Terrenate, for him to come and speak to me; to him, and to such persons as he may bring with him; reserving to myself the disposal of all the rest according to my will, and of this I give security in the name of His Majesty. And I command that no person of this fleet cause any vexation to him, or to anything belonging to him; and that all observe and respect what is herein contained. Done in Terrenate, on the 6th of April, of the year one thousand, six hundred and six years.   DON PEDRO DE ACUÑA.

Within nine days Cachil Amuxa and Pablo de Lima returned to Terrenate, with the king, and prince his son, and others of his kinsmen, Cachils and Sangajes[1], under the before-mentioned safe conduct, and placed themselves in the hands of the governor, who receeived them with friendship and honour. He lodged the king and his son in a good house in the town, with a guard of one company. The king restored the villages of christians, which His Majesty had possessed in the island of the Moor, at the time when the Portuguese lost the fortress of Terrenate. He placed his person and kingdom in the hands of His Majesty, and gave up a quantity of muskets and heavy artillery which he had in some forts of the said island. The governor did not dispossess him of his kingdom, but on the contrary, allowed him to choose two of his own people, who should be satisfactory to the governor, to govern. The king, the prince his son, and his Cachils and Sangajes, swore fealty to His Majesty, and in the same manner, the Kings of Tidore and Bachan, and the Sangaje of La Bua took the oaths, and capitulated and promised not to admit the Dutch in the Maluco, neither them, nor other nations for the clove trade; and

[1] *Sangájy*, a Malay title. *Marsden.*

that as vassals of His Majesty, they should on all occasions come and serve him with their persons, forces, and ships, whenever they were summoned by whoever should have the command of the fortress of Terrenate; and that they should not molest any Muslims who might wish to become Christians, and that if any bad Christian should go to their country to throw off his religion, they should give him up; and other things which were expedient. In this way, the great and small remained contented and satisfied, seeing themselves free from the tyranny with which the King of Terrenate treated them. The governor remitted to them the payment of a third part of the tribute, which they used to pay to the king, and gave other advantages to the Muslims. After that, he traced out another fortress in modern fashion, on an eminent position and very suitable, and left it commenced, and in order that until it was completed, the existing fortification should be in a better state of defence, he reduced it to a lesser extent than what it then covered, making new cavaliers and bastions, which he left completed with ramparts of earth, with fortified gates. In the island of Tidore he left another fortress begun, close to the town in a good site, and having set in order all that seemed necessary in Terrenate and Tidore, and in the other towns and fortresses of the Maluco, he returned with the fleet to the Philippines; he left in Terrenate the master of the camp, Juan de Esquivel, as his lieutenant and governor of Maluco, with a garrison of six hundred soldiers, five hundred of whom in five companies remained in Terrenate, with a large forge and workshop of blacksmiths, sixty-five pioneers, thirty-five quarrymen, two galliots, and two brigantines well armed, and with a crew of rowers: and in Tidore another company of a hundred soldiers, under the command of Captain Alarcon, with munitions and provisions for a year in both fortresses. And the better to secure the state of affairs of the country, he took and brought away with him the King of Terrenate, and his son the prince, and twenty-four Cachils and Sangajes, the nearest relations of the king, giving to all of them good entertainment and much honour, and explaining to them the object for which he was taking them away, and that their return to Maluco depended on the security and tranquillity with which the Muslims should continue to conduct themselves, and on their obedience and service to His Majesty. The three Portuguese galliots returned to Maluco, taking with them the Dutchmen who were in Maluco, and the Portuguese captains and soldiers, who had come in them for this expedition. With the rest of the armament the governor entered with victory, into Manila, the last day of May of 1606, where he was received with joy and praises by the city: giving thanks to God for so fortunate and rapid success in an enterprise of so much weight and importance.

During the time that the governor was in Maluco, the royal High Court of the Philippines governed them in his absence, and desired to turn out of the city a quantity of Japanese, for there were amongst them turbulent people, and of little safety to the town. When this was carried into effect and harm done them, they resisted, and the affair reached such a pitch that they took up arms to prevent it, and the Spaniards were under the necessity of resorting to them also. The business reached the point that both parties wished to give battle, but this was deferred by various means, until by the assiduity of some monks, the Japanese calmed down, and afterwards they embarked those who were easiest to get rid of, though much to their displeasure. This was one of the occasions of greatest peril to which Manila has been exposed, because the Spaniards were few in number, and the Japanese more than fifteen hundred, courageous and high spirited men, and if they had come to an engagement in this conjuncture, the Spaniards would have passed a bad time of it.

When the governor entered Manila, he at once occupied himself with the affairs of the government, and especially with the despatch of the two ships which were to go to New Spain, attending in person in the port of Cabit, to the equipping and lading of them, and the embarcation of the passengers. He felt himself rather indisposed, from his stomach, which obliged him to return to Manila, where he took to his bed : the pain and vomiting increased so rapidly that, no remedy having been able to be found for them, he died in great suffering on St. John's day, to the great grief and regret of all the country. The king of Terrenate especially, showed it and expressed it, for he had always received from him much honour and good treatment. It was suspected that his death had been a violent one, from the severity and symptoms of the illness; and the suspicion increased, because the doctors and surgeons having opened his body, declared from the signs they saw in it, that he had been poisoned, which made his death a greater subject of pity and grief. The High Court buried the governor in the monastery of St. Augustine of Manila, with the pomp and state which was due to him personally and to his office. The High Court having again assumed the government, despatched the ships to New Spain, by which way news was sent to His Majesty of the taking of Maluco, and of the death of the governor.

The flagship which carried Don Rodrigo de Mendoza as general and captain made a speedy voyage to New Spain with these news. The admiral's ship, though it departed from the islands at the same time, was delayed more than six months : it had to throw into the sea eighty persons who died of sickness; and many others infected by it died in the port of Acapulco on landing, amongst whom was the licentiate Don Antonio de Ribera, auditor of Manila, who was coming as auditor to Mexico.

On the arrival of these ships it was understood that since

the death of Don Pedro de Acuña, and the High Court having assumed the government, the affairs of the islands had undergone no change; but that their commerce was limited and narrowed by the prohibition which prevented the sending of more than five hundred thousand dollars each year to the islands out of the proceeds of the sale of their merchandise in New Spain, so that want was suffered, and it appeared a small sum for the many Spaniards and considerable bulk of the trade, by which all classes were maintained, as they had no other gains or means. Moreover, although the conquest of Maluco had been of so great importance, on account of those islands themselves, and the chastisement which would favour the reduction of other revolted islands, especially Mindanao and Jolo, from which the Philippines received so many injuries; this affair was not yet established securely, both because the Mindanao and Jolo men still continued to make descents in their war boats on the provinces of Pintados, and carried off plunder as they were accustomed to do, and this would last as long an expedition was not made against them with much purpose: also because the affairs of Maluco did not fail to give much trouble to the master of the camp, Juan de Esquivel, who governed them, as he had little security on the part of the inhabitants, who as a Mussulman people, and of their own natural disposition, were pliable and inconstant, unquiet and ready for war and disturbance; at every moment, and in different parts, they rose in arms and insurrection, and although the master of the camp and his captains laboured to put them down and pacify them, they were unable to bring the necessary remedies in so great a matter. The soldiery and provisions were being expended, and the succours which were sent from Manila could neither be so well timed nor in such quantity as was desired, on account of the risks of the voyage, and the necessities of the royal exchequer.

No less prejudicial to everything was the arrival at this

time at Maluco of the ships of Holland and Zealand, which were so much interested in the islands, and had put their affairs there on such good footing that they came in squadrons by the Indian navigation, to recover what they had lost in Amboino and Terrenate, and other islands. Supported by them, the Muslims revolted from the Spaniards, who had much on their hands with them, and still more with the Dutch, as they were numerous, and enemies of more importance than the natives.

The interests of the Dutch in these parts are great, both for the trade in cloves and other drugs and spices, and because they are of opinion that in these parts they open a door to the subjugation of the East; for, overcoming all things, and the difficulties of the voyage every day with greater facility, they come to these isles with larger fleets; and if a remedy be not applied to this evil in good time, and very fundamentally, it will shortly grow so much that later it will be incapable of receiving any.

The English and Flemings used to make this voyage by the straits of Magellan; and the first was Francis Drake, and a few years later Tomas Escander,[1] passing by Maluco.

Ultimately Oliver del Nort, a Fleming, with whose fleet that of the Spaniards fought near the Philippine isles, at the end of the year 1600; where his admiral's ship, commanded by Lambert Biesman, was taken, and the flag-ship, with the loss of nearly all the crew, and much battered, took to flight; afterwards it left the Philippines, and was seen in the Sunda and straits of Java in such distress that it seemed impossible for it to navigate, and it was lost, as was related in its place.[2]

This corsair, though so much distressed, had the good fortune to escape from the hands of the Spaniards, and with

[1] This person is the same as Thomas Candlish, whose voyage is sometimes quoted by Oliver de Noort.
[2] See p. 172.

great travail and difficulty returned with the ship *Maurice*, and only nine men alive, to Amsterdam, on the twenty-sixth of August of the year 1601. He wrote a relation of his voyage and of what happened in it, with plates of the battle and the ships, which afterwards was translated into Latin, and Theodore de Bri (German) printed it in Frankfort in the year 1602;[1] and both relations are going about the world as a very prodigious thing, and as containing such great labours and perils.

The same information was given by the pilot Bartolome Perez, of the island of Palma, who, coming from England by way of Holland, spoke to Oliver de Nort, who recounted to him his voyage and hardships; as the licentiate Fernando de la Cueva relates in his letter dated in the island of Palma, the last day of July of the year 1604, written to his brother Marcos de la Cueva, residing in Manila, and one of the volunteers who was on board the Spanish flagship which fought the corsair. It is as follows:—

In this letter I reply to two of yours, one of July of 1601, and the other of July of 1602; and in both you give me an account of having been shipwrecked and having escaped by swimming; and long before that I had seen your letters I had learned the event, and it kept me in great anxiety, and even in much grief, in respect of what was said in these parts, and the belief that you might be concerned in the matter. Thus it was for me a singular satisfaction to be assured that you remained with life and health, with which the rest may be arrived at, and without which human trea-

[1] This German edition of Oliver van Noort forms an appendix to Theodore de Bry's *Ninth Part of America*, printed at Franckfurt, by Wolffgang Richter, 1601: the appendix was printed by Matthew Becker, at Franckfurt, 1602. The plates on copper are different from those of the Dutch edition of Oliver van Noort. This ninth volume of De Bry's America is catalogued 10,003 e in the British Museum. As much as 15,000 francs has lately been given for a complete copy of De Bry's voyages.

sure is of no value. By way of Flanders (whence every day we receive ships in this island) I learned long before all that had happened, though not with so many details; for Oliver de Nort, who was the Dutch general with whom the engagement took place, arrived in safety in Holland, with eight men, and himself nine, and without a penny. When he went out of the rebellious states of Holland and Zealand with five armed ships and merchandise, which were worth, the principal and merchandise, a hundred and fifty or two hundred thousand ducats, his design had been, and he carried orders to trade, buying and selling through the straits, and in the ports where he might be with friends or enemies, and not to attack anybody, but only to defend himself, and to reduce Indians to trade and deal with him. Having all arrived together at the straits, three ships parted company there with storms, and these must have been lost, because till this day there has been no news of them. Seeing that he had suffered such losses, and that he could not by trade restore his loss, or because he did not find an easy entrance and reception among the people of Peru, he determined to exceed his orders, and make this voyage one of robbery, and he posted himself at the mouth of the river to wait for the ships: the rest happened which you know. Oliver de Nort is a native of the city of Rotterdam, whither he arrived with a wooden anchor,[1] without having anything else with which to moor his ship, nor any having remained to him; they say it is of a very heavy wood of the Indies, and it is hung up at the door of his house for its size. He arrived (as I have said) nine men in all, and in great distress, and by a miracle, and he has printed a book of his voyage, with pictures of the ships, and many other particulars of the things which happened to him, and the hardships they underwent in the engagement and during the whole voyage, as

[1] This was the anchor that the Japanese captain gave him, as well as a Japanese cable, in the bay of Manila, on the 3rd December, 1600.

much for his own glorification as to stimulate others to similar deeds. A pilot of this island, named Bartolome Perez, was captured and carried off to England before the peace or truce, and came through Holland, where he talked at length with Oliver, who gave him a long account of all that had happened, which is known to all, and he has spoken of it in this island, before this voyage. Bartolome Perez says that he gave great praise to the people, [the Spaniards] and said that in his life he never saw more brilliant soldiers, and that they had won the deck of the ship, and all the upper parts; and he called out beneath the deck to set fire to the powder, and that with this it was understood that the Spaniards went out of his ship,[1] from fear of blowing up, and they got an opportunity to escape, but so distressed that it seemed a miracle their having reached port. He [the pilot] says that he saw the anchor and the book, and in what concerns the book, here it is. I have given you this relation on account of what you tell me in yours, since you considered them as wrecked, and in order that so singular an event should be known in those parts.

Now the Dutch make the voyage much more speedily and safely, going and returning by way of India, without touching at its ports or coasts, until they enter by the islands of the Javas[1], greater and lesser, and Sumatra, Amboino, and the Malucos; as they know them so well, and have so much experience of the great profits which they there obtain, it will be hard to drive them out of the East, where they have done such great injuries in spiritual and temporal matters.

[1] At p. 150 it is stated that Oliver van Noort's ship had been at the taking of Cadiz by the *Conde de Leste*, that is to say, the Earl of Essex: twenty-two Dutch ships sailed in his fleet.

[2] What we now call Java used to be called Java major, and the island of Bali was Java minor.

CHAPTER VIII.

Account of the Philippine Islands, and of their Inhabitants, Antiquity, Customs, and Government, both during the time of their paganism, and since the Spanish conquest, with other particulars.

The isles of the eastern ocean, adjacent to further Asia, belonging to the crown of Spain, by the demarcation of Castile, and her seas and countries of America, are commonly called by those who navigate to them the western isles; because from first leaving Spain, until reaching them, the navigation to them is by the path which the sun follows from east to west, and for the same reason, they are called eastern by those who navigate by way of Portuguese India, from west to east: both encircling the world by opposite voyages, until they come and meet in these islands, for they are many between great and small, which are properly called Philippines, and are subjected to the crown of Castile. They are within the tropic of Cancer, and extend from twenty-four degrees north latitude, as far as the equinoctial line, which passes through the islands of Maluco. There are many others on the side of the line, in the tropic of Capricorn, which extend as far as twelve degrees towards the south. The ancients affirmed, that one and all they were desolate and uninhabited; now experience has shown that they had been mistaken, there being found in them good climates, many peoples, provisions and other things convenient for human life: with many minerals, rich metals, gems and pearls, animals and plants, of which nature has not been sparing.

All the isles of this great archipelago, between great and small, are innumerable, those which are the Philippines by name and government, may be forty large islands, besides other smaller ones, all continuous; the principal and best known are named Luzon, Mindoro, Tendaya, Capul, Burias,

Mazbate, Marinduque, Leite, Camar, Ylabao, Sebu, Panay, Bohol, Catenduanas, Calamianes, Mindanao, and others of less name.

The first island which the Spaniards conquered and settled was Sebu, where the conquest commenced, and was followed up in all the surrounding islands: these are inhabited by people natives of these same islands, who are named Bizayas, and by another name, Pintados (Picts); because the men of most importance, from their youth, tattoo the whole of their body; pricking it in the appointed places, and throwing over the blood certain black powders, which never come out. But as the capital of the government and the principal town of the Spaniards was transferred to the isle of Luzon, which is a very large island, and nearer and more opposite to Great China and Japan, it will be treated of first, for much of what is said of it applies generally to the others, whose specialities, and whatever particular matters each one may possess, will be noted in their place.

This island of Luzon, from the point or head by which the Philippine islands are entered by the channel of Capul, which is in thirteen degrees and a half north latitude, to the other extremity in the province of Cagayan, which they call the cape of the Boxeador, opposite China in twenty degrees, is more than two hundred leagues in length. In some parts its width is much narrower than in others; especially in the middle the island is so narrow, that from sea to sea there are less than thirty leagues. The whole island is of more than four hundred leagues' circumference.

The temperature of this island is not one only; on the contrary there is much variety in different parts and provinces of it. The head and beginning of the island near the channel, is temperate in the interior, though the sea-shores are hot: and where the city of Manila is built, the site is hot from being low and near the sea; but in the neighbourhood, not far from the city, there are lands and towns which are much cooler, where the heat is not disagreeable: the same is the case at the other extremity of the island, opposite to China and Cagayan. The seasons of the year of winter and summer are the reverse of what they are in Europe, because usually in all the islands the rains are from the month of June till that of September, with many heavy showers, whirlwinds, and storms by sea and land; and the summer is from October till the whole of May, with a serene sky and calms at sea; though in some provinces the winter and the rains begin earlier than in others, and in those of Cagayan, winter and summer are almost similar, and fall at the same time as in Spain.

The people who inhabit this great island of Luzon in the province of Camarines, as far as near the provinces of Manila, both in the maritime districts and in the interior, are natives of this island, of middling stature, of the colour of boiled quinces, well featured, both men and women, the hair very black, scanty beard, of a clever disposition for anything they undertake, sharp and choleric, and resolute. All live by their labour, gains, fishing and trade, navigating by sea from one island to another, and going from one province to another by land.

The natives of the other provinces of this island as far as Cagayan are of the same sort and quality, except that it is known by tradition that those of Manila and its neighbourhood were not natives of the island, but had come to it, and settled there in bygone times, and that they were Malays, natives of other islands and remote provinces.

In various parts of the island of Luzon there are a number of natives of a black colour, with tangled hair,[1] men and women, not very tall in stature, though strong and with good limbs: these men are barbarians and of little capacity, they have no houses nor settled dwellings; they go in troops and bivouac in the mountains and craggy

[1] *Cabellos de pasas.*

ground, changing their abode according to the season from one place to another, maintaining themselves with some little tillage, and sowing of rice, which they do temporarily, and with the game which they shoot with their bows,[1] in which they are very dexterous and good marksmen; also with the mountain honey, and roots which grow in the earth. They are barbarous people with whom there is no security, inclined to murder, and to attack the towns of the other natives, where they do great mischief without its having been possible to take measures to prevent them, nor to reduce them to subjection, nor bring them to a state of peace, although it is always attempted by good and evil means, as opportunity or necessity demands.

The province of Cagayan is inhabited by natives of the same colour as the other inhabitants of the island, though of better shaped bodies, and more valiant and warlike than the rest; their hair is long, hanging down over their shoulders. They have been in insurrection and rebellion twice since they were first reduced to submission, and there has been much work on different occasions to subject them and pacify them again.

The costume and dress of these inhabitants of Luzon, before the Spaniards entered the country, usually consisted of, for men, coats of cangan without collars, sewed together in front, with short sleeves, coming a little below the waist, some blue, others black, and a few of colours for the chief men, these they call *chininas;* and a coloured wrapper folded at the waist and between the legs, so as to cover their middles, and half-way down the thigh, what they call *bahaques;* their legs bare, and the feet unshod, the head uncovered, and a

[1] *Flechan con sus arcos.* This and a statement of De Quiros, p. 68, contradicts an opinion referred to by Mr. Boyle, p. 252 of his *Adventures among the Dyaks of Borneo,* respecting the ignorance of the bow of the Dyaks, which passage seems to imply that other South Sea islanders are supposed to share this ignorance. These aboriginal savages of Manila resemble the Pakatans of Borneo in their mode of life.

narrow cloth wrapped round it with which they bind the forehead and temples, called *potong*. Chains of gold wound round the neck, worked like spun wax, and with links in our fashion, some larger than others. Bracelets on the arms, which they call *calombigas* made of gold, very thick and of different patterns; and some with strings of stones, cornelians and agates, and others blue, and white stones which are much esteemed amongst them. And for garters on their legs, some strings of these stones, and some cords pitched and black wound round many times.

In one province which they call the *Zambals* they wear the front half of their head shaved, and on the skull a great lock of loose hair. The women in the whole of this island wear little frocks with sleeves of the same stuffs, and of all colours, which they call *varos*; without shifts, but some white cotton wraps folded from the waist downwards to the feet; and other coloured garments fitting the body like cloaks, which are very graceful. The great ladies wear crimson, and some silk and other stuffs woven with gold, and edged with fringes and other ornaments. Many gold chains round the neck, *calombigas* (bracelets) on the wrists and thick earrings of gold in the ears, rings on the fingers of gold and precious stones. The hair is black, and tied gracefully with a knot on the back of the head. Since the Spaniards are in the country many Indians do not wear *bahaques* (waist cloths) but wide drawers of the same stuffs and wrappers, and hats on their heads. The chiefs wore braids of beaten gold, and of various workmanship, and used shoes; the great ladies also were daintily shod many of them with shoes of velvet, embroidered with gold, and white robes like petticoats.

Men and women, and especially the great peeple, are very cleanly and elegant in their persons and dress, and of a goodly mien and grace; they take great care of their hair, rejoicing in its being very black; they wash it with the boiled rind of a tree, which they call *gogo*, and they anoint it with oil of sesame prepared with musk, and other perfumes. All take much care of their teeth, and from tender age they file and make them of equal size, with stones and instruments, and they give them a black colour, which is perpetual, and which they preserve till they are very old, although it makes them ugly to look at.

They very generally bathe their whole bodies in the rivers and creeks, both young and old, without hesitation, for at no time does it do them any harm; and it is one of the chief medicines they are acquainted with; when a little child is born, they immediately bathe it and the mother likewise. The women have for their employment and occupation, needlework, in which they excel very much, as in all kinds of sewing; they weave coverings, and spin cotton, and serve in the houses of their husbands and fathers. They pound the rice for their meals and prepare the other victuals. They rear fowls and sucking pigs, and take care of the houses, whilst the men are attending to the labours of the field, their fisheries, voyages and gains. The women, married and unmarried, are not very chaste, and the husbands, fathers, and brothers are but slightly jealous or careful in this matter. They and the women are so interested and covetous, that if money is forthcoming, they easily allow themselves to be overcome, and when a husband finds his wife in adultery, without difficulty he is calmed and appeased; though since they know the Spaniards, some of them who set up claims to know more than others have at times killed the adulterers. In their visits and in going about the streets and to the temples, both men and women, and especially the principal ones, walk very slowly and pay attention to their steps, and with a large following of male and female slaves, and with silk parasols which they carry as a precaution against sun or rain. The ladies go in front and their maids and slaves behind, and behind them their husbands, fathers, and brothers, with their servants and slaves.

Their ordinary food is rice, ground in wooden mortars, and boiled, which is called *morisqueta*, this is the ordinary bread of all the country, boiled fish, of which there is great abundance, and flesh of swine, deer, and wild buffaloes, which they call *carabaos*. They prefer the taste of meat and fish, when it has begun to spoil and stink. They also eat boiled camotes, which are sweet potatoes, French beans, *quilites*, and other vegetables, all sorts of plantains, guavas, pine-apples, custard-apples, oranges of various sorts, and other kinds of fruits and vegetables in which the country abounds.

What is used for drink is a wine made from the tops of cocoa-nut palms and nipal trees, of which there is great abundance, and they are grown and cultivated like vines, though with less labour and tillage. When the sap[1] is taken from the palm, they distil it in retorts with their little stoves and instruments, of a greater or less strength, and it becomes spirits, and this is drunk in all the islands, and it is a very clear wine, like water, but strong and dry; and if it is used with moderation it is medicinal for the stomach, and against colds and all rheums; and mixed with wine of Spain it makes a sweet liquor, very wholesome and well-tasted.

In the feasts, marriages, and meetings of the natives of these islands, the principal thing is to drink this wine, day and night without ceasing, all sitting in a circle, some singing, others drinking, with which they frequently get drunk, without this vice being held amongst them as dishonourable or infamous.

The weapons of these people are, in some provinces, bows and arrows; but in general throughout the isles they use lances with well-made blades of a middling size, and shields of

[1] *Tuba*, Tagal word *licor* and *mosto*. Tagal Dict.

light wood, with their handles fixed on the inside, which cover them from head to foot, which they call *carasas*. At the waist, a dagger four inches wide, the blade ending in a point, and a third of a yard in length, the hilt of gold or ivory, the pommel open with two cross-bars or projections, without any other guard: they are called *bararaos*[1], and are two-edged, in sheaths of wood or buffalo horn, elegantly worked. With these they strike with the point, but more usually with the edge. They are very dexterous, when they reach their adversary, if they lay hold of his hair with one hand, with the other they at one blow cut off his head with the *bararao*, and carry it away; for afterwards they keep them hung up in their houses, where they can be seen, which they do ostentatiously, in order to be considered as valiant men, and as men who have avenged themselves of their injuries on their enemies.[2]

Since they have seen the Spaniards use their arms, many of them handle arquebuses and muskets very dexterously; and before that time they had small brass cannon, and other pieces of cast-iron, with which they defended their forts and towns, though their powder was not as fine as what the Spaniards used.

Their boats and ships are of many kinds, for on the rivers and creeks within the country, they use canoes made of one very large tree, and others with benches made of planks and built with keels; also vireys and barangays, which are vessels very swift and light, and low in the water, joined together with wooden bolts, as slender at the stern as at the bows, which contain many rowers on both sides, who with

[1] *Balarao*, a dagger, Bisay word. Tagal Dictionary of Fray Domingo de los Santos, Manila, 1835.
[2] This contradicts an opinion that head hunting in Borneo was a modern and a recent innovation, which is mentioned in Mr. Boyle's *Adventures in Borneo*, see pp. 318-319, for some very sensible remarks by that unprejudiced observer on this custom; the only other people who now practise it are the Montenegrins.

buzeyes or paddles, and with oars,[1] row outside the vessel, timing[2] their rowing to the sound of some who keep singing in their language, things to the purpose, by which they understand whether they are to hasten or retard their rowing. Above the rowers there is a bailio or gangway made of canes, upon which the fighting men stand, without embarassing the crew of rowers; upon this a number of men go in proportion to the size of the ship, and there they manage the sail which is square and of sail-cloth, and hoisted on sheers made of two thick bamboos which serve as a mast, and when the ship is large, it also carries a foremast of the same form, and both sheers, with their tackle for lowering them upon the gangway, when the wind is contrary, and the helmsman on the poop to steer. They carry another scaffolding of canes on the gangway itself, upon which when the sun is hot or it rains, they spread an awning of mats woven with palm-leaves, very thick and tough, which they call cayans,[3] so that all the ship and its crew are covered and sheltered. There is also another scaffolding of thick canes on both sides of the vessel along its whole length, strongly attached, and which skims the water, without impeding the vessel's way, and serves as a counterpoise, to prevent the vessel from capsizing or foundering, however much sea there may be, or force of wind may press on the sail. And it may happen that all the hull of the vessel will fill with water, for they are undecked, and it will remain just under the surface, until the water is got rid of, and baled out, without sinking on account of these outriggers. These vessels are commonly used in all the islands, from ancient times, and others still larger, which are called caracoas, and lapis, and tapaques, to carry their merchandise, which are very convenient as they are very capacious and draw little water;

[1] *Gaones, gayong*, an oar. Tagal Dictionary.
[2] *Jostrando.*
[3] *Carang*, an awning. Tagal Dictionary.

and they draw them up very easily ashore every night at the mouths of rivers and in creeks, where they always navigate, without putting out to sea or leaving the land. All the islanders know how to row and manage them. There are some so large that they carry a hundred rowers on each side, and thirty soldiers above them for fighting, and the ordinary vessels are varangays and vireys of fewer rowers and people; and now in many of them, instead of the wooden bolts, and sewing of the planks, they nail them with iron nails, and the helms and prow with a beak head are in the Castilian fashion.

The country is in all parts much overshadowed with trees of various kinds of timber, and fruit trees, which beautify it throughout the year, both on the sea-coast and in the interior, in the plains and the mountains; it is very full of large and small rivers, of fresh sweet water running to the sea; and all these rivers are navigable and are full of fish, very savoury and of many kinds. For this reason there is a great abundance of timber, which is cut down and sawn, and is dragged to the rivers, and is brought down by their means. This timber is very good for houses and buildings, and for the construction of large and small ships: and there are many very straight thick trees, light and pliant, for making masts of ships and galloons: so that any ships can be fitted with masts of one piece of timber, without any necessity for fishing them, or making them of pieces; and for the hulls of ships, the keel, futtock timbers, top timbers, and any kind of futtock timbers, compass timbers, transoms, knees, wedges of the mast, and rudders[1], all sorts of good timber is easily to be found, and good planks for the sides and decks, and upper works, of timber very suitable to the purpose.

There are many fruit trees in the country, such as sanc-

[1] *Quilla, estamenaras, barraganetes, y qualquiera otra ligazon, buzardas, puercas, y corbatones, y llaves, y timones.*

FRUIT AND VEGETABLES.

tores, mabolos, tamarinds, jack fruit,[1] custard apples, papaws, guavas, and many orange trees in all parts of different kinds, large and small, sweet and sour, citrons and lemons, plantains of ten or twelve varieties, very wholesome and savoury, many cocoa-nut palm trees of good taste, from which they make wine, and a common sort of oil, very medicinal for wounds, and other wild palms on the mountains, which do not give cocoa nuts; but their wood is useful, and from the rind *bonote* is made, which is tow for cordage and ropes, and this is used for caulking ships. Attempts have been made to plant olives and quince trees, and other fruit trees of Spain, but up to the present time they have not succeeded, except in the case of pomegranates and grape vines, which give fruit in the second year, and bear very good grapes abundantly, three times a year, and some fig trees. Green vegetables of all kinds grow very well and yield abundantly, but they do not form seed, and it is always necessary to bring seed from Castile, China, and Japan.

In the province of Cagayan there are chestnut trees which give fruit, and in other parts there are pine trees and other trees, which give very large pine-nuts, with a strong shell and a pleasant taste, which they call *piles*.[2] There is plenty of cedar, which is called *calanta*,[3] and a finely coloured wood, which is called *asana*,[4] ebony, one kind finer than another, and other costly woods for all sorts of works. The meats which are usually eaten are, flesh of swine, of which there is great abundance, and it is very savoury and wholesome; cows, of which there are large herds in many parts of the islands, of breeds from China and New Spain. Those of China are a small cattle, very good breeders, with very small crumpled horns, and some beasts shake them; they have got a large hump on their shoulders, and they are very

[1] *Nangka*, Malay name.   [2] *Pili*, Tagal.
[3] *Calantas*, Tagal.   [4] *Asana*, Tagal.

gentle cattle. There are many fowls like those of Castile, and others very large, of a breed brought from China, very well tasted, and which make very nice capons; some of these fowls are black in feather, skin, flesh and bones, and of a good taste. There is much rearing of geese, and of swans, ducks, and tame pigeons brought from China. Flesh of wild game is very abundant, such as deer and wild boars, and in some parts porcupines; many buffaloes, which they call *cararaos*, which are bred in the fields, and are very fierce —there are others more tame which are brought from China, of which there are a great number; they are very handsome, and are only used for giving milk, which is thicker and better tasted than that of cows.

Goats and kids are reared, though from the dampness of the country, they have not a good taste, and grow sickly and die from this cause, and because they eat some poisonous herbs. Although ewes and rams have been brought many times from New Spain, they never multiply, so there is none of this cattle, for the temperature and pasture up to the present have not seemed to suit them. There were neither horses, nor mares, nor asses in the islands until the Spaniards had them brought from China and imported them from New Spain; asses and mules are very rare, but horses and mares are in sufficient quantity, and some estates are becoming stocked with them; those which are born in the country, which are of cross breed, (the greater number), turn out well and of good colours, well conditioned, willing to work, and of middling height. Those which are brought from China are small, very sturdy, of long step, vicious, quarrelsome, and ill-conditioned. Some horses of good colours are brought from Japan, well-shaped, of much mane, large fetlocks, leg bones, and front hoofs, that they seem like drayhorses, the heads rather large, hard in the mouth, slow runners, but of a good step, spirited and of much mettle.

The daily feed of these horses is green provender[1] all the year round, and rice in the husk, which keeps them very fat.

Fowls and field birds are in great abundance, also wild birds of extraordinary colours and very showy; but there are no singing birds for cages, although they bring from Japan some larks smaller than those of Spain, very sweet songsters, which are called *fimbaros*.[2] There are many doves, woodpigeons, other doves of very green plumage, of coloured feet and beak, others are white with a coloured spot on their breast, like a pelican. Instead of quails there are some birds which look like them, but smaller, which they call *povos*,[3] and other smaller singing birds.[4] Many wild cocks and hens, very small, and tasting like partridge. There are herons, royal, white, grey, flycatchers (doral), and other shore birds, ducks, wild ducks (lavancos), crested cranes (ayrones), sea crows, eagles, eagle-owls, and other birds of prey, though none are used for hawking. There are jays and thrushes, as in Spain, storks and cranes. There are no peacocks, rabbits, nor hares, although they have been turned out; it is understood that the wild animals which are in the mountains and fields have eaten and destroyed them, such as cats and foxes, badgers, and greater and smaller rats, of which there are great numbers in the country, and other land animals.

In all the islands there is an innumerable quantity of monkeys, large and small, with which sometimes the trees are covered. Parrots, green and white, but stupid at talking, and parroqueets, beautifully marked with green and other colours, which do not talk either. In the mountains

[1] *Camalote*, for *gumalote*, a plant like maize, with a leaf a yard long and an inch wide: this plant grows to a height of two yards and a half; when green it serves for food for horses. Caballero's Dictionary, Madrid, 1856.

[2] Larks; in Japanese, *fi-ba-ri*. Medhurst's *Japanese Vocabulary*, p. 59.

[3] According to Mallat, i, 179, and the Tagal Dictionary, this should be *poyo*.

[4] *Maynelas menores*, diminutive of *maina*, a talking bird.

and towns there are many serpents of various colours, the common ones are larger than those of Castile; some have been seen in the mountains of an extraordinary size, and much to be wondered at. The most dangerous are some slender ones less than an ell in length, which dart from the trees, where they generally remain, upon those who pass under, and bite them, and the venom is so efficacious that the person dies raging within the twenty-four hours.

In the rivers and creeks there are many very large scorpions, and a great number of caymans, very cruel and bloodthirsty, which very frequently drag the natives out of the washing boxes which they use, and they do great mischief to the horned cattle and stud horses when they go to drink, and though great fishing and slaughter of them is made, they never diminish, for which reason the natives put inside the water, in the rivers and creeks, fences and inclosures of thick grating where they bathe in security from these monsters; which they fear so much, that they revere and venerate them as if they possessed a superiority over them, and all their oaths and execrations, and those which are of any importance amongst them—even amongst the Christians—are thus, may the cayman kill him, which they call in their language *Buhaya*, and it has happened that people have sworn falsely or broken their promises, and after that, an accident has happened to them with the cayman, and God has so permitted it for the authority and purity of truth, and the affirming it which they have offended against.

The fisheries of the sea and rivers are exceedingly abundant in all sorts of fresh and saltwater fish, and all the country people use it for their ordinary food. There are plenty of good sardines, congers, sea bream, which they call bacoco, dace, skate, bicudas and tanguingues, soles, plantanos and taraquitos, needle-fish, dorados, eels, large oysters, mussels, parçebes, crabs, shrimps, sea spiders, center fish, and all sorts of shell fish, shad, white fish, and in the river Tagus of Cagayan, in their season, a great quantity of bobos, which come down to spawn at the bar; and in the lagoon of Bonbon many tunny fish are killed in their season, not so large as those of Spain, but of the same make, flesh and taste. In the sea there are many marine fish, such as whales, sharks, caellas, marajos bufeos, and others not known, of extraordinary shape and size. In the year 1596, during a great storm which fell upon the islands, a fish was cast ashore on the coast of Luzon, towards the province of Camarines, so great and deformed, that although it was stranded in water of more than three and a half fathoms deep, it could not again get afloat, and there it perished. The inhabitants said they had never seen a similar animal, nor any other of that form; its head was of extraordinary size and ferocity, and on the forehead it had two horns, which fell towards its back; one of them was brought to Manila, it was covered with its skin or leather, without hair or scales, and it was white, and twenty feet in length, of the thickness of a man's thigh at the root, and it went growing proportionately more slender towards the point; it was somewhat curved, and not very round, and, as far as could be perceived, all solid. It caused much astonishment to those that saw it.[1]

In the island of Luzon, at five leagues from Manila, there is a fresh water lagoon with much fish, into which many rivers enter, and the water issues to the sea by the river which comes out of it, and goes to Manila; it is called the lagoon of Bay. It is thirty leagues in circumference, and has an uninhabited island in the middle, with much game. On its shores there are many towns of the natives, who sail upon it, and cross over it ordinarily in their boats; at times it is very stormy, and dangerous to sail upon with the north winds, which make it rage very much, though soundings are easily found.

There is another lagoon at twenty leagues from Manila,

[1] No fish is known answering to this description.

in the province of Bonbon of the same name, not so large but very full of fish. The method of the natives for catching them, is by making inclosures of *bejucos*, which are canes or reeds, solid and very pliable, and tough, they are slender, and are twisted into cables and other cordage for their vessels. They catch the fish inside these inclosures which are made fast in a ring with stakes, and in creels which they make of these canes; and the most ordinary ways are with watch-towers[1] and fishing-nets, and other small drag-nets, and with strings and hooks by hand. The most usual food of the natives is a fish as small as pejerreys; this they dry and cure in the sun and wind, and cook it in various ways, and they like it better than larger fish, and amongst them its name is *laulau*.

Instead of olives, and other fruits for pickles, they have a green fruit like walnuts which they call *paos*;[2] there are some very small, also a larger size, these when prepared have a good taste; they also put cucumbers into brine pickle, and all sorts of vegetables and green sprouts, which are very pleasing to the taste.

There is much ginger, which is ate green, and with vinegar, and in preserve; and much cachumba, instead of saffron and other spices. The ordinary dainty in all these islands, and in many kingdoms of the mainland, of these parts is the *buyo*. This is made from a tree which has a leaf of the pattern of the mulberry leaf, and the fruit[3] is like an acorn of an oak, and the inside is white; this fruit which is called *bonga* is cut lengthwise in parts, and each one of these is put into a wrapper or envelope, which is made of the leaf, and a powder of quicklime is put in-

[1] *Atarraya*, probably for *atalaya*, a raised stand from which watchers can see when the fish come within the nets.

[2] The Tagal Dictionary translates *paho*, olives.

[3] De Morga describes the leaf and fruit as if they came off the same tree: the *buyo* is the betel, or tambul, or siri, and is the leaf of a creeper; and the *bonga* is the areca or pinang, and comes from a palm tree.

side with the *bonga*, and this composition is put into the mouth and chewed. It is so strong a thing, and heats so much that it brings on sleep and inebriates;[1] and those who are not used to it, it burns their mouths with pain. The saliva and all the mouth become coloured like blood, and marked for a long time; it is not of a bad savour; it is spit out of the mouth when no more juice remains in it which is called *zapa*. Whatever of it has passed into the stomach they find very beneficial, for making it comfortable, and against various illnesses; it strengthens and preserves the teeth and gums from all rheums, decay, and aches, and they relate of it other wonderful effects. What has been seen of it is that the natives and Spaniards, laymen and clergy, men and women, all use it so commonly and habitually, that morning and afternoon, in assemblies and visits, and alone in their houses, all their treats and luxury consist in dishes and salvers for *buyos* much gilt, and well arranged, as chocolate is served in New Spain; in these buyos poison has been given to many persons, of which they have died poisoned, and this is a very common occurrence.

The natives when they go out of their houses, especially the great men, carry with them for state and show their small boxes which are called *buccetas*[2] of buyos ready made up, and the leaf and nut and quicklime separately; with these curious boxes of metal and other materials, and scissors and other tools for making buyos with care and

[1] Apparently De Morga did not use tambul, and his experience seems to resemble Mr. Boyle's, who compares the effect with that of "a schoolboy's first pipe of shag:" he says, however, that the Sarawak officers assured him it never had had any stimulating effect upon them. I never heard of it before as a stimulant, but only as a stomachic: I never tried it however myself.

[2] It is not clear who call these caskets by this name. I imagine it to be the Spanish name, properly spelt *buxeta*. The King of Calicut's betel box is called *buxen* in the Barcelona MS. of the Malabar coasts.

neatness, wherever they stop they make and use them, and in the Parians which are the markets, they are sold, ready prepared, and the materials for making them.

The natives of these islands very commonly use for poisons the herbs which are to be found everywhere of this kind, they are so deadly and efficacious that they produce wonderful effects. There is a lizard usually to be found in buildings, of a deep green colour, a span in length, and of the thickness of three fingers, it is called *chacon*; they put it inside a bamboo box and shut it up; and gather up what this animal slavers during its confinement, which is a very strong poison (as it has been said) when mixed in food or drink, however small the quantity may be. There are other herbs which the natives know and gather for the same need, some dry and others green, for mixing with food or for fumigation; and others which kill by only touching them with the hands, or the feet, or by sleeping upon them; and they are so skilful in making up compositions of these, that they temper them, and apply them in such manner that they produce their effect at once, or after long or short periods as they choose, even should it be at the end of a year; in which way many people frequently die miserably. Especially Spaniards, who are little circumspect, and ill-governed, and abhorred for the ill usage with which they treat the natives with whom they have dealings, either in the collection of their tributes, or in other things in which they employ them against their will, without its being possible to remedy it. There are some poisonous herbs, which when the natives gather them they carry with them a provision of counter-herbs, and in the isle of Bohol, there is one of such quality that in order to cut it from the scrub in which it grows they approach it from the windward, because even the wind which passes over it is deadly. Nature has not left this danger without a remedy, because in the same islands other herbs and roots are found, which possess such power and virtue, as to undo and correct the poison and malice of the others, and they are applied in cases of necessity. Thus, when it is known what poison it is that has been given, it is not difficult, if recourse be had in time, to remedy it by giving the counter-herb which is antagonistic to that poison; and sometimes it has happened that pressure has been put upon the person who was suspected of having done the mischief to make him bring the counter-herb, and so the patient has been cured. There are also other counter-herbs of general use both for preservation against poison, as well as for counteracting it when taken, but the most certain and efficient remedy is some little flies or cochineals of a purple colour, which are found in the isles of Pintados in some shrubs, which when shut up in a clean hollow cane, with the mouth closed, breed and multiply therein; a little ground rice is put inside for them to feed upon, and visiting them every eight days, that rice is taken away and fresh is given them, and so they remain alive. If six of these little flies are taken in a spoonful of wine, or of water, for they have no bad smell, and taste of water-cresses, they produce a wonderful effect; and they are often taken even on going out to invitations, or to dinners which are at all suspicious, and they preserve and make sure against any risk of poison.

All these islands are in many parts rich in gold washings, and in ore of this metal, which the natives extract and work; although since the Spaniards are in the country, they proceed more slowly with this, contenting themselves with what they have already got in jewels, and from a far distant time, and inherited from their predecessors, which is a large quantity, for he must be a very poor and wretched person, who does not possess any chains of gold, bracelets, and ear-rings.

In the province of Camarines, in Paracali, they work some washings and mines, where there is good gold upon copper, also in Ylocos this merchandise is dealt in, because at the back of this province, which is on the edge and coast of the sea, there are some high and craggy mountain ranges, which run as far as Cagayan, on the slopes of which many islanders dwell, in the interior of the country; these are not yet subdued, nor has any entrance been made amongst them, they are named Ygolotes. These possess rich mines, and many of them of gold upon silver, from these they extract only as much as they require for their wants; and they descend with this gold, without completing its refinement or bringing it to perfection, to trade with the Ylocos in certain places, where they exchange the gold for rice, swine, and buffaloes, wraps, and other things of which they are deficient; and the Ylocos finish the refining it, and getting it ready, and by their means it is dispersed over the whole country. And although steps have been taken with these Ygolotes to discover their mines, and how they work them, and the method they possess for extracting the metal, there has been no means of knowing it; because they are apprehensive of the Spaniards, who would go to look them up for the sake of the gold; and they say, that they keep it better taken care of in the earth than in their houses.[1]

In the other islands there is the same plenty of mines and gold washings, especially in the Pintados, river of Botuan, in Mindanao, and in Sebu, where a mine is worked, and good gold extracted, named Taribon, and if the industry and labour of the Spaniards were applied to working the gold mines, as much would be extracted from any of these isles, as from the other provinces in the rest of the world:

[1] *Et sic meliùs situm quum terra celat.* Fernando de los Rios (Thevenot, vol. ii) says that there was much gold in the mountains forty leagues from the city, in the province of Pangasinan, and that Guido de Labazarris, the governor, sent some soldiers to search for it, but they returned in a sickly state, and suppressed all knowledge of the mines, so as not to be sent back there. The Dominican monks also suppressed all knowledge of the mines, on account of the tyranny of which gold had been the cause in the West Indies.

but attending to other gains more than to this, as will be said in its place, this was not attempted with design or purpose.

On some of the coasts of these islands there are pearl oysters, particularly in the Calamianes, and some very large and clean, and orient, have been obtained. Neither is the working of this branch attended to, and in all parts, in the shells of the ordinary oyster, grains of seed-pearl are found, and oysters as large as a buckler, with which they manufacture curious things. Likewise there are very large turtles in all the isles, and the natives obtain their shells, and sell them as merchandise to the Chinese and Portuguese, and other nations, who come to seek them, and value them highly for the rarities which they make with them.

In any of these islands, on the coasts, a quantity of small white snails are found, which they call *siguey;* the natives collect them, and sell them by measure to the Siamese, Cambodians, Pantan men, and other nations of the mainland, where they serve as coin, and they trade with them, as they do in New Spain with cacaos.

The horns of the caravao are goods sent to China, and skins of deer, and coloured wood to Japan. The natives turn everything to use with these nations, and derive great profits from them.

In this island of Luzon, particularly in the provinces of Manila, Pampanga, Pangasinan, and Ylocos, there are to be found amongst the natives, some large jars[1], of very ancient earthenware, of a dark colour, and not very sightly, some of a middle size, and others smaller, with marks and seals, and they can give no account from whence they got them, nor at what period; for now none are brought, nor are they made in the islands. The Japanese seek for them and value

---

[1] *Tibor.* See description of similar jars fetching very high prices, the best called *gusih*, 1500 to 3000 dollars, the second kind 400 dollars = £100 amongst the Dayaks, in Mr. Boyle's *Adventures in Borneo*, p. 93.

them, because they have found out that the root of a herb which they call cha, which is drunk hot, as a great dainty, and a medicine, among the kings and lords of Japan, does not keep or last except in these jars, upon which so high a value is set in all Japan, that they are the most valued precious things of their *boudoirs* and wardrobes; and a tibor is worth a high price, and they adorn them outside with fine gold, chased with great elegance, and they put them in brocade cases; and there are some tibors, which are valued and sold at two thousand taels of eleven reals each, and less, according as each one is, without its detracting from its value, its being cracked or chipped; because this does no harm for keeping tea inside it. The natives of these islands sell them to the Japanese, at the best price they can get, and take pains to find them for these gains; although now few are to be found, on account of the haste with which they have been sought up to this time.

Sometimes the natives have found large pieces of ambergris on the coasts, and as they see that the Spaniards value it, now they know it, and have made profits from it; and last year, 1602, the natives in the island of Sebu found a good piece of ambergris, which when their collector, (*encomendero*) heard of, he took it secretly and exchanged it on account of their tributes; and they say that it weighed a good many pounds. Afterwards he brought it out, and sold it a higher price by the ounce.

In the isle of Mindanao, in the province and river of Butuan, which is pacified and committed to the Spaniards, the natives have another means of gain, bringing much profit, for there are many civet cats, though smaller than those of Guinea; they obtain the civet and barter it. They do this easily, for when there is no moon they go out to hunt them with nets, and catch many cats, and taking the civet from them, they let them go again. They also take a few and put them in cages, and sell them in the islands at low prices.

A great deal of cotton grows in all the islands, and they spin it, and sell it in skeins to the Chinese and other nations who come for it ; and with it they also weave wrappers of various sorts, which they also sell, and others made of plantain leaves which they call medriñaques.[1]

The islands of Babuytanes[2] are several small islands at the head of the province of Cagayan. The principal means of gaining their livelihood of the inhabitants is, coming to Cagayan in Tapaques (skiffs) with pigs, fowls, and other supplies, and lances of ebony, which they sell. These are not placed under Spanish collectors, neither is tribute taken from them, nor are there Spaniards amongst them, as they are people of less reason and culture, and so no Christians have been made amongst them, neither have they magistrates.

There are other islands at the other extremity of the island of Luzon, opposite the province of Camarines, in fourteen degrees north latitude, near the strait of Espiritu Santo, named the Catenduanes. They are thickly inhabited by natives of a good disposition, all placed under Spanish collectors, with churches and catechisers, and a chief alcalde who administers justice to them : the greater part of them till the ground, and others occupy themselves with gold washing, and trading from one island to another, and to the mainland of Luzon, which is very near them.

The isle of Luzon has, on the coast and southern side, at a short hundred leagues from the cape of Espiritu Santo, by which the strait of Capul is entered, a bay thirty leagues round, which has a narrow entrance, and in the middle of it,

---

[1] *Meriñaque*, the modern name in Spain for a crinoline, said to be an Indian word in some dictionaries. Of other words which have passed into vernacular Spanish from the East Indian Archipelago, I have at present only found *champurrar*, to mix liquors, from the Malay *tchampur* of the same meaning; this has passed into Algerine French as *champoraux* (from *champurrado*), meaning hot coffee and spirits in about equal quantities.

[2] This name seems to be Malay, *Babu-utan*, wild swine.

there is an island across, which makes it narrower, called Miraveles, which may be two leagues in length, and half a league wide. It is high ground, and well wooded with many trees; it contains a town of fifty persons, where the watchman of the bay has his house and residence. At both points there are channels for entering into the bay, one on the south side, of half a league wide, with a rock in the middle which is called the Friar; and the other on the north side much narrower, and through both any large ships can enter and go out. All the bay has good soundings and a clean bottom, with good anchorage in all parts. From these entrances to the town of Manila and bar of the river there are eight leagues; and at two leagues to the south of Manila, there is a large cove with a point of land which conceals it, in which is a native town called Cabit,[1] from which this cove takes its name, which serves as a port for ships. It is very capacious, and sheltered from the south-westers, and the winds from the S.S.W., W., W.S.W., N.N.W., and N. points, and has good anchorage, clean, and in easy soundings. Very near the land there is a good entrance of more than a league and a half in width, for ships to go in and out. This bay all round is very well supplied, and abounds in all sorts of fisheries, and is well peopled with natives. Above Manila there is a province of more than twenty leagues named Pampanga, with many rivers and creeks which water it, and the outlet of all this water is into the bay: this province is well peopled by natives, with great abundance of rice, fruit, fish, meat, and other provisions.

The bar of the river of Manila, which is in this bay, close to the town of Manila on one side, and to Tondo on the other, has little water on it, on account of some sand banks, which with the floods change their positions, and

[1] Cavite derives its name from the Tagal word *cavit*, a creek, or bend, or hook, for such is its form. Manila derives its name from a plant called *mani* by the islanders. Mallat, i, 176 and 163.

become obstructions; so that although when once the bar is passed the river contains sufficient depth of water for any ship, yet unless they are frigates, and vireys, and other small craft, they cannot pass to enter the river, and in what concerns galleys, and galliots, and Chinese vessels, which draw little water, they are obliged first to discharge their cargoes, and enter with spring tides and by towing; so they anchor in the bay outside the bar, and as there is not so much security there, they enter the port of Cabit.

At twenty leagues from the channel of Capul, in the same isle of Luzon, there is another good port, sheltered from the south-westers, with a good entrance and anchorage, called Ybalon. Here ships which have put in under stress of the south-westers find shelter, and wait till the wind shifts for entering Manila, which is eighty leagues off.

On the coasts of Pangasinan, Ylocos, and Cagayan, there are some ports and bars into which ships can enter and remain, such as the cove of Marihuma, the port of the Frayle, of Bolinao, the bar of Pangasinan and that of Bigan, the bars of Camalaynga at the mouth of the river Tagus, which goes up two leagues to the principal town of Cagayan, without mentioning other rivers, bars and coves, and shelters of less importance, for smaller vessels, along all the coasts of this island.

Close to this great island of Luzon there are many other islands, large and small, very near to it, peopled by the same inhabitants as Luzon, with gold washings, tillage, and other employments, such as Marinduque, isle of Tablas, Mazbate, Burias, Banton, Bantonillo, and others of less importance. Among these, the nearest to Manila is the island of Mindoro, which is more than eighty leagues long, and about two hundred in circumference. It contains many towns of the same natives, and on the side which is opposite to the provinces of Balayan and Calilaya it is so near and close to the island of Luzon that it makes a strait with strong currents and races, by which ships pass to and fro to go to Manila, with much force of wind and current, and the strait may be half a league wide. In this part the principal town of the isle of Mindoro is situated, with a port called the Varadero, for large ships, besides other roadsteads and bars which the whole island contains for smaller vessels. There are many native towns on all the shores of this island, and all abound in rice and provisions, and gold washings, and woods and game.

The Cape of Espiritu Santo, which has to be sighted to enter the Philippine Islands by ships coming from New Spain, is in an island called Tendaya, in barely thirteen degrees; and twenty leagues further along the coast, leaving this Cape Espiritu Santo to the south, is the island of Viri, and many others are now sighted, through which a passage opens to the isle of Sebu, through a strait called San Juanillo, which these islands make, and which is not very good or safe for large ships. More to the north, having left this passage, the isle of Capul is reached, which makes a strait and channel with many currents and races, through which ships enter. Before reaching this strait, there is a rock or islet in the middle, called San Bernardino. The strait is made by the coast of the island of Luzon and that of the island of Capul: the channel may be a league in length and less in width.

At the outlet of this strait, after having entered it, three small islets are sighted in a triangle, which are called the (naranjos) orange tree islands, they are high and free from rocks, upon which ships are driven with the violent currents, and exertions are made to escape from them. They are uninhabited; but the other islands are large, and contain many towns of natives, and all sorts of provisions and supplies.

From this part towards the south, are the islands of Bisayas, also called Pintados, which are many, and thickly peopled with natives; and those of most name are Leite, Ybabao, Çamar, Bohol, the isle of Negros, Sebu, Panay, Cuyo, and Calamianes. All the inhabitants of these islands, both men and women, are well featured, and of a good disposition, and more well conditioned, and of more noble conduct than the inhabitants of the isle of Luzon, and other neighbouring isles.

They are different from them in their hair, which the men wear cut in a cue, like the ancient Spanish fashion, and their bodies painted with many designs, without touching the face. They wear very large earrings in their ears of gold and ivory, and bracelets of the same material; head-dresses twisted round their heads, very hollow like turbans, with graceful knots, and much striped with gold; jackets with tight sleeves, without collars, with skirts half way down the leg, fastened in front, of medriñaque and coloured silks. They do not wear shirts nor drawers, but bahaques (waist cloths) of many folds, so that their middles are covered when they take off the jackets and skirts. The women are good looking and pleasing, very elegant, and slow in their gait, their hair black and long, and tied up on the head; their wrappers are twisted round the waist, and hang down over them; they are of all colours, and their jackets of the same, without collars. They all go, men and women, without cloaks or other covering, and barefoot, with much adorning of gold chains, earrings, and wrought bracelets.

Their weapons are long knives, curved like alfanges,[1] lances and shields; they use the same boats as the people of Luzon; they have the same labours, fruits, and occupations as all the other islands. These Bisayas are people less inclined to agriculture, and are skilful in navigation, and eager for war and expeditions, on account of the pillage and captures, which they call Mangubas, which is the same as to go out to rob.

[1] Like the Malay *parang latok* of Borneo.

In the island of Sebu, close to the principal town there is a fine harbour for all sorts of ships, with a good entrance; and sheltered in all weather, of good soundings and good anchorage, besides other ports and bars of less name and importance, such as there are in all these islands for smaller vessels.

The isle of Sebu is more than a hundred leagues in circumference, it abounds in provisions, mines, gold-washings, and is inhabited by natives.

Beyond it there are other very good and well peopled islands, especially the isle of Panay, which is large, of more than a hundred leagues circuit, with many native towns, with a very great abundance of rice, palm wine, and all provisions. It has some large rich towns in what is called the river of Panay, and the principal one is Oton, with a bar and harbour for galleys and ships; and stocks for building ships of large size, and great plenty of timber for construction.

There are many natives skilled in building any sort of ships, and close to this island there is an islet of eight leagues in circumference, very full of natives who are all carpenters, and very good workmen; they follow no other employment or livelihood, and without having a tree to speak of in the whole island, they exercise this art with much dexterity and excellence, and all the islands supply themselves with artisans for carpentry from this place, which is called the island of the Cagayans.

After the island of Sebu, next comes the island of Mindanao, which has a circuit of more than three hundred leagues, and Jolo which is small; and lower down the island of Borneo, which is very large, more than five hundred leagues in circumference. All these islands are thickly inhabited, though this island of Borneo is not subdued, nor that of Mindanao entirely, but only the river of Botuan and Dapitan, and the province and coast of Caragan.

Below this island, before reaching that of Borneo, are the islands of the Calamianes, which are a great number of islands, large and small, thickly peopled with natives, with some provisions and tillage; though what they chiefly follow is their voyages for barter and profit from one island to another, and their fisheries; and those who live nearer Borneo go cruising, and plundering the natives of other isles.

The ebb and flow, and the spring and neap tides in these islands, are so varied that there is no certain rule; either on account of the great currents which there are amongst so many islands, or for some other secret of nature with respect to the flux and reflux which the moon causes, of which no certain reason has been able to be discovered; because although during the moon's opposition the tides are higher, and during the March moon they flow higher than during the whole remaining part of the year, yet in the tides of every day there is so much variety, that it causes surprise. Some days there are two equal tides (between day and night), other days there is only one; at other times the flow during the day is low, and that during the night is greater; and generally they have no fixed time; for it will happen that it is high tide at noon, and the next day it will be many hours either earlier or later, and one day the tide will be little, and the following day when it is expected to be less, it will be very much higher.

The language of all the Pintados and Bisayas is one and the same, by which they understand one another, speaking and writing, with letters and characters which they have of their own, and which resemble those of the Arabs; the usual writing of the natives is on leaves of trees, and on canes, upon the bark; for in all the islands there are many with the joints of enormous size, and the roots are very thick and solid trees.

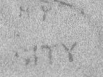

294   LANGUAGE AND WRITING.

The language of Luzon and the islands of its neighbourhood is very different from that of the Bisayas; and in the isle of Luzon the language is not all the same, for the Cagayans have one language, and the Ylocos another; the Zambals have a language of their own, the Pampangos have one different from that of the others; those of the province of Manila who are called Tagals have a very abundant and copious language, with which they express with elegance whatever they wish, in different ways and manners, and it is not difficult to learn nor to pronounce.

They write very well in all the islands, with some characters something like Greek or Arabic, which are in all fifteen; three are vowels, which serve for our five; the consonants are twelve, and they one and all with points and commas combine and signify whatever it is wished to write, as fully and easily as is done with our Spanish alphabet.

The way of writing was on canes, and now on paper, beginning the lines from the right hand to the left, in the Arabic fashion; almost all the inhabitants, both men and women, write in this language and there are very few of them who do not write it very well and with correctness.[1]

[1] A Relation of the Philippine Islands, by a monk who had resided there eighteen years, given by Thevenot, gives a plate (which has been reproduced here) of the Tagal alphabet, which consists of twelve consonants and three vowels, which serve as five: the consonants, when not marked by any point, are pronounced with a; if they bear a point above,

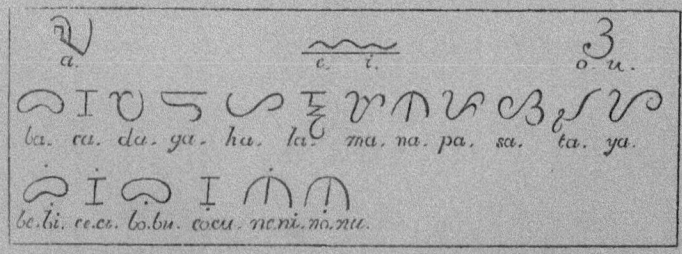

This language of the province of Manila extends over all the province of Camarines and other islands which are not conterminous to Luzon, with little difference between that of one part and another; except that in some provinces they speak with more culture than in others.

The buildings and houses of the natives of all these Philippine isles are of one same kind, and their towns also; because they always construct them on the sea shore between rivers and creeks; the natives usually collecting together in quarters and towns wherever they sow their rice and own their palms, nipa trees, plantain groves, and other trees, and apparatus for fisheries and navigation; and fewer number inhabit the interior of the country, who are the Tinguians, these also seek for sites by rivers and creeks on which they settle for the same objects.

The houses and dwellings of all these natives, are usually founded upon posts and piles (*arigues*[1],) high above the ground, with small rooms and low roofs, covered over and tiled with leaves of the palm, each house by itself, without one joining on close to another. At the bottom they are fenced in with stakes and canes, inside which they rear their fowls and animals, and sift and pound their rice; the ascent into the house is by means of ladders that can be drawn up, made of two bamboos; above they have the galleries[2] open for use, fathers and sons altogether, with little adorning and furniture in the house, which they call bahandin.[3]

they are pronounced with e or i; if the point is below, they are pronounced with o or u. The Tagals have learned from the Spaniards to write from left to right; formerly they wrote from top to bottom.

[1] *Arigues*. M. Mallat, vol. ii, p. 161, says, the theatre is built on high piles, and adds in a parenthesis the word *(arigues)*, so that it is apparently still in use, and must be the Spanish corruption of the Tagal *haligui*, a post, column, pillar. Ang. manga santos, manga haligui sa Santa Iglesia. The saints are pillars of the church. *Tagal Dictionary*, Manila, 1793, reprint of 1835.

[2] *Batalanes*, Tagal word for corridor, gallery.

[3] *Bahay*. Tagal a house.

Besides these houses, which are the ordinary ones, and belonging to people of less importance, there are the houses of the great men, built upon trees and thick piles (*arigues*), very roomy and commodious, well constructed of timber and planks, large and strong, furnished and fitted with all that is necessary, with much more splendour and substance than the others, but like the rest covered with leaves of the palm called nipa, which protect from the rain and sun much more than either shingles or tiles, though there is greater danger from fire.

The natives do not inhabit the lower part of their houses, because they rear their birds and animals in them, and on account of the humidity and heat of the earth, and for the number of rats, which are very large and mischievous both to the houses and seed in the fields: also, because as they are usually built on the beach, and on the shores of rivers and creeks, the lower parts are bathed in the waters, and so they leave them open.

In all these isles, there were neither kings nor rulers who governed them, after the manner of other kingdoms and provinces; but in each island and province, the natives recognised many of their number as chiefs, some greater than others, and each one with his partizans and subjects divided into quarters and families, and they obeyed and respected them; some of these chiefs maintained friendship and correspondence with others, and at times wars and disputes.

These chiefdoms and lordships were inherited by filiation and succession from father to son, and their descendants; and in default of them, the brothers and collaterals succeeded. Their duty was to rule and govern their subjects and partizans, and assist them in their wants and necessities; and what they received from their subjects was, to be greatly respected and venerated by them, and served in their wars, navigation, and labours of tillage and fishery, and the construction of their houses, which they always came to assist in, when they were summoned by their chief, with great punctuality. They also paid them tributes of the fruits which they gathered in, which they called buiz, some giving more, others less; the descendants of the chiefs and their kinsmen, were respected in the same manner, although they had not inherited the lordship, all these being esteemed as nobles, and persons exempt from the services of the other plebeians, who were named Timaguas.[1] The same nobility and chiefship was preserved amongst the women, as amongst the men, and when any of these chiefs was more spirited than others, in war or in other occasions, such an one brought round him a larger number of partizans and of men, and by him the others were governed, even though they were chiefs also: they retained in their own hands, however, the lordship and special government of their own party, which amongst them is named barangai, having *datos* (chiefs) and other special messengers who attend to the administration of the barangay.[2]

The supremacy which these chiefs had over the men of their barangay, was so great, that they held them as subjects, for good and evil treatment, and disposed of their persons, children, and property at their will, without opposition, and without having to give an account to any one; and for small causes of anger, and on trifling occasions they killed and wounded them, and reduced them to slavery; and it has happened, that for having passed in front of the chiefs whilst they were bathing in the river, or for having raised the eyes to look at them disrespectfully, or for other similar causes, that these subjects have been made slaves of for ever.

Whenever any of the natives had suits or differences with others, in matters of property and interests, or with respect to injuries and damage done to their persons, ancients of the same faction were named, who heard them, the parties being present; and if proofs were to be presented they brought

[1] Pronounced Timawa.
[2] In the Tagal dictionary *Balangay*, a quarter, a district.

there their witnesses, and according to what appeared, they at once judged the cause, in accordance with what had been the usage of their predecessors on similar occasions: and that decision was observed and executed without other reply or delay.

In all the islands these laws were, in the same manner, by tradition of the usages of the ancients, without keeping anything written: in some provinces the customs were different from what they were in others; in some matters, though in most things they agree and were in conformity, generally throughout the island.

There are three classes of persons amongst the inhabitants of these islands, and into which their republic is divided; the nobles, who have already been spoken of; the Timaguas who are the same as plebeians; and slaves belonging both to the nobles and the Timaguas.

These slaves were established on several different footings; some were in entire servitude and slavery, like those whom we hold, and these were called Saguiguilires, who served within the houses, and the children who were born of them the same.

There are others who have their own houses inhabited by themselves and families away from the house of their lord, and they come at times to assist them at seed time and harvest, and as rowing crews when they embark, and in building their houses when they build them, and to serve in their houses when there are distinguished guests or ceremony: and they are under the obligation, each time and whenever the lord sends to call them, to come to his house and serve him in these employments without any pay or stipend, and these slaves are called Namamahayes, and their children and descendants are slaves of the same quality. Of these slaves, Saguiguilires and Namamahayes, there are some who are entire slaves, and others half slaves, and others quarter slaves. And it happens in this wise, if the father or the mother were either of them free, and they had an only son, he would be half free and half enslaved; if they had more than one son they were divided in this manner; the first would follow the condition of the father, freeman or slave; and the second that of the mother: and if there were uneven numbers, the last odd one remained half free and half enslaved; and those who descended from these, being children of a free father or mother were only a fourth part slaves, from being the children of a free father or mother. and of a half slave. These half slaves, whether Saguiguilires or Namamahayes, serve their lords every other month. And such is the nature of their slavery.

In the same manner it happens, in partitions between heirs, that a slave may fall to the lot of several, and he serves each one the time which pertains to him. When a slave is not so entirely, but only a half or a quarter slave, he has the right, on account of that part of him which is free, to compel his lord to emancipate him for whatever may be just; and this price is taxed and regulated for persons according to the quality of their enslavement, whether Saguiguilir or Namamahay, half a slave or a quarter slave: but if the slave is so entirely, the lord cannot be compelled to exchange or emancipate him for any price.

Amongst the natives, the common price of a slave, if a Saguiguilir, usually is, at the most ten taels of fine gold, which are worth eighty dollars, and if he is a Namamahay, half of that sum. And the rest are in the same proportion, taking into consideration the persons and their age.

There is no certain beginning or cause from whence these enslavements began amongst these natives, because all of them belong to the islands, and are not foreigners: it is to be understood that they made these slaves during their wars and differences, and what is most certain is that those who were most powerful took and made slaves of the others on slight grounds and occasions; and most frequently on account of loans and usurious contracts, which were current amongst them, the payment, stock and debt increasing with delay, until they remained as slaves. Thus all these enslavements have violent and unjust beginnings, and most of the suits and pleadings between the natives, with which they occupy the judges, are upon these subjects, in the matter of civil law; and with these they occupy the confessors with regard to their consciences.

These slaves are the principal property and resource which the natives of these isles possess, as they are very useful to them, and necessary for their farms and husbandry; and amongst them they are sold, exchanged and bought like any other merchandise, from one town to another, and from one province to another, and likewise from one island to another. For which reason, and to escape from so many lawsuits as there would be if these enslavements were examined into with regard to their origin and foundation, they are preserved and maintained, as they were before maintained.

The marriages of these natives commonly and usually were and are, nobles with nobles, Timaguas with those of the same quality, and the slaves with those of their class; at times the different classes intermarry. They used to have one wife with whom they married, as with the real wife and mistress of the house, who was called Ynasaba ; and besides her, others as friends. The children of the first were held to be legitimate, and complete heirs of their fathers; and those born of the others as not being so, and they left them a portion by appointment, but they did not inherit.

The marriage portion was brought by the man, and his parents gave it him, and the wife brought nothing to the marriage, until she had inherited from her family. The marriage solemnity consisted in no more than the coming to an agreement of the parents and relations of the contracting parties, and in the payment of the portion which was agreed upon, to the father of the bride, and in the assembling together of all the relations in the house of father of the wife, to eat and drink all day till they fell down. At night the husband took her away to his own house and authority, and there it ended. They used to separate and dissolve these marriages for trifling causes, with the consideration and judgment of the relations of both parties, and of the elders who interfered in it: and then the marriage portion which had been received was returned to the husband, whom they name Vigadicaya, unless it happened that they separated on account of a fault on the part of the husband, for in that case it was not returned, and the parents of the wife retained it in their possession.

The property which they had acquired together was divided equally, and each one disposed of his own, and if either had any means of gain in which the consort did not participate or know of, that party acquired the sole possession of them.

They used to adopt one another in the presence of the relations, and the adopted son gave and made over what he actually possessed to him who adopted him; and upon that he remained in his house and power, and with the right of inheriting from him amongst the other sons.

Adulteries were not punishable corporally; on the adulterer paying to the injured man that which was appointed by the judgment of the elders, and was agreed upon by them, the injury was remitted, and the husband had received satisfaction and preserved his honour, and continued living with his wife without there being more talk about that matter.

In the case of inheritance, all the legitimate sons inherited equally from their parents the property acquired by them; and if there were any moveable goods or landed property which they had received from their fathers, and they had no legitimate sons from an Ynasaba, this property went to the nearest relations and collaterals of that stem; this was the case either by will or without one; in executing a will there was no more solemnity than to leave it written, or spoken by word of mouth before known persons.

If any noble was lord of a Barangay, his eldest son of his Ynasaba succeeded him in this, and in default of him, the next; and failing male children, the daughters in the same order: and failing legitimate successors, the succession returned to the nearest relation in the lineage and family of the chief, the last possessor.

If any native who had female slaves entered into relations with any one of them, and had children of her, the children and the slave (the mother) became free;[1] but if he had no children by her, she did not become so.

These children of slave women, and those had of married women, were held to be ill-born, and did not succeed with the other heirs to the inheritance, neither were the fathers under any obligation of leaving them anything; neither if they were sons of nobles did they inherit the nobility or the chieftainship of their fathers, nor the privileges of nobility, but they remained and were reckoned in the number and order of the other Timaguas, plebeians.

The contracts and business treaties of these natives were usually illicit, each one seeking how he might best attend to his own business and interests.

Loans with profit were very ordinary and much practised, very excessive interest being customary, so as to double and increase the debt, all the time it was deferred, to the whole extent of the principal; and the debtor and his children, when he possessed nothing else, became slaves.

Their usual way of trade was by barter of one thing for another, in provisions, cloths, cattle, fowls, lands, houses, crops in the ground, and slaves; also fisheries, palms, nipa

[1] Such is the law throughout most parts of Asia; in Siam the woman becomes free without having children. It is only in America that fathers could and did sell their own children into slavery.

trees, and woods; and sometimes a price intervened, which was paid in gold, according to the agreement made; also in metal bells brought from China, which they value as precious ornaments; these are like large pans, and are very sonorous, and they strike upon them at their feasts, and carry them in their vessels to the wars, instead of drums or other instruments. Often there were long terms and delays for some payments, and sureties who intervened and bound themselves, but always with profits and usurious interest, which was very excessive.

Crimes were punished at the suit of the aggrieved parties; robberies especially with greater severity, by reducing the thieves to slavery, and sometimes by death; it was the same with respect to insults by words, especially those offered to the chiefs; they considered many things and words as the greatest outrage and insult, when said to men or women, and they were less easily forgiven and with more difficulty than things done against the person, such as wounding and actual violence.

No account was taken of seductions, violations, and incests, unless they were done by a Timagua with a noble lady; and it was very ordinary for a man who married to have been for long time living in intimate relations with the sister of the woman whom he was going to marry; and even before living with his wife, to have had access for a long time to his mother-in-law, more especially if the bride were of tender age, until she was grown up, and this in the sight of all the relations.

The bachelors are called Bagontaos, and the unmarried girls, Dalagas. One and all are people of little continence, and from early youth they come and live together with facility and little secresy, and without its being a cause of regret or resentment amongst themselves; neither do the fathers, brothers or relations feel any resentment, more especially if there is any material interest in the matter, as a little goes a long way with any of them.

All the time these natives lived in their paganism, it was never heard that they had fallen into the unmentionable sin against nature; but after the Spaniards entered the country, from communication with them, and still more with that of the Sangleys who have come from China, and who are much given to that vice, something of it has adhered to them, both to men and women, and not a few measures have had to be taken against this matter.

Los naturales de las islas Pintados, especialmente las mugeres, son muy viciosas y sensuales, y la malicia entre ellos a inventado maneras torpes, de juntarse las mugeres y los varones, y an acostumbrado una, que desde muchachos, los varones hazen un agujero, con artificio en su miembro viril, por junto á la cabeza, y encajan en ella una cabezuela de serpiente, o de metal, o marfil, y pasanle un pernete de lo mismo por el agujero, para que no se les salga, y con este artificio, se juntan con la muger, sin poderlo sacar, despues del coito, en mucho rato, de que se envician y deleytan de manera, que aunque vierten mucha sangre, y reciben otros daños pasan por ellos; llamanse estos artificios, Sagras, y ay muy pocas, por que despues que se hazen Cristianos, se anda con cuydado, para quitarselas, y no consentir que lo usen, que se a remediado en la mayor parte.[1]

There were herbalists and sorcerers very generally amongst these natives; they were not prohibited nor punished amongst them so long as they caused no special mischief; which could rarely be ascertained or known.

There were also men who had for employment to ravish and take away the virginity of damsels; and they took

---

[1] Thomas Candish mentions having seen this custom in the island of Capul of the Philippines, and assigns a motive for it different from that given by De Morga. The more probable origin of it is that given by Mr. Eyre for a somewhat similar custom in Australia: "This extraordinary and inexplicable custom must have a great tendency to prevent the rapid increase of the population." *Central Australia*, vol. i, p. 213.

these to them, and paid the men to do it, considering it to be a hindrance and impediment when they married if they were virgins.

In the matter of their religion they proceeded more barbarously and with greater blindness than in all the rest; because, in addition to being gentiles, and having no knowledge whatever of the true God, neither did they cast about in their minds to discover Him by the way of reason, nor did they fix their thoughts on any. The devil deceived them in general with a thousand errors and blindness; he appeared to them in various horrible and fearful forms, and forms of savage animals, so that they feared and trembled at him; and adored him usually by making figures of those forms, which they kept in caverns and special houses, where they offered perfumes and sweet smells, and food and fruit, and they called them anitos.[1]

Others worshipped the sun and moon, making feasts and getting drunk at the conjunction; and some adored a bird which there is in the mountain woods, marked with yellow, which they call batala:[2] and in general they adored and reverenced the caymans, whenever they saw them, going upon their knees, and raising their hands to them, on account of the injuries which they receive from them, under the idea that by this they would be appeased and would leave them.

[1] Mr. Boyle describes (p. 205) two models of a male and female alligator made of mud the size of life in a secluded glade of the jungle, made by the Dayaks of Borneo, encircled by a rough palisade: he was told they were to keep off the antus from the paddy fields; these alligators and a doubtful figure in a *cavern* at Bidi were the only evidence he could gain of any religious feeling among the Dayaks. Mr. Boyle writes antu, which is near the anito of the Philippines. Captain Sherard Osborne, at Keddah, writes untu, and so it is pronounced at Penang; Marsden writes antu.

[2] The dictionary of Fray Domingo de los Santos gives Bathala as the Tagal name for God the Creator, in contradistinction to idols, which it says were called anito, and lic-ha or statues.

The oaths, maledictions, and promises are all, as has been said before: May the Buhayan eat you if you do not speak the truth, or fulfil what you promise, and similar things.

In all these islands there were no temples, nor public houses for the worship of idols, but each person made and kept in his house his anitos, without ceremony or certain solemnity; neither were there priests or monks to administer religious affairs, except a few old men and old women, whom they call Catalonas, great sorcerers and witches who deceive the rest of the people, who communicated to them their desires and wants, and they answered them a thousand absurdities and lies; and they performed prayers and other ceremonies to the idols for their sick, and believed in omens, superstitions which the devil persuaded them to, and according to which they said the sick man would get well, or that he would die. These were their methods of cure and the steps they took, and the use of auguries for all occurrences sought for in various ways. In all this there was so little attendance, show and pomp, or foundation, which God permitted, in order that in these parts the preaching of the holy Gospel should find them in a better disposition, and in order that they should more easily know the truth, and that there should be less to do in taking them out of their darkness, and the errors in which the devil had kept them for many years. Never had they sacrificed men to him, as is done in other kingdoms. They believed that there was another life, with rewards for those who had been valiant and done great deeds, and with punishments for those who had done evil, but they did not know how, nor where this would be.[1]

[1] This description would probably apply better to the Dayaks, than others which have been given of them, denying all religious belief. In the same way Mr. Eyre (vol. ii, p. 355) says: "The natives of New Holland, as far as yet can be ascertained, have no religious belief or ceremonies: a Deity, or great First Cause, can hardly be said to be acknowledged." This statement is however entirely contradicted in the

They buried their dead in their own houses, keeping their bodies and bones in boxes for a long time, and venerating their skulls, as if they were alive, and they had them still present. In their funeral rites they had neither pomp nor assemblages, but only the members of the family and house, where, after having wept for the deceased, all was changed to feasting and drunkenness amongst all the relations and friends.

A few natives of the island of Borneo began to come with their trade to the island of Luzon a few years before the Spaniards subjected it, especially to the towns of Manila

next page by the account given to Mr. Eyre by the natives of the Murray of the origin of the creation, which is, "that there are four individuals living up among the clouds called Nooreele, a father and his three male children, but there is no mother." (This is the Hindu system of creation by a Supreme Power with three emanations.) "The father is all powerful and of benevolent character. He made the earth, trees, etc., gave names to every thing and place, placed the natives in their different districts, telling each tribe that they were to inhabit such and such localities, and were to speak in such and such a language. It is said that he brought the natives originally from some place over the waters to the eastward. The Nooreele never die, and the souls (ludko, literally a shadow) of dead natives will go and join them in the skies and will never die again." Mr. Eyre also quotes the statement of Mr. Moorhouse that the natives round Adelaide "believe in a soul or spirit (itpitukutya) separate and distinct altogether from the body, which at death goes to the west, to a large pit, where the souls of all men go. When all are dead, the souls will return to their former place of residence, go to the graves of their forsaken bodies, and inquire, are these the bodies that we formerly inhabited? The bodies will reply, "we are not dead, but still living." The souls and bodies will not be reunited; the former will live in trees during the day, and at night alight on the ground, and eat grubs, lizards, frogs, and kangaroo rats, but not vegetable food of any description. The souls are never again to die, but will remain about the size of a boy eight years old." So that these natives, so far from being without a religion, recognised the Divinity under the attributes of the Almighty, the Creator, the Eternal, and the Merciful, and believed in the last day, and the resurrection of the dead, and life everlasting: and in this case again it is not possible to assert that there are any children of Adam who do not know their Lord.

and Tondo; and the people of the two islands intermarried. These people of Borneo are Mussulmans, and they were introducing their sect amongst these natives, giving them short prayers and ceremonies and forms to be observed, by means of some gazizes[1] whom they brought with them: and already many, and the greatest chiefs, were beginning (although by piecemeal) to become Muslims, circumcising themselves, and taking Muslim names, so that if the entrance of the Spaniards had been longer delayed, this sect would have extended over all the island, and even throughout the others; and it would have been difficult to have uprooted it from them. The mercy of God remedied it in time; so that, as it was but in the very beginning, it was banished from these islands, and they were free from it throughout all that the Spaniards have subdued, and placed under the government of the Philippines, while it has been much propagated and spread in the other islands which are outside of this government; for already the natives of nearly all of them are Mahomedan Moors, directed and instructed by their gazizes and morabits, who come to preach and teach them continually, from the straits of Mekkah and the Red Sea, from whence they navigate to these islands.

The entrance of the Spaniards into the Philippines since the year 1564, and the subjection and conversion which has been effected in them, and their mode of government, and that which during these years His Majesty has provided and ordered for their good, has been the cause of innovation in many things, such as are usual to kingdoms and provinces which change their faith and sovereign. The first has been that, besides the name of Philippines, which they took and received from the beginning of their conquest, all the islands are now a new kingdom and sovereignty, to which His Majesty Philip the Second, our sovereign, gave

[1] *Kasis.* This is another instance of the misapplication of this Arabic term, which means exclusively a Christian priest.

the name of new kingdom of Castile, of which, by his royal privilege, he made the city of Manila the capital, giving to it, as a special favour among others, a coat of arms with a crown, chosen and appointed by his royal person, which is a scutcheon divided across, and in the upper part a castle on a red field, and in the lower part a lion of gold, crowned and rampant, with a naked sword in the dexter hand, and half the body in the shape of a dolphin upon the waters of the sea, signifying that the Spaniards passed over them with arms to conquer this kingdom for the crown of Castile.

The commander-in-chief, Miguel Lopez de Legazpi, first governor of the Philippines, founded the city of Manila, in the isle of Luzon, in the same site in which Rajamora had his town and fort (as has been said more at length), at the mouth of the river which pours out into the bay, on a point which is formed between the river and the sea. He occupied the whole of it with this town, and divided it among the Spaniards in equal building plots, with streets and blocks of houses regularly laid out, straight and level, leaving a great place, tolerably square, where he erected the cathedral church and municipal buildings; and another place of arms, in which stood the fort, and there also the royal buildings: he gave sites to the monasteries and hospital and chapels which would be built, as this was a city which would grow and increase every day, as has already happened; because, in the course of time which passed by, it has become as illustrious as the best of the cities of all those parts.

The whole city is surrounded by a wall of hewn stone of more than two and a half yards in width, and in parts more than three, with small towers and traverses at intervals; it has a fortress of hewn stone at the point, which guards the bar and the river, with a ravelin close to the water, which contains a few heavy pieces of artillery which command the sea and the river, and other guns on the higher part of the fort for the defence of the bar, besides other middling-sized field guns and swivel guns, with vaults for supplies and munitions, and a powder magazine, with its inner space well protected, and an abundant well of fresh water; also quarters for soldiers and artillery-men, and a house for the commandant. It is newly fortified on the land side, in the place of arms, where the entrance is through a good wall, and two salient towers furnished with artillery which command the wall and gate. This fortress, named Santiago, has a detachment of thirty soldiers, with their officers, and eight artillery-men, who guard the gate and entrance in watches, under the command of an alcayde who lives within, and has the guard and custody of it.

There is another fortress, also of stone, in the same wall, at the distance of the range of a culverin, at the end of the wall which runs along the shore of the bay; this is named Nuestra Señora de Guia: it is a very large round block, with its courtyard, water and quarters, and magazines and other workshops within; it has an outwork jutting out towards the beach, in which there are a dozen of large and middle-sized guns, which command the bay, and sweep the wall which runs from it to the port and fort of Santiago. On the further side it has a large salient tower with four heavy pieces, which command the beach further on, towards the chapel of Nuestra Señora de Guia. The gate and entrance of this is within the city, it is guarded by a detachment of twenty soldiers, with their officers, and six artillery-men, a commandant, and his lieutenant, who dwell within.

On the land side, where the wall extends, there is a bastion called Sant Andres, with six pieces of artillery, which can fire in all directions, and a few swivel guns; and further on another outwork called San Gabriel, opposite the parian of the Sangleys, with the same number of cannon, and both these works have some soldiers and an ordinary guard.

The wall is sufficiently high, with battlements and turrets for its defence in the modern fashion: they have a circuit of a league, which may be traversed on the top of the walls, with many stairs on the inside at intervals, of the same stonework, and three principal city gates, and many other posterns to the river and beach for the service of the city in convenient places. All of these gates are shut before nightfall by the ordinary patrol, and the keys are carried to the guard-room of the royal buildings; and in the morning, when it is day, the patrol returns with them and opens the city.

The royal magazines are in the parade; in them are deposited and kept all the munitions and supplies, cordage, iron, copper, lead, artillery, arquebuses, and other things belonging to the royal treasury, with their special officials and workmen, who are under the command of the royal officers.

Close to these magazines is the powder magazine, with its master, officials, and convicts, in which, on ordinary occasions, thirty mortars grind powder, and that which is damaged is refined.

In another part of the city, in a convenient situation, is the cannon foundry, with its moulds, furnaces, and instruments, founders, and workmen, who carry on the works.

The royal buildings are very handsome, with a good view, and very roomy, with many windows opening seaward and to the parade; they are all of hewn stone, with two courts and high and low corridors with thick pillars. The governor and president resides in them with his family; there is a hall for the Royal High Court, which is very large and stately, a separate chapel, a chamber for the royal Seal, offices for the clerks of the council of the court, the clerk of the court,[1] and the clerk of the government, and other

[1] *Escribano de camara de la audiencia, escribano de la audiencia.*

rooms for the royal exchequer, and the administration of the royal officials, and a large porch opening to the street, and two large doors where the guard-room is placed; it contains a company of paid hackbut-men, who every day enter with their banner to mount guard. There is another house opposite, across the street, for the royal exchequer and the person who has it under his charge.

The houses of the municipality, which are in the great square, are of hewn stone, and have a good look out, and handsome halls; in the lower part is the prison, and the court-houses of the ordinary alcaldes.

In the same square is situated the cathedral church, built of hewn stone, with three naves, its chancel and choir, with stalls and seats, surrounded with gratings, and ornamented with an organ, lecterns, and the rest of what is requisite, with a sacristan and his apartments and offices.

Within the city is the monastery of St. Augustine, which is very large and well supplied with dormitories; it has a refectory and offices; a temple is being completed, which is one of the most sumptuous edifices that there are in those parts; this convent in general contains fifty monks.

The monastery of St. Dominic is within the walls, and may consist of forty monks; it was of stone, and very well constructed in regard to the church, dwelling-house, and all the offices; it is being newly rebuilt much better than it was, for it was entirely burned in the fire of the city in the year 1603.

The monastery of St. Francis is further on; it is well built of stone, and a new church is in the course of construction; it may consist of forty barefooted monks.

The college of the company of Jesus is founded close to the fort of Nuestra Señora de Guia; it is composed of twenty monks of their order, with a good house and church of stone; they promote the study of latinity, the arts, and cases of conscience, and close to them a college and assemblage of

Spanish students, with their rector, who wear cloaks of reddish yellow frieze and coloured hoods.[1]

In another part there is a good conventual house, with its stone church, called San Andres and Sta. Potenciana, a royal foundation, in which lives a lady rector, and other confidential assistants, with a parlour and circular door, where women in distress and maidens of the city are taken in under the form of religious retirement; and some go forth thence to be married, and others remain there permanently in the workshops and choir; His Majesty assists them with a part of their maintenance, and the rest is provided out of their own labour and property; they have their major domo and a priest as administrator.

In another part there is a royal hospital for Spaniards, built of stone, with a doctor, apothecary, surgeons, administrators, and servants, with its church, sick rooms, and set of beds, in which all Spaniards are cared for and attended; in general it is very full. It is under royal patronage, and His Majesty provides it with most of what it requires; it has as superintendents three barefooted Franciscan monks, who are of great use for the corporeal and spiritual cherishing of the sick. It was burned down in the fire of the past year of 1603, and is now being rebuilt.

There is another hospital of Mercy, under the charge of the community of that name, which was founded in the city of Manila by the brotherhood of Mercy of Lisbon, and the other brotherhoods of India; and, under Apostolic Bulls, for the purpose of works of charity, burying the dead, maintaining shamefaced poor people, portioning orphan girls, and relieving many misfortunes; in this hospital they take in the sick slaves of the city, and give lodgings to poor women.

Close to the monastery of St. Francis is the hospital for the native inhabitants, under royal patronage, which was founded, by means of alms, by a holy Franciscan lay friar,

[1] *Becas*, stripes or strips of stuff added to students' gowns.

named Fray Juan Clemente, in which a great number of natives are cured of all sorts of infirmities, with much care and delicate attention; it has a good house and offices of stone, and the barefooted Franciscan friars administer it; in this are employed three priests on the establishment, and four lay brothers of exemplary life, who are doctors, surgeons, and apothecaries of the hospital; they are so skilful and well qualified that many wonderful cures are wrought by their hands, both in medicine and surgery.

The streets of the city are well lined with houses, most of them of stone, and some of wood, many of them roofed with clay tiles, and others with nipa palm leaves; they are goodly houses, high and spacious, with large rooms, many windows, and balconies, and iron gratings to deck them out; and every day more are being built. There may be about six hundred houses within the walls, without reckoning as many more of wood, outside in the suburbs; all these are the dwellings and abodes of Spaniards.

The streets, squares, and churches are in general very full of people of all sorts, especially Spaniards, all dressed and equipped neatly in silks, men and women, with very choice clothes, and all sorts of costumes, on account of the facility which there is for this. So that this is one of the towns most praised by the strangers who flock to it of any in the world, both on this account, and by reason of the great plenty and abundance of provisions and other necessaries for human life which are there to be found, and at moderate prices.

Manila possesses two outlets for recreation, one[1] is by land by the point named Nuestra Señora de Guia, nearly a league along the beach, which is clean and very smooth, and

[1] The "Calzada," the Hyde Park of Manila, is often a double line of carriages extending nearly half a mile in length, and containing elegantly dressed women going out for evening exercise. Manila is really a gay, populous, and expensive place. Mr. Consul Farren, April 22, 1845.

by a street and town of the natives called Bagunbayan, as far as a chapel, an object of great devotion, named Nuestra Señora de Guia, and the road continues for a good distance as far as a monastery and mission of St. Augustine monks, called Mahalat.

The other promenade is by a gate of the city[1] to a native town named Laguio, from which it continues to a chapel of San Anton, and to a monastery and school of barefooted Franciscans, a place of much devotion named La Candelaria, near to the city.

This city is the capital of the kingdom, and of the government of all the islands, and the metropolis of the other cities and towns; in it reside the High Court and Chancery of His Majesty, and the governor and captain general of the islands.

It possesses a Town Council, with two ordinary alcaldes, twelve perpetual magistrates,[2] a chief constable,[3] a royal standard bearer, a clerk of the council, and other officials.

The archbishop of the Philippines resides in this city, with a metropolitan church, with all its dignities, canonries, prebends, and half prebends, chaplains, sacristans, choir of music and of organ-chaunt, and minstrels, and all the pomp and decoration with which the divine service is celebrated gravely and solemnly; it has, as its suffragans, the three bishops, who are in the islands of Sebu, Cagayan and Camarines.

There is a royal chest with three royal officials, factor, accountant, and treasurer, through whom the royal revenue of all the islands is administered.

From this city of Manila the ships are despatched, which every year perform the voyage to New Spain, with the merchandise and ventures of all the islands, and thither they return from New Spain with the proceeds of this merchandise, and with the usual succours.

---

[1] By the gate of Santa Lucia. Mallat.   [2] *Regidores.*
[3] *Alguazil mayor.*

Here is permanently established the camp of paid soldiers, which His Majesty ordered should be kept up in the islands.

In Manila, likewise, are stationed some galleys with their general and captains, and other armed ships of lofty bulwarks, and smaller craft in the country fashion, to attend to the necessities of all the islands.

The great mass of ships from China, Japan, Maluco, Borneo, Siam, Malaca, and India, which come to the Philippines with their merchandise to trade, all flock to the bay and river of Manila, and there sell and exchange for transmission to the other islands and towns.

The city of Segovia was founded in a province of this same island of Luzon, in the time of Don Gonzalo Ronquillo, the third governor; it consists of two hundred Spanish inhabitants, dwelling in wooden houses on the banks of the river Tagus, two leagues from the sea and port of Camalaynga; it has a fort of stone close to the city, for the defence of it and the river, with some artillery, and its commandant; in general it contains, besides the inhabitants, one hundred paid soldiers, arquebusiers, with their officers, under the command and rule of the chief alcalde of the province, who is commander in warlike affairs.

A bishop resides in this city, with a church, though at present without dignitaries or prebendaries; there is a town council, with two alcaldes, six magistrates, and a chief constable; it abounds in all sorts of provisions and delicacies, at very cheap prices.

The city of Cazeres was established in the province of Camarines, of the same isle of Luzon, in the time of Dr. Sande, governor of the Philippines; it may consist of one hundred Spanish inhabitants, with a town council, alcaldes, magistrates, and officials. A bishop of this province has his residence there, with a church, but without dignitaries or prebendaries, and there is a monastery of barefooted Franciscans. The government and affairs of war of this province are entrusted to a chief alcalde, who is commander in war time, and resides in Cazeres. It is a place well provided and supplied with all sorts of victuals at very cheap prices; it is in the interior of the country, four leagues from the sea, built on a river bank, of wooden houses.

The fourth city is that of the most holy name of Jesus, in the island of Sebu, province of Bisayas or Pintados, which was the first Spanish settlement, and was founded by the commander-in-chief, Miguel Lopez de Legazpi, the first governor. It has a fine sea-port, with a clean bottom and easy soundings, capable of holding a good many ships; it has a very good stone fort, with a quantity of artillery, with its commandant and officers, to guard the port and defend the city, with a sufficient garrison of paid troops, under the orders of the chief alcalde, and captain of the province in war time, who resides in the city. The town may contain two hundred Spanish inhabitants, with houses of wood; it has a town council, two ordinary alcaldes, eight magistrates, a chief constable, and his officials; it also has a bishop with his church, and, like the other cities of these islands, without prebendaries.

This city is well provided with supplies, and the ships which come from Maluco to Manila touch here by the permission of His Majesty. They have got a large ship for cargo, which usually leaves their port for New Spain with merchandise, consisting of the fruits and produce which are collected in these provinces. This city has a monastery of Augustine monks and a college of Jesuits.

In the island of Oton, the town of Arevalo was settled, in the time of the governor, Don Gonzalo Ronquillo, close to the sea; it may contain eighty Spanish inhabitants, and has a monastery of the order of St. Augustine, and a parish church, with a vicar and secular priest, belonging to the diocese of the Bishop of Sebu.

It has a town council, alcaldes and magistrates, and other

officials, also a chief alcalde and commander-in-chief for war of these provinces: the town is very well supplied with all sorts of provisions at very low prices.

The town of Villa Fernandina, which was founded in the province of Ilocos, in the isle of Luzon, is without Spanish inhabitants; there are very few Spaniards in it: it has a church with a vicar and a secular priest, of which no mention is now made on account of what has been said; the chief alcalde of the province resides in it, and it belongs to the diocese of the bishop of Cagayan.

Since the conquest and pacification of the Philippine isles commenced, the preaching of the holy Gospel was undertaken in them, and the conversion of the natives to our holy Catholic faith; and the first who set their hands to this work were the monks of the order of St. Augustine, who came over with the commander-in-chief Legazpi in the fleet which came to discover these islands, and those of the same order who came later to occupy themselves with this work: and they laboured in it with much fervour and care, in such a manner that, finding the harvest ripe, they gathered in the first fruits of it, converting and baptising many pagans in all parts of these islands.

After them, and at the fame of this conversion, there came over to these islands, by way of New Spain, barefooted monks of the order of St. Francis, and later, monks of the order of St. Dominic, and of the Company of Jesus, and more lately barefooted ascetic Augustine monks; one and all establishing themselves in the islands, they laboured in converting and instructing the natives. In this way they have effected that there are at present in all the islands a great number of baptised natives, besides many others, who, for want of ministers, are waiting in many parts in the expectation of this benefit, and of priests to administer it to them. As to instruction by secular clergy, up to the present time there is little of it, as few of them have come over to these islands, and but few have been ordained in them, for want of students.

The order of St. Augustine has many schools in the islands of Pintados, and established monasteries, and other visitations and missions; and in the isle of Luzon those of the province of Ylocos, and some in Pangasinan, and all those of Pampanga, which are many monasteries; and others which are very good in the province of Manila and its neighbourhood.

The Dominican order holds the schools of the province of Cagayan, and others in the province of Pangasinan, in which they have many monasteries and missions, besides others which they also administer around the city.

The Franciscan order has some schools and monasteries around Manila, and all the province of Camarines and the coast opposite to it, and the lagoon of Bay, which make a large number of schools.

The Company of Jesus has three large schools around Manila and many missions, and several others in Pintados in the isles of Sebu, Leite, Ybabao, Samar, and Bohol, and others of that neighbourhood, with good persons, careful of the conversion of the natives.

These four orders have produced much fruit in the conversion of these isles, as has been said, and in strictest truth the affairs of the faith have taken a good footing, as the people have a good disposition and genius, and they have seen the errors of their paganism and the truths of the Christian religion; they have got good churches and monasteries of wood, well constructed, with shrines and brilliant ornaments, and all the things required for the service, crosses, candlesticks, chalices of gold and silver, many brotherhoods, and religious acts, assiduity in the Sacraments and being present at Divine service, and care in maintaining and supplying their monks, with great obedience and respect; they also give for the prayers and burials of their dead, and perform this with all punctuality and liberality.

CONVERSION.

At the same time that the monks have taught the natives matters of religion in their schools, they labour to make them more skilful in things for their advancement, by holding schools of reading and writing in Spanish for the boys; teaching them to assist in the church, plain song, and chanting with the organ, and playing upon instruments, to dance and to sing, in which there is already great skill, especially round Manila; so that there are very good choirs of singers and musicians composed of natives, who have skill and good voices: and there are many dancers and musicians of other instruments who solemnize and adorn the feasts of the most holy sacrament, and many others in the course of the year; and they represent dramas and plays in Spanish and in their own language very gracefully. This is due to the care and assiduity of the monks, who, without ever wearying, are engaged in what may be of profit to them.

In these islands there is no province or town of the natives which resists conversion, and does not desire it; but, as has been said, in some, their baptism is delayed for want of labourers to remain with them to prevent their retrogression or reverting to their idolatries. In this matter the best that is possible is done, the divisions of the country for instruction being very large and extensive; and, in many places, the monks avail themselves of natives, who are well instructed and clever, to assist in their missions, by teaching the rest to pray every day, and to look after them in other matters touching religion, and bring the heads of families to mass, and so preserve and maintain them.

Till now the orders which carry on this religious instruction (by omnimodo and other apostolic regulations) have effected the conversion, and administered the sacraments, and managed the spiritual, temporal, and ecclesiastical affairs of the natives, and have given them dispensations in their hindrances; but now that there is an archbishop and bishops, this is being diminished, and the management of these affairs is being established in the hands of their vicars, although the administration of these natives is not so settled or arranged, by means of justices, or of the visitation and superintendence of the bishops, as it is attempted on their part.

The governor and High Court of Manila give their aid as far as is fitting, promote, and set on foot, by the best measures and expedients, the increase of the conversion, and administration, and religious instruction of the natives; such, for instance, as by obliging the tax collectors to come to the aid of the monks and churches within the collectorates which they enjoy, by furnishing the stipends and necessary expenses of the missions; also providing from the royal exchequer that part which corresponds to it in this matter, which is not the least portion; and ordaining, in any other matters which require providing for, or remedying, with regard to the said missions and improvement of the natives, that also aid should be furnished by the archbishop and bishops in what is under their charge and office as pastors.[1]

[1] A letter of Pope Clement VIII, dated March 25, 1592, addressed to the Bishop of Manila, and to the governor, clergy, monks, council, magistrates, nobles, encomenderos, and all the people of the Philippine Islands, congratulates them on the spread of Christianity, and expresses satisfaction at the mission to Rome of Alfonso Sanchez, a professed Jesuit priest who had been sent to the late Pope Sixtus V, and to those who had followed him; it exhorts them to persevere in faith and obedience, and in their exertions for the conversion of the heathen, and with that object in view, requires them to conform to Catholic precepts and make their lives a good example by their humanity and good treatment, not only of the Christians, but also of those not yet brought into the faith. Here is the original paragraph, especially addressed to the old Christians from Spain:—

"§ 5. Quoniam vero ad vitæ cujusque vestrum exemplar nationes istæ (vetustiores Christianos alloquimur), ut videtis, suas tamquam Christianis, atque Catholicis institutis consentaneas vivendi rationes facile conformaturæ sunt, a vobis requirimus, ut vestram humanitatem, benignitatemque tum Christianis, tum cæteris ad fidem nondum conversis, illis, ut confirmentur, his, ut ad veram Religionem alliciantur, quibuscumque

The Holy Office of the Inquisition, which resides in Mexico of New Spain, keeps in Manila, and in the bishopricks of the islands, its commissioners, familiars, and officials, for causes pertaining to the Holy Office, in which there is no want of constant work, on account of the entrance of so many foreigners in those parts. But this holy tribunal does not take cognizance of causes relating to the natives, as they have been so recently converted.

All these islands are peaceful, and are governed from Manila, having chief alcaldes, magistrates, and lieutenants, each of whom governs and administers justice in his province and district; appeals from their acts and sentences go to the High Court; and in what concerns the administration and war, the governor and captain-general provides and attends to it.

The chiefs, who before held the other natives in subjection, have now no power over them, in the arbitrary manner which they were accustomed to; this was not the least benefit which the natives have received by having come forth from such servitude. It is, however, the fact that, as regards the slavery, it has remained from former times on the same footing as before, and the King our Sovereign commanded, by his royal orders, that the honours should be paid to the chiefs that belonged to them, and that the rest should recognise them, and assist them with certain labours, such as they used to execute in the time of their paganism. This is the course followed in the case of the lords and possessors of Barangays, for those that are of the Barangay are under their governance; and when the lord gathers in his rice they go for a day to assist him, and likewise if he builds his house or repairs it; and this chief, lord of a Barangay, collects tributes from his followers and takes them under his charge to pay them to the tax collectors.

in rebus poteritis impertiri velitis."—*Bullarium Magnum*, Rome, 1753, tom. v, p. iii, p. 112.

Besides these, each town has a governor, who is elected, and who, with his constables, who are called vilangos, is the ordinary administrator of justice amongst the natives, and hears their civil suits in a moderate quantity; appeals lie from him to the first magistrate or chief alcalde of the province. The election of these governors takes place each year by the votes of all the married natives of that town, and the governor of Manila confirms it, and bestows the title of governor on the elected, and bids him take the place of the one who has vacated the office.

This governor, besides the vilangos and clerk before whom he passes his acts in writing, in the language of the natives of the province, also has the chiefs, lords of Barangays, and those chiefs who are not so, under his command and government, and at his disposition and orders, for whatever may occur, collection of tribute, and division or distribution of personal services; and they do not suffer the chiefs to do any injury to the timaguas or slaves whom they have in their power.

The customs which these natives observed in their paganism, these same, in as far as they are not contrary to natural right, they observe since they have become Christians, especially in their slavery, successions, inheritances, adoptions, wills, and lawful contracts; and, in their lawsuits, they always allege and prove the customs, and according to that, judgment is given; this is by royal orders; and in other causes, where there is no usage, and in criminal matters, the case is decided by law, as among the Spaniards.

All these islands and their inhabitants, when subdued, were from the first assigned[1] to the Royal Crown, that is, the capital towns, ports, and dwellers in cities and towns; there were also places and particular towns in all the provinces assigned for the requirements and expenses of the royal exchequer; the rest was all assigned and committed[1] to the

[1] Encomendar, encomienda: an encomendero is more like a Multezim

conquerors and settlers who had served and laboured in the conquest and pacification and in the war; and this is under the charge of the governor, who looks to the merits and services of the claimants. In the same manner, they always re-assign the towns which become vacant; the assigned districts are many and very good in all the islands, and very profitable, both on account of the quantity of tribute they yield, and for the value of what they give in tribute. An assignment lasts by the laws and royal orders, and by the order and manner of succession in them, for two lives, and, by permission, it may be extended to a third life, and afterwards it remains vacant, and is again assigned and newly filled up.

The tributes which the natives pay to the collectors were fixed by the first governor, Miguel Lopez de Legazpi, in the provinces of Bizayas and Pintados, and in the isles of Luzon and its neighbourhood, at a sum of eight reals,[1] as the whole yearly tribute of each tributary; this they paid in the produce which they possessed, gold, wrappers, cotton, rice, bells, fowls, and the rest of what they possessed or gathered, a price being fixed and a certain value for each thing, in order that when making payment of the tribute with any one of these articles, or with all of them, it should not exceed the value of the eight reals. In this manner it has gone on till now, the governors raising the prices fixed and valuations of the produce as has seemed expedient to them at different times.

The tax collectors have derived very great profits from collecting in kind; because, after the produce came into their possession, they used to sell it at a higher price, by which they largely increased their incomes and produce of

or Iltizamjy than a tax-collector, by which name I have translated encomendero.

[1] These reals are larger than reals de vellon, as eight of them go to a dollar instead of twenty.

their collectorates, until a few years previously, when, at the petition of some monks, and the instances which they made upon the subject to His Majesty, orders were issued that the natives should pay their tributes in whatever they chose, either in kind or in money, without being compelled to anything else; so that having given their eight reals they would have fulfilled their obligation. This has been carried out, and experience has shown that, though this appears to be a compassionate ordinance, and one favourable to the natives, it does them a great injury, because, being as they are of their natural disposition inimical to labour, they neither sow, nor weave, nor work the gold, nor rear fowls, or other provisions, as they used to do when they had to pay the tribute in these things; and they easily, without so much labour, acquire the sum of money with which they acquit themselves of their tribute. From this it follows that the natives, from not working, possess less property and substance, and the country, which was very well supplied and abounding in everything, commences to feel a want and scarcity of them, and the holders of the collectorates, both His Majesty, as well as the individuals who held them, have experienced great loss and reduction in their value.

When Gomez Perez Dasmariñas went to take the government of the Philippines, he brought royal orders for the formation in Manila of a camp of four hundred soldiers enrolled on the pay list, with their officers, galleys, and other warlike implements, for the defence and security of the country, in which at first all the Spanish inhabitants had been employed without any pay. Then it was ordained that an increase should be made, for each tributary, of two reals more, in addition to his eight reals, which should be levied by the collectors at the same time as the eight reals of the tribute, and that they should bring and pay them into the royal chest, in which they were placed to a separate account apart from the rest of His Majesty's revenue. They were applied in this manner—a real and a half for the expenses of the said camp, and the remaining half real for the stipend of the prebendaries of the church of Manila, whom His Majesty supplies additionally from his chest, so that their tithes and revenue may suffice for their maintenance.

These tributes are levied upon all the natives, Christians and pagans, in the entire sum; excepting in the collectorates in which there are no missions, the fourth part of the eight reals, which are two reals, are not taken by the collector for himself, since he has no religious schools, nor the expense of them, but he brings them into Manila to a chest, which is called that of the fourth parts, the proceeds of which from this source are applied to and spent upon hospitals of natives and in other works for their advantage, as the governor may see fit; and as they go on obtaining missions and monks, the receipt of these fourths and expenditure of them on these special works ceases.

In some provinces the number of natives has been reckoned; thus, by these reckonings, the tribute is levied, and the two reals are assigned.

In the greater number there has been no census, and the collection is made by the collectors and their tax-gatherers, with the chiefs within the collectorate who are present together at the time of collection, with the registers and accounts of past years, from which they strike off the deceased and those who have gone away, and add those who have grown up or newly come into the collectorate; and in making up the accounts, when a shortcoming is observed, an account is again required, and is made.

The natives are at liberty to change their residence from one island to another, and from one province to another, and they pay their tribute for the year in which they make their change of residence in the place to which they remove; and they remove from a Christian town where there is religious instruction to another town which has it too, but not in the contrary manner may they move from where there is instruction to a place where there is none,[1] nor, in the same town, may they remove from one barangay to another, nor from one faction to another. With respect to this, the necessary instructions are given by the administration, and ordinances are issued by the High Court, so that this order be observed, and that all inconveniences should cease from the permanent removal of the inhabitants from one part to another.

Neither are they allowed to go away from their towns, on trading expeditions, unless with permission from the governor or the chief alcalde or justices, and even from the monks, who have frequently been embarrassed by their going away on account of the religious instruction; this is to prevent the natives from wandering about without necessity away from their homes and towns.

[1] This was forbidden by paragraph 6 of a Papal Bull:—
X. Diversæ ordinationes circa Indos Insularum Philippinarum ad Christianam fidem conversos.
     Gregorius Papa XIV.
  Ad perpetuam rei memoriam cum sicuti nuper accepimus.
Datum Romæ apud S. Petrum sub Annulo Piscatoris die 18 Aprilis, 1591. Pontificatus nostri An. I.
§ 6. Et quia nonnulli earundem Insularum, & ordinum prædictorum rerum novarum curiosi de una ad aliam partem vagantes, aut transeuntes nuper conversos, et Baptizatos deserunt, ac propterea sunt in causa, ut interdum, quod maxime dolendum est, ii ad Idolatriam facile revertantur, & quod multi alii, qui alias ad fidei agnitionem venirent, et accederent ad Baptismum, ob defectum ministrorum id negligant, aut in Infidelitate permaneant; et è contra ipsi Religiosi etiam Idiomatis illarum partium ignari, in dedecus suorum ordinum contemnantur, ac debitos fructus suæ prædicationis in Vinea Domini non producant, difficilioremque Indorum conversionem reddant. Nos huic malo opportunum remedium adhibere cupientes, omnibus & singulis cujusvis Ordinis Religiosis, ac aliis quibuscumque circa Infidelium conversionem, & doctrinæ Christianæ eruditionem incumbentibus sub excommunicationis pœna, ne de pacifica ad non pacificam Terram accedere audeant, aut præsumant, nisi de ejusdem Episcopi, & Prælatorum Religionum expressâ licentiâ, & mandato in scriptis obtenta districte interdicimus, atque prohibemus."—*Bullarium Magnum*, Rome, 1751, tom. v, part i, p. 259.

The natives who hold slaves pay their tributes for them if they are saguiguilirs [domestic slaves], and if they are namamahays living out of their houses [serfs owing corvée] they pay it themselves for possessing, as they do, their own houses and means of gain.

The Spaniards used to hold some of the slaves of these natives, whom they had bought from them, and others whom they had acquired as prisoners in some expeditions during the conquest and pacification of the islands. This was abolished by a Brief of His Holiness[1] and by royal letters; so that all these slaves, natives of these isles, who were in the possession of the Spaniards, in whatever way they had been acquired, were set at liberty; and it was prohibited for the future for Spaniards to hold them, or to make them captives, for any reason whatever, nor under colour of there being war, nor in any other manner; and the service which they obtain from these natives is by pay and daily wages, and the other slaves and captives whom they hold are caffers and negroes, brought by the Portuguese by way of India,

---

[1] By paragraph 7 of the Bull cited above—

"§ 7. Postremo, cum sicut accepimus, charissimus in Christo filius noster Philippus Hispaniarum Rex Catholicus prohibuerit, quod nullus Hispanus in prædictis Insulis Philippinis Mancipia, sive servos, etiam jure belli justi & injusti, aut emptionis, vel quovis alio titulo, vel prætextu propter multas fraudes inibi committi solitas facere, vel habere, seu retinere audeant, & nonnulli adhuc eadem mancipia, apud se contra ipsius Philippi Regis edictum, vel mandatum detineant. Nos, ut ipsi Indi ad doctrinas Christianas, et ad proprias ædes, & bona sua libere, & secure absque ullo servitutis metu ire, & redire valeat, ut rationi congruit, & æquitati; omnibus & singulis cujuscumque status, gradus, conditionis, ordinis, & dignitatis existant, in eisdem Insulis existentibus personis, in virtute Sanctæ obedientiæ, & sub excommunicationis pœna præcipimus, & mandamus, quatenus publicatis præsentibus, quæcumque mancipia, & servos Indos, si quos habent, seu apud se detinent, ac omni dolo, & fraude cessante, liberos omnino dimittant, & imposterum, nec captivos, nec servos ullo modo faciant aut retineant, juxta dicti Philippi Regis edictum, seu mandatum." From the Bull of Gregory XIV, dated April 18, 1591. *Bullarium*, etc., Rome, 1751, tom. v, pt. i, p. 259.

obtained with justification for the enslavement, in conformity with the provincial councils and licences of the prelates and justices of those parts.

The natives of these islands also have personal service which they are obliged to render to the Spaniards, in some parts more than in others, and in different manners; this is commonly called the Polo: for where there are chief alcaldes and justices, they give and distribute to them by the week some natives for the service of their houses, paying them a moderate day's wages, which usually amounts to the fourth part of a real each day, and rice to eat; the same is done for the monks of the missions, and monasteries and churches, and for works belonging to these, and for other works of the community.

They also give rice and provisions of all kinds for prices which are sufficient and pass amongst these natives, which are always very moderate; and the chiefs, bilangos (constables), and fiscals make the division, gather, and take them from the natives; and in the same way they supply their tax collectors when these come to levy taxes.

The chief service which these natives render is on the occasion of war, giving rowers and crews for the vireys and ships which go on expeditions; and pioneers for what is most necessary in the course of the war, though they are paid their daily wages.

In the same way they appoint and distribute natives for the king's works, such as the construction of ships, felling timber, the yard for making cordage, the cannon foundry, and the service of the royal magazines, paying them their stipend and daily wages.

For the rest, in the matter of service of the Spaniards, in their voyages, works, or any other service which the natives render, it is voluntary and paid for by agreement; because as up to the present time the Spaniards do not work mines, nor have been addicted to the profits of agricultural labour, there is no need to employ them in anything of this sort.

The Spaniards who are in the Philippines reside for the most part in the city of Manila, which is the capital of the kingdom, and the chief seat of trade and commerce; and some tax-collectors live in their provinces and districts, and other Spaniards dwell in the cities of Segovia, Caceres, the most holy name of Jesus, in Sebu, and in the town of Arevalo, where they are settled, and most of them hold collectorates.

In the Indian towns Spaniards are not allowed,[1] except for the collection of the tribute, when the time for that arrives, and excepting the chief alcaldes, magistrates and justices; and these are not allowed to remain always in one town of their district, but they must visit it as much as they can; and every four months they must change their house and residence to some other central town or village, where all the natives may have access and obtain the fruit of their assistance, and that it may be less onerous for them in the matter of their maintenance and their ordinary service.[2]

The governor makes appointments to all offices, and when an office is fulfilled or vacated, the High Court sends to take an account of it, and issues its sentence thereupon; and until this is despatched, the official is not appointed to another post or office.

The governor also appoints commandants of forts, of companies, and other military offices, in all the cities, towns and villages of the islands.

Some offices of magistrates and clerks have been sold for one life, by a royal order, and the sale of them has now been desisted from, as it appeared that the price given for

[1] In Java also the Dutch restrict Europeans from roaming about the country; this is a good regulation for the protection of the inhabitants.

[2] These are most salutary regulations: the ordinary service refers to the service which the natives had to render by turns to the magistrates, as related above.

them was not of much importance, and that the drawback and disadvantage of making them thus perpetual was greater.

The elections of ordinary alcaldes in all the Spanish towns are held on New Year's Day by the town council and magistracy; and His Majesty orders the accounts of these alcaldes and town councils to be taken at the same time that accounts are taken from the governor and captain-general of the isles, and they give an account of the administration of their revenues and corporation estates; notwithstanding this, before this, each year, and at any time whenever it may seem to him expedient, the governor can call for their accounts, and have the balances gathered in; and with his opinion and authorisation the expenditure is made for things which the towns call for.

The city of Manila possesses a sufficient quantity of corporate property in the fines[1] which its judges impose, for certain years, and in the corporation estates within and without the city, and in the charges for reweighing merchandise, and the rents of all the properties, and sites of the Parian of the Sangleys, and in the monopoly of playing cards; all this was granted to it by His Majesty, especially for the expense of the fortification, and they expend their resources upon this and the salaries of their officials, and the agents whom they send to Spain, and in the city holidays, the chief of which are the day of Santa Potenciana, the 19th of May, on which the Spaniards entered and took the city; and St. Andrew's day, 30th of November, which was when they conquered and drove away the corsair Limahon. On this day the citizens bring out the city standard, with a procession to vespers and mass in the church of St. Andrew, at which all the city, the town council and magistracy and High Court are present, with all solemnity: the same takes place at the reception of the governors who newly arrive in the country, and at festivals for the marriages

[1] *Penas de camara.*

of the sovereigns, and births of princes, and honours and obsequies of those that die, and on all these occasions as great a demonstration as possible is made.

The other cities and towns have not, up to the present time, got as many estates or corporate property, nor requirements upon which to make expenditure, although, within the measure of their means, they take their part in all that is of the same kind.

The Spaniards who are in the islands are divided into five sorts of persons: these are prelates, monks, and ecclesiastical ministers secular and regular; tax-collectors, settlers, and conquerors; soldiers, officers, and officials of war, by sea and land, and of navigation; merchants and persons employed in trade and commerce; officials of His Majesty for the government, justice, and administration of the royal exchequer.

The ecclesiastical prelates, it has been already said, are the Archbishop of Manila, who resides in the city as metropolitan, with his cathedral church; he has four thousand dollars stipend, which is paid yearly from the royal chest: and the stipend of the dignitaries, canons, prebendaries, and other officials of this church is paid in the same way, for the whole is a royal patronage, and the appointments are made conformably. His office and jurisdiction is, and extends over all that is spiritual and temporal and ecclesiastical, and the governance of it.

The bishop of the city of the most holy name of Jesus, in Sebu, and the bishop of Segovia in Cagayan, and he of Caceres in Camarines, possess the same jurisdiction and office in their dioceses as suffragans of the metropolitan of Manila, to whom appeals may be made from their sentences: and he summons and assembles them for his provincial councils, when it is expedient. Each of these bishops has five hundred thousand maravedis[1] as stipend for his main-

---

[1] Equal to 735 dollars, 5 reals, and 30 maravedis.

tenance from the royal chest of Manila, besides the offerings and his pontifical rights, all which together, in consequence of the cheapness and plenty of the country, is amply sufficient for their maintenance. For the present they have not got churches with prebendaries, nor is any stipend allowed them for that purpose.

The regular prelates are the provincials of the four mendicant orders of St. Dominic, St. Augustine, St. Francis, the Company of Jesus, and the barefooted Augustines, each of whom governs his order and visits it: these have in their hands almost the whole of the religious instruction of the natives, in what concerns the administration of the sacraments and conversion (by favour), and in conformity with their privileges and Apostolic Bulls; in this they maintain themselves up to the present time: and in judicial matters they are as vicars of the bishops, with nominations and powers from them. The barefooted Augustines up to the present time have no missions, as they have recently arrived in the islands.

The monasteries are maintained out of some private revenues which they possess or have acquired, especially the Augustines, and those of the Company, and by succours and allowances which His Majesty has given them. The Dominicans and Franciscans do not possess nor accept revenues or properties; and they and the others principally depend upon alms, offerings, and the money offered for the deceased in the parts where they reside and officiate; for this is done both by the Spaniards and also by the natives with much piety and in abundance, and they also receive the stipend which the collectorates pay to them for the religious instruction which they administer: so that they are well off and have the necessary comforts.

The collectors, conquerors and settlers, who are of the first comers to the islands, and those who have descended from them, maintain themselves honourably with the proceeds of their collectorates, and with some trade and means of gain which they enjoy like the rest. Of these there are many persons, who each reside and own houses in the city and town of Spaniards in the province where they hold their collectorate, so as not to abandon it, and to be nearer at hand for their requirements and receipt of the tribute.

There are now few living of the first conquerors who won the country, and came over to its conquest with the commander-in-chief, Miguel Lopez de Legazpi.

The soldiers and military and naval officials used to be the whole of the dwellers and residents in the islands, who without any pay or allowances bore arms, and used to go on all expeditions and pacifications which offered; and they guarded the forts and strongholds, the cities and towns; and this was their principal exercise and occupation, being at the discretion of the governor, who, according to their merits and services, appointed them to collectorates, offices, and common lands of the country.[1]

In that time the soldiery of the islands was the best existing in the Indies, of great experience and practice at sea and land, esteemed and respected by all those nations: they took a pride in their arms and in giving a good account of themselves.

After that Gomez Perez Dasmariñas entered upon the government, a camp of paid soldiers was established of four hundred men; the arquebusiers had six dollars monthly pay, and the musketeers eight dollars: there were six captains at four hundred and twenty dollars yearly pay each, with ensigns, serjeants, corporals, banner bearers, and drummers with pay in proportion; a master of the camp, with pay of one thousand four hundred dollars a year; a serjeant-major, with captain's pay; an assistant of the serjeant-major and field-captain, with ten dollars pay a month; two wardens and commandants of the two fortresses of Manila, each one

[1] *Aprovechamientos*, or profits.

with four hundred dollars a year, with their lieutenants and squads of soldier and artillery-men; a general of the galleys with eight hundred dollars yearly pay; a captain to each galley with three hundred dollars a year; with boatswains, second boatswains, coxswains, alguazils of the galleys, soldiers, gunners, carpenters, riggers, sailors, pressed men,[1] and the rabble of galley slaves, Spaniards, Sangleys, and natives condemned for crimes. And when convicts are scarce, good rowers are got from the natives by payment, for the time that the expedition or occasion for the voyage lasts.

In despatching fleets of large ships for the voyage to New Spain, the ships which are sent carry a general and vice-admiral, masters and boatswains, storekeepers, stewards, alguazils, gunners, and artillery-men, sailors, pilots and their aids, ship-boys, carpenters, caulkers, and coopers, in the pay of His Majesty, from whose royal chest in New Spain they are paid, according to what was there established and settled, and all that is necessary for the fleet is there provided. Its supplies and appointments are attended to by the Viceroy of New Spain, whom this has hitherto concerned, although the ships may have been built in the Philippines and sail thence with the cargo of merchandise for New Spain, whence they return with the succours of soldiery and munitions, and the rest of what is required for the camp, and with passengers and monks, and with the money proceeding from the sale of the merchandise.

After that the camp of paid troops was founded for the forts and expeditions, the other inhabitants and residents continued to be enrolled, and under the banners of six land captains, without pay, for indispensable occasions of the defence of the city, but relieved from all other services pertaining to soldiery, unless they were to offer themselves of their own free will for any expedition or special occasion, in order to possess merits and good service by which they

[1] *Concejeles*, men sent to service by order of a Municipal Council.

might be employed in collectorates which became vacant, or in offices, or gain grants of land; they are not obliged nor urged to this if they do not hold collectorates. In this way all have turned to trade, having no other occupation, but not for that letting themselves forget their military exercise.

His Majesty prohibits all those who draw his pay for the army in these islands from being merchants, and orders the governor not to suffer it, nor to embark their goods for New Spain; and if this was carried out, it would not be ill.

The merchants and traders form the greater part of the residents in these islands, on account of the quantity of merchandise which flows in to them (in addition to the produce of the country) from China, Japan, Maluco, Malacca, Siam, and Camboja, Borneo, and other parts, with which they make their ventures, and every year embark them in ships which sail for New Spain: and now for Japan, where raw silk is very profitable, and whence the proceeds are brought to them on the return to Manila, and up to this time the gains have been great and brilliant.

As this trade had so much increased, it had inflicted great loss and injury on the merchandise of Spain which was embarked for Peru and New Spain, and upon the royal duties which used to be levied upon them, and the men of business in Mexico and Peru had grown eager to trade with the Philippines by means of their agents and factors; so much so, that the trade of Spain was, in the greater part, coming to an end; and they used to send much silver to the Philippines for their purchases, which in that manner every year flowed out of the realms of His Majesty into the possession of the pagans; it was prohibited that any persons of New Spain or Peru should trade with the Philippines, and they were not to bring Chinese goods to those parts; and licence was given to the dwellers and residents in the Philippines by which they alone might trade in those said goods, and load and embark them, provided that they take or send them with persons belonging to the islands, in order that they should sell them, and that of the proceeds of the said merchandise no more should be sent in coin to the Philippines than five hundred thousand dollars each year.[1]

Usually there come from great China to Manila a large number of somas and junks, which are large ships, laden with merchandise; and each year thirty usually come, and sometimes forty ships, and although they do not come in together in the form of a fleet or convoy, they come in squadrons, with the monsoon and settled weather, which most generally is in the new moon of March. They are from the provinces of Canton, Chincheo, and Ucheo, whence they sail; they perform their voyage to Manila in fifteen or twenty days, and sell their merchandise, and return in time before the south-westerly gales set in, which is at the end of May and in the first days of June, so as not to be exposed to danger in their voyage.

These ships come laden with goods, and bring great merchants, the owners of the goods, with servants, and the agents of other merchants who remain in China; and they come out of that country with permission from their viceroys and mandarins. The goods which they usually bring, and sell to the Spaniards, are raw silk, in bundles of the thickness of only two strands, and other silk of inferior quality, soft untwisted silk, white and of other colours in small skeins, much smooth velvet, and velvet embroidered in all sorts of colours and patterns; and others with the ground of gold and embroidered by hand with the same material; stuffs and brocades of gold and silver upon silk of various colours and design, many other brocades, and silver twist in skeins, upon thread and upon silk, but all the spangles of gold and silver are false and upon paper;

[1] De Morga has already said (page 287) that this restriction of the money sent from Mexico for goods from the Philippines to 500,000 dollars was felt as a hardship in the Philippines.

damasks, satins, taffetans, and gorvarans; glossy silks, and other stuffs of all colours, some finer and better than others; a quantity of linen made of grass, which they call handkerchief stuff,[1] and white cotton tablecloths of different kinds and sorts, for all sorts of uses; musk, benzoin, ivory, many ornaments for beds, hangings, coverlets, and curtains embroidered on velvet; damask and gorvaran of many shades of colour, tablecovers, cushions, carpets, caparisons of horses of the same stuff, and with bugles or seed pearl; some pearls and rubies, sapphires, stones of crystal, basons, kettles, and other vases of copper and cast iron, large assortments of nails of all sorts, sheet iron, tin, lead, saltpetre and powder, wheat, flour, preserves of oranges, peaches, viper-root, pears, nutmeg, ginger, and other fruits of China, hams of pig, and other salt meats, live fowls of good breed, and very fine capons, much fresh fruit, oranges of all kinds, very good chestnuts, walnuts, pears, *chicueys* fresh and dried, which is a very delicate fruit; much fine thread of all kinds, needles, knick-knacks, little boxes, and writing boxes;

[1] *Lencesuelo*. This fabric is now called *Piña*. It is made of threads stripped from fibres of the leaf of that plant or fruit, and which are never longer than half a yard. It cannot be woven at all times, as extreme heat or humidity affects the fibre. The machinery employed is of wood, unmixed with any metal, and of rude construction. This fabric is stronger than any other of equal fineness, and its colour is unaffected by time or washing. The pieces are generally only 1½ feet wide: the price varies from 1s. 4d. to 2s. 6d. per yard. Piña of a yard wide is from six reals to a dollar (of eight reals) a yard. All the joinings of the threads are of knots made by the fingers. It is fabricated solely by native Indians in many parts of the Philippines, but especially in Ilo-Ilo. The use of this stuff is extensive, and the value is estimated at 500,000 dollars, or £120,000; the value of the annual export of it to Europe for dresses, handkerchiefs, collars, scarves, and wristbands, which are beautifully embroidered at Manila, is estimated at 20,000 dollars annually. Signor Ortiz of Ilo-Ilo employs continually upwards of two hundred weavers upon this fabric; and he has sent a piece made expressly for the Exhibition of 1851.—Mr. Consul Farren, January 21, 1851.

beds, tables, chairs, gilt seats painted with all sorts of figures and designs, tame buffaloes, geese like swans, horses, some mules and donkeys, and even caged birds, some of which talk and others sing, and they make them play a thousand tricks; and a thousand other gewgaws and ornaments of little cost and price, which are valued among the Spaniards; besides much fine crockery of all sorts, *cangans*, and *sines*, and black and blue wrappers, *tacley*, which are beads of all kinds, and cornelians in strings, and other beads and stones of all colours; pepper and other spice; and curiosities, to recount all which would be never to come to an end, nor would much paper be sufficient for it.

As soon as the ship arrives at the mouth of the bay of Manila, the watchman who is in the island of Miraveles goes out to meet it in a light vessel, and having examined it, he puts on board two or three soldiers as guards, for it to go and anchor at the bar near the city, and that no one should land from the ship, nor enter it from without, until it has been inspected; and by the signal which the watchman makes by fire from his island, and the notice he sends in haste to the city of what ship it is, and from whence it comes, and what people and goods it brings, before it comes to anchor, the governor and the city generally know all about it.

On arriving and casting anchor, the royal officers go to inspect the ship and bills of cargo and entry of the goods which it brings, and at the same time a valuation is formally made of what they are worth in Manila; because it at once pays three per cent upon all of them to His Majesty. When the list and valuation have been made, the merchandise is at once taken out and discharged in champans, and carried to the parian, or to other houses and warehouses, which they have outside the city, and they sell it in full liberty.

No Spaniard or Sangley, or other person is allowed to go and buy or barter merchandise or provisions, nor anything else in the ship, nor, when they have got their goods on shore in their houses or warehouses, is it allowed to take or buy them by force or violence; but the trade must be free, and the Sangleys may do with their property what they like.

Usually the price of the raw silk, and silk stuffs, and wrappers, which is the bulk of what they bring, is settled at leisure, and by persons who understand the business, both on the part of the Spaniards and of the Sangleys, and what is given them for it, is silver and reals, for they do not like gold, nor any other goods in exchange, nor do they carry any to China: and all the purchase must be made within the month of May, a little more or less, in order that the Sangley may be able to return, and in order that the Spaniard may have it all in readiness to load it in the ships which by the end of June sail for New Spain; though indeed those who are most careful of gain and well provided with money usually effect their bargains later at more moderate prices, and keep their goods till another year. Some Sangleys with the same object remain in Manila with a part of their merchandise, when they have not had a good sale for it, and go on selling it more at leisure. They are very experienced and intelligent people in trade, and of great coolness and moderation for the better carrying on of their business; and they are ready to trust and give liberal facilities to whomsoever they know deals with them honestly, and will not fail in his payments at the time which is appointed: on the other hand, as people without a faith or conscience, and so avaricious, they are guilty of a thousand frauds and tricks in their merchandise, so that it is necessary to be very attentive, and to know the goods, for the buyers not to be taken in; they, on their side, are quits with their bad payments and frauds, so that between both of them the judges and High Court have much with which to occupy themselves.

There come likewise every year from Japan, from the port of Nangasaki, with the north winds at the end of October, and during the month of March, a few ships with merchandise, Japanese and Portuguese, which enter and anchor off Manila observing the same order; the bulk of what they bring is wheaten flour of a very good quality, for the supply of Manila, salt meats that are highly prized, some silk stuffs of combined colours, and very smart screens painted in oil,[1] and gilt, fine and well fitted up; all sorts of cutlery, many collections of arms, lances, catans, and other halberds, curiously wrought, small writing boxes, boxes and caskets of wood, varnished and of curious workmanship, and other baubles pretty to look at, very good fresh pears, barrels and kegs of good salted tunny, cages of larks which are very good, and which they call fimbaros, and other trifles. In this trade some purchases are also made, without royal duties being levied upon these ships, and the greater part of these goods are used in the country, and some serve for cargoes to New Spain. The price is chiefly paid in reals, though they are not so set upon them as the Chinese, as they have silver in Japan; and generally a quantity of it is brought in plate as merchandise, which they supply at moderate prices.

These ships return to Japan at the season of the south-westerly gales in the months of June and July; they carry their purchases from Manila, which consist of raw silk from China, gold, stags' horns, and Brazil wood for their dye; and they also take honey, manufactured wax, palm wine, and wines from Castile, civet cats, tibor jars for keeping their tea, glass panes, cloth, and other rarities from Spain.

Some Portuguese ships come each year to Manila from Maluco and from Malacca with the south-west monsoon; the goods they bring are cloves, cinnamon, pepper, black and Caffre slaves, cotton cloths of all sorts, fine muslins, *caniqui*,

---

[1] *Bionos al olio*, perhaps a misprint for *biombos*.

fine stiff cotton stuff (*bofeta*), gauze (*caza*), *rambutis*, and other sorts of stuffs very fine and costly, amber and ivory, embroidered stuff of aloes, ornamental coverings for beds, hangings and rich coverlets of Bengal, Cochin, and other countries, many gilt things and curiosities, jewels of diamonds, rubies, sapphires, topazes, balashes, and other fine stones, set and separate; many pendant jewels for head-dresses and rarities from India, wine, raisins and almonds, delicate preserves, and other fruits brought from Portugal and prepared in Goa, carpets, and small carpets of silk and fine wools from Persia and Turkey, writing cases, drawing-room chairs and other furniture daintily gilt, made in Macao, needlework on white stuffs and silk of combined colours, chain lace and royal point lace, and other work of much delicacy and perfection. All these things are purchased in Manila, and paid for in reals and in gold, and these ships return in January with the north-east winds, which are their fixed monsoon; and for Maluco they take away provisions of rice, wine, crockery, and other baubles which are in request there, and to Malacca only gold or money, excepting a few particular gewgaws and rarities from Spain, and emeralds: the king's duties are not levied on these ships.

Smaller vessels come likewise from Borneo, belonging to the natives of that island; they come with the south-westerly gales, and return with the north-east winds: they enter the Manila river, and sell what they bring inside their ships, which consists of very fine palm mats, highly finished; some slaves for the natives; sago, which is a certain food of theirs made of the pith of palm trees; tibors and large and small jars, glazed black, very fine, of much durability and use; fine camphor, which is produced in that island; and although on its opposite coast fine diamonds are found, they do not come to Manila by this way because the Portuguese of Malacca barter for them in that part. The purchases of these Borneo articles are made more by the natives than by the Spaniards, and what they take in return are supplies of rice and wine, cotton wrappers, and other baubles of the islands which are wanting in Borneo.

A few ships come on rare occasions to Manila from Siam and Camboja: they bring some benzoin, pepper, ivory, cotton cloths, rubies and sapphires badly cut and set, a few slaves, horns of the female rhinoceros, the hide, hoofs, and teeth of that animal, and other trinkets; and on the return they take those (the trinkets) which there are in Manila. Their coming and return is between the north-easters and south-westers, during the months of April, May, and June.

The Spaniards make their purchases, gains, and shipments for New Spain of these goods and with the produce of the islands, which are gold, cotton cloths, medriñaques, white and yellow wax in cakes; each one does as best suits him, and they load them in the ships which are to make the voyage, valuing and registering them, because they pay two per cent. export duty into the royal chest of Manila before they sail, besides the freight of the ship, which is forty ducats of Castile per ton, which is paid in the port of Acapulco in New Spain into the royal chest of that port, besides the duties of ten per cent. on the importation and first sale in New Spain.

Since the ships which are despatched with this merchandise are on account of His Majesty, and no others are allowed to navigate, there is usually a great pressure and difficulty in shipping all the purchases; the governor divides the shipments amongst all the shippers according to their respective capital and deserts, examined into by intelligent persons whom he names for that purpose; so that each one knows by the distribution made how much he can ship, and that quantity only is received into the ship, with full account and care taken by confidential persons who are present at taking in the cargo, leaving space for the provisions and passengers which the ships have to take. When they are laden and ready to sail, officials are put at the disposal of the general who take the merchandise under their charge, and they set out on the voyage at the end of the month of June, with the first south-westers.

This trade and merchandise is so considerable and profitable, and easy to administrate (because it only lasts three months of the year, from the time that the ships arrive with the merchandise until those that go to New Spain take it away), that the Spaniards have not applied themselves to nor undertake anything else. So that there are neither agricultural works nor undertakings of any importance, nor do they work mines or gold washings, of which there are many, nor do they devote themselves to many other things, which they might do with great profit if the trade with China should come to be interrupted; this trade has been in this respect very detrimental and prejudicial, and also for the occupations and labours which the natives used to be employed in, for now they are abandoning and forgetting them: besides the loss and detriment of so much silver leaving this port every year to go into the possession of the pagans, which will never return by any way into the possession of the Spaniards.

The ministers of His Majesty for the government and justice, and the royal officials for the administration of His Majesty's finance are the governor and captain-general of all the islands, who at the same time is president of the High Court of Manila. He has as salary for all his offices eight thousand dollars[1] a year, and his guard of twelve halberdiers, with a captain of the guard, with three hundred dollars yearly pay: he issues orders, and despatches by himself all that pertains to war and government, with consultation with the auditors of the High Court in arduous cases; and he takes cognisance of criminal causes in the first instance in the case of the paid soldiers, and appeals from this process go to the High Court.

[1] *Pesos de minas.*

He appoints many chief alcaldes, chief magistrates, lieutenants, and other justices, in all the isles and their provinces, for the carrying on of the government and of justice and affairs of war, in the presence of the chief secretary of the government, appointed by His Majesty, who takes part with the governor.

Together with this, he is present at the High Court as its president in all that pertains to it; in which there are four auditors and a fiscal, each one with a salary of two thousand dollars a year, a reporter and a secretary, a chief constable, with his lieutenants and the warden of the prison of the Court, a chancellor and registrar, two porters, a chaplain and sacristan, an executioner, attornies and clerks.[1] The High Court takes cognisance of all causes civil and criminal which are brought before it from all the provinces of its district; these are the Philippine islands, and the mainland of China, discovered and yet to be discovered; and it has the same powers as the Chanceries of Valladolid and Granada in Spain. Together with this the High Court provides what is fitting for the good administration, accounts, and order of the royal exchequer.

The chest of the royal exchequer of His Majesty in the Philippines and its tribunal consists of three royal officials whom His Majesty appoints, a factor, accountant, and treasurer, each of them with a salary of five hundred and ten thousand maravedis[2] a year, with their clerk of the mines and registers of the royal finance, officers for executions and officials, who reside in Manila; from whence they administer and despatch all that pertains to the royal exchequer in all the islands.

His Majesty possessed, belonging to his royal crown of the Philippines, a quantity of encomiendas in all the provinces of the Philippines, which are collected into his

---

[1] *Procuradores y recetores.*
[2] Seven hundred and fifty dollars.

royal chest by means of the king's officials, and the collectors whom they send for that purpose; these, one year with another, amount to thirty thousand dollars, free of costs and expenses.

They collect eight thousand dollars from the tribute of the Sangleys, Christians, and pagans, one year with another.

They also levy fifths upon all the gold which is obtained in the islands; and by a special favour granted for a limited time, instead of a fifth a tenth is taken. Upon this there is a declaration that neither fifths nor other duties should be paid upon the jewels and gold which the natives held from their ancestors before that His Majesty came into possession of the country; for the clear specification of this, and for the certifying of those jewels, and of those which have once paid a tenth, and for the measures which are to be taken in the matter, sufficient provisions have been made.

One year with another ten thousand dollars are raised from these fifths, for many are kept back.

There enters into the royal chest and is made over to it the sum of two reals assigned from each tributary for the pay of the soldiery, and stipend of the prebendaries, which the collectors receive and bring, in conformity with the account by which they collect the tributes,[1] which is worth and amounts, one year with another, to thirty-four thousand dollars.

The fines and costs of justice are taken possession of by the treasurer of the royal exchequer and enter the royal chest, and one year with another are worth three thousand dollars.

The duties of three per cent. on the merchandise brought from China by the Sangleys ships are worth, one year with another, forty thousand dollars.

The duties of two per cent. which the Spaniards pay for

[1] These two reals are those which were added to the tribute of eight reals, see page 325.

the export of the merchandise which they ship to New Spain, one year with another, amount to twenty thousand dollars, and the duties on the merchandise and money which are brought from New Spain to the Philippines amount to eight thousand dollars more: so that from these sources, and small matters of less importance, which belong to the royal exchequer, His Majesty receives in the Philippines every year a hundred and fifty thousand dollars, a little more or less.

Besides these, as this is not sufficient for the expenditure which is made, every year a succour in money is sent from the royal chest in New Spain to that of the Philippines, more or less in quantity, according as the exigency requires; because His Majesty has made this provision for it from the proceeds of the duty of ten per cent. which is levied upon the merchandise from China in the port of Acapulco of New Spain. This succour enters into the custody of the royal officials of Manila, and they take charge of it with the rest of the finance which they administer and gather in.

Out of the mass of this finance of His Majesty the salaries of the governor and High Court are paid, also the stipends of the prelates and ecclesiastical prebendaries, and the salaries of the justices, and the royal officials and their assistants, the pay of all the military officers and paid troops; all the payments pertain to His Majesty in the way of stipends for religious instruction and sums for the fabric and ornaments of churches, gratuities and money to assist certain monasteries and private persons, the construction of sea-going ships for the navigation to New Spain, and of galleys and other vessels for the defence of the islands, expenditure for gunpowder, munitions, cannon-foundry, and the dock-yard, and the expenditure which has to be incurred for expeditions and particular enterprises in the islands, and for their defence, and for voyages and business with the neighbouring kingdoms, which are very ordinary and obligatory: in such sort, that the resources which His Majesty possesses in these isles being so limited and the expenditure so great, the royal exchequer is drained, and straits and indigence experienced.

Moreover, the proceeds of the duty of ten per cent. and freight of the ships, which are levied in Acapulco of New Spain upon the merchandise which is shipped thither from the Philippines, although they are copious, yet they are not always sufficient for the expenses which are incurred in New Spain for the ships, soldiers, munitions, and other things which are sent every year to the Philippines; these expenses usually mount up much higher, and the royal chest of Mexico supplies the deficiency. So that up to the present time the king our sovereign has no financial profit whatever in the Philippines, but on the contrary no small expense out of his revenues in New Spain; and he only endures them for the sake of Christianity and the conversion of the natives, and with the hope of better results, in other kingdoms and provinces of Asia, which are looked for by this means and opening, whenever God shall be so pleased.

Each year the High Court calls for the accounts of the royal officers of the king's revenue, and the balance is made; and the accounts are sent to the Tribunal of Accounts of Mexico.

In the city of Manila, and in all the Spanish towns in the islands there are Sangleys who have come from great China, besides the merchants; they have fixed quarters, and occupy themselves with various employments, and come to seek their livelihood; they have their parians and shops, and others go after fisheries and other means of gain throughout the country among the natives, and they trade from one island to another with large and small champans.

The ships which come every year from great China bring these Sangleys, especially to the city of Manila, in great numbers, for the sake of the profits which they make by their passage money: and as people are superabundant in China, and the gains and daily wages run short, whatever they obtain in the Philippines is of much importance to them.

From this arise great difficulties and disadvantages; because, besides there being little security in the country with so great a number of pagans, they are bad and vicious people, and from dealing and communicating with them, the natives make little improvement in their Christianity and morals: and as they are so many, and great eaters, they raise the price of provisions and consume them.

It is true, that the city can neither go on nor maintain itself without these Chinamen, because they are the workmen in all employments, they are very industrious, and work for moderate wages. But for this a fewer number would suffice, and the disadvantage would be avoided of so many people as there usually are in Manila at the time of the shipping; besides many who go about the islands under colour of trade with the natives, and who commit a thousand evils and offences: and at least they explore all the country, rivers, creeks, and ports, and they know them better than the Spaniards do; and in case of any insurrection or the coming of enemies to the islands, they will be very detrimental and prejudicial.

In order to remedy all this, it is ordained that the ships shall not bring so many people of this kind, with penalties which are put in force, and that when they go away to China, they should carry them back again, and that there shall not remain in Manila any others than a suitable number of merchants in the Parian, and the artisans of all necessary trades, with a written licence, under severe penalties. In this an auditor of the High Court is each year employed by special commission, without other assistants; and in general he leaves, at the request of the Town-Council, the Chinamen who are required for the service of all the trades and employments, and the rest they put them on board ship and oblige them to go back in the ships which return to China, with much force and pressure which is used for that purpose.

These merchants and workmen who remain in Manila, previous to the insurrection of the year 1603, had their dwellings in the Parian and its shops, which is a large closed silk-market, with many streets, at a considerable distance from the city walls, close to the river, at the place they call San Graviel,[1] in which there is a commandant of its own, with his court and prison, and officials who administer justice to them, and watch over them day and night, that they may be in security, and not commit disorders.

Those who cannot find room in this Parian live opposite, on the other side of the river, on the side of Tondo, in two towns called Baybay and Minondoc, under the charge of the chief alcalde of Tondo, and under the administration of the Dominican monks who undertake their conversion, and by that means know the Chinese language.

They have two monasteries, with the requisite ministers, and a good hospital for the cure of Sangleys; they have, in a quarter separate from that of the pagans, a settlement of baptised Sangleys, with their houses, wives, and families, to the number of five hundred inhabitants, and every day they go on baptising others, and establishing them in this settlement. Few turn out well, being despicable people, restless and vicious, and of bad morals; and their having become Christians has not been on account of a desire for their salvation, but for the sake of the temporal comforts which they there enjoy:[2] and in the case of some of them, the not being able to return to China for debts and offences which they have committed there.

All of them indifferently, Christians and pagans, go un-

[1] (?) San Gabriel.   [2] This is still the case.

armed, and with their own costume, which consists of long robes with wide sleeves, made of blue cangan, or white stuff for mourning; and the great men wear black silks and coloured, wide drawers of the same stuff, short stockings of felt, very wide shoes in their fashion of blue silk, embroidered with braid, with many soles, well sewn together, and other stuffs, the hair long, very black and well cared for, tied up on the head with a knot, under a small hood or skull-cap, made of horsehair, close fitting, coming to the middle of the forehead, and a high round cap of the same horsehair on the top of all, of different patterns, by which the employments and quality of each man are distinguished.

The Christians only differ from the rest in wearing their hair cut short, and hats like the Spaniards.

They are white people, tall in stature, with little beard, large limbed, and very strong, industrious workmen, and ingenious in all arts and trades, phlegmatic, people of little courage, treacherous and cruel when they see their opportunity, and very covetous; great eaters of all sorts of meat, fish, and fruit, but drinking little, and what they do drink, hot.

They have a governor of their nation, a Christian, with his officials and ministers, who hears their suits in their family and business affairs; appeals from him go to the chief alcalde of Tondo or of the Parian, and from all of these to the High Court, which also pays especial attention to this nation, and to all that concerns it.

No Chinaman may live or have a house outside of these settlements, the Parian, Baybay, and Minondoc, nor are natives allowed to live in their houses, nor to establish themselves around the Chinese; nor may a Chinaman go out amongst the islands, nor two leagues from the city without express permission; and much less remain at night within the city when the gates are shut, under pain of death.

There usually are in Manila Japanese, both Christians and pagans, who remain from the ships which come from Japan, though there are not so many of them as of the Chinese. These have a particular quarter and a site outside the city, between the Parian of the Sangleys and the quarter of Laguio, close to the monastery of Candlemas, where the Franciscan barefooted monks administer them, with interpreters whom they keep for that purpose. They are spirited people, and of good disposition and valiant; they wear their own costume, which consists of garments (*quimon*)[1] of coloured silk and cotton reaching half way down the leg, open in front, wide short drawers, close fitting boots of chamois leather; shoes like sandals, the sole of straw well interwoven; their heads bare, the top shaven as far as the crown, and the back hair long, tied upon the head with a graceful bow; they wear large and small catans in their waists, and little beard; they are people of noble condition and conduct, of much ceremony and courtesy, with much point of honour, and very estimable, and determined in any case of necessity or difficulty.

Those who are Christians turn out well, and are very devout and observant of their religion, because nothing moves them to receive it except the desire for their salvation, on which account there are many Christians in Japan; and so they return easily and without reluctance to their country. The most of this nation that may be in Manila, for they do not go to other parts of the islands, may be five hundred Japanese, and from being of the quality of which they are, they return to Japan without remaining long in the islands, and so in general very few of them remain: in everything good treatment is offered them, as they are people who require it; and such is expedient for the good relations of the islands with Japan.

Few people arrive of the other nations, Siamese, Cambodians, Borneans, Patanis, and of the other islands outside of the Philippine government, and they return immediately

[1] *Vestis—quiru mono.* Collado's *Japanese Dictionary,* Rome, 1632.

with their ships: so that there is nothing particular to be said of them, except that care is taken to receive and despatch them well, and to get them to return shortly to their own countries.

Having related with as much brevity as was possible what the Philippine islands are, and what is current and practised among them, it will not be out of place to treat of the navigation which is made to them from New Spain, and of the return voyage, which is not a short one, nor devoid of many risks and difficulties, and of the voyage which is made in the eastern direction.

When the islands were conquered in the year 1574,[1] the Spanish fleet, in which the general was the commander-in-chief Miguel Lopez de Legazpi, sailed from the port of Navidad in the South Sea, on the coast of New Spain and province and district of Xalisco and Galicia, where the High Court of Guadalajara resides. For some voyages later they continued to sail from the same port, until, for improvement and greater convenience, the despatching of these ships was removed to the port of Acapulco, more to the southward on the same coast, in sixteen and a half degrees latitude, eighty leagues from Mexico, and in its district; which port is good, sheltered from all weathers, with a good entrance and anchorage, a good neighbourhood, better supplied and with more population than that of Navidad. There a chief alcalde has been established, with many Spanish inhabitants, and a treasury of His Majesty, with royal officers who attend to this despatch.

The departure of the ships which are to sail for the Philippines, which are despatched yearly on account of His Majesty, must necessarily be in the season of the northeast winds, which begin from the month of November and last till the end of March, and this voyage could not be performed at any other time, because from June there are southwesterly gales which are contrary to it.

[1] This should be 1564.

The usual practice is for these ships to be despatched and to sail at the end of February, and at latest the twentieth of March; they go westward, making for the islands of Las Velas, also named the Ladrones, and the island of Guan, which is one of them, is in thirteen degrees latitude: and because sometimes on leaving Acapulco the ships meet with calms, they decrease their latitude from sixteen and a half degrees, in which that port stands, until they find the northerly winds, which is ordinarily the case in ten or eleven degrees. On this course they always sail with the wind astern, and without altering the set of the sails, with fresh and favouring north-easters and other moderate weather, a distance of eighteen hundred leagues, without sighting any land or island, leaving to the southward the Barbudos and other islands, they increase their latitude gradually to thirteen degrees, until they sight the island of Guan, and above it, in fourteen degrees, the Carpana: this voyage to the Ladrone Islands is commonly one of seventy days.

The natives of these islands, who are naked people, strong-limbed and barbarous, as soon as they discover the ships at a distance of four or six leagues, come out to sea, making for them, with many vessels, made of one piece of timber,[1] very light and slender, with a counterpoise of bamboo to leeward, and the sail made of palm leaves lateen-shaped; in these go two or three men with paddles and oars, and a cargo of flying-fish, dorados, cocoa-nuts, plantains, sweet potatoes, water canes, and some fine mats, and on reaching the ships they barter them for iron of barrel hoops and pieces of nails, which are of use to them for their works and for constructing their vessels. Since the shipwreck and putting in in distress of some Spaniards in these islands, some monks and Spaniards have remained with them, and they approach our ships more readily, and enter inside.

Our ships pass between the two islands of Guan and

---

[1] Or, with one mast.

Carpana, making for the Philippines and cape of Espiritu Santo, which is three hundred leagues further on, in barely thirteen degrees latitude, which is a run of ten or twelve days with the north-east winds: and it happens that by sailing rather late south-westerly gales are met with, which put the navigation in peril, and the islands are entered with much labour and difficulty. From the Cape of Espiritu Santo ships pass through the strait of Capul to the islands of Mazbate and Burias, and from there to Marinduque, and along the coast of Calilaya to the strait of Mindoro, and to the shoals of Tuley, and to the mouth of the bay of Manila, and thence to the port of Cabit, which is a course of a hundred leagues, since entering among the islands, this is traversed in eight days: with that this navigation ends, which is good, and most generally without accidents, if made in the right season.

The return voyage from the Philippines to New Spain is now made by these ships with great difficulties and perils, on account of the navigation being long, and accompanied by many storms and various temperatures: on which account the ships set out very well provided with stores, and equipped in a suitable manner, for each one makes its voyage singly, making what sail it can, without one waiting for the other, nor seeing one another during the whole voyage.

They sail from the bay and port of Cabit with the first setting in of the south-westers, passing between the same islands and straits, from the twentieth of June and later, for there is hard work passing between islands, with storms of rain, until getting out of the strait of Capul. Having got out to the open sea, they take advantage of the south-westerly gale, shaping their course eastward as much as possible in the latitude of fourteen or fifteen degrees.

Then the north-east wind sets in, which is the wind which generally prevails in the South Sea, especially in low latitudes, and as this is a head wind, the course is changed and the ship's head put between north and east as much as the wind allows of; by which they increase their latitude, and so the ship is kept on until the south-west wind returns, and with it, in the latitude in which the ship may be, it makes its course to the east, and follows it as long as the wind lasts; and when it falls light, they set the ship's head as the wind best allows between north and east, and if the wind should be so contrary as to be north or north-west, and that course cannot be made, the other course is shaped, so as to continue and keep on the voyage without falling off. At four hundred leagues from the Philippines, the volcanoes and ridges of the Ladrone isles are seen, which run towards the north, as far as twenty-four degrees, and amongst them there are frequently great storms and hurricanes; and the Cape of Sestos, the headland of Japan, lies to the north, six hundred leagues from the Philippines. The ships pass between other islands which are rarely seen, in thirty-eight degrees,[1] with the same perils and storms, the temperature cold in the neighbourhood of the islands, *Rica de oro* and *Rica de plata*, and which are seldom reconnoitred: having left these islands there is a wide open sea, where the ship can run free with any weather; this is traversed with the winds that are met with for many leagues as far as forty-two degrees latitude, making for the coast of New Spain and looking for the usual winds which prevail in that latitude, and which in general are north-westerly, and at the end of a long navigation the coast of New Spain is reached, which, from the Cape Mendozino, which is in forty-two degrees and a half, runs for nine hundred leagues to the port of Acapulco, which is in sixteen and a half degrees.

[1] This is probably an error for twenty-eight degrees, and these islands would be the Mounin-Sima Islands, between 26° 35' and 27° 45'; and Lot's Wife in 29° 51', and Crespo in 32° 46', which are supposed by the *Univers Pittoresque* to be the Roca de Oro and the Roca de Plata of the ancient maps; and De Morga's phrase, "rica de oro, rica de plata," the names of islands in the old maps, is to be found in other contemporary documents.

When the ships are near the coast, and in general they sight it between from forty degrees to thirty-six, the cold is very great, and the crews suffer and die of it. Three hundred leagues before reaching land, signs of it are seen in [portions of] bad water, of the size of a hand, round and purple, with a crest in the middle like a lateen sail, which they call *caravels*. This sign lasts until reaching a hundred leagues from the land, when they next discover some fishes, half the body of the form of dogs, which go frisking one with another close to the ship; after these little dogs are seen the knobsticks *(porras)*, which are sprouts of grass, hollow and very long, yellow, with a ball at the end, which come floating on the water, and at thirty leagues from the coast are many very large clumps of grass, which the large rivers which are in the country bring down into the sea: these are called floats (*balsas*), and many dogs by turns with all the other signs. After this the coast is discovered, which is very high land, and a clean coast, and without losing sight of it, the ship runs along it with the north-west, north-north-west, and north winds, which are usually met with on this coast, by day towards the land and by night back again to the sea; decreasing the latitude, and entering a warmer temperature the island of Cenizas is sighted, and afterwards that of Cedars; from thence they go on to sight the cape of San Lucas, which is the mouth of California. From there they cross the eighty leagues which it has in width until sighting the islands of Las Marias, and the Cape of Currents, which is on the other side of California in Val de Vanderas, and the province of Chametla; thence they pass by the coast of Colima, and of Sacatul los Motines and Ciguatanejo; and the port of Acapulco is entered, without any port having been touched at or a landing made since the channel of Capul of the Philippines during the whole voyage, which usually lasts five months, a little more or less, and frequently six months or more time.

By way of India a voyage may be made from the Philippines to Spain, by shaping the course to Malacca, and thence to Cochin and to Goa, which is a distance of twelve hundred leagues, and it has to be done with the north-east winds. From Goa the navigation is by the Indian voyage to the Cape of Good Hope, and to the Azores Islands, and from them to Portugal and the port of Lisbon, which is a long and laborious navigation, as is experienced by the Portuguese, who pursue it every year. From India they are in the habit of transmitting letters and despatches to Spain by the Red Sea, by the hands of the Indians, who send them through Arabia and Alexandria, and thence by sea to Venice, and from there they go to Spain.

A galloon is usually despatched and sails in some years from the fortress of Malacca, which goes to Portugal by the open sea, without touching in India, nor at any of its coasts: it arrives much more speedily at Lisbon than the ships from Goa. Its ordinary departure is on the fifth of January, and it does not delay beyond that time, nor are they used to anticipate it. Though these voyages, one and all, are not practised by the Castilians, and are prohibited to them; but only that voyage which is performed by way of New Spain, going and returning, as has been related, and without any better or more speedy way having been discovered by the South Sea, although it has been attempted.

₊ This translation was begun on the 2nd of April, 1867, and ended on the 27th of May of 1867. The printing of it was commenced in the beginning of July 1867, and was not finished till April 1868.

Laus Deo.

APPENDIX I.

Á Don Cristoval Gomez de Sandoval y Rojas, Duque de Cea.

Ofresco á V. Excelencia este pequeño trabajo, tan digno de buena acogida, por la fiel relacion que contiene, cuanto desnudo de artificio y ornato; conociendo mi pobre caudal, lo comence con temor, animome á pasar adelante, entender, que si lo que se dà, hubiese de tener igual proporcion con quien lo recibe, no habria quien mereciese poner en manos de V. Excelencia, sus obras, y quedarian en olvido, las que en estos tiempos han hecho nuestros Españoles, en el descubrimiento, conquista y conversion de las islas Filipinas, y varios sucesos que á vueltas han tenido en los grandes reinos y gentilidades que las rodean; que como de partes tan remotas, ninguna relacion ha salido en publico, que lo trate de proposito, desde sus principios hasta el estado que ahora tienen. Suplico á V. Excelencia, reciba mi voluntad, postrada á sus pies; y cuando esta breve escritura no diere el gusto que me representa el amor propio (enfermedad del ingenio humano), use V. Excelencia conmigo como suele con todos; leyendola y disimulando sus imperfecciones, de su prudencia y mansedumbre, como tan rico destas y otras virtudes, que hacen con fuerza divina que las cosas altas no estrañen á las humildes, y han puesto á V. Excelencia sobre su propia y natural grandeza, en el lugar que tiene, para bien destos reinos, premiando y favoreciendo lo bueno, corrigiendo y refrenando lo contrario, en que consiste el buen estado de la republica, que dio motivo á Democrito, filosofo antiguo, para llamar al premio y al castigo verdaderos dioses. Para gozar desta felicidad, no hay que desear ningun tiempo pasado, sino contentos con el presente, rogar á Dios nos guarde á V. Excelencia por largos años.

D. Antonio de Morga.

APPENDIX II.

SUBSEQUENT HISTORY OF CALDERA AND MINDANAO.

After De Morga's time the Mindanao men, in 1616, burned the dockyard in Pantao, a port of the isle of Luzon, although it was defended by soldiers and cannon; they continued to infest the coasts of Macalilum, Camarines, Albay and other places till 1634, when they sacked and burned the town of Tayahas, eighteen leagues from Manila, and very nearly captured the Archbishop Fray Miguel Garcia Serrano. Various fleets were sent against them, and Juan Xuarez Gallinato, the master of the camp, went a second time to chastise them, and returned with little better success than the first time. In 1635 the fort of Samboangan was erected by Captain Juan de Chaves, two leagues from the old fort of Caldera in the isle of Mindanao. Shortly after the erection of this fort King Corralat had ravaged the Philippines, and on his return to Mindanao he was attacked by the Sergeant-major Nicolas Gonzalez, from Samboangan, who routed his fleet and recovered most of the plunder: in March 1636 the governor of the Philippines took King Corralat's town, burned a hundred vessels and sixteen villages, and ruined his kingdom: after that he returned to Samboangan, and subjected the Basilan men and town of Buhayen. Some of the Mindanao towns which had been subjected again rose, and Corralat gave more trouble: in 1657 he brought a fleet against Marinduque and Mindoro; and though the fleet from Manila did nothing against the Mindanao fleet, the Spaniards burned several towns of King Corralat. Shortly after the Chinese corsair Cogsen, who retook the island of Formosa from the Dutch, threatened the Philippines and demanded tribute from them. For the defence of the islands, the abandonment of the forts of Terrenate, Samboangan, Calamianes, and Iligan was decreed. That of Terrenate could not maintain itself, those of Calamianes and Iligan were useless; there was doubt about that of Samboangan, which kept in check the Sulu and Mindanao men, and it was decided to leave in it a garrison of fifty men, and withdraw the rest and the artillery to Manila. With so short a garrison it could not maintain itself, and came to an end in 1662. A royal order of the queen regent of December 30, 1666, was issued for the re-establishment of the fort of Samboangan, and others in 1672 and 1712; nevertheless, it was not re-established till the year 1719, by order of the Marshal Bustamante, governor of the Philippines. Between 1719 and 1734 the Spaniards sent seven expeditions against the Mindanao men. In 1736 Fray Joseph Torrubia wrote his *Dissertation on the Philippines*, with the object of urging the maintenance of the fort of Samboangan, under the idea that that was the only means of checking the incursions of the Mindanao men. Though that garrison was maintained, and a stone fort erected, the most important after that of Manila, and four other Spanish settlements made in the island, one at Missamis in the bay of Panguil, in the middle of the northern coast, the second at Dapitan on the same coast, and the third at Caraga on the north-east coast, the fourth Pollok, in the south, yet the incursions of the Mindanao men into various islands of the Philippine group continued till the year 1848, previous to which year from 800 to 1,500 persons are said to have been carried away annually. The real cause of the cessation of these incursions was the increase of the number of steam vessels. Mr. Rienzi, the author of three volumes of the *Univers Pittoresque* on Oceania, gives a short account of the Philippines, written a little before 1830: he states that the name of Maïn-danao signifies peoples of the lake, and that the language of Maïndanao is allied to that of the Bisayas. The southern part of the island is independent, and obeys a sultan, who holds in his dependence the small group of the Mengui Islands, situated between Maïndanao and the Moluccas. The residence of this prince is at Sélangan on the Pélandgi: the population, comprising the few inhabitants who still live in the ancient town of Maïndanao, situated on the other side of the Pelandgi, and which is now almost entirely abandoned, may be as many as 10,000 or 12,000 souls. The whole population of Mindanao is estimated at 800,000 by Mr. Rienzi, and at 300,000 by Mr. Farren.

HISTORY OF SULU.

Since the period embraced in De Morga's account, the Spaniards attempted the conquest of the Sulu isles in 1628, 1629, 1637, and 1731, and only succeeded in doing more or less damage; in 1746, according to Mr. Rienzi, they attacked the islands with a fleet of thirty vessels and took the principal island of Holo, which they abandoned later. Since then the patriotic Sulu men have preserved their independence. They have been frequently bombarded in more recent times: amongst other attacks made upon them was one, in February of 1848, by Manila troops on the island of Balanguingui; its fort contained fourteen guns; more than eighty Malays were killed there; in an interior fort 340 people, including women and children, were killed by the Tagal troops, who lost only forty killed and one hundred wounded in the attack.

In June of the same year a Dutch corvette and brig came before Sulu and claimed two Malay captives, and on their not being given up by the fourth day, they fired on the town for some hours. The only result was five Sulu men killed and twenty wounded, and the setting fire to the Chinese quarter and to an Englishman's house.

In January 1851 an expedition left Manila consisting of a 30-gun ship, a 12-gun ship, three war-steamers, four companies of infantry, and one hundred artillerymen: they went to Tonquil Island, between Basilan and Sulu, and destroyed upwards of six hundred houses, and killed forty-five of the inhabitants of the island, from which some piratical vessels were reported to have sailed. The fleet then appeared before Sulu, where a few shots were exchanged. In March of the same year another Spanish expedition, with reinforcements, went against Sulu, and destroyed the town and forts; not many Sulu men were killed. The population of Sulu is estimated at 100,000 souls and 20,000 fighting men, a considerable increase since De Morga's time.

The account of a French attack on Basilan and the destruction of a town, in revenge for an officer having been killed in a dispute by a Malay, is given by Dr. Yvan, in his book called *De France en Chine*.

CAPTURE OF MANILA BY THE ENGLISH.

In 1762, an English expedition of seven ships of war and 10,300 men came to Manila and took it on the 6th October. During the siege the Canon Anda collected 6,000 of the islanders and nearly succeeded in raising the siege. General Draper demanded of the town a ransom of twenty million francs; only a quarter of this sum could be raised, with which the general contented himself, and embarked part of his troops, leaving only Sepoys behind him. The English, after establishing themselves in the capital, proceeded to subjugate the provinces, and aided by the Chinese, gained the battle of Boulacan. The Canon Anda then raised all the provinces of Luzon, and the English forces were hemmed in inside Manila, and on the point of being reduced by famine, when an English frigate arrived with news of the conclusion of peace. The Sepoys evacuated Manila, and the Canon Anda and the Hispano-Tagal forces entered it March 31st, 1764. A little while after Canon Anda was named governor of the Philippines in reward for his services. (From the *Univers Pittoresque*.) According to the Annual Register of 1763 the English force consisted of nine ships of war, two store-ships, and 2,300 men, including the 79th Regiment and a company of the Royal Artillery. Spanish official documents state the number of ships at thirteen.

CHINESE INSURRECTION IN MANILA. — GOVERNMENT OF THE CHINESE.

Of the insurrection of the Chinese in Manila, and of their massacre, Mr. Rienzi says: "In 1603 they had begun to surround with a stone wall the quarter of the town which they inhabited; the Spaniards, naturally suspicious, thought they saw a hostile project in that measure. The Chinese population consisted of 35,000 men; 23,000 were massacred, and the rest of these unfortunates fled to their country. The celestial emperor had an inquiry made into the cause of this massacre. The Spanish historians pretend that the conduct of their government was fully justified. The absence of documents prevents our deciding upon that question. In the year 1639 the Chinese population had again increased, and amounted to 40,000 individuals, the most part engaged in agriculture: they again revolted, and their number was reduced to 7,000.".....""In 1709 all the Chinese were expelled from the Philippines. They were accused of plotting and monopoly, and this accusation was probably well founded, for these foreigners, restless and intriguing, have often deserved the same reproach at Batavia, Kalemantan, and in other places. Nevertheless, their conduct did not deserve extermination. In spite of the edicts of expulsion, the offscouring of the celestial empire continued to penetrate into Manila."

Mr. Rienzi saw some persons amongst the Sangleys who were pointed out to him as descendants of the Christian Japanese in Manila.

The Spanish historians alluded to by Mr. Rienzi justify the slaughter of the Chinese on the ground of the excesses committed by them, and the allegation that they had prepared 100,000 men in China to invade the Philippines.

The reader will have seen from the Chinese document given by De Morga, and from the statements of De Morga, that it is very improbable that the Chinese government had any design of invading the Philippines, and the insurrection is to be attributed to panic on the part of the Spaniards, which drove the Chinese into insurrection: it also appears that the Celestial government did not consider the massacre of the Chinese as justified, but that it declined to act in behalf of men whom it considered as bad subjects from their having deserted their country by permanently settling in a foreign land, also because political and military considerations obliged the Chinese government so to act. The position of the Chinese in many European settlements is very much the same at the present day as it was when described by De Morga. But the duties of European governments towards these Chinese guests are much increased by the obligations of reciprocity, since those governments have broken down the barriers which secured China from foreign troubles, and have exacted from its government an unrestricted right of way through the empire for their own subjects; and in addition, that these, though frequently in no ways more trustworthy than the Chinese emigrants, should be exempted from Chinese jurisdiction and taxation.

In 1636 the Chinese in the Philippines had again increased, for in that year they amounted to 25,000. They then inspired no apprehension, from their pacific and spiritless disposition: the governor had given during six months of the preceding year nineteen thousand licenses to Chinese settlers, which had brought in more than 170,000 dollars, and he expected to levy 200,000 dollars in the year 1636. The Chinese were then made to pay nine dollars less one real, and those who lived out of the Parian, or Chinese quarter, had to pay ten dollars and two reals.

In Manila the Chinese pay about four times as much tribute as the Philippine islanders; and a sum of 100,750 dollars raised on patents of the Chinese traders appears in the last budget: in

Australia the local governments have been suffered to put exceptional imposts upon the Chinese who go to try their fortune at the gold mines.[1] It is not easy to see what cause of dislike the Chinese give, beyond that their greater industry and sobriety allow them to compete successfully with all other classes, and give rise to accusations of monopoly; their separate language also contributes to the ill-will with which they are frequently looked upon. De Morga mentions how much their absence was felt. Mr. J. Lannoy, formerly Belgian Consul at Manila, in a work on the Philippines printed at Brussels in 1849, recommends the Spanish government to encourage the Chinese settlers. M. Mallat speaks of them now as indispensable to Manila, and says that numerous attempts have been made to enlighten the Philippine government as to the danger from the Chinese, and royal ordinances have been issued to keep them in a very subordinate position, but they have been eluded or neglected. M. Mallat also says that the Chinese are, at least in appearance, the most pacific people, but he admits that they have numerous enemies who consider them dangerous. Mr. Consul Farren writes some years later, in November 1862: "A considerable number of Chinese are settled at Manila: a class of them monopolise in fact, though without any legal prescription, the retail business of foreign trade; by their industry, intelligence, economy, and system, they have acquired the confidence of the British merchants here, and have become (with a few exceptions, in which the same qualities have enabled some mestizos and natives to share that confidence) the almost exclusive mediums of trade between the foreign importers and the consumers of merchandise in general. The Chinese are scattered through the provinces, and there sell in wholesale quantities to the natives articles of foreign goods, and are the chief clayers of sugar, and the shopkeepers and hucksters of every village. This position of the Chinese is very enviously regarded by a number of Spaniards at Manila and in the provinces, from trade jealousy, and they have been striving, as opportunities offered, for many years to induce the government to expel the Chinese from the provinces, and it was taken into consideration to establish provincial commercial agencies of Spaniards to supersede the Chinese."

[1] I have heard it said that these exceptional imposts have been removed within the last six months.

Mr. Farren mentions further proofs of the ill-will existing against the Chinese, and the vigilance and precautions of the Spanish governor.

The Spanish authorities in Manila are too enlightened to give way to this unjust jealousy of the Chinese, and they have since an early date taken the best measures for preventing the Chinese feeling themselves slighted and treated as aliens by the rest of the community. They have, as has been mentioned by De Morga (p. 234), and as M. Mallat states, given the Chinese of Manila a *Gobernadorcillo*, or little governor; he and his constables wear, as a distinctive mark of their office, a European hat above their Chinese skull-cap, and carry in their hand a cane with a cord to it; this cane is a sign of command throughout the Philippines (ii, 137). He also says that the natives of each parish each January, by means of their twelve most ancient electors, elect in the town-hall, in the presence of the alcalde, priest, notary and others, three candidates, whose names are submitted to the governor, who chooses one as gobernadorcillo. He usually takes the first name on the list...... The Chinese of mixed race, wherever they are sufficiently numerous, have the privilege of electing a gobernadorcillo; he is, however, inferior to a gobernadorcillo of the natives of the Philippines...... These gobernadorcillos judge civil causes of two taels of gold (220 francs); they draw up criminal informations, and supervise the gathering in of tributes and money belonging to the treasury (i, 352-354).

I have been informed by various Spaniards who have served in the Philippines, amongst others by an ex-governor, that this system works well, and that there are but few appeals against the decisions of the gobernadorcillos.

Some similar recognition of the interests of our Chinese subjects in the Straits Settlements, by giving them headmen with an official position, and consequently greater facilities for the better making known their wants to government, and the conferring upon them responsibility along with authority over their fellow-countrymen, would do much to prevent the frequent recurrence of faction fights, such as that which broke out last summer among the Chinese at Penang.

ADMINISTRATION OF JUSTICE.

M. Mallat says: "The weakest part of the administration of

APPENDIX II. 367

the Philippines is that of justice, which is owing to several different causes, which we will attempt to present, not without feeling some fear that the confusion which reigns in this department may introduce itself, in spite of us, into what we are going to say" (i, 359). Part of this confusion he attributes to the ignorance of the gobernadorcillos and interpreters of the Spanish language, and to all causes being sent to Manila. M. Mallat, however, describes the royal audiencia as: "that respectable, great and noble institution, the only one of its kind in the Philippines, and which forms a counterpoise to the vast powers of the governor general. The governor general is *ex officio* president; he has under him a regent, five auditors or judges, and two fiscals or solicitors general, one for civil, the other for criminal causes" (i, p. 361.) Since M. Mallat wrote, one of the captain generals of the Philippines thought it necessary to establish a permanent court-martial for the repression of incendiaries: the audiencia did its duty, for it is said to have protested against this as illegal.

Mr. Rienzi insinuates vaguely a great deterioration in the administration of justice, and though in general he sneers at the monks, he says: "It must be owned, however, that these monks often defend the Christians of this great archipelago with an infinitely laudable zeal and courage against the despotism and cupidity of certain alcaldes."

To judge from Mr. Consul Farren's reports, extending over a long period, there was not more to complain of latterly in the administration of justice than in other places inhabited by various races: the chief grounds of complaint would be legal delays, and that imprisonment during the collection of evidence depended on the discretion of the judge whether he should take bail or not. It was said in 1862 that the removal of this evil was contemplated in a pending revision of the Spanish commercial code.

Nevertheless, no government should remain satisfied, neither can it feel security, if justice is not administered in its dependencies by men of as much learning and integrity as those whose services it can command at home.

By a royal decree dated July 4, 1861, the powers of the Audiencias in the Spanish colonies were limited to judicial matters, and administrative councils were established for the consideration of matters formerly submitted to the Audiencias.

The council of the Philippines consists of three councillors. The whole expense of the council for salaries of the councillors, secretaries, etc., amounts for the current year, 1867-68, to 30,543 dollars. This innovation is the subject of regret, since the class from which councillors are taken cannot offer men of equal weight, experience of government, and respectability of character as the judges and auditors who compose the Audiencia.

LINEAL DESCENDANT OF VINCENT YANEZ PINZON.

One of the auditors of the High Court of Manila was D. Ignacio Pinzon, who died there in the beginning of September 1852. He was a lineal descendant of the companion of Columbus. When Mr. Washington Irving was preparing his history of Columbus he visited the family of the deceased in search of information, and it was, to a great degree, through his recommendation to the government at Madrid, that the deceased was appointed a judge at Manila.

THE FIRST GOVERNOR OF THE PHILIPPINES.

A portrait of Miguel Lopez de Legazpi exists in the house of the municipality at Manila, and a copy was obtained in 1863 for the government house of Tolosa, the capital of Guipuzcoa, his native province (see frontispiece). Legazpi's house is still to be seen at a few paces from the railroad station at Zumarraga: the lower part is of solid masonry, with two loopholes; the upper part is patched up with bricks. Legazpi died on the 20th of August, 1572, not 1574, as stated by De Morga.

ATTEMPTED INSURRECTION OF PHILIPPINE SPANIARDS.

Besides the danger to the Spanish rule in the Philippines, that would ensue from the falling off of the High Court of Justice, Mr. Rienzi points out a danger from the Philippine-born Spaniards, or Spaniards of mixed race, whom he thinks likely to follow the example of the colonists; and in support of his opinion, he states the following: "In 1823, a certain number of half-breeds, assisted by some officers of the Manila garrison, and by some Spanish merchants excited by the ideas which the Spanish revolution, and that of the Spanish American colonies, had given rise to, resolved to declare the independence of the Philippines. The insurrection broke out on the 2nd of June. The conspirators took possession of one of the city gates, from there they marched to the city arsenal. The Captain General Martinez shewed the greatest cowardice; but, Lieutenant Colonel Santa Romana conquered the insurgents, who were few in number. The fidelity of the troops, and the capture of Novales and Ruiz, the two insurgent chiefs, changed the parts. The conquerors of the morning were the vanquished in the evening. They were thrown into prison, and some sent to Spain, others to the convict establishments in the Philippines. These degenerate men were only guided by material interests, and ambitious of the places occupied by Europeans, these men necessarily failed. The holy fire of liberty can only be maintained by pure hands, and not by political mountebanks and by greedy men."

This accusation made by Mr. Rienzi against General Martinez is not in any way justified, since, according to official statements, that general, as soon as he heard of the outbreak, put himself at the head of the artillery and the remnants of four battalions, and routed the insurgents who had got possession of the palace and town-hall; besides Colonel Santa Romana, the two Serjeants Romero and Domingo greatly contributed to put down the movement. General Martinez is also completely exonerated by the statements of an eye-witness, M. Paul de la Gironière, a Frenchman, who at the time was surgeon of a revolted regiment, and who acted with the artillery and the governor.

Mr. Rienzi rather exaggerates the independent disposition of the Philipinos and of the mestizos; but some, who are best entitled to form an opinion, say that the Philippine government ought to simplify education, and by stimulating the study of agriculture, botany, and chemistry, seek to provide the islands with useful settlers rather than with lawyers in search of employment and place-hunters; and that whilst care is taken not to affront or humiliate the mestizos, the government should not allow the ancient privileges of the indigenous race to be diminished, nor allowed to fall into desuetude. Much may be done to advance agriculture by taking advantage of the vanity and rivalry of the chiefs of barangays, by offering premiums, decorations, etc.; in this manner, when a sum of money was offered to those who should plant a certain quantity of coffee plants, a great number were planted, but as there was no supervision, or subsequent inducement to take care of the plants, the plantations were neglected and abandoned. There are still many barbarous tribes in Luzon and in the other islands, and the civilising of these should be attempted by the priests by slow degrees, rather than by military expeditions which devastate the country, and often produce little result besides that of exciting jealousy among those who take part in them.

TOO FREQUENT CHANGES IN THE ADMINISTRATION.

Another defect in the administration, which has been complained of, is the too frequent change of the officials, who have not time to become acquainted with the country and its requirements, nor to study the means of satisfying them. That this complaint is well founded is shewn by the fact, that from 1844 to 1865, there were nine captain generals, governors of the Philippines, and two lieutenant or acting governors. The first only, filled his post for five years.

SALARY OF THE GOVERNOR.

Mr. Rienzi states, that the salary of the governor of the Philippines is 18,000 dollars (= about £4,000), of which 4,000 dollars are placed in the royal treasury, as a guarantee against peculation. (In 1863 this salary was raised to about £8,000.) He also says, that there is a regulation, that when a new governor has arrived at Manila, his predecessor must remain there six months longer as a private individual, to give an account if necessary, of certain acts of his administration, or to pay his debts. This wise and prudent measure is too often eluded."

This regulation dates from the times written of by De Morga, and does not appear ever to be attended to now.

POPULATION.

Mr. Rienzi (1830) estimates the superficies of all the Philippine islands at 12,900 square leagues, and the total population at 4,500,000 souls, of these 2,530,000 Christians and Pagans are under Spanish rule, and about two million inhabitants are under independent Pagan chiefs, or the Mussulman princes of the isle of Mindanao. He divides the population under Spanish rule thus:

Native Indians,	2,397,330
Mestizos and Sangleys,	118,030
Chinese,	8,640
White men of all sorts,	6,000
	2,530,000

APPENDIX II. 371

In 1851, Mr. Farren stated the whole population of the Spanish possessions in the Philippines, at 3,800,000 souls, without reckoning the unsubdued tribes; the population of the town of Manila he reckons at 200,000, and all the Europeans in the colony, at 7,000.

REVENUE AND EXPENDITURE.

Mr. Rienzi before 1830, estimated the total revenue from all sorts of imposts in the Philippines at a gross produce of 2,721,979 dols. And the expenses to be deducted - - 807,700 „

Net produce, - - 1,904,279 „

In 1849, the net produce from three sources of revenue was 3,681,693 dollars, viz:

Tobacco, 2,119 058 dols, after an expenditure of 1,796,167
Spirits, 426,586 - - - - - 222,170
Tributes, 1,126,049 - - - - -

3,681,693

"During the three years, 1846–48, nearly a million of dollars has been spent in Manila alone, on necessary but unproductive works, such as embellishments of the governor's palace, sea embankments, a new quay, fortifications, military hospital, officers' barracks within and without the city, old debts or bills of the Madrid government paid off in Manila, and 120,000 dollars for the passage of political offenders.[1] At the same time, the official salaries of all the chief members of the government have been raised, a new police has been formed, the excise and coast-guard organised, and a considerable addition made of officers and non-commissioned officers from Spain, and the salaries increased of the Alcaldes or provincial magistrates, in lieu of commercial privileges.

In 1853 there was a surplus of 2,000,000 dollars owing to the increased cultivation of tobacco, and a more rigid enforcement of the capitation tax or tribute. This was after paying for an effective military force of upwards of 8,000 men, an organised police, and coast-guard, a flotilla of a steam frigate, three smaller war steamers, a gun brig, fifteen armed cutters, and forty-three

[1] It would be better for the Philippines if the Spanish government could dispose of its offenders, political or others, elsewhere, in places where they would not do so much harm by corrupting the inhabitants.

gun-boats manned by 1,736 men, and a large naval staff, besides the departments of ecclesiastical, civil, and judicial administration, and public works, and the consular establishments in Singapore and China ; at one time the expense of a Spanish legation in China, amounting to about £5,000 a-year, was defrayed by the Manila treasury. In 1853, the Intendant General published that the treasury would pay 110,000 dollars borrowed from public bodies in Manila towards the building of three government steamers, and 15,000 dollars borrowed for an expedition to Sulu. In 1854, the captain governor called for a loan of 180,000 dollars from the societies called *Obras Pias*, for the purchase or construction of three mail steamers." (*Extracts from Mr. Consul Farren's dispatches.*)

The foregoing description of the flourishing condition of the Philippine colony and treasury is likely to be contradicted by their condition during the last few years, notwithstanding that in 1865, a new intendant of finance denied that the treasury was in a state of distress. Here is a list of the calamities and losses which fell upon the Philippines before and during the year 1865, taken from official reports.

June 3rd, 1863.— An earthquake took place at 7.30 P.M. at Manila. The cathedral, palace, churches, markets, and barracks, public and private buildings of stone, were in a few seconds rent, and injured or overthrown. The British consular office fell in, and the books were buried under the ruins. The estimate of personal injury is 400 lives lost, and 2,000 individuals wounded, eight million dollars, or more than a million and a half sterling, lost. On the 4th of July the loss was stated to be 289 people killed, and it was supposed that there were more bodies under the ruins of the cathedral. Manila was like a town bombarded: great loss to government in public buildings.

March 1864.—Arrival of Spanish minister in China. Renewal of this charge on Philippine treasury which had been discontinued in 1849.

June 1864.—Mr. Consul Farren broke his leg, and about the 10th July part of his house adjoining his bedroom fell in, in consequence of the earthquake. He died on the 23rd of August of acute dysentery and inflammation at Santa Ana in the suburbs.[1]

[1] Dysentery is the chief illness to which foreigners are subject in the

Mr. Vice-Consul Webb reports:—

November 1864.—Cholera has been in the Philippines for the last twelve months; it formerly only attacked natives, this time it had attacked Europeans; the Governor's wife died of it. Chlorodyne had been found to be the most efficacious remedy. The disease had been so severe as to cause much loss to Government of the tributes from the numerous deaths.

February 1865.—A fire destroyed the village of Hermita and the government barracks. Loss to Government of about 150,000 dollars; private loss similar.

March 1865.—Fire in village of Lallo of Cagayan. Government tobacco factory burnt with 38,000 quintals of tobacco, each quintal equals 104 lbs., worth 21 dollars.

May 1865.—Fires on April 30th and May 2nd have devastated the suburbs of Tondo, Sta. Cruz, and Quiapo. Forty lives lost, and two million dollars.

July 4th, 1865.—Royal order from Madrid prohibiting metal roofs from fear of electricity and lightning.

July 29th, 1865.—Lightning fell on the magazine on the point of Cañacao, and blew up five tons of gunpowder.

September 27th, 1865.—A fearful typhoon passed over Manila; seventeen ships were driven ashore, trees torn up, and houses injured. He forwards printed meteorological observations by the Jesuit fathers.

October 19th, 1865.—A fearful earthquake in the province of Albay, where the volcano of Mayong is situated; no lives lost, but much property; the sea invaded the towns of Tabaco and Malinao. Slight shocks at Manila.[1]

I beg leave gratefully to acknowledge the courtesy of the Colonial Office at Madrid, and the kind offices of Count Vistahermosa, the Spanish minister in London, to which I am indebted for a copy of the Budget of the Philippine Islands for the current financial year, 1867-68. It is a very carefully prepared document, and enters into the most minute details. I have added

---

Philippines, which otherwise are not unhealthy; a voyage to China for change of air is the most efficacious remedy.

[2] Some unreasonable complaints are frequently made at the numerous fires in countries subject to earthquakes; if the houses are built of stone, instead of with light and inflammable materials, the loss of life during an earthquake is much greater.

at the end of this appendix a table of expenditure and revenue as it was in De Morga's time; this table is very incomplete, as De Morga has not given the figures of all the items of outlay which he mentions. The modern budget of the Philippines is drawn up in *escudos* of ten reals, or half a dollar, which unity is now adopted in Spanish accounts for the sake of the decimal system. In the table of the budget here given of the current year, I have converted the *escudos* into dollars, as being more convenient for comparison with the figures of De Morga, and those given by Mr. Farren. I have also prepared from the budget a table of the division of the Philippines into parishes, with the number of tributes, representing heads of families, and the amount of stipends paid to the parochial clergy.

TAXATION.

Reals in the Philippines are the old Spanish reals called reals of silver, which are worth rather more than double the modern reals of Spain called *reales de vellon*, twenty of which go to the dollar, whilst eight of the old reals of silver, or Philippine reals, make a dollar.

The tribute of the Indians was originally fixed at eight reals, and in De Morga's time was increased to ten reals: that of the mestizos or men of mixed parentage, was twenty reals, or two dollars and a half, and that of the Chinese, six dollars. These tributes appear to have been the same in 1736, when Fray Torrubia wrote, but he mentions other imposts in kind. One of these was, that the government levied measures of rice called 'caban,' for provisioning the troops, and which were named 'purchased,' because it paid two reals each for them, though they were worth four reals or more, and in the neighbourhood of Manila never less than three: and the same with regard to wheat, though with wheat the Indians did not lose much. Besides this, he says the Indians cut wood for the ships, for monthly wages of sixteen reals, which did not suffice for their tools, which they found themselves; and they worked as soldiers, sailors, carpenters, &c., for three, four, even five years, without pay, only in order to obtain an employment in the Acapulco ship. In 1635, when the garrison of Samboangan was renewed, Padre Juan de Bueras, provincial of the Jesuits, advised that the Indians of the province of Pintados, who, from their neighbourhood to Mindanao, were most interested in its maintenance, should add half a ganta[1] of rice to each tribute. This advice was followed, with the augmentation of two gantas, which make one of clean or sifted rice, and it was extended to all the islands, which paid it at the time he wrote.

Fray Torrubia seems to have thought that the Indians were overtaxed, and estimates the annual value of this contribution of two gantas of rice, at two thousand five hundred dollars: he also thought it a special hardship, that this tax should have been continued during fifty years, in which there was no garrison at Samboangan, which was the motive for laying it on. He then proposes a *Monte de Piedad*, or *Obra Pia*, for the purpose of redeeming this impost. This opinion of Fray Torrubia of the Indians having been at one time overtaxed is confirmed by an archbishop of Manila, who in 1662 reported on the wretched condition of the natives on account of the numerous burdens imposed upon them; and remonstrances were made against the continuance of the cutting timber and other tasks being imposed upon the islanders without wages being paid them.

As I find no mention of this impost of rice in modern works, it has probably been commuted, since M. Mallat says, that now one tribute represents five persons, and it is now fourteen reals of silver, (nine francs, twenty *centimes*) of which eleven reals are for the government, and three for the church: he also says, that to the ancient tribute of ten reals there had been added for the

	Indians.	Mestizos.	Sangleys.
For the municipal chest	1 real	1 real	6 reals
For public worship.	3 reals	3 reals	
Total of tribute	1 dollar 6 reals	3 dollars	6 dollars 6 reals

The municipal chest (*caja de comunidad*) is for the payment of schoolmasters, vaccination, defence of prisoners, and parish affairs.

Mention has been made above, from Mr. Consul Farren's reports, of large sums recently borrowed or exacted by the captain generals of the Philippines, from religious bodies, for purposes of

[1] Ganta, from the Malay gantang, a measure of rice, salt, and other dry goods, equal to a kulak, or the 800th part of a koyan, a measure which varies: on the west coast of Sumatra it is 800 koulabs, at Palembang a koyan is estimated at 48 piculs, or 6400 lbs. English; so that a Malayan koulah or ganta is equal to 8 lbs. (Marsden's Dict.)

state, such as expeditions, building steamers, etc. Those levies were not, however, of the nature of exactions, those chests having been founded for similar purposes, as will be explained by the following extract from Fray Torrubia's Dialogo Cortesano Filipino.

"*Philipino.*—There is, in Manila, a *monte de piedad*, (establishment for lending money) called the table of Mercy, of such eminence, that the crown of Spain may boast of having its foundations in those isles based upon such exalted charity. This was founded in the year 1594, by the venerable Juan Fernandez de Leon, in imitation of that which the lady Doña Leonor, wife of Don Joan II., erected in Lisbon, in the year 1498. From the year of its foundation until that of 1730, in which the accounts were reckoned up, this house had portioned 23,300 orphan girls, daughters of Spaniards; it had expended in their maintenance, 508,916 dollars. It had supplied to our catholic monarch in urgent cases, 409,018 dollars. It had expended for Divine service 155,785 dollars; and it had given in alms 4,113,207 dollars.

Cortesano.—I am astonished at this expenditure, and it seems to me that it will not have been surpassed by the Royal Mercy of Lisbon.

Philipino.—This expenditure is positive, and derived from the original books of that House. In the life of the venerable *Fray Simon de Roxas*, lib. viii, folio 418, it is related as unexampled that the Mercy of Lisbon had given in alms in one year 30,000 ducats, the Manila House gives every year 71,824 dollars. See if that does not surpass the other? The most wonderful part of it is that all this machinery was founded upon fourteen cargoes and a few packages.

Cortesano.—And how did it increase so much?

Philipino.—The increase of this House depends upon the risks they run with the ships which trade with New Spain and with India; and in order that you may perceive it, I will give you an example. Some one devotes a sum of three thousand dollars for various pious objects (such as saying masses for souls, portioning girls, entertainment of guests, &c.), and he places this sum in the *Monte de Piedad*, which divides it into three parts of a thousand dollars. One it gives at a venture for New Spain, receiving upon it fifty per cent., and it gains five hundred dollars a year.

The other thousand dollars are given for Canton for a return of twenty-five per cent., and they gain two hundred and fifty; or for India or the coast, and they gain at thirty-five per cent. three hundred and fifty. The remaining quantity, the other thousand dollars remain as stock in the deposit of the House to meet any loss, and if it is lent at low interest of five per cent., it produces annually fifty dollars; and thus you see how the three thousand dollars in one year only produce eight hundred or nine hundred dollars. Of these four hundred are spent for pious purposes, and the five hundred are laid by with the principal of the ventures, and as this goes on increasing, the gains augment at the wonderful rate I told you of.

Cortesano.—I admire and wonder at the method which you have explained to me.

Philipino.—Well, my friend, this is what is observed by the regulations laid down by the foundation statutes, and the ordinances of this *Monte de Piedad*, which bind the administrators under mortal sin, by the oath which they take to observe them, and which they fulfil without interesting themselves either personally or by the interposition of any one else, in the emoluments of these risks."

The societies of the *Obras Pias* probably do not make anything like these profits at the present day, yet they may have plenty of available funds, which the government has a claim upon in emergencies, since these societies are more or less government establishments under the direction of religious or clerical persons. It is said that the administration of the *Obras Pias* is much in need of reform.

The *Monte de Piedad* in Spain is a government pawnbroking establishment conducted by civil employés, and lending money at two and a half per cent. It is generally used by the population, without any disgrace attaching to it. There is no Monte de Piedad in the Philippines, and its establishment is much wanted for poorer persons: the *Obras Pias* assist a richer class, and the government in undertakings such as banks and those mentioned by Mr. Farren.

PRODUCE.

Since De Morga's time the Philippines have been enriched by

two new products, tobacco and hemp, and a third, sugar, has been greatly developed.

TOBACCO.

Mr. Consul Farren wrote of this in December 1848:—"The monopoly of tobacco is one of the principal sources of revenue to the government of these possessions, amounting annually to about £300,000, chiefly derived from its manufacture into cigars. The plant is chiefly cultivated in the northern provinces of Cagayan, and the provinces south of Manila. That of the north has been entirely at the disposal of the government, and the natives there are not permitted to cultivate rice, indigo, sugar, nor any other general produce without permission; the government desiring to constrain their occupation to the culture of tobacco for which that soil is peculiarly favourable. In the southern provinces a different course is pursued; there is no restraint on cultivation there; and though no leaf tobacco can be sold for exportation from the Philippines without the consent of the government, the purchase of it from the growers for the purpose of export, or for sale to exporters was entirely free. This right of purchase is now abolished by an order of the Intendant General, that henceforth growers must sell to the government alone. Regulations have been fixed for the classes of tobacco, and a tariff of prices established which are a slight advance on average valuations and not considered to be oppressive. The design of the government has been to centre in itself the whole of this branch of industry and revenue in these possessions, and to acquire the profits hitherto gained by the natives (chiefly mestizos), who purchased and resold the tobacco from the growers.

"Thirty-seven thousand quintals or 1,652 tons of leaf tobacco are sent from hence annually to Spain, 45,000 quintals from Cuba, and 60,000 from the United States; making 6,352 tons valued at £426,000, and producing a revenue of £1,350,300 for the monopoly there. Unless the new measure be administered liberally, and very judiciously, it may diminish in the southern parts the produce of tobacco which hitherto has been facilitated by the private advances made by traders to the cultivators; on the other hand the cultivators will receive better prices for their produce. The result entirely depends on the administration.

APPENDIX II.   379

Should the supply not be diminished the foreign trade may benefit, it is supposed, by purchasing from the government and at auction, instead of having to buy from private speculators who are under restrictions by government."

Two years before this, the export of tobacco to England from Manila in less than a year, was reported at 1,456 tons, worth 79,000 dollars.

"The importance of this tobacco trade is so great that the freights amounted to 150,000 dollars a year. The Intendant-General was of opinion that a saving to the treasury of the Philippines of 100,000 dollars a year might be effected by purchasing or building ships and attaching them to the Royal Navy, employing them as transports, and having on board of each an officer of the civil service, to take charge of the government cargo and of its accounts. The estimate of the Intendant may perhaps not be exaggerated."

The royal decree dated May 6, 1867, sanctioning the budget of the Philippines for the year 1867-68, fixes the quantity of tobacco to be sent in leaf to the Peninsula during that year at 135,000 quintals, and orders the payment in Manila of 101,250 dollars as half the freight of it.

This proposal of using government transports instead of freighting ships would be merely a return to the course described by De Morga.

A model school or plantation for growing tobacco figures in the budget at an annual cost of 600 dollars.

HEMP.

The quality of Manila hemp appears to be very good, and the demand for it in England and the United States exceeds the production. In 1854, the export of hemp to the United States was the preponderating article of trade.

In 1854 it amounted to 228,516 piculs, or 14,282 tons.
„ 1855   „   „   214,579   „
„ 1856   „   „   312,453   „   19,528 tons.

This hemp is not the plant so called in Europe, but is produced from a plant called abaca, a kind of plantain; there are more than seventeen plants in the Philippines, from which cords, thread, and paper can be made.

SUGAR.

The production and trade in sugar received a great impetus from the change of law and sugar duties in England in 1844.

Mr. Farren wrote in 1845 that sugar was grown by very small proprietors, and refined by the Chinese. The provinces of Pampangos and Taal about Manila, and the isles of Sebu and Panay were the chief sources of supply. "The Alcaldias repress all competing influences on agricultural improvement, and a peremptory order from Spain prohibiting the Alcaldes from engaging in local traffic is under consideration; but unless liberal salaries be assigned them, the order would probably be evaded, for their profits are now very large. The sugar of these islands is cheaper than anywhere else in the East and has been sent at times to Amoy; the price has not advanced though demand has increased."

However, the price of sugar had gone up in 1857 since a few years from 4 and 5 dollars a picul to 12; oil from 3 dollars a picul to 7; rice from 1½ dollars the cavan[1] to 4; and house rent had increased 50 per cent.

The exports of sugar from Manila were in the years

	Clayed Sugar.	Unclayed.
1835	11,462 tons.	140 tons.
1840	10,254 ,,	6,309 ,,
1844	15,450 ,,	6,078 ,,

The quantity exported in 1844 was divided as follows:—

England and Colonies.	Spain.	America.	France.
8,167 tons.	608 tons.	4,173 tons.	70 tons.

The exportation of sugar from Ilo-Ilo in the island of Panay sent to England and Australia, at first through Manila, and after the opening of that port in 1856, exported directly, increased steadily. The quantities were—

In 1856	-	-	-	-	850 tons.
,, 1857	-	-	-	-	1,800 ,,
,, 1858	-	-	-	-	1,290 ,,
,, 1859	-	-	-	-	5,427 ,,
,, 1860	-	-	-	-	7,048 ,,
,, 1861 first six months	-	-	3,904 ,,

[1] In 1736, according to Torrubia, this measure of rice was worth half a dollar, more or less.

TRADE.

In 1855 it was decided, that new ports should be opened in the Philippines to foreign trade, and in July orders were given for the establishment of custom-houses at Sual, a port of Pangasinan, Ylo Ylo in Panay, and Samboangan in Mindanao. British vice-consuls were appointed at Sual and Ylo Ylo in 1856. In 1862 or 1863 the port of Sebu was opened. In 1841, according to M. Mallat, the total value of the imports into the Philippines was £643,720, and of the exports, £868,720. In 1864, according to Mr. Farren, the imports amounted to 11,910,900 dollars, equal at 4s. 6d. to £2,679,052: and the exports amounted to 10,205,237½ dollars, or £2,296,178 8s. 9d.

AGRICULTURE AND MANUFACTURES.

De Morga stated (p. 241) that the inhabitants of Manila had forgotten the exercise of those arts with which they were acquainted before the arrival of the Spaniards. This was probably owing to the great quantity of goods imported by the Spaniards, and the same unfortunate result has followed, in too many places, the inordinate introduction of cheap and tasteless European goods, for the production of which, millions are crowded together, to lead a dreary life in close and unwholesome cities. The manufactures of the Philippine islanders were not, however, entirely ruined throughout the islands, as appears from the following pleasing description written by Mr. Loney, the British vice-consul in Hilo-Hilo, in April 1857.

"Considering that the Philippines are essentially an agricultural, rather than a manufacturing region, the textile productions of goods may be said to have reached a remarkable degree of development. Nothing strikes the attention at the weekly fairs held at the different towns, more than the abundance of native-made goods offered for sale, and the number of looms at work in most of the towns and villages also affords matter for surprise. Almost every family possesses one or two of these primitive-looking machines, with a simple apparatus formed of pieces of bamboo. In the majority of the houses of the mestizoes, and the more well-to-do Bisayans, from six to a dozen looms are kept at work. I have heard the total number in this province computed at 60,000, and though these figures may rather over-represent the actual quantity, they cannot be much beyond it. All the weaving is done by women, whose wages usually amount to from seventy-five cents to one dollar fifty cents per month. In general—a practice unfortunately too prevalent among the natives in every branch of labour—these wages are received for many months in advance, and the operatives frequently spend years—become, in fact, virtually slaves for a long period—before paying off an originally trifling debt. There are other workwomen employed at intervals to " set up " the patterns in the looms, who are able to earn from one dollar to one and-a-half per day, in this manner."

Governments, such as those of the Philippines and of Bengal, ought to exercise a strict supervision over this system of advances to the labourer, beyond what he can pay off, on finishing the piece on the loom, or gathering in his crops, and they would do well to take into consideration the introduction on behalf either of the Bisayan weavers, or of the Bengal indigo growers, or the labourers of any other places similarly circumstanced, of a statute of limitations, restricting the recovery of such advances within a period of, say two years, and preventing the labourer from being involved in a succession of advances, from which he can never extricate himself; though, as appeared from the report of the indigo commission, the natural difficulty of the ryot in paying off these debts, was increased by the practices of some of the planters.

I believe that under the Dutch Government in Java such advances have to be made under the supervision of a Government officer, and entered into his books, so as to prevent abuses.

The power of purchasing crops by anticipation is one of great profit to the speculator, and ought to repose on mutual confidence and advantage, and not become a means of extortion and oppression, into which it is likely to be developed, especially where the speculator and the labourer are not of the same nation and language.

The following project of a regulation for the establishment of magazines of grain in the chief towns of provinces was framed and proposed with the object of providing for the necessities of the Philippine Islanders, assisting them in periods of scarcity, and supplying them with grain for their maintenance, and sums of money for the cultivation of their land, and even for their undertaking a trade, with the payment of a small interest for what they receive; and for the avoiding by this means the abuses caused by exorbitant usurers amongst the cultivators. This projected regulation was appoved of in the Philippines, but had not been carried into effect. A similar one exists in Spain, where in all considerable villages magazines named *Posito* are under the charge of the municipal authorities, and lend corn at the rate of a celemin ($\frac{1}{12}$ of a fanega) per fanega per annum. In Wallachia and Moldavia there are village magazines of reserve against scarcity. In ancient Hindu India each village had a similar reserve magazine. This regulation deserves study for application in India and other countries, especially since the calamities which have befallen Orissa and Algeria.

Article I.

Grain shall be deposited in the granaries of the Town-hall or convent, and where that is not possible, a magazine shall be built for that purpose : this shall be constructed by the inhabitants, the bringing the materials and labour of building being considered as personal service : it shall be closed with three keys, which shall be held by the Alcalde, the parish priest, and the administrator of rentas estancadas (excise), or else by the Gobernadorcillo.

Article II.

In the chief town of each province, the Alcalde, the administrator, and parish priest shall form a committee for the administration of the magazine.

Article III.

A register shall be kept of all the operations of the committee : besides that, another which shall be signed by the Alcalde at the beginning of each year, in which shall be written the obligations and guarantees in favour of the magazine, and signed by the borrower and guarantors, and if they do not know how to sign, a witness shall sign with the clerk. The Alcalde, administrator, and parish priest shall also sign.

Article IV.

The obligations (*debts*) entered in the book mentioned in the preceding article shall have the legal bearing of escrituras garantigias (bonds), according to the provisions of section 79 of the Royal Instructions of May 31, 1753, and shall be payable with a preference over other obligations.

Article V.

When the chief officer of the province knows that the magazine should be opened to the public, either for the scarcity of grain, or at the time of sowing, or any other circumstance, he shall announce it by proclamation, so that the inhabitants who require palay, rice, or maize may present themselves on the day or days appointed, before the committee, to which they will apply. The committee will then take information and will distribute to each claimant the quantity which the borrower and his guarantors can reasonably answer for, without other formalities than those expressed in Article III.

Article VI.

The borrowers of grain shall restore to the magazine after the following harvest the quantity which they received with an additional quantity of six per cent., without any delay being allowed; the alcalde, administrator, and parish priest are responsible for this, and will have to make good whatever they cannot recover: to avoid which they will take all necessary precautions before making over grain. A register will be kept by the alcalde, in which shall be written down all the grain that goes out of and that comes into the magazine, and the operations of each day will be entered and certified.

Article VII.

During the fifteen days preceding that on which the debts of grain become due, the committee will draw up a list of the debtors and their guarantors, and of the quantities which they have to replace in the magazine, as appears from the register of operations and loans, and the committee will publish the day on which the debts become due, and will set up copies of the list of debtors in the tribunals and other public places, and order the replacement of the grain; and make a note of it in the register of obligations, which shall be equivalent to filing the debt in court against the borrower.

Article VIII.

At the end of every year a duplicate report of all operations shall be drawn up, of which one shall be sent to the Supreme Government, the other remaining in the archives of the magazine.

Article IX.

Whenever the alcalde, administrator, or priest is removed from his office, an examination and measuring of the grain shall take place, in the presence of the committee, certified by the clerk and witnesses, and the keys, books, papers, etc., belonging to the magazine shall be handed over with the inventory, which shall remain in the archives under the charge of the alcalde, and a copy shall be sent to the Supreme Government.

Article X.

The books and papers of the magazine shall be kept shut up under three keys.

Article XI.

The committee shall name a keeper of the magazine and four men, whose duty it will be to measure the grain which is distributed and received; these men, whose services will be gratuitous, shall, in consideration of them, be reserved from corvées and personal service, and these services of the keeper of the magazine shall be taken account of in all honorary matters in the village, for which reason care shall be taken that these persons shall be selected from the first and most honourable of the village.

Article XII.

If any borrower should be unable for any circumstance to replace the kind of grain which he received, he shall be bound to pay in currency at the price which the committee shall determine.

Article XIII.

To commence the establishment of the magazine, the committee shall meet and determine the quantity to be bought of rice, palay, and maize, according to the quantity of each required for the consumption of each province.

Article XIV.

The following measures shall be taken to provide funds for the purchase of grain:—

1. Every alcalde on his appointment shall give a hundred dollars to this fund.

2. The gobernadorcillos of villages exceeding six thousand tributes, shall contribute twelve dollars on taking possession of their post; those of villages of between five and six thousand tributes shall pay eleven dollars; those of four to five thousand tributes, ten dollars; those of three to four thousand, eight dollars; those of two to three thousand, four dollars; and those of villages of less than a thousand tributes shall pay two dollars; the gobernadorcillos of villages of Tinguianes,[1] in the provinces where there are any, shall pay one dollar, however many tributes they may contain.

[1] Unconverted Indians.

3. The sum paid by Indians on moving from one village to settle in another, which usually disappears and remains in the possession of the chief of the Barangay, shall also be applied to this fund, for which purpose the alcaldes shall keep a register in each village of those that leave it.

4. With respect to the Royal order authorising the Supreme Government to dispose of the surplus of the cajas de comunidad (municipal chests), the fourth part of this shall be applied to the magazine funds at the end of each year.

5. All vessels of a hundred tons and upwards going from one province to another, shall contribute one dollar for each voyage.

6. The produce of fines imposed for breaches of the regulations of the police and of public order, shall be applied to this fund.

7. Every chief of a Barangay, on receiving his title, shall be invited to contribute voluntarily whatever he may choose for this fund.

Article XV.

A register of all sums received for the magazine shall be kept and signed by the members of the committee.

Article XVI.

Whenever there is a surplus of money in the magazine funds, which has not been spent in purchasing grain, it may be lent at interest of six per cent. with the securities which the committee may think sufficient; the committee being responsible for its repayment, should the borrowers not repay it at the end of the period, which must never exceed a year.

Article XVII.

Since the establishment of the magazine has for object to prevent the advances which are made by rich persons to the peasants and producers of sugar and indigo, to their great prejudice, by reason of the excessive interest which they exact from them, inhumanely abusing the straits and need in which some peasants are frequently situated; all kinds of advances by private individuals to Indians are entirely prohibited; because, besides the injury done to them by the excessive usury, they are induced to spend money which, in many cases, is not necessary to them, and besides it appears to be unadvisable to give money in advance for rice, indigo, etc., four or five months before it is sown, without knowing what may be the result of the harvest.

TROOPS.

M. Mallat wrote, before 1846, of the military forces in the Philippines: "The regiments are almost entirely composed of Indians, and it is certain that now there are not a hundred Europeans amongst them. The remainder of a regiment of Asia has been sent back, which was composed of one thousand men, and had come from Spain to remain in Manila; but the misconduct of the soldiers made it apparent that it was better to do without Europeans, who have almost always been the cause of disorders, which would not have occurred but for them. A great number of men of this regiment died at Manila from their excesses. We cannot too often repeat it, so long as the Catholic religion and its ministers shall preserve their influence over the minds of the Indians, no troops will be required to restrain them. The Philippines have been conquered, aggrandised, and preserved by them; but will this happiness be their lot for long, and is it not to be feared that the philosophers will preach in this archipelago also, which now is so peaceful, and will persuade its fortunate inhabitants to exchange their prejudices for a pretended liberty, which would at once deprive them of their well-being and tranquillity?"—*Mallat*, ii, p. 3. This, however, is what several Spaniards have lately been injudiciously attempting to do in the Philippines.

About ten years ago five hundred Spanish artillery-men were sent out. The Philippine army is raised by conscription: it amounts to nearly twelve thousand men, and consists of nine regiments of infantry, four squadrons of cavalry, 1,200 Philippine artillery, 700 Philippine engineers, and the Peninsular artillery-men. There is also the *Resguardo*, or force to prevent smuggling, of 1,986 men, and a metropolitan police force of 160 men. Besides these, the authorities can, and do, avail themselves of the military service of the Igorrotes or Ygolotes, uncivilised men, accustomed to mountain warfare.

There are thirty thousand natives registered as seamen in the Philippines. There are some of these in each of the P. and O. steamers, as sail-makers and steersmen, who receive higher wages than the other men on board those vessels.

I desire to take this opportunity of again thanking Lord Stanley, the Secretary of State, for having kindly permitted me to make the foregoing extracts from the consular despatches.

It ought to be unnecessary to add that I am alone responsible for any conclusions or opinions expressed upon these extracts.

May I be allowed to conclude with a tribute to the memory of Mr. Consul Farren, who seems to have done good service during twenty years that he resided at Manila.

APPENDIX III.

The following account of recent discoveries of sunken rocks in the neighbourhood of the Philippines, though they have been reported to the Admiralty, and do not possess any general interest, yet seem to deserve a place in the publications of the Hakluyt Society.

A rock was discovered in the Sulu seas by the Spanish steamer *Magallanes*, commander Don Miguel Lobo, on the 3rd July, 1849. It was on a level with the surface of the water, and surrounded by breakers on the Takút Pabúnúwan Bank, the least depth of water on which, according to Horsburgh, is three fathoms, and six according to Captain Dalrymple's chart. "It is a rock of an elliptic figure, distant seventeen or eighteen miles from the southwest part of Pilas; is nearly on a level with the water, but it showed a little above water at the time it was examined: soundings nine to twelve fathoms all round it at a boat's length from the breakers; three or four fathoms further off no bottom with twenty-five fathoms Bearings N.E. islet of Duo Bolod S. 65° E. S.W. islet of Duo Bolod S. 61° E., the island of Vitinan S. 15° E.; and the centre of the most northern part of Pilas Island N. 38° E. Rock in latitude 6° 17' north, and longitude, according to Capt. Dalrymple's Chart, 127° 31' E. of Cadiz. It is situated three miles from the N.E. part of the bank described by Horsburgh. We steered from it S.W.¼W. for about three miles, and found ourselves in shallow water, and sounded successively 11, 7, 6, 5½ 5, and 4 fathoms of water."

A coral rock was discovered on the 29th October, 1849, by F. A. Hipps, master of the U.S. ship *Columbia*, in the China seas. which appeared not to have more than six or eight feet of water. It is in latitude 9° 36' N., and longitude E. of Greenwich

110° 30′ 0″, and 2° 29′ E. of the Northern Natuna by the chronometer: the rock is twenty feet long, and about twelve feet wide.

December 1, 1849. The discovery is announced of a new reef on passing Bontton, in latitude 5° 30′ N., and longitude 129° 38′ E. of Cadiz; it runs from E. to W.; it is visible towards the west side, and accessible on the north side, with soundings of 10 to 30 fathoms, which increase to 115 fathoms at the distance of a ship's length. *Extracts from Consul Farren's Despatches.*

APPENDIX IV.

GAZETTE OR BROADSHEET, PRINTED AT SEVILLE IN GOTHIC LETTER, BY ALONZO DE LA BARRERA, 1574.

[*First page, large type, Summary.*]

Very true and certain account of that which has newly been known of the new Islands of the West, and of the discovery which they mention of China, which was written by Hernando Riquel, Secretary of the Government, of them (the islands) to a friend of his in Mexico, which came in the ships which had put into the port of Capulco, and of their great riches, and of the trade and merchandise of China, and of the manner in which they extract and work gold: and another relation of the news which has arrived from Italy, and the fortification of Tunis, and of the fleet of the Great Turk: and how the city of Geneva has treated of returning to the obedience of the Holy Mother Church, and finally the death of the most Christian King of France, and of that which is going on in Paris and in Flanders. There is also the epitaph which has been found here of the blessed King Don Fernando, who conquered Seville. M.D. lxxiiii.

[*Second page, smaller type.*]

We reside in this isle of Luçon, whither the camp of his Majesty has passed, as it is the best of all these districts; in it there are many mines of gold in many parts, which have been seen by Spaniards, and all say that the natives work it as they work silver mines in New Spain. And the metal has a continuous vein like the silver ore. Trials have been made, and the mineral presents itself so plentifully, that I do not write about it lest they suspect me of exaggeration; but it is sufficient to say that I swear, as a Christian, that there is more gold in this island alone than there is iron in Biscay. The Moors use this gold and mix it with silver and copper so cunningly, that they might take in the most dexterous and cunning artificers of Spain. In this country there are tilled lands of the best that have been discovered in any part of the Indies. I do not write particulars about them, as those who go there will know all about it.

Since a year, that the camp is in this island of Luçon and city of Manila, which is built in it on the river named Manila, there came three ships from China, which brought some goods thence, as they are in the habit of doing as they come every year to these islands to trade. When they came in sight of the port, they sent from the sea to beg a safe-conduct from the Governor, which was given them, and he ordered that they should be well treated. What they brought were trifles from China, though in small quantity. Because the Moors chiefly use, and they bring for them large jars, coarse earthenware, iron, and copper, this in abundance; and for the chiefs they bring some pieces of silk, and fine porcelain, and this is not a great curiosity. They also brought some fine earthenware, which they sold very well and all the rest, because all we who are here have much money and are short of things to sell to the Chinese. They were so allured by this, that they promised to come again in seven or eight months, and bring very precious goods in great quantity and abundance. They brought samples of various articles which they have in their country, in order to ascertain the prices at which they might sell them; such as quicksilver, gunpowder, pepper, and very fine cinnamon, cloves, sugar, iron, copper, tin, brass, silk in skeins, silk stuffs, fresh flour, sweet oranges, rice, gold dust, wax like that of Spain, and realgar, and many other things which other nations do not use or bring.

They also brought images of crucifixes, and very curious chairs in our fashion. The cause of this arrival, besides the usual one which influences them, was, one of the Chinese who has been amongst us for more than a year's time, and who, returning to his country, gave information of this settlement, and that in it all the things they possessed might be traded in. And with this understanding, they made the voyage, and came with the before-mentioned ships, in which they brought what has been said, and other things, which it would be long to relate. We understand that they will keep their word and return when they said, and bring very choice things which will be much esteemed in Spain.

To perpetuate these settlements, the Governor has distributed a few villages of Indians in the district of this city of Manila, and a settlement has been made of what each tributary has to give in the year, which is a fringed cloth of four ells long and two wide; it is a fine stuff which they use to clothe themselves, and a hen; this they can give without pain. At present matters are conducted lightly with regard to them; later, when they are able to bear the yoke, they will give tribute of more importance.

These ships which at present go to the kingdom, left last year, and as it was late, they met with contrary winds at sea, and they were obliged to put into port; and so this year they have sailed in this month of July of seventy-three years. May God bring them in safety. There were other little details out here of which to advise you, but I leave them to other authors who are more unoccupied. The most especial of the affairs of this country is what I have related. At present there is satisfaction in it from the much that its richness and trade promise. May all be so, that his Majesty fulfil his holy desires, and that so the Lord may be served. So far the account goes. What is written and known from Mexico is, that the affairs there and all the province, through the medium of what comes from China, were greatly increasing and growing; because, besides many people being encouraged to go to those parts, many companies are being formed for the trade in merchandise. The Viceroy desired to send his Majesty a long relation of what there is there, and of what he had heard of the three ships which had arrived.

APPENDIX V.

[*Note to page* 126.]

Colonel Fernando de los Rios says that the demarcation between the crowns of Castile and Portugal began at three hundred and seventy leagues to the west of the Cape Verde islands, whereas the Bull of Pope Alexander VI of 1493 drew the line at one hundred leagues (or 400 miles) to the west of the Cape Verde islands. The reason of this discrepancy is that, D. Joan II of Portugal had appealed against this bull, and had requested to have the line drawn more to the west, so that it should not interfere with the Portuguese settlements in Africa. The King of Portugal had sent ships with geographers to visit all the coast of Africa, if it were possible; after this the King of Spain, desirous of peace, came in to this arrangement, and instructions were sent to the Portuguese and Spanish Ambassadors at Rome to draw up a new agreement before the Pope, with the consent of the King of Spain to the meridian of separation being placed 1,080 miles further west beyond the 400 miles at which it had been drawn. This was confirmed in the town of Tordesillas, on the 7th of June, 1494. The Spanish monarchs (says Gomara) whilst thinking that they would lose countries by giving up the 1,080 miles, on the contrary gained the Moluccas and other rich islands. But Osorius is of another opinion, for he states that the mouth of the Indus is ninety degrees east of Lisbon and the Moluccas forty-two degrees east of the Indus, which make one hundred and thirty-two, and adding the thirty-six degrees west of Lisbon to the meridian of demarcation, the whole distance would be one hundred and sixty-eight degrees. After the return of Juan Sebastian del Cano with Magellan's ship the *Victory*, Charles V was going to send more ships to the Moluccas, but the King of Portugal begged him first to ascertain to whom they belonged. After the interchange of some communications, they agreed that the difference should be settled by the most eminent geographers and experienced pilots. The delegates of the Emperor and of the King set out to Badajos and Elvas, towns close to the frontiers of the two kingdoms, at the beginning of the year 1524. After losing much time in ceremony and discussion, where the first interview should be held, and who should speak first, they at last agreed to meet and salute one another at the stream Caya, which separates the two kingdoms, half way between Badajos and Elvas, and after that they were to meet one day at Badajos and the other at Elvas. They passed many days examining globes, charts, and reports by pilots, then they discussed the degrees of longitude of the first discoverers of the Moluccas, and each side tried to make good his cause. Navarrete has printed several of the opinions given by the Spanish pilots and geographers, among them one of Hernan Colon. A letter from a Portuguese agent in Spain to the King of Portugal (the text of which is given at the end of this note) mentions sending a book written by Christopher Columbus upon the demarcation of the Castilian and Portuguese limits, which the Portuguese agent obtained through the Condesa de Lemos. It appears to have been favourable to the Castilian claims, since the agent says that the king should bid his cosmographers look at it, since theologians likewise read the Koran.

The geographers were two months without deciding anything; at last the Spanish delegates pronounced their sentence on the banks of the Caya in favour of their Emperor, which was not approved of by the Portuguese, and so they separated without coming to an agreement. The historian who relates this (Gomara, folio 57, translated by Simon Goulard, 1581) says, there then happened a laughable case; but which, nevertheless, is worth mentioning. As the Portuguese delegates were coming to their usual meeting, and passed by a river named Guadiana, a child who was taking care of some linen which his mother had washed and hung out to dry, asked them if they were the persons who were coming to divide the world with the Emperor. When they had said that they were; the child turned round, lifted up his shirt, and said aloud, draw your line through the middle of this. This trait of ridicule at once spread abroad everywhere, and some laughed at it, others considered that the child had been put up to it by some one to laugh at the pomposity of the Portuguese geographers, or rather at both the Portuguese and Spaniards together.

After the ill success of the geographers, negotiations continued with respect to the possession of the Moluccas; the archives at Lisbon contain a great number of letters from the King of Portugal to Antonio d'Azevedo de Coutinho, his ambassador in Spain, upon this subject. At length the question was settled by a treaty executed in Saragossa on the 22nd of April 1529, and ratified by the King of Portugal in Lisbon, June 20, 1530. By this treaty Charles V pledged his rights, dominion, property, and possession or quasi-possession, and all rights of navigation and commerce in the Moluccas to Portugal for a sum of three hundred and fifty thousand ducats or cruzados, to be worth in Castile 375 maravedis each. This treaty is preserved in the Torre do Tombo, Gav. 18, M. 8, No. 29, and it has been published with part of the documents by Navarrete. The first instalment of 150,000 cruzados was paid in Lisbon to Lope Furtado, ambassador of Charles V, by a royal order or *alvara* to Fernam de Alvares, the treasurer, dated June 1, 1529. By this treaty a line of demarcation was drawn by a semicircle from the N.E. and a quarter E., at a distance of nineteen degrees from the Moluccas, which corresponds with barely seventeen degrees distance at the equator: this line would pass over the islands of Las Velas and Santo Thome.

In a letter to Azevedo Coutinho, dated Lisbon, January 13, 1529, D. Joam III says that he desires to prevent his subjects and the Castilians meeting and quarrelling in those distant seas. He objects to allowing of any exception for those who pass the line in ignorance, since those who navigate in those parts must have with them pilots and persons of much experience in navigation, and it is not in reason that so wide a door should be left open, as to say that any one passed the line in ignorance, and with this excuse give rise to these scandals which it is the object of this treaty to avoid.

This new demarcation would include the Philippines or part of them within the Portuguese limits: accordingly we find that D. Jorge de Castro, governor of Ternate and the Moluccas, protested under the treaty, on July 3rd, 1543, against Ruy Lopes de Villa Lobos, for having come with five ships and a galliot to Mindanao and other Moluccas islands. This protest was served upon Villa Lobos on the 9th of August, 1543. (See De Morga, p. 14.)

The protest accuses Villa Lobos of ravaging and burning towns and capturing inhabitants within the limits of Portugal. Villa Lobos replied when the protest was given him, that the island of Antonia or Maludo, as the Portuguese named it (where he then was), was within the Spanish limits, and that he was sorry for any damage he had done, as such was not his intention, but only to chastise some treacheries done to him by the natives of these islands. He recognised that he was bound by the treaty and by his instructions not to come within the Molucca limits, and would not send ships there except with letters to the Portuguese governor, as is usual among the vassals of kings who are brothers. He added that from the inconvenience of the island of

Antonia he was getting his ships ready to seek another settlement further off from Maluco, and he requested the Portuguese governor to send his reply with the protest, whenever he sent the protest to his sovereign.

D. Jorge de Castro replied on September 2, 1543, to Villa Lobos with politeness, but requesting him to leave the island of Mindanao, which he had confessed he had no right to enter, and with further polite excuses he told him that he was entering by cunning and stealth places in which he had no business, and he rejected Villa Lobos' notion that the islands of Maluco meant only the Clove Islands, which would be to suppose the treaty to have been made with artifice. He also complained that Villa Lobos was remaining in Mindanao, and that according to report he had sent a ship to New Spain to obtain succour and instructions, as if he intended to settle in the country; and he said that as Charles V had ceded the Moluccas to Portugal, he had also ceded the entrances to them, as no one would give his house and keep back its door. He complained that an island called Cabedo, and also Maludo, where the Portuguese used to find provisions, are now so ruined that there are only dead bodies of the natives in them. He therefore, once, twice, and three times, required Villa Lobos to withdraw from Mindanao; and if, on his return voyage, he required provisions or repairs or cables, to address himself to him and he would assist him. If Villa Lobos did not do as required, he was requested to send a reply, authenticated by Gaspar de Castilla, the chief clerk of the fleet, for the security of the governor of Moluccas.

Villa Lobos replied that whatever he did or said did not affect the rights of the King of Portugal, and that there was no ground for serving him with requisitions, that the islands of Maluco were known by name, and it was known what a different thing it was to trade with countries or to subject them, and that if it were understood that all the countries where navigators passed and bought provisions with their money belonged to the sovereign of those navigators, all the world would already belong to one prince. As to the complaint of the governor of Maluco that he would not let Antonio d'Almeida see his fleet, there were things which he would not show even to his own brother; and as for the governor's insinuation that his polite reply was cunning and empty compliment, in truth he was not accustomed to use compliments : and he begged of the governor, as their sovereigns were brothers, not to give occasion for quarrels to arise between Castilians and Portuguese. Dated Island of Antonia, September 12, 1543. This collection of documents was drawn up by Graviel Rebello, judge for the deceased, and signed by others. February 7, 1544. (Torre de Tombo, Gav. 18, Maço 8, No. 31.)

There is no trace of any protest by the Portuguese against the occupation of the Philippines by D. Miguel Lopez de Legazpi.

CARTA DE D. DUARTE DE ALMEIDA A EL REY.
(Torre do Tombo, Gav. 18, *Maço* 8, No. 7.)

Senhor,—Porque nom sey se seraa dada a V.A. huma carta mynha em que lhe escrevya que me ficavão tresladando hum livro do almyrante das Indias que fezera Dom Cristovão Colon seu pay das demarcaçoês dos mares e terras de V.A. cos de Castela, lho torno a escrever agora, e o livro ja o tenho mandado a V.A. e ainda que aquylo nom seja verdade como me parece, todavia devyao V.A. de mandar ver por cosmografos porque tambem os Teologos vem o Alcorão. A condessa de Lemos mo mandou treladar, e estemou que nom se entregasse ao Conselho das Indyas, que o pidya muy apertadamente ao almirante que he seu sobrinho, e muito seu amigo della; e o livro vai concertado por mym co propreo que fica em poder da Condesa pera se nom poder fazer delle nada, senão o que for servyço de V.A. e mays anda me sabendo por via do almirante em que asentarão aqueles cosmografos que se aquy ajuntaarão sobre que V.A. me screveo e quem tem este zelo e deseja tanto de o servir parece que lhe devera V.A. de fazer a merce que lhe pedia, que assi me salve Deos, que soo porquem ela he, sem estoutras circustancias, que importão muyto lha ouvera V.A. de fazer, e ela estaa muy desconsolada por lha V.A. negar e nao creo que por ysso deyxara de o servyr Nosso Senhor: a vida de V.A. com muyta saude, e seu estado real guarde e prospere por muytos anos pera seu servyço.

De Valhadolid a vynte cynco de Noviembre [ ]? Beyjo as Reales mãos de V.A.

Dom Duarte de Almeida.

[*Note to page* 22.]

The Sultan of Egypt's embassy to Rome was addressed to

Pope Alexander VI, according to De Barros and San Roman; Osorio states that it was received by Pope Julius.

[*Note to page* i.]

No copy of *De Morga* exists either in the Escorial Library or the Biblioteca Nacional of Madrid. There is one in the Library of San Isidro, Madrid, and in the public library of Lisbon, and Mr. Gayangos possesses a copy.

[*Note to page* 169.]

A copy of a letter in the Hydrographic Department, Madrid, to the Conde de Monterrey, Viceroy of New Spain, 1600, compared by Navarrete, June 23, 1794, with the original in the Archives of the Indies in Seville, gives a detailed relation of the naval action with Oliver Van Noort which agrees with De Morga's account, and adds the following particulars:—

When De Morga's ship was getting very full of water, a Jesuit named Padre Santiago, with a crucifix in his hand, called out, "See now, Christian Spaniards, where is your courage? see that this is the cause of God: die then, die like good soldiers of Jesus Christ, and do not become food for fishes; see that of two evils which threaten us, the least is to enter the enemy's ship, and if we lose one ship we gain another." At this exhortation some sprung on board, others held back because of the fire on board the enemy caused by some cartridges which they lighted on purpose to frighten the Spaniards. When the ship was going down, De Morga stripped off his clothes at the persuasion of a servant of his named Joseph de Naveda, who gave him a mattrass of . . . (blank in the original, probably straw of maize), and the two stripped of their clothes threw themselves into the sea, as did many others, but the lesser number reached land. Some reached the enemy's ship seeking succour, where those heretics received them with spears and thrust at them with much cruelty. Amongst them Captain Gomez de Molina received a lance wound, and with it swam to shore, where he died on the beach of loss of blood.

This letter says that Juan de Alcega took with the Dutch consort nineteen men alive who surrendered, and that the Spaniards lost one man killed by a shot, named Juan Baptista de Mondragon, nephew of the precentor of the cathedral of Manila;

another man, from the Canary Islands, was drowned leaping from one ship to the other, and a few were wounded: they captured eight large cannon of cast iron and four small ones.

Juan de Alcega sent the prisoners alive to Manila and received an order to follow the enemy, which he did, and on his return " the governor ordered him to be arrested and afterwards set at liberty: I do not know the justification that there was for the one or for the other." [This shows that this letter was not written by the governor nor by any high official.] "After that the governor ordered, and with much justice, notwithstanding the word which the Admiral Juan de Alcega had given them, that the garrote should be given to all the prisoners. This was done, and thirteen of them were executed, because the rest were boys; and they are distributed among the monasteries; I do not know with what object, for they are not very young. Twelve died very good Catholics, and converted with many tears, so much so that it obliged the monks to give them the most holy sacrament of the Eucharist. The Brotherhood of Holy Mercy buried them with much charity. The one that would not be converted was the admiral, the most dogged and pertinacious heretic that I ever saw in my life."

[*Note to page* 81.]

A law-suit is at present going on between the two towns of Vergara and Beasain, in Guipuzcoa, each of which claims the Japanese martyr Fray Martin de la Ascencion; one town pleads that his name was Aguirre, the other that it was Loynes. The contemporary authority of De Morga, who has printed a letter from this martyr, stating his name to have been Aguirre, ought to be sufficient to establish that as having been his name. There was, however, at that time in Japan another Martin de la Ascencion; and a MS. book in the library at Evora, cxv, 2-2, by Padre Alexander Valignano, Visitor of the Company of Jesus in Japan, dated October 9, 1598, was written to refute the calumnies of Fray Martin de la Ascencion against the company. It consists of thirty-one chapters, and the last three are refutations of the statements of Fray Geronymo de Jesus, who fills so large a space in De Morga's history. This book states that Fray Martin Loines de la Ascencion, a Basque by nation, had written treatises against the Jesuits, and had directed a Portuguese friend of his, a secular priest, named Miguel e Roxo, to correct them. This priest was much scandalised at the calumnies they contained. The Visitor complains of Fray Martin for having been so facile in believing and so hasty in speaking, for he had not been more than five or six months in Japan, for he came in the year 1596 from the Philippines, and he had not been in the country more than three months when he wrote these treatises since he began to write them in Nangasaki. The Visitor forbears to speak of Loines as he deserved, because he had quitted this life *(por ser pasado de esta vida)*, a phrase which seems to indicate a natural death, and not that by martyrdom. (I had not time to read the whole book through, but in those parts which treated of the martyrdom the Visitor only names one of the martyrs.)

In the twenty-sixth chapter the Visitor replies to the calumnies against the Jesuits of causing the loss of the galloon *San Felipe* in Urando of the kingdom of Tosa, and says that what happened was only in accordance with the law of Japan, and other neighbouring kingdoms, that when a vessel is lost, it and its goods belong to the lord of the country. He says that Taicosama sent Yemonojo to take possession of the galloon, and that the friars negotiated with him about it, without ever informing the Jesuits of their business. He speaks of De Morga as a man of much authority, and of a letter having come into his hands which had been written by Fray Pedro e Bautista, to Fray Marcello de Ribadeneira about the galloon. The Visitor also gives the story of the imprudent speech of the Spanish pilot to Yemonojo, the confidante of Taicosama, and attributes the execution of the friars to that cause alone; for he says the Jesuit's house was not closed, and they were not molested, though three Jesuits were crucified by mistake, and a Christian, whom Padre Organtino had sent after the friars to assist them on the road. Further on he says that Taicosama was moved by the pilot's report to kill the Manila friars; and that "he was not fanatical, and believed the feasts of the Bonzes to be lies, and that there is no other life for men than the present one, and he does not abhor our faith, but said he did not want it in Japan, as it seemed to him to be an invention for the conquest of countries, and so he wrote clearly to D. Francisco Tello." The Visitor gives Taicosama's reply of 1597 to D. Francisco Tello's letter, sent by D.

Luis de Navarrete, rather more at length than it is given by De Morga; see p. 84.

The Visitor states that the friars complained of the company objecting under the Brief of Gregory XIII to their proceedings, and that they attempted to override that Papal Brief by the rights of the King of Castile under the general grant of the islands and countries to be discovered in the Indies. The Company of Jesus seem to make out their case well, and the wisdom of the Brief, and to have shewn themselves superior to the friars through being solely devoted to the advancement of their religion, whilst the friars mixed up projects for the subjection of those countries under the influence of national and so-called patriotic feelings.

In the twenty-seventh chapter the Visitor says the friars resorted to another plan to conceal the mischief they had done in Japan, and to cast blame on the Company; this was to make great festivity and processions in honour of those friars who had been slain, publishing that they were martyrs, and that the men of the Company knew very well how to take care of their lives and to run away from martyrdom.

In reply to this the Visitor observes that the three Jesuits who had been crucified by mistake with the Manila friars had died with as much constancy as the others; one of them, named Aligi Paulo, had been a Jesuit brother for more than twelve years. The Jesuits were not jealous of the martyrs, but thought that their canonisation was a right reserved to the Holy Father, and that till then the friars should not have distributed their relics. He also blames the martyrs for having made so large a list of Japanese Christians and given it to Gibunoxo (Ximonojo), the lieutenant of Taicosama, who from prudence did not shew it to Taicosama, so as not to compromise so many important persons.

The Visitor then denies the miracles which the friars attributed to the martyrs. 1. Though their bodies did not become corrupt during the first few days on account of the cold, they did so later, and were as unpleasant as any others. 2. It was stated that the body of Fray Pedro Baptista shed blood many days after his death: this was only the corrupted humours, which, with the intestines, found an exit. 3. It was pretended that a vial of their blood remained uncorrupted and liquid. The truth was that Juan Baptista Bonacina, a Milanese, mopped up their blood with a napkin, and carried it home, and squeezed it out into a China porcelain bottle and stopped it up, and kept it in a chest, with the intention (as he told me) of taking it back with him to Italy for his own devotion, and to relate there what he had seen with his own eyes. When he went to Macao, and I arrived shortly after from India, he brought me the bottle with joy to shew it me, as the blood still moved and was liquid, and he thought it was miraculous, and the greater part of the blood was from Fray Aligi Paulo. The bishop D. Pedro Martins, who had been expelled from Japan, and D. Luis, who was going there as bishop, were both in Macao, and I took the Milanese and the bottle to them, and they opened it and put a thin paper in, but by the colour it could not have been known for blood, but only from its very bad smell. After well considering the matter all three of us, we stoppered the bottle with a cloth as it was before, and gave it back to Juan Baptista, without saying what we thought, so as not to disturb his devoutness, but afterwards we were of opinion that there was nothing miraculous about it: moreover, we thought that from the blood having been collected with a cloth and squeezed out, it would naturally remain liquid, as the thicker parts would remain in the cloth. The friars got hold of the bottle later, and made no mention of the name of Aligi Paulo, and carried it off to the Vicar of Macao, an unlettered man: he, without communication with our fathers or the bishops, was induced by the friars to make out a paper certifying that the blood of the friars was liquid, and that it seemed to be marvellous its being thus preserved; all this without mentioning its bad colour and bad smell. The Bishop D. Pedro heard of this, and sent for the Vicar and reprimanded him for having done such a business in a concealed manner, whilst there were two bishops there and so many fathers of the Company, among whom were five or six who read or had read theology."

There is also an original Portuguese document in the library of the Madrid Academy, which is a protocol of a conference drawn up by Mattheus de Cours, ecclesiastical notary, dated Nangasaqui, September 23, 1598, and signed by those who were present at it, who were Dom Luis Cerqueira, Bishop of Japan, the Visitor of the Company Alexandro Valignano, the Viceprovincial Pero Gomez, the Superiors Francisco Pasio, Diego de Mesquita, Melchior de Mora, Affonço de Lucena, Alonzo Gonzalvez, and the Fathers Organtino Soldo, Francisco Calderon, Gil da Mata, Celso Confalonero, Valentim Carvalho, and Ruy Barreto. The protocol complains of the mischief done by Fray Geronymo de Jesus and his companion Fray Gomes de San Luis, and other Manila friars who had come in opposition to the Brief of Gregory XIII, and saying that their prelates had sent them. The protocol states the opinion of the meeting that the Bishop of Japan might, and ought, as soon as he could, take up and re-embark, and send away all such friars as came without authority.

[*Note to page* 30.]

Padre Alonzo Sanchez was sent from Manila to Macao to take the oath of allegiance from the Portuguese on the accession of Philip II to the throne of Portugal. The library of the Academy of History, Madrid, contains a Chinese copy of a chapa, by which the mandarins of Canton allowed a Portuguese ship to come and fetch Padre Alonzo Sanchez and the despatches from Machan (Moluccas).

APPENDIX VI.

LETTER OF LUIS VAEZ DE TORRES TO HIS MAJESTY, RELATING HIS VOYAGE THROUGH THE TORRES STRAITS, DATED MANILA, JULY 12, 1607; RECEIVED JUNE 22, 1608.

(J 2, Biblioteca Nacional, Madrid, apparently a copy of a document mentioned by Navarrete as existing in Simancas.)

As I find myself in this city of Manila at the end of a year and a half of navigation and discovery among the lands and seas of the unknown southern parts; and since until now they have not been pleased in this Royal Audiencia of Manila to despatch me, in order to finish the voyage as Your Majesty ordered; and as I was in the hope of being the first to give Your Majesty a relation of what has been discovered, with the rest, and as I am detained without knowing whether they will despatch me from this city of Manila, I have chosen to send a person to give an account to Your Majesty, who is Fray Juan de Merlo, of the order of St.

Francis, one of the three monks whom I brought at my charge; which relation he will give to Your Majesty as a person who was present at all; which account, on my part, is the following:

We left the port of Callao, of the city of the Kings, of Peru, on the 21st December, with two ships and a launch, in the year six hundred and five:[1] the chief of them was Captain Pero Fernandez de Quiros, and I as his second in command. We steered, keeping well in company, the S.W. by W. course, and we sailed on this course for eight hundred leagues, and in the latitude of twenty-six degrees. It seemed fit to our commander not to go beyond this on account of certain shifts of the wind: and I gave him my opinion, signed with my name, that it was not a very prudent thing to go lower than that, until arriving at thirty degrees and more, if the wind should leave us; my opinion did not prevail, because from the said twenty-six degrees we went down soon after by the course N.W. by W., and we went by this course as far as twenty-four degrees and a half. In this neighbourhood we found a flat islet, uninhabited, and about two leagues long, without bottom for anchoring the ships. From there we departed steering west and a quarter north-west as far as twenty-four degrees: in this neighbourhood we found another uninhabited island without anchorage; it might have about ten leagues circumference.[2] We gave it the name of San Valerio. Thence we departed steering for one day west and a quarter north-west, and then to north-west by west until reaching twenty-one degrees and a third. In this neighbourhood we found another flat islet,[3] without soundings, uninhabited, and divided into portions: we went forward by the same course, and after going twenty-five leagues, we found four triangular isles of five or six leagues each, flat, uninhabited, and without soundings.[4]

---

[1] At three in the afternoon, says the pilot Gaspar Gonzales de Leza, Quiros in the galleon *S. Pedro y S. Pablo*, and Torres in the *S. Pedro*; the patache was named *Tres Reyes*, and was commanded by Pedro Bernal.

[2] The first island was reached on the 26th January, named Anegada by De Leza, and said to be in 25°, and 1,000 leagues from Callao; the second island (Sin Puerto) was reached on the 29th January: it was in 24¾°, and 1,075 leagues from Callao.

[3] The 2nd February the ships parted company for some hours; on the 3rd they saw an island in 21¼°.

[4] Four islands reached on the 4th and 5th February in 20° and 21°: they were three or four leagues apart.

We gave them the name of the Virgins: here our needle varied to the north-east.[1] From hence we went out steering to the north-north-west as far as nineteen degrees. In this neighbourhood we saw an islet on the east side about three leagues off from us; it was like those left behind: we gave it the name of Santa Polonia.[2] From hence, diminishing our latitude half a degree, we saw a flat island with a point to the south-east full of palm trees: it was in eighteen degrees and a half;[3] we came to it, it had no anchorage, we saw people on the beach: the boats went to shore, and when they got there they could not land on account of the rocks and high sea. The Indians on shore called out to them, and two Spaniards took to swimming,[4] and the Indians received them very well, and throwing down their arms on the ground embraced and kissed them on the cheeks. With this friendliness there came one of their chiefs on board the flagship to speak, with an old woman,[5] and they clothed and treated them, and set them on shore again at once, because they were much frightened. In return for this benefit they sent a bunch of hair and some poor feathers, and some carved shells of pearl oysters. All these were their finery: they were very wild people, dusky, and corpulent. The arms which they use are some very long and thick lances. As we could not land nor find an anchorage, we went forward, steering to the west-north-west, and we went by this course, sighting the land of this island, we could not reach it after the first occasion, on account of the strong contrary wind, with many showers. It was all very flat, and in parts the water washed over it. From this neighbourhood, in

[1] De Leza says—"On the 7th February they set fire to the oven, and water artifice, and began to produce it with much facility, and this day they obtained three earthen jars full, and it was to make a trial of the machine, which water was seen by all to be very clear, sweet, and good to drink." I have been informed that a machine for condensing sea water is mentioned as early as 1518 as used by one Domingo Rivera.

[2] Sighted on February 9, in 19°.

[3] This point was seen on the 10th February, in 18° 10'.

[4] Francisco Ponse and Miguel Morera swam ashore: they were well received, and two others swam ashore. Torquemada mentions these same names.

[5] On the 11th February, De Quiros sent a boat with ten men and the ensign Pedro Lopez Gojo on shore; they found an old woman damaged in one eye and one arm; they brought her on board and gave her presents; she had with her a small white dog like ours; where she was

sixteen degrees and a half,[1] we went steering to the north-west and a quarter north until reaching ten degrees and three-quarters; in this neighbourhood we saw an island which was understood to be San Bernardo, as it was in pieces, but it was not, from what was seen later. We found no anchorage in it, although the boats went on shore to see if there was water, as we were short of it, and they found none, but only some cocoa-nuts, and they were small. Our commander, considering that we were short of water, decided that we should go to the island of Santa Cruz, where he had been with the Adelantado Alvaro de Mendaña, saying that there we should provide ourselves with wood and water, and a decision would be taken as to what should be most convenient for the service of Your Majesty. At this time the crew of the flag-ship were in a mutinous disposition, and enter-

found there were many graves; in this island they found half of a pulley of cedar, wrought on the coast of Nicaragua or Peru. They found no water in the island, but got many cocoa-nuts. On taking back the old woman, they found a chief and some canoes of fourteen or fifteen men each: the chief's canoe had twenty-six men; it was very well built, not of one piece of wood, and as good as could have been made in Castile. They got the chief away with much trouble, and almost by force, leaving seven Spaniards on shore; the chief would not come on board, so Quiros went down to him in the boat, and pacified and soothed him, giving him quince preserve and other things to eat, but he would not eat them and put them by. Quiros then gave him a taffetan robe, and a hen which he asked for, and sent him ashore, to the great joy of his people. The islanders gave to the Serjeant Pedro Garcia a turban of feathers, which seemed to be of Pangiles. On coming on board they found amongst the feathers a quantity of woman's hair like a diadem: the general valued it much; the hair was very long and very yellow, like threads of gold. The Indians also sent two large shells, in which a fowl could be served up; and their knives are made of shells. They then left the island, and all night the crews did not cease talking of what they had seen, and of the good conduct of the islanders.

[1] 12th February. They ran along the island, which was twenty-five leagues long and ten broad: all the middle is sunk, as though one said a piece of the sea surrounded by land. They saw a small island five leagues to the north of this, which they did not visit. 13th February, in 16¼°, saw another island.

On the 13th February Quiros placed an order on the mainmast that no one should swear by the name of God in vain under pain of a fine of a patacon for the departed souls: that no one should meddle with the affairs of others and put his hand to the knife, and if he did, he should be fined thirty patacones.

tained the design of going straight to Manila. For this cause he
sent me the chief pilot under arrest to my ship, without com-
mencing legal proceedings against him or against others.[1] He
was importuned by me to punish them or allow me to punish
them, for they had the name of traitors, and he did not choose
to do so; for which reason there happened to him that which
Your Majesty will already have known, for they made him turn
out of his course, as will be mentioned further on, and he will
have related it in the royal court of Your Majesty. We went
away from this above-mentioned island to the west and a quarter
north-west. Here we found that in this meridian the needle
varied to the north-east by about a quarter. We sailed by this
course as much as fully ten degrees: in this neighbourhood we
found a low island of five or six leagues,[2] flat and without soundings; it was inhabited, and the people and arms were of the
fashion of those we had left behind; but different boats came
near to the ships to speak to us, and taking what we gave them,
and asking for more, and stealing whatever was hanging to the
ships,[3] and thrusting at us with lances, as it seemed to them that
we could not do them any harm: since there was no anchorage,
from the want of water that was felt, our commander sent me
ashore with the two boats and fifty men; when I reached land
they resisted my entrance, without ever consenting to peace, by
which they obliged me to skirmish with them: after some harm

The 14th February they saw another island in 15°, and De Leza found
they had gone 1,475 miles from Callao, and in a straight line 1,398
leagues; in all this time they had received only a quartillo of water, and
provisions had been short too, and the heat had been very great: the
general endured the same privations.

The 19th, in 10¾°, making for Santa Cruz Island; 21st, 10⅓°, saw an
island; on the 22nd found a bay in its west side, but no anchorage, 10½°;
some said it was San Bernardo, others the Solitaria, and it was never
settled which it was: the general, seeing the little advantage that it
was, made for Santa Cruz.

[1] A summary of Quiros' voyage, by the accountant Juan de Iturbe,
Mexico, 25 March, 1607 (J 2), says that on the 22nd March Quiros called
a council, and afterwards the chief pilot Juan Ochoa de Bilboa went
over to Torres' ship, being disgusted with the captain Quiros. Leza does
not mention this.

[2] Sighted an island with many cocoa-nut trees on the 2nd of March, of
three or four leagues.

[3] Leza says they carried away our hawsers (orinques) to shore, upon
which they fired upon them and wounded them.

had been done them, three of them came forth to offer me peace, singing with branches in their hands, and one with a lighted match, upon his knees. I received them well, and embraced them, and then clothed them, as they were chiefs, and on asking them for water, they would not show it me, pretending that they did not understand; and keeping the three chiefs with me, I sent the serjeant with twelve men to seek for water, and when they fell in with it, the Indians sallied out again and attacked them, and wounded a Spaniard. Seeing their treachery I attacked and routed them without other injury, the country remaining in my possession, I ran all over the village without finding more than only dry oysters and some fish, and plenty of cocoa-nuts, with which the country was well provided: I did not find birds or animals, except only some little dogs. I found many covered boats, with which they are used to sail to other islands with lateen sails, very cleverly made of straw, and the women are clothed with shirts and petticoats of the same stuff, and the men with not more than their waists and middles covered. We went out from here with the boats laden with water: from the much sea they were swamped, with much risk to our lives; and so we had to continue our voyage without taking water from this island, to which we gave the name of La Matanza. We went out, steering by this parallel for thirty-two days: in all this course we found that there were very great currents and many drifts of wood and snakes, and much litter.[1] All these were signs which showed that there was land on either side: we did not venture to seek for it nor to leave the altitude[2] of the island of Santa Cruz; for it seemed to us to be always near, and that was reason, if it was in the place where they had marked it the first time that it was discovered; but it was much further on, as will be seen by the narrative. So before reaching it about sixty leagues, and 1,940 leagues from the city of Lima, we found an islet of about six leagues, very high, and with a good bottom all round it, and other islets near it;[3] under shelter of which the ships remained at anchor. I went out with the two boats and fifty men to reconnoitre the inhabitants, and I found a village at the dis-

[1] *Pagereria.* Gaspar Gonzales de Leza says they saw many sea snakes on the 18th March.
[2] From the 5th March till 9th April Leza always gives 10° or 10° 30'.
[3] Leza names this island and islets Nuestra Señora de Loreto, in 10° 10'.

tance of a gunshot from the island, surrounded by a wall with
only one entrance, and without a gate; while I was near it with
the two boats with the intention of attacking it, because they
would not give signs of peace, at last there came out a chief with
water hung at his neck and a staff in his hand, and without fear
he came straight to the boats. I received him very well, and by
signs, with which we understood each other very well, he told
me that his people were much afraid of the arquebuses, and so
he begged me not to land, as they would bring me water and
wood on supplying them with vessels. I said to him that it was
absolutely necessary to remain five days on shore to rest. Seeing that he could do no more, he quieted his people, who were
much disturbed, and things turned out in such manner that no
missiles were discharged either from his side nor from ours. I
landed in the fort in perfect safety, and calling on them to halt,
made them give up their arms; and I bade them take their
chattels out of their houses, all which were not worth much, and
go with them to the island to other villages which were there.
They thanked me much: the chief remained all the time with
me. Then they named the country. All came to make peace
with me, and all the chiefs came to assist me, making their
people bring us wood and water and take it aboard of the ships.
We employed six days in this. The people of this island were
of very good conversation; we understood each other very well,
and they were desirous of learning our language and of teaching
us theirs. They were great seafarers, all well furnished with
beards, great archers and throwers of javelins, and very venture-
some: their boats, which are very large, could go a great distance: they gave us information of more than forty islands, large
and small, and all inhabited, naming them by their names, and
telling us that they fought with several of them. They also gave
us information of the isle of Santa Cruz, and of that which
happened there to the Adelantado Alvaro de Mendaña;[1] the
people of this island are of ordinary sized bodies; there were
amongst them white people and others red, other native Indians
of the colour of those of the Indies, and others black, swarthy,
and dusky. They practise slavery.[2] Their victuals are some

[1] Leza says they sent a canoe to Santa Cruz to give information of
Quiros' arrival.

[2] Leza says the people of this island fought with other islands, and
used the captives as slaves for their tillage.

yams and fish; they have plenty of cocoa-nuts; they possess pigs and fowls. This island was called Taomaco, and the name of the chief of it was called Tomay. I took leave of them, having caught four Indians, at which they were not much pleased, and as we got water and wood here, we were not obliged to go to the island of Santa Cruz, which as I say was sixty leagues further on in this parallel. So we left this place, steering to the south-west as far as twelve degrees and a half, where we found an island of the size of that of Taomacoy, with the same sort of people; it was called Chucupia. There was only one small anchorage in the whole of it, and going along it I reached the shore in a little boat with only two men. They came out to offer me peace, and at the same time they presented the husk of a tree, which looked like a very fine cloth, of four ells in length and three spans in width, with which they clothe themselves; with this I took leave of them. From hence we departed, steering to the south; a very strong wind from the north fell upon us, which obliged us to beat against it[1] for two days. At the end of that time there were opinions that as it was winter we should not go beyond fourteen degrees latitude in which we then found ourselves, although my opinion was always very much to the contrary. It was decided that we should seek the islands named by the Indians of Taomaco; so we left this neighbourhood, steering to the west, and after a day's sail we discovered a volcano, very high and thick, more than three leagues in circumference, very thickly wooded, and with black inhabitants with thick beards. To the west, and in sight of this volcano, at the distance of eight leagues there was an island, not very high, and very pleasant to look at. It had few places of anchorage, and they were very close to the land. It was well peopled with black inhabitants. Here two were caught in some boats, and they were clothed and fed, and the next day put on shore. In return for this they wounded a Spaniard with an arrow, though it is true that it was not in the same port, but a gunshot further on; they are people who on seeing their opportunity do not let it pass. In sight of this island and all round it there were many very high and large islands, and we went to the south side as it was so large, and where they wounded one of our men, we named it Santa Maria. Leaving this, and going southwards towards this

[1] *A echar de mar entraves.*

large island which we saw, we discovered in it a very large bay,[1] well inhabited and very fertile, with yams and many fruits, pigs, and fowls. All these people are black and naked; they fight with arrows, javelins, and large clubs. They never would be friends with us, although we spoke together many times, and I treated them; I never set foot on shore with their good will, as they always wished to oppose it, and we always fought with little risk. This bay is very fresh, and has many and large rivers; it is in fifteen degrees and two-thirds latitude, and will have twenty-five leagues circumference.[2] We gave it the name of the Bay of St. Philip and St. James, and the land that of Espiritu Santo.[3] Here we remained fifty days. We took possession in the name of your Majesty of the interior of this bay, and from the most sheltered part of it there went forth the flagship at one o'clock after midnight without telling us or making signals for us to know of it.[4] This happened on the 11th of June, and although

---

[1] Iturbe and Leza say they anchored in this bay on the 3rd May, but they reached it on the 1st.

[2] Iturbe says fifteen or sixteen leagues in circumference.

[3] This is the largest island of those now called the New Hebrides.

[4] Juan de Iturbe de Quiros' accountant, who is by no means favourable to Quiros, thus relates this parting company of the ships:—

"On Thursday, 8th June, the ships went out of the bay (as they had done the week before, the crews being rather sick from eating fish), and on coasting to the eastward there came a storm from the south-east which obliged them to put into the bay. Sunday the 11th day of St. Barnabas, as the *Almiranta* and *Fragata* were going in front, they anchored early, and the flag-ship, as a better ship and going better on a bowline as they were then going, arrived at nine at night near the anchorage, when a sudden squall fell upon her, and as her sails were set she heeled over, but righted on striking them, and again went out of the bay, which being of clean bottom and wide, they might have remained in it that night going on one and other tack, or have anchored where they thought fit, but they only chose to return to the danger from which they had fled, leaving their companions at anchor. They were two days off the entrance, tacking about without being able to fetch it, and on the third day, seeing that they had fallen off, although they might have sheltered themselves under the land and waited till the wind fell, and rejoined the *Almiranta* and *Zabra*, the captain only chose to take the course for New Spain, setting the ship's head north-east, and on Thursday, the 15th June, we discovered a large and a small island: these had been already seen from the island of the Virgin Mary to the north-east of it.

Gaspar de Leza says, "We sailed on the morning of the 8th with the

I went out at one next morning to look for it, making all due diligence, it was impossible to find them, since they did not

people now well, for which we thanked God, for the dogs, cats, and pigs which had eaten the entrails of the fish had died. On the 9th there came a gale at three in the afternoon from the S.E. and S.E.E.; we had to sail under courses only to wait for the *Almiranta*: when it came up to us, they said where were we going, and that this weather caused the ships to open, and that it was necessary to take care of them. Our general then ordered to put back into the bay, and we were all Saturday and Sunday beating to windward with the wind S.E. and S. till sunset. The 11th our patache reached the port at evensong (after sunset), and we did not see nor know whether it anchored or not, for we were a league and a half or more from the port, the flag-ship, and *Almiranta*, though at this time the *Almiranta* went more to windward than we did half a league. On that tack the two ships made for the anchorage, and when we were near and were going to take in the mainsail, we heard the people of the *Almiranta*, who seemed to be taking in their sails and anchoring, and this would be at nine o'clock at night; and we had left behind us lights, and were in doubt whether they belonged to fishermen or to the patache. We went on sounding to see if we could find anchorage, as it was dark, and we never could find any, because in all this bay, as has been said before, there is none except in that corner. During this there came so violent a wind from the land, that without fail, if we had not furled our mainsail, we should have passed an ill time of it. When we saw that we could not find anchorage, and that we saw more fires on the beach separate from one another which could not be our vessels, since if they were our vessels they must have been close together, for the anchorage so required it, and seeing ourselves with little sail and the wind increasing in violence, and we could now only carry the foresail, it was agreed by the officers and the general that we should put about and take the middle of the bay, for we were near the rock, and until striking on it, no bottom was found, as we had learned; and all these ships of Peru are bad for handling with little sail, and so we might strike before the ship went round. We put about, and a man aloft said he had seen the *Almiranta* at anchor to windward of us, which we never were able to reach, because each time we put about we fell off very much, as the wind was so violent, for which reason it was determined by the same persons to wear the ship and run with only a bowsprit square-sail (*sevadera*), striking the topmasts, and put ourselves under shelter of the point to windward, and this was done.

"The 12th, at dawn, we were about four leagues from the land out to sea outside of the bay; we carried our lantern lit all the night before for the ships to follow us, which they did not do. We tacked about in the mouth of this bay in sight of the port, with the weather always the same, without their coming outside. With this weather and our topmasts always struck we went on for three days, until, at the end of them, we found ourselves some nine leagues to leeward.

"The 13th our general saw, and the other officers agreed with him, that go by a straight road or with right intention, so I had to return to the bay to see if perchance they would return there, all which

the ship laboured greatly, and as the lives of all depended on its preservation and the giving information to His Majesty—so he decided on returning to land to see if the weather improved, and to return to the same bay to seek our *Almiranta*. In this manner we went on, from the 13th to the 19th, attempting to re-enter, but we never could do so. On the 19th they were in 12°. The 20th, as the wind did not go down, our general, to encourage the people, agreed that if the weather did not permit, on reaching $10\frac{1}{2}°$ he would go to Santa Cruz, where we should wait for our companions and take in what we wanted, since this was the order they had received, that whoever arrived there first should wait three months, and if the other did not arrive should follow out the rest of the order. On the 21st they found themselves in 10° 30′, and not knowing whether they were east or west of Santa Cruz, and fearing to get embayed on the coast of New Guinea, they decided on steering north for the island of Guan and the Philippines. On the 23rd July they found themselves in the latitude of Guan, $13\frac{1}{2}°$; and on the 24th Quiros ordered the pilots to make the course for Acapulco. They reached the port of Navidad in New Spain on the 20th October, 1606, and on the 15th November they went out, making for Acapulco, which they reached on the 23rd."

The following account of the manner in which Quiros and Torres parted company differs from the three given above, whilst it exculpates Quiros from having abandoned Torres, and explains why Quiros did not persevere in pursuing his voyage of discovery.

Letter of D. Diego de Prado, dated Goa, 24 December, 1613.
(*Madrid Library, MSS. J 2 copy*).

I send to His Majesty, by means of the Viceroy of the Indies, the map of the discovery which was effected by Luis Vaez de Torres, captain of the *Almiranta* of Pedro Fernandez de Quiros, who followed the instructions given by the Conde de Monterrey, which discovery was the island called by us La Magna Margarita, which has 680 leagues of coast, as your worship will see by the said map. That which was discovered by Pedro Fernandes de Quiros, the liar, were those rocks and small islands, because his crew mutinied at the bay of the island Espiritu Santo. I came as captain of the flag-ship,[1] and had knowledge of what was being arranged in the ship: I informed him of it, and as it was a most difficult and delicate matter to tell him of, and of what was best for His Majesty's service, he could not stand me. So I disembarked in Trumaco, and went on board the *Almiranta*, at which there was great joy in the flag-ship, as they could better carry out their design. On the 11th of June of 1606,

---

[1] Gaspar Gonzales de Leza gives the name of D. Diego de Padro y Tobar, who was appointed Depositario General when Quiros appointed officials in the bay of St. Philip and St. James for the new colony.

I did for greater good faith in this bay, and I waited for them fifteen days. At the end of this time I took out your Majesty's orders, and calling to a council the officers of the patache also, it was agreed that we should follow those orders, though it was against the will of many, I might say of the greater number, but my temper was different from that of Captain Pero Fernandez de Quiros. Finally I came out of this bay in obedience to the order. I intended to double the island, but the weather did not permit of it on account of the great currents, though I ran along a large part of it, in which I saw very high mountain ranges. It has many ports, though some of them are small; throughout there is much water and rivers full of water. At this time I had only bread and water, and it was in the greatest rigour of winter, the sea and wind being contrary, and the dispositions of the men evil. All this was not sufficient to stop or hinder me from reaching the altitude, which I passed by a degree, and it would have been more if the weather had allowed me, for the ship was good, and it was just and right to act in this manner, since these

being in the bay, as we were coming from an island which was near, there came a rather fresh wind from the south at eight in the evening, upon which the mutineers carried out their evil design; and as it was night and far from us, they put the ship about, and the prattler did not see it, as he was in his cabin in the stern, and in the morning the country from which they had come out did not appear: he did not venture to speak; on the contrary, he was told to get into his cabin and hold his tongue, on which account they spared his life and landed him at Acapulco. His own companions told the Marquis of Montesclaros who he was, and how they might as well tie him up as mad, and he treated him as such a man as he was. I do not know what respect the Spaniards of Piru were to have for a man who yesterday was a clerk of a merchant ship, and a Portuguese: if they knew him as Captain Alonso Corzo knows him, those gentlemen of the state would end by knowing that they ought not to take account of such low and lying men. I shall leave for Ormuz on the 8th of February of next year, if it please God, to go by land to the port of Leppe (Aleppo), and thence to Venice, and I shall not stop till I reach the court to kiss the hands of his Majesty; and, your worship, I send an Indian of the country which was discovered as a witness to certify it, who is taken at the charge of Señor Ruy Lorenzo de Tavora, the ex-viceroy of India, with directions not to give him up to any one unless by order of your worship or mine. The death of the Secretary Andres de Prada has given me much sorrow, but as it is the journey we all have to take, I recommend him to God. May He give to your worship the health which your servant desires for you. From Goa, 24th December, 1613.   Don Diego de Prado.

are not voyages which can be made every day, nor would your Majesty be convinced, be it understood, by following this course in this latitude.[1] By the south-west course I did not find any signs of land, thence I turned to the north-north-west as far as eleven degrees and a half. Here I fell in with the beginning of New Guinea,[2] the coast of which trends from east to west, a quarter north-west and south-east. I could not go up it by the east side, so I went coasting to the west, and on the south side it is all the land of New Guinea. It is peopled by Indians who are not very white, and naked, though their middles are well covered with the bark of trees, after the manner of cloth, much coloured and painted; they fight with javelins and bucklers, and some stone clubs, with many gaudy feathers about them. There are along the coast other inhabited islands. Along the whole coast there are many large ports, with very large rivers, and many plains. Outside of these islands there extends a reef and shoals, and between them and the mainland are the islands; within there is a channel. We took possession in these ports in the name of your Majesty, with whose decision this remains. Having run three hundred leagues of coast, as has been said, and decreased our latitude by two degrees and a half, so that we remained in nine degrees, at this point there begins a bank of from three fathoms to nine, which stretches along the coast until seven degrees and a half, and the extremity of it is five [degrees?] We could not go forward on account of the numerous shoals and strong currents which there are throughout, so we had to go out by the south-west course by the said deep channel until eleven degrees, and the shoal is lower there. There were some very large islands, and more were seen towards the south. They were inhabited by black people, naked, and very corpulent. They have for weapons some thick and long lances, many arrows, very uncouth stone clubs. We could not send any of their weapons. I caught in all this country twenty persons of different nations, in order, by means of them, to give your Majesty a better account; they give much information of other peoples, although, up to this time, they do not make themselves well understood. We went along this shoal for two months. At the end of that time we

[1] *Ni podia Vuestra Magestad ser desengañado, entiendese, ir haciendo esta derrota al altura.*
[2] The southern point of Louisiada.

found ourselves in twenty-five fathoms water and in five degrees latitude, and ten leagues from the coast, and we had gone four hundred and eighty leagues. Here the coast trends to the north-east. I did not reach it, because the bank is very shoal, so I went on running to the north in twenty-five fathoms water as far as four degrees, when we fell in with a coast which also stretched from east to west. We did not follow it to the end on the east side, but we understood that it joined on with the coast we had left behind, as the shoal reached to it, and on account of the great calmness of the sea. This country is inhabited by black people, different from all the rest. These people are more gaudily adorned; they also use arrows and javelins, and very large shields, and some blow-pipes of cane full of lime which they discharge, so that in fighting they cut down their opponents. Lastly, we ran along to the west north-west beside the coast, always finding these people, though we landed in several places. I here also took possession in the name of your Majesty. Here it was in this country where I found the first iron and bells of China, and other things from there, by which we understood more certainly that we were near the Moluccas, and so we went following this coast, a distance of a hundred and thirty leagues, so that the extremity would remain at fifty leagues distance. Before reaching the Moluccas there are a quantity of islands towards the south, and very large, and for the want of provisions I did not touch at them, for I doubt that in ten years one could see the coast of all the islands which we saw. Observations of the needle were made throughout all this country of New Guinea until the Moluccas; throughout the needle is fixed, and this country falls in the meridian of the Ladrone Islands and the Philippine Islands. At the extremity of this country we found some clothed Moors, with artillery for service, such as falconnets and swivel guns, arquebuses, and white weapons. They go conquering these people who are named Papuas, and preach to them the sect of Mahomed. These Moors traded with us, selling us fowls, and goats, and fruit, and some pepper and biscuit, which they call Sagu, which lasts more than twenty years, although there was little of all, because they wanted stuffs and we had not got them, for all the goods for barter which had been given us were carried away with the flagship, and even the tools, and medicines, and other things, which I do not mention, as there was no remedy for it; but the Lord favoured us without them. These Moors gave us news of the events in the Moluccas, and of Dutch ships, though they had not reached here, although they say that there is much gold throughout all this country, and other good things of spices, such as pepper and nutmeg. From here to the Moluccas there is nothing but islands, and in the southern direction there are also many which meet with those of Bandayan bueno, where the Dutch have trade. I arrived in these parts at the islands of Bachan, which are the first of the Moluccas, where I found a Theatine monk with a matter of a hundred Christians in the country of a friendly Moorish king, who asked me to reduce for him one of the Isles of Ternate, which was in the hands of some rebellious Moors, which D. Pedro de Acuña had bestowed upon him to hold it in the name of your Majesty. When I had sent advices from here to the Master of the Camp, Juan de Esquivel, who governed the Isles of Ternate, of my arrival, and to ask whether it was suitable to give this succour to the King of Bachan, he answered me that it would be doing a great service to your Majesty if I had with me sufficient forces for it. Upon this I determined to do it with forty Spaniards and four hundred Moors of the King of Bachan. With these I made war upon them. In four hours only I routed them and took the fort, and put the King of Bachan in possession of it in the name of your Majesty, to whom I administered the customary oaths, making an agreement with him that he should never fight against Christians, and that he should always be a faithful vassal of your Majesty. I did not find these people so valiant and courageous as those I had left behind. It must have been caused by the powerful hand which in so many labours and victories as I have encountered, always made things easy for me, and that my only loss in all my wanderings was one single Spaniard. I do not relate them to your Majesty because I hope to give it much at length. Having put the king in possession, I left Terrenate, which was twelve leagues from this island where Juan de Esquivel was, by whom I was very well received, for he was very short of men, and the people of Terrenate were in revolt, and they were much amazed at seeing succour brought in so circuitous a manner. He had arrived since a few days from Manila, which was very desirable, as he had lost half the men whom Don Pedro de Acuña had left there, and he was short of provisions, because, as I have said, the islanders were in revolt: but with the prudence of the master of the camp, Juan de Esquivel, the affairs of these islands are being set to rights, although a succour of money is wanted. Here I left the patache and a matter of twenty men, as that would be altogether fitting for the service of your Majesty. I then left for the city of Manila, where they despatch my affairs so ill, as I have said, nor up to this time, which is a space of two months, have they given provisions to the crew; and so I do not know when I shall be able to go from this place to render an account to your Majesty, whom may the Lord preserve in prosperity as lord of the world. Dated in Manila, the twelfth of July of 1607.

The Servant of your Majesty—LOUIS BAEZ DE TORRES.

Quiros, on his return from this voyage, tried to induce the Spanish Government to send him to the Austral Islands to colonise and settle them: at the end of one of his letters to the king, he says of the Austral regions, "Parece que guardó Dios para la postre las mejores y mas ricas tierras, y un hombre de tan buena voluntad." "It seems that God has reserved till the last the best and most fruitful lands, and a man of such good will and enterprise. Despatch, Sire, despatch then the business in accordance with the greatness and necessity of this cause, since it must be done at once." A minute of a consulta of the council of state, dated Madrid, July 1609, upon the discoveries of Quiros and the letters of Iturbe, his accountant, shows that Quiros' proposals were not accepted for various reasons; the first of these, and the one that was given to Quiros for not at once employing him as he requested, was the difficulty of finding money for the enterprise. Besides these reasons, there was a certain jealousy of Quiros on the part of his subordinates, on the ground of his being a Portuguese, and they accused him of refusing to take counsel and of being very vain. Quiros, in the various documents relating to him, is described as the discoverer of the Austral mainland, but he does not appear ever to have seen anything else than islands in these voyages of his which have been recorded. In one of his letters to the king, dated Mexico, March 25, 1607, Juan de Iturbe, the accountant, accuses Quiros of having neglected the opportunities he had, and of having discovered nothing more than islands which were known before, and of having disobeyed his instructions, which were to go as far as 40° S. latitude. He also says that Quiros, on being refused some requests by the Viceroy of Peru, used improper language in public, to the effect that the Conde de Monterey was sent by the Council of the Indies, but that he was sent by the Council of State and by the Pope, and it would be seen who had most influence. Iturbe also throws some ridicule upon Quiros for having established an order of the Espiritu Santo, with habits of blue taffetan, and for having on that day given their liberty to two Negro cooks who were not his, and who remained in the same slavery. The pilot, Gaspar Gonzalez de Leza, gives an account of the speech which Quiros made on the 14th of May, 1606, on taking possession of the port of St. Philip and St. James and of the Austral regions to the pole, in virtue of the permission of Pope Clement VIII and the orders of Philip III, and of the government officers whom Quiros named out of his crews for the city of New Jerusalem, which was to be founded in 15° 20' in the Bay of St. Philip and St. James. In the minute, the Conde de Lemos' opinion is given as contrary to the pretensions of Quiros, as his enterprise was neither just nor possible, and he thought that Quiros had got into his head that he was to be another Columbus, which was his weakness. Fray Luis Aliaga, the king's confessor, is also quoted: he was of opinion that Quiros, with whom he had conversed, was a good Christian and a well-intentioned man, and his principal object was the conversion of souls, and reduction of those people to obedience to his Majesty; nevertheless, he did not hold the conquest to be lawful, nor the repartition of Indians, which the said captain proposes to make; but that conversion should rather be attempted by means of the ministers of the gospel, and that the Indians should be induced to submit voluntarily to his Majesty. The minute then states that a former council, in September 25 of 1608, recommended that Quiros should not be employed in this enterprise, but that to prevent his offering his services to any other state, he should be employed in Spain as cosmographer. The Cardinal of Toledo was of opinion that no resources existed for the proposed enterprise, and that to avoid indisposing Quiros, he should be told so, and some favour granted him to prove that it is necessity and not disfavour that prevents the undertaking his enterprise. The Cardinal added his fears that, from the little secrecy kept in business, Quiros would hear of the counter-despatch to the Viceroy of Peru, and in his indignation would betake himself to other princes.

P.S.—A translation of the above letter of Torres by Dalrymple has been printed in the appendix to vol. ii of Capt. James Burney's *Voyages in the South Sea*, London, 1806; and the reader is referred to Mr. Major's remarks upon this voyage of Torres, and the character of Quiros, in his introduction to *Early Voyages to Terra Australis*, Hakluyt Society, 1859.

London, June 2, 1868. H. S.

TABLE OF PAROCHIAL CLERGY (1867).

PROVINCES.	No. of Parishes.	No. of Tributes.	Amount of Stipends.
Luzon.			Dollars.
Manila, two priests of the sacristy at 900 dollars each, and one sacristan at 150 dollars	...	...	1,950
Albuy, the priests of each parish, at the rate of 180 dollars for every 500 tributes	37	65,210	23,475½
Abra {Missions with fixed stipends	5	1,555	1,500
{Parishes at the rate of 180 dollars for every 500 tributes	3	4,208	1,515
Bulacan, parishes at 180 dollars for every 500 tributes	23	61,111	22,163
Batangas, parishes at 180 dollars for every 500 tributes	20	73,971	26,629½
Bataan, parishes at 180 dollars for every 500 tributes	11	12,950	4,662
Cavite, the priest of the port, 600 dollars; the sacristan, 91½; parishes at 180 dollars for every 500 tributes	...	...	11,016
Camarines Sur {Parish priest of the cathedral of Nueva Caceres, 183¼ drs.; parishes at 180 drs.	15	28,679	14,675
{Parishes at 280 dollars for every 500 tributes	28	40,253	1,352
Camarines Norte, parishes at 180 dollars for every 500 tributes	5	1,647	3,076
Cagayan, two missions, and parishes at 180 dollars for every 500 tributes	8	8,544	7,816¼
Laguna, chaplain of Los Baños, 120 dollars; parishes at 180 dollars	17	19,840	13,645
Lepanto, mission of Cayan	28	37,569	540
Manila, sacristan at Ermita, 92 dollars; parishes at 180 dollars	...	...	23,807¼
District of Morong, parishes at 180 dollars	30	64,765	4,366
Nueva Ecija, parishes at 180 dollars	11	11,733	9,511
Nueva Vizcaya {Six parishes at 444 dollars each	22	23,488	2,664
{Three missions	6	3,620	1,880
Pampanga, mission of Capaz and Patling, 288 dollars; parishes at 180 dollars	24	50,983	18,930
Pangasinan, parishes at 180 dollars	28	72,083	25,950
Tayabas, parishes at 180 dollars	17	28,250	10,213
Union, parishes at 180 dollars	13	22,873	8,504½
Ilocos Sur, parishes at 180 dollars	22	45,317	16,314
Ilocos Norte, parishes at 180 dollars	15	35,703	12,853

Isabela, five missions, and five parishes at 180 dollars	10	8,600	4,229
Zambales, parishes at 180 dollars	16	21,861	7,870
Alhambra	1	...	360
ADJACENT ISLES.			
Batanes Islands, five parishes at 450 dollars each	5	...	2,250
Mindoro, parishes at 212½ dollars for every 500 tributes	10	10,994	5,751
Masbate and Ticao	9	3,220	1,800
Burias, San Pascual	1	490	480
Calamianes { Mission of Dumaran, and four parishes at 212½ dollars for every 500 tributes { Sacristans of cathedrals of Nueva Segovia and Nueva Caceres, 92 dollars each	5	5,000	2,588½
			184
BISAYAS.			
Sebu, parishes at 212½ dollars for every 500 tributes	75	102,000	43,324
Capiz, parishes at 180 dollars	36	51,079	19,507
Isla de Negros { Parishes at 180 dollars	24	38,100	13,717½
{ Four missions	4	...	1,380
Iloilo, parishes at 180 dollars	39	106,518	38,777¼
Leite, parishes at 212½ dollars for every 500 tributes	39	42,249	17,955½
Samar, parishes at 212½ dollars	19	36,560	16,938
Antique { Parishes at 180 dollars	13	14,598	6,255½
{ Parishes at 212¼ dollars	6	6,030	2,192½
MINDANAO.			
Zamboanga	...	2,626	1,116
Misamis { Parishes at 212½ dollars for every 500 tributes	32	16,450	7,817½
{ Mission of Santa Isabel	...	...	500
Surigao, parishes at 300 dollars for every 500 tributes	18	11,910	7,544½
Davao, Vergara	1	808	816
Bislig, parishes at 308 dollars for every 500 tributes	12	3,220	2,742
Total	757	1,196,725	475,194¼

APPROXIMATIVE TABLE OF THE EXPENDITURE OF THE PHILIPPINE ISLANDS IN 1600.

	Dollars.
Salary of the Governor, Captain-general and President	8,000
Four auditors and a fiscal at 2,000 dollars each	10,000
Reporter, secretary, chief constable and other officials	
Three officers of the Treasury at 750 dollars each	2,250
Archbishop of the Philippines	4,000
Three bishops at 735 dollars each	2,205
Grants to the monasteries	
Pay of 400 soldiers	33,600
Master of the camp	1,400
Six captains at 420 dollars each	2,520
Ensigns, serjeants, corporals, drummers in proportion (say about 2,040)	(2,040)
Serjeant-major, 420; adjutant, 120	540
Two wardens of forts of Manila, 400 each	800
Lieutenant wardens (at say 200 each)	(400)
Military force...	41,300
General of the galleys	800
Captain of each galley, 300 dollars	
Officers and crews of the galleys	
Building galleys, stores and munitions	
Building ships for voyages to New Spain	

APPROXIMATIVE TABLE OF THE REVENUE OF THE PHILIPPINE ISLANDS IN 1600.

	Dollars.
Tributes of the Philippine islanders	
Tributes paid into the exchequer by the royal encomiendas or assigned districts	30,000
Tributes of the Christian and pagan Sangleys	8,000
Fifths on gold (at present (1600) tenths only)	10,000
Two reals in addition to tribute of eight reals	34,000
Fines imposed by justice	3,000
Three per cent. import duty on Chinese goods	40,000
Two per cent. export duty on China goods going to New Spain	20,000
Import duties on goods brought from New Spain	8,000
	153,000

The ten per cent. import duties levied at Acapulco on Manila goods might amount to 100,000 dollars, out of which the necessary succour was sent to the Philippines.

Forty ducats of Castile per ton freight paid into the royal chest at Acapulco.

TABLE OF THE

EXPENDITURE OF THE PHILIPPINES IN 1636.

	Dollars.
Department of Justice employs 32 Spaniards, costs	37,977
Department of Public Worship, conversion, sustenance of convents, employs 73 Spaniards, costs	53,715
Presents to neighbouring kings	1,500
Royal Treasury employs 19 Spaniards, costs	11,550
Military establishment consists of 1,762 Spaniards and 140 Indians, costs	229,636
Military establishment for Moluccas consists of 612 Spaniards and 200 Indians, costs	97,128
Naval Department and Dockyard consists of 882 Spaniards and 200 Indians, costs	283,184
Department of provisions, stores, and munitions employs 8 Spaniards, costs	153,302
Total	**850,734**

REVENUE OF THE PHILIPPINES IN 1636.

	Dollars.
Tributes of Crown Encomiendas, of islanders, Chinese, and Japanese, 44,763 tributes at ten reals each	53,715
Encomiendas held by individuals, 84,429 tributes, upon which two reals are levied on each tribute, leaving eight reals to the encomenderos	21,107
Annual licenses to Sangleys to remain in the isles, 14,000 of whom pay eight dollars each	112,000
Tribute of these Sangleys at five reals each	8,250
The fifths and tenths levied on the gold owned by the islanders	750
Ecclesiastical tithes levied as royal property, because with it all the clergy is paid	2,750
Freight of passengers to other parts in royal ships	350
Fines of justice, annually	1,000
Customs on goods of China, India, etc.	38,000
Customs, freights, and dues levied in New Spain on Philippine goods, reckoned as Philippine revenue, and remitted to Manila, by royal order of February 19, 1606	300,000
Dues of one month's pay for the clergy and half a year for the secular clergy	6,000
Total	**543,932**

The deficit of the Philippines is supplied from New Spain by royal order. Some people complain that the Philippines cost much and are of little use; but the deficit is only apparent, for the Moluccas belonged to Portugal till 1607, and their expense, which is now defrayed by the Philippines, and which amounts to 290,000 dollars, equals the deficit in the Philippine revenues; for the share of the Moluccas in the second, third, and fourth branches of the expenditure, the whole of the sixth, half of the seventh, and a third of the eighth amounts to that; and from their distance from Goa they used to cost the crown of Portugal 400,000 dollars. (Taken from a memorial to the king by Don Juan Gran y Monfalcon, Madrid, 1637.)

EXPENDITURE OF THE PHILIPPINE ISLANDS IN 1867.

	Dollars.
Salary of the Governor and Captain General, 40,000 dollars. Total expense of civil government, including salaries of council, deputy-governors, government buildings, postal and telegraphic service, prisons, grants to hospitals	202,880
Salary of Regente of the Audienera, 8,000; two judges at 5,500 each; four auditors at 5,000 each. Total expense of department of justice	165,503
Archbishop of Philippines, 12,000; four bishops, 6,000 each. Total expense of the clergy, colleges, pious establishments and missions	649,610
Total expense of the department of war, artillery and engineers	2,260,265½
Chief naval officer, 16,392. Total expense of navy and dockyards	1,555,479½
Intendant General of Finance, 15,000. Total expense of the revenue department, including customs, taxes, stamps, and the mint, 47,687.	5,252,191
Fomento, Public Instruction (Naval Academy, School of Drawing, of Botany and Agriculture, Professors of Calculation and Languages), 12,966½; commercial tribunal, 4,105; ports and lighthouses, 22,826½; telegraphs, engineers, etc. Total	67,521½
Spanish minister in Pekin, 12,000; his staff, consuls in China, Hong Kong, Singapore, and Saigon. Total expense	56,708
General obligations, including various classes of pensions to 1,812 persons amounting to 434,031, concession to the Duke of Veragua, in virtue of the capitulation granted by the Catholic monarchs to Christopher Columbus of 23,400 dols. upon the countries of America, which grant has been imposed upon the colonial treasuries by royal order of Feb. 12, 1820; 4,000 of which are paid by the Philippines; grant of 1,500 dollars to Marquis of Bedmar on the office of assayer and founder of the mint of Potosi being incorporated with the crown of Spain; other items ...... Total	510,190½
Total	10,890,391

The supplementary budget of extraordinary expenses assigns 12,126 dols. for the construction of a wooden gunboat, inclusive of workmen's wages.

REVENUE OF THE PHILIPPINE ISLANDS IN 1867.

	Dollars.
Tributes of islanders, 1,166,120 tributes = 1,837,700 dollars ,, Mestizos 52,704 ,, = 161,100 ,, ,, Chinese 20,293 ,, = 120,350 ,, The Chinese who are not cultivators pay 6 dollars each, the cultivators pay 3, and others 2 dollars; of the above number 425 only are agriculturists. Tribute of vassalage of pagans, 29,059 tributes = 13,000 dollars; predial tenths, 13,500 dol.; tenths of those who are excused from paying tribute for old age or sickness, 102,532 persons, or by privilege, 65,872 persons, making an eighth of a dollar each; = 21,000 dollars; taxes on the villages of Abra, Union, and Ilocos, 123,145 tributes = 88,000 dollars, tax on production of rum, 123,150 dollars. Total of tributes and imposts on property	2,378,100
Patents of Chinese traders, 100,750 dols.; patents for sale of rum, 235,700	336,450
Customs duties	962,800
Monopolies, regalia, stamps, tobacco (7,058,245 dols.), opium, etc.	7,636,020
Lottery, sale of tickets	700,000
State property and domain	55,250
Eventual or possible income (proince of the mint, 55,250 dols.)	210,050
Income from the Navy (mail steamers, sale of old stores)	52,632
Total	12,331,302

INDEX AND GLOSSARY.

Abaca, Tagal hemp of plantain, 379
Aconsi, Siamese official, 45
Acuña, D. Pedro, appointed governor, 199; his death, 259 (June 24, 1606, official despatch)
——— D. Tomas, 229, 236, 238
Advances to cultivators and workmen, necessity of government supervision, Appendix, 382
Aetas, barbarous tribe in the interior of the Philippines, 267
Affairs of Cambodia, 43-53, 62, 87, 91, 93-113, 131-137, 221-223
——— China, 119-129, 216-220, 244-247
——— Cochin China, 52, 62
——— Japan, 33, 42, 76-86, 142-149, 200-210, 248, 398-402
——— Mindanao, 53, 54, 57-62, 87, 137-142, 190, 211, 260, 292, Appendix
——— Moluccas, 28, 196, 214-216, 225-229, 249-258, 392-396, 416
——— Siam, 43, 44, 133, 194
——— Sulu, 23, 88, 192, 211, 362
Aguirre, Juan Tello y, 133, 158, 165, 205
——— Fray Martin, 80, 81, 398-402
Agurto Pedro, 55, 89
Alarcon, Pascual de, 252, 257
Alcega, Juan second in command with de Morga, 158; his misconduct, 167, 170, 173; his death, 235-237; 397
Aliaga, Fray Luis, his opinion against forcible conversion of Indians, 418
Almanack of Manila, its rectification, 18
Almeida, Duarte, letter to King of Portugal, 393, 396
Alphabet, Tagal, 294
Ambergris, 286
Anacaparam, 47, 49, 101
Anda, Sr., 363

Anito, Tagal, Malay, an idol, a spirit, 305
Arellano, D. Alonzo, 16, 17
Arevalo, foundation of, 24; defence of, 141; description of, 317
Arias, Sr., prize essay, ix
Arigue, Tagal, a pile, 54, 295
Arms of the Philippines, 309
Arrieta, Domingo de, 168
Arrows, use of, 268
Asana, Tagal, kind of wood, 275
Ascencion, Fray Martin de la, dispute as to his identity, 398; *see* Martin Aguirre.
Audiencia, first establishment, 28; removal, 31, 33; second establishment, 56, 89; its powers, xvii, 91, 344, 345, 113; its buildings, 311; its merits, viii, 367; government carried on by it, 258-261
Australia, prognostication of by Quiros, 417
Azambuja, Diego de, 25
Azebo, Gaspar, government secretary, 157, 158, 161

Babuytanes Islands, 287
Bacoco, sea-bream,
Bagontao, Tagal, a bachelor, 303
Bahandin, a house, 295
Bahaque, Tagal, a waist cloth, 268
Balarao, Bisaya, a dagger, 272
Barangay or *balangay*, Tagal, a boat, 272; also a quarter, district, sept, 297, 322
Barreto, Doña Ysabel, 64-74
Barrier reef of New Guinea described by Torres, Appendix, 414
Basilan Island,
Batala, Tagal, a deity, 305
Batalan, Tagal, a corridor, 295
Bay, lagoon of, 279
Beatrix, Doña, 74
Belloso, Diego, his adventures, 44, 93; his death, 136; author's opinion of him, 221

INDEX AND GLOSSARY.

Belver, D. Luis, 168
Benavides, Fray Miguel, 55 ; Archbishop of Manila, 220, 231, 243
Bernard, St., Island, 69
Betel chewing, 280-282
Biesman, Lambert, lieutenant of Van Noort, 150, 168, 176 ; his execution, 169, Appendix, 398
Bilango, Tagal, a constable, 329
Bisayas Islands, 19, 266, 291, 292
——— language, 293
Bishops, 332
Boats of the Philippines, 272, 274
Bonga, Tagal, areca nut, 280
Bonote, Tagal, tow, oakum, 275
Boyle, Mr., book on Dayaks, vii. 268, 272, 281, 285, 305
Bronce de cuchara, guns loaded with a ladle, 150, 152
Brosses, President de, iii, 64, 74
Buhahayen town, 53, 58
Buhayan, Tagal, a crocodile, 278, 306
Buiz, Tagal, tribute,
Bulls, Papal, xxi, 225, 321, 327, 328, 400, 402
Burial, 307
Buyo, Tagal, betel leaf, 280
Buzeyes, paddles, 213, 273

Cachil, Malay, a chief, 50, 59
Cagayan, province, 25, 268
Calanta, Tagal, a cedar tree, 275
Caldera, fort, 61, 138, 141, 360, Appendix
Calleway, John, 150, 180
Calombiga, a bracelet, 269
Camarines, 267, 316
Cambodia, *see* Affairs of.
——— river, its rapids, 108
Campilan, Malay, a sword,
Candish, Thomas, his voyage, 29, 175, 261, 304
Cano, Sebastian del, *see* Elcano.
Canton, aversion to foreigners, 127 ; cold, 128
Carabau, Malay, a buffalo, 276, 285
Caracoa, a canoe, 273
Caraza, a large shield, 272
Castro, Fernando de, 42, 65, 75, 187
Catalona, Tagal, a witch, 306
Catan, Japanese, a sword,
Catenduanes Islands, 287
Cattle, 275, 276
Cavan or *gaban*, Tagal measure of rice, etc., 372, 380
Cavite, port of Manila, 288
Cazeres, city, 316
Cea, Duke of, dedication to, 5, 359
Cervantes, Juan, 253

Champan, kingdom of, 113
Change of residence of islanders, 327
Changes, too frequent in the administration, 370
Chaves, D. Pedro, 22, 64
——— D. Juan, Appendix
Chiefs of the islanders, 296, 297, 302, 322
Chincheo, 242, 245
Chinese, domination in the Philippines, 19
——— mission to Manila in search of Eldorado, 217-220
——— insurrection in Philippines, xii, 231-240 ; massacre and letter thereupon from Chinese authorities, 244-247, 363-364
——— gobernadorcillos, 351, Appendix, 366
——— government of in Straits settlements, Appendix, 366
——— aversion to them in Philippines, 125, 349, Appendix, 365
——— condition of in Philippines, 348-351, 365 ; in Australia, 365
——— trade, 337-340
Chininas, Tagal, dress of Luzon, 268
Chiquiro, Japanese official, 148, 200, 205
Chofa, Siamese and Cambodian title, 93
Cholera, Appendix, 378
Chordemuco, 43, 223
Chupinanu, Chupinanon, and Chupinaqueo, 51, 100-108
Circumnavigation of the globe by Magellan, 1519, 13, 14
Drake, 1577, 29
Van Noort, 1598, 174-187
Civet cats, 286
Clemente, Fray Juan, founds hospital for natives of Manila, 313, 314
Columbus, his book about demarcation between Castilian and Portuguese possessions, 393, 396 ; sum assigned to him and his heirs still paid, Table of Revenue of 1867, 424
Combaco, sovereign of Japan, 80
Concejeles, pressed men, 335
Condensation of sea-water, 404
Constantin, author of French collection of Dutch voyages, 174
Conversion of Philippines, 318
Coral islands, 405, *Note* 1
Coshenga, Chinese corsair, 360
Coutinho, Azevedode, 393, 394
Crocodiles, 278, 306
Cueva, Fernando, letter to his bro-

INDEX AND GLOSSARY. 427

ther Marcos about Van Noort, 262-264
Cueva, Marcos, 120, 262
Cuevas, Captain Juan, 252, 253
Customs, 270, 304

Daifusama, 200, 247; letter to governor of Manila, 248
Dalaga, Tagal, a maiden, 303
Dasmarinas, Gomez Perez, governor, 32-41
────── Luis, governor, 38-87, 113-119, 129; his death, 234-237
Dato, Malay, a chief, 297
Demarcation of Pope Alexander VI, xxi, xxii, 11-13, 121, 126, Appendix, 391-396
Dongon libor, 60
Dias, Marcos de Febra, 197, 198
Dilao, village, 238
Disputes between Spaniards and Portuguese, 121,126,130,Appendix
Dominicans, 318, 319; they urge the expedition to Cambodia, 46, 52, 87, 196
Drake, Sir Francis, his voyage through the Straits of Magellan, 29; his piety, 30
Dysentery, 89, 143, Appendix, 372

Earthquakes, Appendix, 372, 373
Elcano, Sebastian de, 14
Encomiendas, 323, 345
Enslavement of Philippine islanders, 298-300; prohibited, 329
Esquivel, Juan de, 249, 257, 260, Appendix, 416, 417
Essex, Earl of, takes Cadiz, 150, 264
Expenditure, *see* Revenue.
Eyre, Governor, xi, xvi, xviii, 304, 306, 307

Faranda quiemon, Japanese, 33, 85, 143
Farren, J. W. P., British Consul at Manila, vi, xx, 314, 338, 365, 371, 372, 378, 379, 380, 381, 388
Figueroa, Esteban Rodriguez de, 23, 37; expedition to Mindanao, 53 (in April 1596, with 36 vessels, 212 Spaniards, and 1,500 Indians; despatch of D. Francisco Tello); his death, 54; his widow, 56, 57
────── Melchior de, 168
────── Cristoval Suarez, iv
Fimbaros, Japanese, larks, 277
Fish, 279
Foreign jurisdiction, xi-xvi
Fortifications, 28, 32, 252, 310
Fragment of Mendaña's voyage to Santa Cruz Islands in the British Museum, iv, v, 73
Froude, Mr. A., his defence of Drake, 30
Fruit, 275

Gallinato, Juan Xuarez, 94; expedition to Cambodia, 46; abandons the expedition, 50; blamed by the adventurers, 62; expedition to Sulu, 210; expedition to Ternate and praise of Portuguese general, 227, 228; expedition against Mindanao men, Appendix, 360
Gandullo, Fray Luis, 241
Garcia, Juan, de Sierra, gallant defence of Arevalo and death, 141, 142
Gauna, Martin Lopez, 2
Gayan, mats or screens, 273
Gayangos, D. Pascual, commission to examine colonial archives, vi
Gayong, Tagal, an oar, 273
Gazette or broadsheet of 1574, with a letter from a Philippine colonist, Appendix, 389
Geronymo, Fray, 145-149, 200-204, 231, 398, 402
Goiti, Martin, 18, 21
Gold, vii, 283, 284
Gomez, Alonso, pilot, 161, 168
Gomez de, Molina, 397
Gonzalez, Gaspar, de Leza, pilot of Quiros in 1605; Appendix vi
Govea, Japanese adventurer, 134
Governors of the Philippines—
Miguel Lopez de Legazpi 1564-72
Guido de Labazarris 1572-75
Dr. Francisco de Sande 1575-80
Gonzalo Ronquillo 1580-83
Diego Ronquillo 1583-84
Dr. Santiago de Vera 1584-90
Gomez Perez Dasmariñas 1590-93
Luis Dasmariñas 1593-96
Francisco Tello 1596-1602
Pedro de Acuña 1602-1606
Juan de Silva 1608-17
Alonzo Faxardo de Tenza 1618-24
Geronymo de Silva 1624-28
Juan Niño de Favora 1628-33
Juan Cerezo Salamanca 1633-35
Sebastian Hurtado de Corcuera 1635-44
Diego Faxardo 1644-62
Sabiniano Manrique de Lara 1662-
(The dates of the Governors subsequent to D. Pedro de Acuña are approximatively correct, and are

INDEX AND GLOSSARY.

taken from despatches written by them.)
Guevara, Fray Diego, 203, 207, 241
Gutierrez, Fray Juan, 161

Harbours, 288, 289
Hara-Kiri, Japanese, belly-slice, 210
Hemp, Appendix, 379
Heredia, D. Cristoval de, 168
Hilo Hilo, see Ilo Ilo.
Horses, 276, 277
Hospitals, 313
Houses, 295

Ibarra, Francisco, 177
Ichthyology, 278-280
Ilo Ilo, 338, 381
Inquisition, did not meddle with Philippine islanders, 322
Insurrection of Chinese, see Chinese.
———— Philipinos, Appendix, 368
Iturbe, Juan de, accountant in Quiros' voyage, 1605, Appendix, vi

Japan, see Affairs of Japan.
Japanese, condition of in Manila, 352
———— martyrs, 79-82, 84, 398, 402
———— request assistance in ship-building, 147, 201
———— trade in Manila, 341
———— wooden anchor given to Van Noort, 184, 263
Jesuits, opposition to Manila friars, 77, 399-402
Juan, friar, devotes himself to stay with shipwrecked Spaniards in the Ladrones, 189; he and the others are recovered, 206
Justice, administration of, Appendix, 367

Labazarris, Guido, governor, 21
Lacsamana, Ocuña, 51, 136, 221, 222
Landa, Francisco de, pilot, his imprudent speech to confidante of Taicosama, 78, 79, 87, 399
Landecha, Mathia, 75, 82
Langara, Phra-uncar, King of Cambodia, 43, 51; his letter to De Morga, 92
Language of Luzon, 294; of Bisayas, 293
Lanchan, town of Cambodia, 50, 198
Lapis, a Philippine boat, 53, 273
Lau-lau, a small fish, 280
Laws of Philippine islanders — Adoption, 301; adultery, 301, 303; divorce, 301; illegitimate children, 302; inheritance, 301, 302; loans, 302; marriage, 271, 300; service to their chiefs, 297; slavery, 298-300; maintenance of part of these laws by Spaniards, xvii, 300, 323
Legazpi, Miguel Lopez, governor, 15-20, 309, 324; his portrait and house, 368
Lima, Pablo de, 255, 256
Li-ma-hong, Chinese corsair, 21
Lozano, Alonso, 168
Luzon, Id., 266

Mabolo, fruit, 275
Magalat, Philippine chief, 63, 64
Magellan, 13, 14, 16
Malaver, D. Antonio, 134, 193
Maldonado, Gabriel, 168
———— Fray Juan, 133, 137, 195; letter to his order dissuading them from expeditions such as that to Cambodia, 196
Mallat, work on Philippines, v, xxi, 288, 365, 366, 367, 387
Manila, settlement of, 19; bay of, 288; description of, 309-15; capture of by English, Appendix, 362
Manufactures, 287, 338, 381
Martinez, Juan de Chave, pilot, 133, 195
———— General Juan Antonio, Appendix, 369
Mathia, General, see Landecho.
Mendaña, Alvaro de, discovery of Santa Cruz islands, 64-74, 408
Mendia, Captain Martin, 211
Mendoza, Andrea de, Portuguese general, 213, 224-229
———— Francisco, 168
———— Juan, 132, 137, 193-195
———— Rodrigo, 252, 259
Meriñaque, Tagal, stuff made of plantain fibre, and in Spanish, a crinoline, 287
Monasteries, 312, 333
Monks, xix, xx, 318-320, 333
Monte de Piedad, Appendix, 377
Montesclaros, Marquis of, 242, 413
Morales, Fray Francisco de, 203
———— Pedro Coleto de, 193
Morga, Dr. Antonio de, appointed auditor in Manila, 41; in Mexico, 229; President of the Audiencia, in Quito, ii; he opposes the Cambodian expedition, 46, 92; his preparations against Van Noort, 152-155; his sea-fight with Van Noort, 166-169; certificate of the Governor, 170; further details about the action taken from ar-

INDEX AND GLOSSARY. 429

chives of the Hydrographic Department, Madrid, Appendix, v; leaves Manila, July 10th, 1603, 229; his book very rare, i, Appendix, v; his wife Doña Juana, 82, 128; contemporary testimony in his favour, 399
Municipal Authorities, 323, 328, 331
Naguatato, Japanese, interpreters, 218
Namamahay, Tagal, serfs, 298
Nambajy, Japanese, Christians, 77
Navarrete, D. Luis Fajardo, mission to Japan, 83, 400
Navigation, 290, 353-358
Navy, 335, Appendix, 387
New Jerusalem, city projected by Quiros, 412, 418
Noort, Oliver Van, 149, 261; his own account of his voyage and inhumanity, 174-187; Dutch editions of his voyage, 186, 188; German edition, 262; French editions, 174, 188; English abridgements, 174

Obras, Pias, 313, Appendix, 372, 376
Ocuña de Chao, 51, 100-106
―――― Lacsamana, *see* Lacsamana.
Odia, 44, 193
Œcumenical Council, xxiv
Organtino, Padre, 399, 402
Ornithology, 277
Ortiz, Luis, 63, 116, 131, 135
Osseguera, D. Pedro de, 88
Oton Island, 24, 139, 292, 317

Palay, Tagal, rice in the husk,
Pampanga province, 288
Panay, 291
Pao, Tagal, fruit for pickles, 280
Parian, Tagal, market, bazaar,
Parishes, Appendix, table, 420
Pearls, 285
Piles, Tagal, pine-nuts, 275
Piña, Cambric, 338
Pingré, astronomer, iii-v, 74
Pintados province and islands, *see* Bisayas.
Pinzon, descendant of Yanez Pinzon, Appendix, 368
Pogo, Tagal, a quail, 277
Poisons, 282, 283
Polo, Tagal, personal service, 329
Population of Philippines, 370
―――― of Sulu, 88
Potong, Tagal, wrap for the head, 269
Prado, Diego, letter about Quiros and Torres, Appendix, 412

Prauncar, King of Cambodia, 51, 92; his death, 137
Protection of Philippine islanders by Spanish authorities, vii, x, 181

Quanto, Japanese province, 144, 147, 203
Quimon, Japanese, a garment, 352
Quiros, Pedro Fernandez, iii-v; his narrative of Mendaña's voyage, 65-74; his voyage in 1605; Appendix vi; insubordination of his crew, 405, 412; consultation of Council of State respecting him, 417, 419

Rajamora, chief of Manila, 18, 19
Regulations of government, xvii, xviii, 330
―――― others suggested, Appendix, 366, 369, 377, 382, 386
Religious belief of the Philippine islanders, of the Dayaks, of the Australians, 305-308
Revenue and Expenditure, 346, 347, Appendix, 371, tables, 422-424
Rica de oro, and Rica de plata, 356
Ricci, Matthew, the Jesuit, 127
Rienzi, Mr., his statements, 361, 363, 364, 367, 368, 370, 371; contradiction of one of them, 369
Rios, Fernando de los, 39; letter on China, 119-129, 284, 391; lived thirty years in the Philippines, 39
―――― Gaspar de los, 168
Rivera, Antonio, de Maldonado, new auditor in Manila, 1601, 27; refuses to wait in fair weather to pick up shipwrecked Spaniards at the Ladrones, he is wrecked off the Philippines, 188, 189, 211; his death, 259
―――― Gabriel, 25, 27 (He served the King in Flanders and St. Quentin, and came to the Philippines with Legazpi)
Rodriguez, Augustin, 202, 203
―――― Francisco, 168
Rojas, Pedro de, 27, 33, 38, 41
Ronquillo, Diego, governor, 27
―――― Gonzalo, governor, 23-26
―――― Juan, 57
Ruy Faleiro, cosmographer, 13
Ruys, Blas, letter to De Morga, 93-112; author's opinion of him, 221

Saguiguilir, Tagal, household slave, 298
Sago, 415

Salary of the governor, 344, Appendix, 370
Salazar, Fray Domingo, first bishop of the Philippines, 26, 40, 41, 55
Samar Island or Çamar, 266, 291, 319
Sanchez, Padre Alonso, 26, 30, 31, 321, 402
Sande, Dr. Francisco, governor, 22
Sangajy, Malay, a chief, 256
Sangley, Chinaman of Philippines, 120, 125
Santa Cruz Islands, 70-72
—————— communication of islanders with island of Taumaco, Appendix, 408
Santiago, Fray Diego, 161, 168
Sebu Island, 14, 16, 266, 292
Segovia, town, 25, 316
Serpana, or Çarpana, or Seypan Id., 73, 354
Serpents, 278
Serrano, Francisco, 12
—————— Juan, 12, 14
Siguey, white snails, 285
Silonga, Mindanao chief, 139, 141
Silva, Nuño da, his account of Drake's voyage, 29
Sistor, town of Cambodia, 48
Slavery, see Laws and Enslavement.
Solitary Id., 69
Sugar, Appendix, 380
Sulu Islands, first dealings with, 23; subsequent attacks on them, 190-193; subsequent history, 361
Sunken rocks, 388

Tagal language, 293; alphabet, 294; dictionary, 295, 305
Taico-sama, his letter to governor of Manila, 33; martyrdom of friars, 80, 81; reply to Navarrete's embassy, 84, 399; his death, 79, 142
Taomaco Id., 409
Tapaque, a boat, 273, 287
Taxation, 324-326, 346, Appendix, 374
Tea, 286
Tello, D. Francisco, governor, 55, 75
—— D. Pedro, 158, 168
Ternate, Island, expedition to it, 249; its conquest, 254, Appendix, 416
Tibor, Chinese jars, 205, 285
Tides, ebb and flow of, 293
Tidore Island, king's letter to Dr. Morga, 198
Timava, Tagal, plebeians, 297
Timber, 274
Tingues or Tinguianes, uncivilised tribe, 240, 385

Tobacco, Appendix, 378, 379
Torres, D. Luis Vaez de, his voyage through Torres Straits, Appendix vi
Torrubia, Fray, book on the Philippines, i, Appendix, 375, 376, 361
Toxicology, 282, 283
Trade, 123, 336-343, Appendix, 381
Tribute, 324, 326, 329, Appendix, 375
Troops, 334, Appendix, 387
Tuba, Tagal, liquor, juice, 271

Ulloa, Lope de, driven into Japan by a storm, fights his way out of port, 206-209, 229
—————— Alonzo, 209
Urdaneta, Fray Andres, a Biscayan, 15
Urdiales, Augustin de, 158, 168
Usury, 300, 302, Appendix, 382-386

Valdes, Fray Francisco, 161
Valignano, Padre, Visitor of the Jesuits, his book in the Evora library, statements about Japanese martyrs, 398-402
Vargas, Gregorio, 50; his death, 168
Vegetables, 271, 275
Velasco, D. Luis, governor of Peru, v, 1, 151
—————— D. Luis, 238, 239
Vera, D. Francisco Gonzales de, archivist at Alcala de Henares, vi
—————— Dr. Santiago, governor, 28-31
—————— Juan Bautista, 233
Vergara, Captain, 252, 253
Victoria, Magellan's ship, 14
Viesman, see Biesman.
Vigadicaya, Tagal, a husband, 301
Villafañe, Luys, 135, 193
Villagra, Captain, 137-252
Villalobos, Ruy Lopez de, 14, 394

Weapons, 272, 291
Wreck of *Sant Antonio*, 243
—————— *San Felipe*, 75, 76, 142, 399
—————— *San Geronymo*, 188
—————— *Jesus Maria*, 250
—————— *Santa Margarita*, 188
—————— *Santo Tomas*, 190
—————— *San Juanillo*, 23
—————— D. Luys Dasmariñas' flagship, and *Almiranta*, 117

Xara, Juan de la, 53, 57
Xicoraju, Japanese official, 143
Ximenes, Fray Alonso, 53, 87, 95, 105, 115, 130
Ximonojo, Japanese official, 78, 79, 143

Yemondone, or Yemonojo, Japanese official, 79, 399, see Ximonojo.
Yeyasudono, Japanese regent, see Daifusama, 143-149
Ygolotes, uncivilised tribe in interior of Luzon, 284, 387
Ylocos, province, 20, 284
Ylo-ylo, see Ilo Ilo.
Ynasaba, a wife, 300; *Ina*, Tagal, a mother

Zacate, long grass, reeds, and zacatal, a thicket, place where zacate grows, 53, 220
Zambales, province, 33, 269, 294
Zamudio, D. Juan, 84, 114, 128, 168
———— Juan, notary, ii
Zoology, 277

ERRATA.

Page 2, l. 15, *for* GANNA *read* GAUNA.
,, 35, l. 14, *for* 1563, *read* 1593.
,, 113, l. 11, *for* nighbouring *read* neighbouring.
,, 261, note, *for* Candlish *read* Candish
,, 266, l. 1, *for* Ylabao *read* Ybabao.
,, 269, l. 32, *for* peeple *read* people.

CORRIGENDA.

Page 415, l. 14, *for* cut down, *read* blind.
,, 416, l. 7, *for* Bandayan bueno *read* Banda and Amboyna.

LONDON: T. RICHARDS, 37, GREAT QUEEN STREET.